The name Dolmetsch has always been

DOLMETSCH

THE MAN AND HIS WORK

Arnold Dolmetsch, aged 44, 1903

DOLMETSCH

THE MAN AND HIS WORK

BY

MARGARET CAMPBELL

University of Washington Press

Seattle

University of Washington Press edition first published, 1975

Library of Congress Cataloging in Publication Data

Campbell, Margaret.
  Dolmetsch: the man and his work.

  Bibliography: p.
  Includes index.
  1. Dolmetsch, Arnold, 1858–1940.
ML424.D65C3   781.9'1'0924[B]   75-4558
ISBN 0–295–95416–7

Printed in Great Britain by
Western Printing Services Ltd, Bristol

TO THE MEMORY OF
RUDOLPH AND RICHARD DOLMETSCH

Contents

List of Illustrations

Foreword by Robert Donington

ARNOLD DOLMETSCH meant a very great deal to me in those formative years on the verge of early manhood when life takes on its coming patterns; and I have every personal as well as public reason to be pleased with the remarkable story which Margaret Campbell has pieced together here with such indomitable persistence and such integrity of vision. Appropriately so; for these are the very qualities which stand out most abundantly in the great man who is her subject. She has served him, it seems to me, in the only way a biographer really should or could, by finding out all she can and holding very little back. Great men are not less human than other people: if anything, they are more human, having both our good qualities and our bad in more than ordinary measure. And the good and the bad are as inseparable as the two sides of a single coin. Just such a man was Dolmetsch in his genius, his suspiciousness, his vision, his intolerance, his lovableness, his irritability, and whatever else went to make him the perfectly glorious human phenomenon he was. To tell less than the truth about such a man is no tribute at all: we want him as he really was, in full confidence that this is how he will show to best advantage. We do not want to be defrauded of any part of him; for it is as a whole that we so highly rate him.

The Dolmetsch family, unlike the Wagner family in somewhat similar circumstances, have evidently taken this constructive view, helping Margaret Campbell with admirable openness. Indeed they had nothing to fear: she is so warmly on his side, and so I think will most of her readers end up by being. Many of them will learn here for the first time the public reason why Arnold Dolmetsch deserves a good biography. The very success of his own life's work has helped to conceal the pioneering quality of it. For Arnold Dolmetsch was the first among modern musicians to take early instrumental music seriously, and with it the early instruments and performing styles which we all now agree (but no one else imagined then) are so necessary to any really satisfactory performance of it. What many thousands of active musicians across the world now take for granted had to be conceived with rare vision and fought for with rare tenacity when Arnold Dolmetsch embarked on his half-century of un-compromising crusading, way back in the 1880s, to the applause of fellow prophets like Bernard Shaw but the patronising indifference of the majority of the musical profession.

Then came the years, well into the present century, when this in-difference gave place before a growing recognition and even some modest measure of practical support. Arnold Dolmetsch himself was so accustomed to being in opposition that he could never quite bring himself to trust the novel experience of being admired and sought out: he was never altogether able to let his defences down; and he remained, to his own loss, a prickly and difficult man long after the need for it was past. But what of it? The work got through, if the man did not; and now the world of music is so resonant with the results of it that not one enthusiast in a thousand knows that it all pretty much began, as such movements must, in a single man's visionary initiative. Arnold Dolmetsch, for example, was the first man who found out, with some considerable difficulty, how to make a recorder in modern times; and it is hard now to imagine a world without recorders. But so it was; and that is the pioneer whose story Margaret Campbell has told here with as much fulness as the surviving documents, and the memories of that dwindling band of us who were his friends and followers, allow. I think a great many lovers of early music, and lovers of a good story well told, too, will enjoy her book.

The State University of New York   ROBERT DONINGTON
   at Buffalo, Spring, 1974

Introduction

THE great danger with men who become legends in their own lifetime is that posterity tends to retain the legend and discard the truth. Arnold Dolmetsch was a legendary figure who brought with him into the 20th century a nostalgic air of late 19th century romanticism: a link with the Pre-Raphaelites and beyond. For most people the early Haslemere festival performances conjure up visions of aesthetic young men and elderly ladies in Liberty smocks and sandals; a mode of dressing, incidentally, that has now become commonplace. But what of the music itself? It is for this, the discarded truth, that Dolmetsch should be remembered. From the late 1880s right through to his death in February 1940, he made a serious and intensive study of 16th-, 17th- and 18th-century music, working on old scores and manuscripts in museums and libraries in many parts of the world: he became an authority on early music and its performing styles that had no equal among his contemporaries. Therefore, for the sake of musical history, we must attempt to isolate the scholarship from the myth.

If in this biographical study I can awaken new interest and a willingness to take a fresh look at the work of this very great man on his own terms, I shall have achieved what I set out to do.

London, 1974   MARGARET CAMPBELL

Acknowledgements

I would like to thank all the publishers who have allowed me to print extracts from their books, each of whom is listed in the Bibliography and in footnotes. In addition I would like to thank: Alleyn's College of God's Gift (Dulwich College), for an extract from *The Alleynian*, Macmillan of London and Basingstoke, Macmillan Company of Canada and St. Martin's Press, N.Y., for *Grove's Dictionary of Music and Musicians*, the Society of Authors, the Trustees of the British Museum, the Governors and Guardians of the National Gallery of Ireland and Royal Academy of Dramatic Art for published and unpublished writings of George Bernard Shaw, the Society of Authors (on behalf of the estate of Holbrook Jackson), Faber and Faber Ltd., the Viking Press, Inc., N.Y., Random House, Inc., N.Y., the Bodley Head, and the Society of Authors for quotations from the published writings of James Joyce. Published and unpublished writings and an unpublished drawing by Sir William Rothenstein appear by courtesy of Sir John Rothenstein and Mr. Michael Rothenstein.

For permission to print unpublished extracts from letters and diaries I am grateful to the following: Lord Ponsonby of Shulbrede *Sir Hubert Parry*, Mr. Roger Machell *The Countess Valda Gleichen*, Dr. Konrad Sasse of Händel-Haus Museum *Chrysander*, Mr. Lance Thirkell *Sir Edward Burne-Jones*, Mr. J. C. Medley *George Moore*, Professor Kenneth Leighton *Frederick Niecks*, Mrs. Pamela Diamand *Helen Coombe*, Mrs. John Dunn, The Library of Congress *Theodore Roosevelt*, Mr. J. E. Image *Professor Selwyn Image*, Mrs. G. Dugdale *Herbert Horne*, Lady Inès Burrows, M. Camille Aubery *Auguste Tolbecque*, Mrs. Winifred Whelen *F. T. Arnold*, Herr Günther Hellwig, Mrs. Marjorie Claisen, Yale University (Belle Skinner Collection of Musical Instruments) *Otto Kingkeldy*, Mr. G. C. Allfrey *Charles Sanford Terry*, Mrs. Ella Grainger, Mr. Stewart Manville, The Percy Grainger Library Society and the Library of Congress *Percy Grainger*, Mr. Edgar Hunt, Mr. Ralph Kirkpatrick, Dom Anselm Hughes, Miss Suzanne Bloch, Devar Surya Sena, Wallace and Guthrie *Sir Donald Tovey*, Mrs. Mary Parkin (on behalf of the late Mrs. Vera Newman's Estate) *Ernest Newman*, The Free Library of Philadelphia

Jean Sinclair-Buchanan, Group Captain, the Earl of Ilchester *A. H. Fox-Strangways*, G. Schirmer Inc., *Carl Engel*, New York Public Library (Berg Collection) *Dolmetsch letter to W. B. Yeats*.

I have made every effort to trace the owners of the copyright in all material quoted; for any unintentional omissions I can only apologise.

For permission to quote from personal interviews I would like to thank: Dame Sybil Thorndike, the late Sir Lewis Casson, Dame Marie Rambert, Professor Robert Donington, Mr. and Mrs. Robert Goble, Sir Robert Mayer, the late Kathleen Salmon, Mr. Richard Appel, Mr. John Challis, Mlle. J. F. Gaisser and Miss Lucy Norton for the late Philippa Strachey.

To all who so generously offered help and information I am most grateful and in particular I would like to thank: Dr. Gerald Abraham, Professor Karl Beckson, Sir Adrian Boult, Miss Penelope Barker-Noyes, Miss Enid Bagnold, Mr. W. S. Bristowe, Comtesse de Chambure, Mr. Maurice Card, Mr. Montagu Cleeve, Mrs. Melba Coolidge, Miss Margaret Donington, Admiral H. E. Dannreuther, Mr. Oliver Davies, Comtesse de Divonne, the late William Darby, Commander G. J. Dodd, Mr. William Dowd, the late Ruth Daniells, Dr. Ian Fletcher, Mrs. Helena King, Mr. Hugh Gough, M. Yves Gérard, the late Dame Adeline Genée, Sir John Gielgud, Mr. Ambrose Gauntlett, Mr. Michael Holroyd, Miss Elizabeth Hartman, Dr. and Mrs. John Hsu, Mrs. Lois Howard, Miss Jane Harington, Frau Uta Henning, Sir Rupert Hart-Davies, Miss Margaret Field-Hyde, Professor Norman Kelvin, Mr. Desmond Shawe-Taylor, Mr. John Kelly, Mr. Robin Langley, Dr. Mary Lago, Mrs. Janet Leeper, Professor Dan Laurence, Sir Anthony Lewis, Mr. E. W. Lavender, M. Jean Mongrêdien, M. Georges A. Mongrêdien, Miss Agnes Mongan, Lady Ruth Mott, the late Basil Maine, M. Leonide Massine, the late Sir Compton Mackenzie, A. C. N. Mackenzie, Younger of Ord, Colonel P R. Maciver, Mr. Richard Nicholson, Mrs. Jean Nathan, Mr. Guy Oldham, Sẽnor Antonio Orzabel, Mr. Frank Phillips, Miss Diana Poulton, Mr. Omar Pound, Mrs. Phyllis Pye, Mrs. Mary Potts, Mr. Marco Pallis, Miss Margaret Pace, Dr. Lillian M. Ruff, Mr. Layton Ring, Mr. George Roberts, Mr. Richard Rephann, the late W. C. Retford, Mrs. Jean Sapir, Miss Madeau Stewart, Mr. Lionel Salter, Miss Hope Stoddard, Mrs. Lois Sieff, Mr. Robert Spencer, Professor Ronald Schuchard, Mr. Joseph Saxby, Mr. Miles Tomalin, Commendatore and Mrs. J. A. Tigani, Lady Tweedsmuir, Miss Pamela Weston, Mr. H. A. J. Woolfenden, Sir Jack Westrup, Miss Narcissa Williamson, Mr. and Mrs. David Wilkins, Mrs. Lee Wurlitzer-Roth, Mr. W. S. Wright, Mr. Michael Wilson, Mr. Arnold Yates, Mr. Ian White, Mr. W. M. Whitehill and Senator Michael Yeats.

I have received inestimable help from the staff of the Newspaper Library at Colindale, the Reading Room of the British Museum, Mr.

Alex Hyatt King of the Music Department; and from Novello and Co., who allowed me constant access to archive copies of the *Musical Times*. My thanks are due also to: the Bodleian Library, Boosey & Hawkes Ltd., the Boston Public Library, the Brussels Conservatoire, the Boston Museum of Fine Arts, Cornell University Library, the Music Department Columbia University, the Courier-Journal Louisville Ky., E.M.I. Archives Dept., Eton College, the Fogg Museum, the Folger Shakespeare Museum, the Grosvenor Museum, the Houghton Library Harvard, Maison Kerner Le Mans, the Lute Society of America, the Library of Performing Arts Lincoln Center, the University of London Library, the Royal College of Music, the Royal Academy of Music, the William Morris Gallery, the University of Minnesota, the Bibliothèque Municipale Le Mans, New England Conservatory of Music, National Library of Ottawa (Music Division), the Smithsonian Institution, the Rowe Library King's College Cambridge, the Victoria & Albert Museum, the Director-General and Trustees (in particular the Dowager Lady Alexander of Tunis and Sir Trenchard Cox) of the Winston Churchill Memorial Trust and the English-Speaking Union.

For invaluable assistance with translations I am grateful to Verena Belart, Barbara Hurter, Sally Knight, Ursula Müller, Bernadette and Jean Morand, Corinne Orde and Evelyne Pierotti. Janet Dunbar's initial encouragement prompted me to start writing the book and the support over the years from Dorothy Darrell-Ward and John Thomson helped me to finish a task that occasionally seemed impossible. I am indebted to Graham Watson and Roger Machell for making the project a reality and to Pamela Lincoln for her meticulous typing of the manuscript. Chalmers Burns and John Bishop have generously read every word of the typescript and many of their valuable suggestions have been incorporated in the text. I am also grateful to Dr. Burns for compilation of the Index.

My thanks are due to the Chairman and Governors of the Dolmetsch Foundation and to the Dolmetsch family *in toto*, who have allowed me unrestricted access to private letters, diaries and documents from their personal papers and the Dolmetsch Library. Without the approval and understanding of Dr. Carl Dolmetsch and the assistance of Miss Greta Matthews my work would never have been completed. Lastly, I am grateful to my husband who has helped with a patience and optimism that passes understanding.

London 1974   MARGARET CAMPBELL

CHAPTER I

Early Years

WHEN Johann Konrad Ludwig Dolmetsch died in Stüttgart in 1789 he left his thriving bakery business to the eldest of his fifteen children. But Johann David had no liking for the trade. Within a short time he had dissipated the profits, declared himself bankrupt and signed everything, including his wife and eight children, over to one of his younger brothers. He then took himself off to Russia and was never seen again. It is unlikely that this profligate's adventures would be of any interest today had he not begotten a ninth child, out of wedlock, by a Swiss girl from Zürich. The records show that he registered the birth of a boy, Friedrich Rudolph, in his own name and made full provision for his welfare and education right up to the time of his own disappearance.[1]

Sporadic musical talent had manifested itself in the Dolmetsch family over several generations of millers, merchants and protestant clergymen, but it was in this natural son that the gift appears to have taken root and been nurtured for the first time. The boy was adopted by his teacher, the composer Johann Egli, who naturally saw to it that he was given a first-class musical education. In adult life, Friedrich was made a Buerger of the City and enjoyed a place of distinction in the musical life of Zürich: he became Director of the Singgesellschaft des Studenten and in 1876 founded the Saengerverein Zürich: his many accomplishments included composition and a number of his part-songs pass today for 'old Swiss' melodies.

When Friedrich married he, too, produced a large family, but all born to the same wife and well within the bounds of respectability. They all received musical instruction at a very early age and were expected to give a fair account of a number of the Bach preludes and fugues on the clavichord. This is an interesting link for in the years since Bach's death in 1750, public performances of his works were rare. This is further borne out by the fact that Dolmetsch was a close friend of Nägeli, of the famous publishing house, and it is claimed that it was due to Dolmetsch's influence that they published *Das Wohltemperierte Klavier* from the Zürich MS in 1801.

Two of Friedrich's sons migrated to France: the eldest, named after himself, settled in Nantes, where he became director of the Municipal Orchestra. The second son to travel westwards was Rudolph Arnold, born in 1827 and Frédéric's junior by 17 years—a fact he was seldom allowed to forget. Rudolph's interest lay in organ-building and thus it was that at the age of 19 he was apprenticed to Armand Guillouard of Le Mans in the province of Sarthe.

The Guillouards had their origins in Savoy but had settled early in the 19th century in Le Mans, where they had opened a music shop at 11 rue de la Préfecture, in the old part of the town. They were a good-looking family, small of stature and dark-skinned. When Rudolph Dolmetsch arrived to take up his apprenticeship he fitted into the picture very well for he too was short, with a complexion still tanned from the Alpine sun. Within ten years he had become a permanent part of the scene: he was managing the rapidly expanding piano department and had married his employer's eldest daughter, Marie Zélie.

Their first child, Eugène Arnold,[2] born on 24 February 1858, was so small and frail that his survival seemed unlikely. It is an old French provincial custom to feed such weaklings on white wine. This diet, administered by his grandmother, appears to have worked effectively, for Arnold was never again known to be sick in childhood. And whether it stemmed from this incident or not, throughout his life he retained an uncommonly fine taste for wine.

Although four more children were born to the Dolmetsches, the two families still continued to live over the shop and, despite cramped conditions, set apart one room for their music-making. Rudolph played both organ and piano and his wife the 'cello: often they were joined by their brother-in-law, who lived next door: a talented violinist, Anasthase Boblin had studied with Delphin Alard in Paris. So for the child Arnold there had never existed a home without music.

Rudolph and Marie Dolmetsch were both strong characters, thrifty and industrious with a highly developed sense of family pride. Of the two, Marie was the more affectionate and certainly the most flexible, although she too could be obstinate when severely crossed. Rudolph was a difficult man by anyone's standards: irascible, dogmatic, demanding and, like his brother in Nantes, lacking in humour, a characteristic that did not endear him to the French. He was a rigid disciplinarian with his children, but as a craftsman he excelled and his work was admired all over the town and beyond. He had no eye for the clock when there was work to be done and there is no denying that he was a valuable asset to his father-in-law.

Old Armand Guillouard would have protested that none of his grandsons was his favourite: but every New Year's Day he gave Arnold a gold ten-franc piece whilst the others had to be content with one franc each. Arnold spent much of his time with the Guillouards and without question it was his grandfather who exercised the strongest influence on him. It was in these formative years that he acquired a respect for the antique that enabled him to discriminate for the rest of his life. The perceptive old man had noticed that his grandson's musical sense was developing early. Whenever it was possible he would take the boy with him on his travels around the countryside when he had to tune and repair the organs in the parish churches. The great Cathedral at Chartres was on his itinerary and Arnold's first sight of this magnificent building in the early morning light was one of his most vivid memories. While other children played games in the sunlight, Arnold wandered through the dimly-lit churches absorbing a unique world of his own. He was taught to recognise each period of architecture; how to seek the beautiful and reject the grotesque. His hands were trained to feel the surface of fine woods so that at a very early age he could define a noble piece of carving with astonishing accuracy. It is also likely that it was during this time that his gift of perfect pitch was discovered, for he is said to have assisted his grandfather with the actual tuning when still a young child.

When Arnold was four he was given piano lessons by a bandmaster who had served at Waterloo. The picture of him arriving for the first time—a tall, haughty man, cane-in-hand, perpetually twirling his huge black moustache—was one which remained vividly in Arnold's memory. His method, not unknown at the time, was to rap the knuckles of his erring pupils every time they played a wrong note; needless to say, the man was given plenty of opportunity to use his cane. Fortunately for everyone concerned, the bandmaster soon exhausted what little patience he possessed and finally abandoned his pupil as 'Untalented, unmusical and unteachable!' Brief though it was, this unhappy experience was to have a disturbing effect on the child's musical development, and only much later did Arnold overcome his dislike of the keyboard: in some respects the damage was permanent for he never properly came to terms with the modern piano.

Soon after the bandmaster's departure Arnold came across an old violin[3] in the loft, but could find nothing better than a double-bass bow with which to try his skill. Whatever sound he produced at the time with this somewhat unorthodox combination of equipment, it certainly instilled in him a desire to learn the violin. The first teacher to give Arnold instruction was an impoverished gipsy violinist who walked into their shop one day to borrow an instrument. With uncharacteristic recklessness Rudolph struck a bargain with the man, agreeing to lend him a violin free of charge if in return he would give Arnold some lessons. It seems that the 'mysterious stranger', as he was called, remained anonymous throughout the period of their acquaintance. Occasionally the man was invited to dine with the family and would recount stories of his adventures, which were enjoyed though not necessarily believed. There was, however, nothing dubious about his facility on the violin. Arnold always had great pleasure in relating the story of how he discovered one of the man's 'tricks', which he would only consent to perform if hidden behind a screen. The sound which came forth was more like that of a string quartet than a solo instrument. Arnold was curious beyond endurance and crept up to look through one of the slits in the silk cover. He saw the man undo the frog of the bow and weave the hair through the strings so that when he rescrewed the frog and bowed, all strings were being played together: in fact, by deft stopping he could play almost any combination of notes with a single stroke.[4] One day the man vanished as suddenly as he had arrived, still in possession of the borrowed violin. Arnold spent the next few years learning the basic techniques from his Uncle Boblin, a less romantic but more reliable teacher.

At the age of six Arnold attended the Lycée du Mans. Life was hard for children in these times: they had to be in their places by six in the morning, and walked to school with their hands in their pockets clutching hot baked potatoes. The hours were interminably long—the morning in particular. Indiarubber was not then in general use, so the children were given pieces of stale bread to serve as erasers: by lunch time every fragment had been consumed. Despite these hardships Arnold threw himself vigorously into the excitement of more learning: his power of concentration was very marked in one so young and his obvious enjoyment in acquiring knowledge for its own sake had clearly manifested itself by this time. In reports the teacher frequently wrote 'excellent' and at the end of term Arnold invariably won first or second place.[5] He seems to have been reasonably gifted in most subjects, with a slight advantage in science: in fact it was because of his progress in this subject that it was suggested Arnold should try for an exhibition scholarship to university. Music still had the stronger appeal but his knowledge of science and physics was to prove extremely useful in the career he finally chose for himself.

*   *   *

In July 1870 the Franco-Prussian War brought both excitement and disaster into their lives. The citizens of Le Mans, who were later to become so heavily involved in the fighting, mustered a local army for which Rudolph Dolmetsch was one of the first to volunteer: but he was rejected on account of his Swiss birth.[6] As French nationality stems from the father, Arnold, too, was Swiss, but since he was so young when war broke out the question of fighting did not arise. However, in the last days of the preliminary training for battle he was allowed to serve as a drummer-boy. When the extent of his musical ability was discovered, he was asked to write out the time-honoured bugle calls, which added considerably to his self importance.

An amusing story dating from this time shows both Arnold's curiosity and astuteness to perfection. When the Prussians occupied the town in January 1871, the proud citizens of Le Mans closed their shutters in protest; but Arnold could not resist peeping through the slats to watch, fascinated as battalion after battalion marched through, each preceded by its own band. After a while he recognised the same faces reappearing at regular intervals and saw through the Prussians' ingenious plan of marching their entire forces—consisting of one ragged battalion and one band—in a circle like a recurring mechanical toy[7] to give a false impression of strength.

* * *

Arnold was 14 when he left school and entered the family workshop as an apprentice: it was during this time that he learnt the craft of making and repairing keyboard instruments and assisted with the restoration of all the other instruments that came into the shop. By the age of 16 he was thoroughly trained in workshop technique.

His wood-working skill had advanced with the years. A fine example of it can be seen today in the Haslemere home of the present Dolmetsch family: a small chest of drawers in cedarwood with mahogany veneer, originally intended to hold tools, it is an exquisite piece of craftsmanship, with no evidence of deterioration in the hundred years since it was made.

Genius is often impeded by incipient laziness but Arnold never suffered any such handicap: he always generated a tremendous capacity for hard work and never seemed to tire. In these adolescent years, even after a long day at the bench, he continued to practise his violin in the evenings and was still fresh enough to join in the family music-making. Nevertheless he nursed a growing regret that he could not give sufficient time to systematic music study and resolved to repair this deficiency at the first possible opportunity. This plan was brought to a sharp halt in the winter of 1872, when the first real tragedy of his young life sent Arnold to the family graveside to mourn the death of his grandfather. A rare affinity had existed between the two and the boy took some time to recover from the effects of his loss. Old Guillouard had bequeathed his grandson two of his own most treasured personal possessions: a beautifully executed drawing of an organ destined for installation in the church of the Notre Dame de la Couture, and his canvas bag of tools. Arnold cherished these for the rest of his days.[8]

After Guillouard's death the organ-building side of the business ceased to function but the piano department went from strength to strength. Arnold had assisted his father for so long that he was now a considerable tuner in his own right. But the imperious Rudolph, slow to acknowledge his son's increasing skill, never permitted the boy to work without supervision. In 1874 when an epidemic of Russian influenza swept the country, Rudolph fell a victim and died within a few days. The 16-year-old boy was suddenly faced with the problem of looking after the family business aided only by his mother and ageing grandmother. The piano-tuning clientele became his responsibility overnight.

As a grown man he was barely five feet tall: at 16 he could not have been a very impressive figure, so that it is not surprising that the housewives were unwilling to allow him inside when he stood on their doorsteps calmly announcing that he had come to tune the piano. Fortunately for Arnold there were a few ladies with more curiosity than scepticism: the wildfire of local gossip spread fast and from a mere child the boy became a child wonder overnight.

But Arnold's troubles were not over. His uncle Frédéric Dolmetsch had heard of his reputed success and without prior warning arrived from Nantes demanding vociferously that the boy should tune a piano to *his* satisfaction before he could consider himself qualified. Arnold evidently managed to satisfy this overbearing gentleman's requirements, although he admitted it had been the most formidable tuning in his whole experience.

No doubt Frédéric returned to Nantes congratulating himself on having such a clever nephew but it was not long before his finger was in the domestic pie again. This time it concerned money. An interesting document dated 1876, drawn up at Frédéric's instigation and written in both French and German, is still in existence:[9] its function was to prevent Marie Dolmetsch from having free access to her late husband's money, and the lengthy clauses (according to Swiss law) bound her to the extent that he was unable to sell the business, or in fact to use the money for any other than the purpose outlined.

Rudolph had left some 12,000 francs in excess of Marie's dowry, which amounted to 4,000 francs: each of the children was to receive his inheritance on reaching the age of 21; meanwhile the money was to be kept in the business. Frédéric made certain that there was no loop-hole in the contract; he allowed Marie partial control of the money until her sons should reach their majority, but until then she had to accept full responsibility for its ultimate payment, regardless of the fortunes of the business: indeed, an ironic proviso considering that it had originally belonged to the Guillouard family.

On the change to petticoat rule, family music-making declined and Arnold began to seek his amusement outside the home. His first independent move was to join the local orchestra, where he played the violin and learnt a vast amount of light music and *opera bouffe*. It is also the first time we learn of him having found a friend of the same age, a 'cellist by the name of Provost. After a while they tired of the monotonous repertoire and joined a small chamber group who were engaged for concerts and private parties. It was through one of these engagements that they met a well-to-do young widow who played the piano. She lived in a fine house in the fashionable part of the town and invited them to join her one afternoon to make music *à trois*. As Arnold's home music had been neglected since the death of his father, he welcomed the idea.

Marie Morel was a lawyer's daughter from Nancy who had settled in Le Mans when she married. She was 29, slight of stature and still very attractive. Arnold at 19 had grown into a handsome young man with italianate features dominated by large, expressive brown eyes. It was inevitable that passions would be roused. Unfortunately both young men fell deeply in love with the lady, a situation that brought about fierce and bitter rivalry between them. It was Arnold who finally succeeded in winning Marie's affections and it seems that poor Provost arrived one day for rehearsal just in time to learn that the trio had become a duet.

The confines of Arnold's matriarchial home had bound him so fast that until now he had had no opportunity to enjoy friendships with members of the opposite sex. His life had consisted of work and music and even that according to the dictates of the family. It was therefore not surprising that the first close association with a young woman should have so overwhelmed him. The perspicacious ladies at the rue de la Préfecture were furious when they heard that their breadwinner wanted to marry a widow nine years his senior. In their usual fashion they forbade him to see her under any circumstances whatsoever and considered the matter closed.

Obviously their judgement had been faulty for the next we hear is that the couple had eloped to Nancy, where their daughter Hélène was born on 14 April 1878, and that the birth was registered in the name of Dolmetsch. There was no question of them being married in France since parental consent was necessary for anyone under 21. But Marie's family appear to have accepted the situation sympathetically for they took entire charge of the infant soon after its birth. They also continued to provide their daughter with a generous allowance, fully aware that she would have to support Arnold until he had found suitable employment. Someone must have suggested that English law was less exacting than the French for as soon as Marie recovered from her confinement the couple travelled to London and, taking rooms at 18 Maddox Street, were married on the 28th of May at the Register Office in the parish of St. George's, Hanover Square.

The marriage certificate abounds with inaccuracies: Marie describes herself as a spinster and Arnold falsifies his age to 21, his 'rank or profession' becomes that of a 'gentleman'—a curious deceit quite out of character with the man, who was never ashamed of being a craftsman. It is possible that Marie's pride constrained her from admitting her husband was in 'trade'.

England's capital made little impression on the newly-weds: Marie did not speak the language at all and Arnold's limited vocabulary of school English was unintelligible to the natives. One day he accidentally strayed into Soho, where he was amazed to hear French and Italian spoken all around him. So enchanted was he that he stopped strangers in the street and engaged them in conversation. But even the charms of London's Latin quarter could not tempt them to remain.

After a brief return to Nancy they set out for the USA in one of the primitive steam-packets of the time. The boat was overcrowded and the going rough: passengers were obliged to take their own food for the entire voyage and their diet varied from salted fish for the immigrants travelling steerage to live pigs and sheep, which were slaughtered when needed for the first-class passengers. Virtually nothing is known about their life at this period except that which appears in Mabel Dolmetsch's book:

> On landing, they travelled to the town of Louisville, doubtless attracted by its name, and established themselves in a boarding house. The cuisine was novel and they were frequently regaled with wild turkey and cranberry sauce, which they thought delicious. Madame Arnold Dolmetsch gave piano lessons and her young husband worked up a round of piano-tuning and regulation and found himself warmly welcomed in the outlying farms.[10]

The actual date of their return is uncertain but, whenever it was, one of Dolmetsch's first undertakings was to take his wife and baby daughter to Le Mans to make peace with the family and at the same time collect his father's legacy, which had now become due. All was forgiven, in the manner of the best romantic fiction, but when the embracing was done, Arnold's mother introduced him to her newly-acquired husband, Alphonse Gouge, a young man about the same age as himself who had come into the business as his successor.

Soon after this marriage the business was renamed 'Dolmetsch-Gouge' and it was thus that it prospered for many years to come. In addition to the increase in the sale of musical instruments, it now had a thriving piano department. This was largely due to Albert, second eldest of the Dolmetsch boys, who had inherited his father's ability for tuning and repairing and was now in complete charge. Albert was then only on the threshold of what was to become a successful and distinguished career as a tuner *par excellence*: later he was for many years personal tuner to the celebrated Polish pianist, Jan Paderewski, who took him on his concert tours and is reputed to have refused to play unless the piano had been tuned by Albert. When Paderewski retired from the concert platform and entered politics, he offered him a post in the government, but Albert declined, preferring to spend the rest of his days making pianos in the little town of Colombe.

The next recorded date is that of 25 October 1879, when the Dolmetsches arrived in Brussels via Ghent, where Arnold's registration is entered enigmatically as 'Dolmetsch dit Dawning'. They took lodgings at 82 rue de la Longue Haie, just off the fashionable Avenue Louise, and Dolmetsch began his private studies on the violin with Henri Vieuxtemps. It was no doubt due to Vieuxtemps' influence that Dolmetsch later achieved a place at the Conservatoire in Brussels, then the centre of the French-speaking musical world and celebrated for its excellence in string teaching. Vieuxtemps had been associated with the Conservatoire for many years, as a teacher and orchestral director from 1871–73 and later in an advisory capacity. Unfortunately, a severe illness induced paralysis of his left side and Vieuxtemps retired to Algiers, where he died in June 1881, two months after Dolmetsch had entered the Conservatoire.

A number of related incidents during the Brussels period lead us to believe that it was here that Dolmetsch was first exposed to the influences of early music. On 23 December 1879 he attended a 'Concert Historique' at the Conservatoire which included the music of Rameau, Handel, Lulli, Guédron, Bach, Couperin, Boccherini, Scarlatti, Mathias Van den Gheyn and L. Jouret. The instruments used were a two-manual harpsichord (1679) by Vincent Thibaut, a pair of Virginals (1628) by Jean Ruckers, a positive organ from the time of Louis XIII, a Bible Regal from the reign of Henry IV, a treble viol by Nicholas Bertrand (Paris 1701) and a viola da gamba of unknown origin. The inevitable lack of a positive record as to how the viols were held, what kind of bow was used or whether the interpretations were authentic, precludes retrospective comment: nevertheless it was an exceptional undertaking for the time. Dolmetsch, when recalling this concert, was greatly impressed by the music he heard, but he also remembered sensing instinctively that 'something was not quite right'. His knowledge of the period was still strictly limited but the first question had been asked.

Another curious outcome of this particular concert was that Auguste Tolbecque, the distinguished 'cellist and composer from the well-known family of Belgian musicians, played both 'cello and viola da gamba at the performance. Also a skilled restorer and maker of early instruments, Tolbecque happened to be in Brussels at the time, working on some of the instruments in the Conservatoire Collection.[11] However, Dolmetsch and Tolbecque did not meet then: it was not until 1899, when the older man wrote to Dolmetsch introducing himself as a fellow enthusiast, that a meeting took place and a warm friendship that engendered some valuable correspondence was established.

The musical scene of the day was painted on a large canvas in glowing colours. Richard Wagner had brought spectacle into the opera in Germany and the Frenchman Hector Berlioz had livened up the concert platform with ever-increasing dramatic orchestration. The English, too, favoured enormous choirs performing large-scale choral works at the Albert Hall; whilst singers with big voices like Melba and Madame Albani were all the rage. But the embodiment of prevailing taste throughout Europe was that idol of the piano, Franz Liszt, hailed as 'King of the Keyboard'. The adulation he received, especially from the ladies, can only be compared with the excessive admiration lavished upon the 'Pop' groups of our own time. The following account of one of his London concerts is reprinted from an editorial in the *Musical Times* of May 1886:

> Conceive people with their animal spirits at their highest, all shouting with one accord, and all eager to obtain a favourable view of the hero of the day, and you will have it. Those who were not tall enough to see over their neighbour's shoulders got upon the seats and stood there, the example being so greatly followed that soon the floor of the concert room presented the extraordinary and somewhat absurd spectacle of an audience standing on the benches.

Music on an intimate level was restricted to the home: the chamber ensemble was enjoyed by musicians more as a private luxury, although there were a few public performances by small groups: Joachim, in particular, was responsible for bringing the string quartet to the concert platform. When Arnold Dolmetsch took his place at the Conservatoire he was not yet interested in 'small' music. Since his first study was the violin he was keenly interested in the music of Brahms, but the composer that he still preferred to all the others was Hector Berlioz.

Dolmetsch took part in many activities at the Conservatoire, one of which was membership of the well-known professor-student orchestra. He also played the viola in a chamber group. Fortunately for him the director at this time was the celebrated François Gevaert, who had been elected a member of the French Académie des Beaux-Arts in 1873 and two years later brought out his *Histoire et théorie de la musique dans l'antiquité*, 'a work remarkable for much new matter, the result of careful and original research'.[12] It was Gevaert who first taught Dolmetsch the importance of ornamentation and further inspired him to take an interest in the instruments of early music, although admittedly more out of curiosity than scholarship.

Another professor who exerted a strong influence was his teacher for harmony and counterpoint, Ferdinand Kufferath, with whom Dolmetsch formed a close friendship which lasted until the older man's death in 1896. Kufferath was the first to recognise that Dolmetsch was no ordinary student, and it was he who persuaded Dolmetsch to take up serious study of the pianoforte. It happened when the professor was lecturing on the shortcomings of a musical career based on limited knowledge of the compass of a wind or stringed instrument. In pointing out that harmonic progressions are far easier to work out and understand when played first on a keyboard instrument, he advised his students to acquire a working knowledge of the piano. This was particularly hard on Dolmetsch: ever since his treatment by the bandmaster from Waterloo he had resisted the piano: at best he regarded it as an accompanying instrument, at worst a means of livelihood that he had already mentally rejected. His respect for Kufferath, however, was uncommonly high and despite his prejudices he made good progress when placed with the celebrated Arthur de Greef for lessons. Once again, the association developed into friendship and he and his master kept in touch for many years after they had gone their separate ways.

Ironically enough, it was through the piano that Dolmetsch made his first acquisition in antique instruments. He came across an old square piano in a junk shop and bought it for a trifling sum. It was in need of a complete overhaul and when Dolmetsch inquired at a number of dealers to know the cost of the work, he was surprised to be met with a refusal even to look at the instrument. Most were curt and indifferent: some were good enough to explain that the demand for such work no longer existed and in consequence the craftsmen were not practised in that particular skill: one unusually contemptuous man retorted that such instruments were only fit for museums and were not meant to be played!

As it turned out, it was the best thing that could have happened. It suddenly occurred to Dolmetsch that he had his grandfather's tools and he could do no harm by attempting to carry out the job himself. As soon as he set to work he began rediscovering the skill he had acquired in his boyhood. In the end the long and laborious task resulted in a major restoration of the instrument but it gave Dolmetsch immense satisfaction. Most important of all was the excitement he felt when he touched the keys and heard them speak for the first time.

The second instrument with which Dolmetsch became acquainted at Brussels was the viola d'amore. A fellow student and close friend, Louis Van Waefelghem, was a fine performer on this instrument, much in neglect at that time and only a little less today. The honey-sweet tone appealed to Dolmetsch and he often borrowed the instrument to play on himself. When Van Waefelghem suggested they should take some instruments from the Conservatoire collection and form a group, Dolmetsch welcomed the proposal and helped to round up a number of similar enthusiasts.

The instruments were rather more in displaying than playing condition, and the students had to be careful not to cause any damage. When Dolmetsch recounted the incident himself, he would also provide the sequel which, in the light of what we now know, is of the greatest importance. It appears that, shortly following the students' experiment, one of the professors decided to give his own lecture on early wind instruments. A number of students were chosen to demonstrate and when they came to the early recorders, the professor allotted them to the instrumentalists who were, in his opinion, playing the modern equivalent: the bassoonist was given the bass recorder, the clarinettist the tenor, and the flute and piccolo players the treble and descant. Musicians familar with the fingering of any of these instruments will know instantly how disastrous the result of such an experiment would sound: to those 19th-century ears, who knew nothing of the early recorder or its fingering, it must have been a severe shock. The fingering of the recorder is altogether different from that of other wind instruments, and the experiment would have resulted in loss of pitch and faulty intonation. Derisive laughter greeted every attempt and one student remarked that he could not understand our forebears using such dreadful instruments. 'How could they be so unmusical?' he asked. But Dolmetsch was not at all satisfied at this total rejection of the instruments, and thereby in a sense also the music, of a bygone age: he remembered thinking that we do not dismiss the painters and writers of the same period merely because their style is not identical to our own. So a second question formed in Dolmetsch's mind: one that was to remain unanswered for a very long time.

*   *   *

When Dolmetsch was nearing the end of his stay in Brussels he received the following letter:

Monsieur,

Vous avez eu il y a quelque temps, l'amabilité de m'offrir votre concours pour le cas où je désirerais faire de la musique chez moi. Je me permets aujourd'hui de vous rappeler cette bonne promesse. Il vient de paraître un quintette de Brahms pour instruments à cordes. Je suis très curieux de le connaître et si cela vous arrange nous pourrions l'essayer jeudi prochain à 8½ h. du soir.

En vous remerciant d'avance je vous prie, Monsieur, de recevoir l'assurance de mes meilleurs sentiments.

Ferdinand Kufferath
12 rue de la Charité.

ce Mardi 26 Dec. 1882.[13]

Brahms was in his late forties and already an established composer. Dolmetsch was 24 and still an unknown student. It is well known that Kufferath and his pupil were good friends and that in the vacation Dolmetsch was a frequent visitor to the professor's summer home at Blankenburg; but it cannot be assumed that Kufferath was predisposed to invite Dolmetsch for this historic try-out when he could have chosen any of his students for the purpose, some of whom were, probably, better performers. Why then did he ask him? Was it that the shrewd old man had recognised the sixth sense that Dolmetsch undoubtedly possessed, that ability to see inside the music that his later achievements proved he had in abundance? Regrettably there is no record of how the evening progressed. Nevertheless, Kufferath's curiosity must have been satisfied, for the work turned out to be the first quintet for strings that Brahms ever wrote, the Opus 88 in F major, known as 'The Spring', dedicated to Th. Engelmann and published the following year.

* * *

Marie Dolmetsch remained very much in the background during their stay in Brussels, and when her husband terminated his studies in April 1883, with excellent reports on every subject, it was with some relief that she looked forward to their return to France, where she could pick up the threads of their old life again. But she was not to have her way. Her unpredictable husband came home one day brimming with fresh plans: a new college of music was soon to be opened in London. He now wished to be trained all over again: this time, in English.

NOTES

1. *Stammfolge*. Haslemere.
2. For some reason unknown the first name was dropped altogether.
3. Later known to be a converted treble viol.
4. Such a man was said to have been known in Poland in the latter half of the 19th century: it was his practice to perform tricks in sideshows all over Europe.

5. School reports, Haslemere.

6. When the post-war conferences took place between the ruling forces and the civic authorities, Rudolph Dolmetsch was at last able to contribute to the war effort by acting as interpreter: he was said to be the only person in Le Mans who could speak German.

7. Dolmetsch, Mabel, *Personal Recollections of Arnold Dolmetsch*, Routledge & Kegan Paul, London, 1958, p. 5.

8. Haslemere.

9. ibid.

10. Dolmetsch, Mabel, *Personal Recollections of Arnold Dolmetsch*, Routledge & Kegan Paul, London, 1958, p. 8.

11. When J. F. Fétis, celebrated musicologist and director of the Conservatoire, died in 1871, the Belgian government purchased the contents of his library and 74 musical instruments and presented them to the Conservatoire. Other collections were added later and it was opened to the public in 1876. It was Victor Charles Mahillon, the first curator, who increased the number of instruments to 1,500 and it was he who established a workshop within the building where research, re-construction and restoration took place. It is important to remember that the latter expansion took place long after Dolmetsch had left Brussels.

12. Grove's *Dictionary of Music* 5, 1954, p. 621.

13. Some time ago, you were so good as to offer me your services should I wish to make music at my house. Today I take the liberty of reminding you of that generous promise. A quintet for strings by Brahms has recently appeared: I am keenly interested to know what it is like and if it suits your arrangements we could try it out on Thursday next at 8.30 in the evening.

with many thanks,
Yours most sincerely,
Ferdinand Kufferath
12 rue de la Charité

Tuesday, 26 December 1882.

CHAPTER II

Discovering the Elizabethans

THE Royal College of Music was formally opened by the Prince of Wales with much pomp in the presence of Mr. Gladstone, the Prime Minister, on 7 May 1883, in the building which had previously belonged to the National Training School and is today occupied by The Royal College of Organists. It had only 30 classrooms and conditions were severely cramped so much so that when the college moved to its present site in Prince Consort Road, Hubert Parry recollected it as being 'about the worst constructed for any purpose'. Sir George Grove, the college's first director, presided over a professorial board abounding with eminent names, amongst whom were Walter Parratt, J. F. Bridge, Hubert Parry, C. V. Stanford and one lady, Madame Lind-Goldschmidt, more popularly known as Jenny Lind, 'The Swedish Nightingale'.

Dolmetsch and his wife again took rooms at Maddox Street, but there are no records of their private life at this time. However, we may presume that, even if Marie deplored her husband's perennial studentship, she continued to support him in every respect: certainly financially, for Arnold's legacy had long since dwindled and Maddox Street was both fashionable and expensive.

Dolmetsch's first study was once more the violin: this time under Henry Holmes, a gifted musician who some years later, following involvement in a private scandal, was forced to resign and live abroad. Bridge was his professor for harmony and counterpoint and Parry took him for composition.

When shown the work that Dolmetsch had completed at Brussels, these celebrated gentlemen expressed doubts as to whether they could teach him any more. Nonetheless, he stayed five terms and his name appears on each of the programmes of the first five concerts ever given at the college: these were all performances of string quartets with his friend, Emil Kreuz, later to become a celebrated soloist, as first violin; Dolmetsch played the viola part.

The general pattern of his behaviour and achievement closely resembled that of his time in Brussels. Reports read: 'Capital progress . . . studies conscientiously . . . shows improvement in almost every respect . . . a valuable member,' a record in fact that was the essence of conformity, even to the extent that in all 18 months of his studying period he was absent only seven times on account of illness and twice without leave.

However, beneath the surface of formal education there were disturbances. Without knowing his real objective, Dolmetsch felt compelled to keep a vigilant eye on the junk shops, and he voraciously read every book on music that came his way.

*   *   *

Sir George Grove, who 'exercised a remarkable stimulating and fruitful influence on his pupils' and was 'a most lovable and delightful man, with a genius for friendship with young and old alike . . . was not able to conceal a preference for instrumentalists over singers'.[1] It was Dolmetsch's good fortune to be in the care of such a man, and as his interest in the music and instruments of the past increased he found Sir George both sympathetic and enthusiastic. However, this study was still speculative when in his last term he approached the director about his future career. Both were then thinking in terms of teaching and it was through Sir George's influence that E. D. Rendell, music Master at 'Alleyn's College of God's Gift' (more commonly known as Dulwich College), took on Dolmetsch as a part-time violin teacher.

This new appointment necessitated the Dolmetsches' removal from London and they took rooms at 4 Alleyn's Crescent in West Dulwich. Here houses were few and the wide, tree-lined streets afforded an uninterrupted view of the Kentish countryside. To Dolmetsch's supreme delight there was a garden. His affinity with the soil and the pleasure of growing things was inborn; he once insisted that gardening was more important to him than music. Although this story errs on the tall side, Dolmetsch undoubtedly had green fingers, most likely inherited from his maternal grandmother, who had always tended the large garden of their own house in Le Mans with such care.[2]

There is another side to the coin. Dolmetsch's enthusiasm for horticulture is remembered with mixed feelings by some of the children who now survive him. His Gallic streak tended to influence his preferences, and when a batch of plants arrived from France the children were taken away from whatever they were doing and told to prepare the ground for the new arrivals, the excuse being that the fresh air was good for them. Then, in his manner pontifical, with the family in obsequious procession, Dolmetsch would commit the plants to the earth: having exercised his *triportage*, their future growth was ensured. The practice, however, had a habit of being reversed when the children wished to play in the garden and their father considered it more important to rehearse for a forthcoming concert.

Although Dolmetsch is not mentioned as being on the staff of the college until 1887, when he became assistant violin master, there is ample proof that he was concerned with the school music-making from a much earlier date. An account in *The Alleynian* of a concert that took place in March 1885 states that he 'led the violins and played violin solos'. It is also recorded that he took part in another concert in July of the same year. A letter from one of his pupils, written in 1928, gives some idea of the way he was beginning to inspire those who came to him to learn:

> 40 Loxley Road,
> London S.W.18.
> Jan 24th. 1928

> I don't suppose you remember me but from 1885–1889 I was one of your pupils at Dulwich College, where I have been a master since 1898 . . . I still play the violin and it is to you that I owe my love of the ancients. You introduced me to Purcell and I still remember some of your talks about Elizabethan music.

> H. E. Adams.

Also on the staff during Dolmetsch's first year was A. H. Fox-Strangways, then a young mathematics master, who left for Wellington College in 1886. Later he relinquished the teaching profession to become one of the most distinguished and respected musical critics of the day, at one time on the staff of *The Times* and later with *The Observer*. Drawn together by common interest, Dolmetsch and Fox-Strangways were closely associated in their Dulwich days; much later, when Dolmetsch had become totally immersed in his work on the ancients, Fox-Strangways was a frequent visitor to Haslemere at festival time.

It was at Dulwich that Dolmetsch instituted the controversial method of teaching that was to have such a profound effect on his later work. The school permitted the boys only half an hour's music practice each day and he soon found that it was useless to burden them with technique. Dolmetsch was essentially a man who, if the means were not available, could invent as the necessity arose: so he taught the boys to hear first and thereby develop their musical sensitivity. He would allow them to play tunes right away on the open strings and once they had accepted the violin as an instrument related to their own efforts, not merely as a means of conveying sound, he could safely introduce technique.

As for learning the finger positions, he placed frets on the fingerboard, as recommended by Playford.[3] This obviated all the initial fumbling that bedevils most learners of the violin, and indeed is often the reason for early abandonment of the instrument.

It worked well for Dolmetsch, and even the most timid beginner would develop a sense of pitch in a remarkably short time: when they had mastered the finger positions the frets were removed.

Dolmetsch's critics persistently ridiculed this particular unorthodoxy but he achieved results regardless and was frequently complimented on the fact that his boys played in tune, a rare occurrence in youthful string players, as any teacher will know. At Dulwich he brought the numbers of violin pupils up from a pitiful handful to more than 40 and his time there was marked by greatly increased musical activity. His choice of music, too, was out of the ordinary: he gave the boys the lesser-known works of Handel to play, besides those of Corelli and Purcell. On a performance of music by the latter composer a local critic remarked that 'the music sounded fresh in spite of its age'; at another concert a reviewer wrote: 'Of the string performances, without doubt, the *Sarabande for Eight Violins* by Handel, conducted by Mr Dolmetsch, was the most striking and the best rendered.'

Perhaps the best illustration of the kind of inspiration that Dolmetsch gave to his pupils was the case of Will Boxall, who at 15 was the school's 'black sheep'. He was moody, lacked concentration, worked only in spasms and was the despair of the entire staff, with the exception of Dolmetsch, who found his behaviour exactly the opposite when he came for his violin lesson. Dolmetsch persuaded the headmaster to allow Will more time for his music and undertook personally to see that his other lessons were not neglected in consequence. Will underwent a complete metamorphosis: his academic work improved, his personality took on a new vitality, and his violin-playing reached a standard of excellence that Dolmetsch had not yet encountered in any of his pupils. W. A. Boxall went on to study at the Royal College of Music and from there to the Brussel's Conservatoire. He became a first-class violinist, playing in leading European orchestras and the Queen's Hall Orchestra in London. He was music-master at Charterhouse until the outbreak of the First World War and from 1918 onwards played with the London Symphony Orchestra for many years; he was coaxed from retirement on a number of occasions in response to a personal invitation from Sir Thomas Beecham to play in opera at Covent Garden. Boxall remained grateful to his old teacher throughout his life and when Dolmetsch was giving his first concerts, in the 1890s, his name is often to be seen on the programmes of that era.

In spite of his strange appearance, wild gesticulations, quick temper and thickly accented voice, Dolmetsch was to Will Boxall and many others a man who inspired them to reach across the boundary where formal teaching and imagination meet, and in so doing attain a fuller realisation of their own capabilities. Such methods are common practice today, but the Victorians worked on straight lines and regarded all non-conformity with suspicion.

Marie Dolmetsch's own money still provided for the family's basic needs as her husband's income was by no means sufficient, even after he had been promoted to the staff at Dulwich. He augmented his earnings by taking on a number of private pupils, one of whom resided in St. James's Palace: she was the 20-year-old daughter of Rear Admiral Prince Victor Ferdinand, Count Gleichen, a relative of Queen Victoria. In addition to her talent for the violin, Valda Gleichen[4] had an attractive mezzo-soprano voice which she intended to use professionally at the first opportunity. This young friend at court was to open many doors for Dolmetsch in the years to come.

Although teaching still occupied most of Dolmetsch's time, research was gradually depriving him of more hours than he could spare. He paid more and more visits to the Royal College of Music, making good use of their fine library,[5] reading MSS and copying down music that attracted him: Purcell's *Golden Sonata* and some pieces from the *Fairy Queen* were both acquired in this way and were first performed by Dolmetsch's pupils at Dulwich.

At the same time he was slowly building up a library of his own. There was then little demand for books on the ancients and so by assiduously combing the secondhand shops he was able to purchase some rare volumes for a fraction of their real worth.

With the dexterity of an octopus, Dolmetsch managed to handle an incredible number of activities at the same time: in addition to his teaching and research he also found time for composition: a number of his pieces for strings (curiously enough, 19th century in style) were performed by his pupils and were well received by the critics. Dolmetsch also had a gift for arrangement and the first of his two books of Corelli sonatas for violin and piano were published by Novello, Ewer and Co. in 1888. The second book came out in July of the same year. He sent copies to several of his academic friends; as he had hoped, he received some appreciative replies. M. Colijns, one of his violin professors at Brussels, wrote;

> 2nd August 1888
>
> I wish to say that I am doubly charmed, primarily because I found the work very interesting and well constructed and then because it proves to me that you progress in an interesting way.

The professor goes on to say that he intends adopting the work for his own students both at Brussels and Antwerp. From this letter we learn of Dolmetsch's intention to devote more time to studying the ancients:

> I will always be happy to receive your news and to know that your career continues to prosper. Besides you have taken the right, the only right course.
>
> (translation)

This was two years before Dolmetsch applied for his first ticket to the Reading Room of the British Museum.

During this period three more of Dolmetsch's writings were published by Novello, Ewer: *Twelve Easy Pieces* of his own composition for violin and piano, six Corelli trio sonatas for violin, 'cello and piano, and six Handel sonatas for violin and piano. The trios he dedicated to his friend and teacher, Dr. Parry. The following letters suggest that the brew was very much to the professor's taste:

> Knight's Croft,
> Rustington,
> Worthing
> July 31st 1888
>
> My dear Dolmetsch,
>
> I am very glad indeed to see your edition of Corelli Trio Sonatas and am much obliged to you for sending me the copies, and for putting my name on the inside. Indeed, they are beautifully got up, quite a treat to look at! I have been through a good deal of it, and it seems to me most excellently well done. Just in the right sort of style and spirit. I'm going to get my little girls[6] to learn some of them as soon as possible. I'm very glad too that you have made such a good arrangement with Novellos. I hope you will have a very good sale, as it deserves.
>
> Wishing you all success with it and all else you do.
>
> I am,
>
> Very sincerely yours,
> C. Hubert Parry

When the Handel sonatas appeared, the *Musical Times* of March 1890 reviewed the work with enthusiasm:

> The form in which they are presented will make them very acceptable, not only to violin players but to students of Handel's works. The original figured bass has been cleverly translated, so that the piano part is a complete accompaniment, with small touches of fancy suggested by the character of the themes. . . . Mr. Dolmetsch has not only written out the accompaniments in full, but he has added marks of expression, and, in fact, has fulfilled his self-imposed task in an artistic manner.

To have achieved success with his first published work might well have encouraged Dolmetsch to devote himself entirely to the manuscript resuscitation of early music; but another of those stranger-than-fiction incidents that seemed to mark every change in his life sent him headlong in quite another direction.

Whenever Dolmetsch was passing one of the London salerooms he could not resist the temptation to look in on the off chance of finding a bargain. On one such occasion he strolled in during an auction and was just in time to bid for what appeared to be a viola, which he secured for a very low price. On closer examination he discovered the instrument to be a viola d'amore by Testore, a handsome instrument, deep chestnut in colour with its finely carved angel's head intact.[7] Dolmetsch was overjoyed. Ever since the Brussels days he had wanted a d'amore and to have acquired one at such a price was a two-fold achievement. Dolmetsch did not know it then but he was richer by far than the price of a fine old instrument.

Knowing from experience that he would have little response from a violin dealer should he ask to have his d'amore cleaned and restored, Dolmetsch carried out the work himself and, guided only by the instructions given in one of the text-books in his own library, he provided the instrument with a completely new set of strings. All he now needed was some music so that he could play it. The Royal College of Music Library had seemed the most likely source, but he was disappointed. Even after weeks of searching he found little that was not already known to him, and he soon became aware of what is unfortunately still true today—that the viola d'amore, a distant relative of the viols, is one of the most neglected of this truly gentle family of instruments.[8]

It was this lack of success with music for the d'amore that suddenly brought home the realisation that he had passed over an abundance of music for viols: fantazies, ayres, galliards, pavans, sparkling with the dance-rhythms of those superb amateurs, the Elizabethans, that had been lying undisturbed for the best part of 300 years. Today we take this music for granted but how ready were the public in 1889? An editorial in the *Musical Times* deplores the 'Worship of bigness' and goes on to describe a work for soloist, chorus of 2,000 and four orchestras to be performed at the Paris Exhibition for a cost of £12,000. 'Shades of Berlioz', groans the writer, 'You aren't in it!'

In the same issue of this periodical we learn that 'in Brussels a society has been formed for the study and practice of instruments once in general favour but now almost unknown in our concert rooms, such as the clavicembalo, the viol da gamba, the viol d'amore etc., and that members of this body have already given historical concerts with much success. As many of these instruments are freely used in works of Bach, Handel, Couperin, Rameau, etc., it is to be hoped that performances of such deep

interest to musicians may shortly be heard in the metropolis.' The prophecy was in part accurate, but not in the way that the writer had visualised. The society[9] attracted a certain following for a few years but never
really became an established group giving regular performances. The
metropolis was indeed to hear such music on the instruments for which it
was written, but the 'deep interest to musicians' was still very wide of the
mark and destined to remain so for many decades to come.

The acquisition of a repertoire of Elizabethan music was now of paramount importance to Dolmetsch, who, with the zeal that he applied to
everything, spent most of his time to this end. By early 1890 he had
extended his researches to the British Museum: it is generally believed
that it was here that Dolmetsch made his first discoveries and in fact he
states it as being so himself in numerous autobiographical notes with the
date 1889. But there is no record of Dolmetsch having visited any of the
reference libraries of the museum until April 1890, when he took out a
three-day ticket. He did not go there again until 22 October of the same
year; on 25 November he was given a three-monthly pass and thereafter
held yearly tickets until 1916.

It seems odd that Dolmetsch, usually accurate in statements relating
to his work, should have 'misremembered' the facts in such an important
phase in his life. Yet we know that Hélène played a Simpson *Division on a
Ground* on the 'cello at a concert in June 1889 from a MS found in the
RCM Library and on the programmes which follow this date there are
very accurate descriptions of the exact source of each item; the majority
are certainly from the RCM. The only feasible explanation is that Dolmetsch quarreled with the RCM at a later stage and therefore felt less
inclined to give them credit for being his first source of discovery.

However, Dolmetsch was still on the friendliest terms with his *Alma
Mater* in 1890 when he reached what was to be the turning-point in his
career. It was then that he made the decision that singled him out from
his contemporaries. Dolmetsch knew instinctively that it would be useless
to attempt the interpretation of the music of an earlier period on modern
instruments so he decided to start collecting a chest of viols.[10] Instruments
were not then the prey of collectors as they are today, and now that
Dolmetsch knew what he was looking for, the right ones were not so hard
to come by. It was often possible to pick up a viol that had been re-
modelled and re-strung as a violin or a viola and, provided no positive
destruction had been wrought, it was usually a fairly simple matter to
restore the instrument to its former shape.

Dolmetsch's first acquisition was a fine six-stringed bass or viola da
gamba by Barak Norman; then followed a treble, a tenor, an alto, a
pardessus de viole and eventually a violone made by Maggini. He intended

to form a family consort and immediately set about giving some instruction to his wife, his daughter and a few of his pupils.

One of the earliest reference books to which Dolmetsch had access was Christopher Simpson's *The Division Violist*.[11] Prior to the study of this work, Dolmetsch had believed, in common with his contemporaries, that the viol should be played in the same position as their modern counterparts, i.e., the smaller instruments under the chin and the larger ones on the knees or the floor. He soon found this to be an incorrect assumption. He learned that all viols except the violone are played between the knees and also (later) that they should be played with the early outcurved bow, not the Tourte model designed specifically for the violin during the latter part of the 18th century—a complete reversal of the early bow.

It was 300 years since Elizabeth I's Golden Age had been at the peak of its creative powers, and 200 of these had passed since the viols had enjoyed any real popularity. Having formed his consort, unearthed the music and the tutors he needed, Dolmetsch finally made up his mind to devote himself to the 'authentic interpretation of early music on the instruments for which it was written'—a phrase now indelibly associated with the name of Dolmetsch everywhere.

The first person with whom he discussed his future plans was Sir George Grove. Trained originally as an engineer, Sir George could be relied upon to take a logical approach to most situations: a useful asset when dealing with musicians, who are not always endowed with this quality. Whilst he was impressed with Dolmetsch's enthusiasm and indeed his intentions, he issued a salutary warning on the difficulties that would beset him every inch of the way. There was little money to be made from such research and the Establishment would not be encouraging. But if Dolmetsch was prepared to take this path, regardless, his services to music would be invaluable. Dolmetsch's tenacity provided him well for dealing with obstacles, so there was no argument. It is also fair to say that Sir George's advice was not given lightly: throughout the years he was to remain a strong advocate of all Dolmetsch's activities.[12]

In order to see Dolmetsch's early work in perspective, it is necessary at this point to assess what had already been achieved by his predecessors and examine what was being done by his contemporaries. It is difficult to prove that any one person's work is the first in a particular field: the reaper and the sower may not be one and the same person, but each is dependant upon the other's good husbandry. Dolmetsch knew better than anyone how much he owed to Agricola, Mersenne, Praetorius and other learned writers of musical history: he had been a voracious reader of the ancients long before he took up the practical study of their teaching. In the history of researches into early music there are isolated cases of both individual and collective attempts to gather together, restore and perform upon instruments which had fallen into disuse, although in general the accent is more upon collection and performance than restoration and reconstruction.

There was Stafford Smith, the English organist, tenor singer and composer, who collected a vast and important library of books and music; but when he died in 1836 his affairs were settled by an incompetent auctioneer and no trace was kept of any but a few items.[13]

The German-born Pepusch edited the Corelli sonatas in score but is better known for the arrangements and overture he wrote for John Gay's *The Beggar's Opera*. He also took an active part in the establishment of the Academy of Ancient Music. In 1776 a society known as 'The Antient Concerts' was founded by a committee with several noblemen on the board: their aim was to perform only music that had been written more than 20 years prior to the date of their foundation. It attracted members of the Royal Family and, as a mark of interest, George III personally wrote the programmes, so that it was afterwards known as 'The King's Concerts'. There was also a Purcell Society, but in November 1886 a correspondent in the *Musical Times* bemoans the failure of the organisation to achieve anything at all.

No mention of early music could omit the name of Carl Engel, early 19th-century writer on musical instruments. His famous *Descriptive Catalogue of the Musical Instruments in South Kensington Museum* (1874) has been described as 'a masterpiece of erudition and arrangement, and a model for the subsequently written catalogues of the Paris and Brussels Conservatoires and of the Kraus Collection at Florence'.[14] During his close association with the Victoria and Albert and the British Museums, Carl Engel became known as a leading authority on early instruments, and his private collection of books and instruments could hardly be rivalled except by those in a few public institutions.

Nearer Dolmetsch's time was A. J. Hipkins, specialist employee of Messrs. Broadwood and authority on the harpsichord, upon which instrument he gave lecture-recitals from 1883 onwards. A greatly respected writer of books on the pianoforte, it was said of him that when Chopin visited this country he refused to play on a piano unless Hipkins had been personally responsible for its tuning.

Then there was Dolmetsch's eminent contemporary, Canon Francis Galpin,[15] born on Christmas Day in the same year as Dolmetsch—1858: his scholarly writings and fine collection of instruments have been of the greatest value to succeeding generations of students and organologists. His scholarship and knowledge are above reproach but it seems doubtful if his performances were up to the same standard. There is in the *Musical World* (22 November 1890) an interesting account of a 'graphic lecture on music common in England during the reign of "Good Queen Bess"' given by Mr. C. F. Abdy Williams in which the Rev. Mr. Galpin and his wife took part using instruments from their private collection. The reviewer was not impressed by what he heard: the sound produced by the Bible regal 'somewhat resembled an assemblage of ducks at feeding time' whilst the *Lyra Mendicorum*, or beggar's fiddle, in which the strings are put in vibration by a revolving wheel, 'sounded like wheezy bag-pipes'. The critic continues;

> Illustrations were also played by Mr Galpin on the *Recorder*, which may be described as a bass flute of soft and rich tone quality, but played *à bec*, on a waite, practically a flageolet, and from which we derive our title for certain persons who make night hideous at Christmas-time, and the original of the cornet, a straight conical tube, with lateral holes. The effect of *Ein feste burg* played on the latter instrument, and accompanied on the Regal, is indescribable, and fully accounts for our ancestors' partiality for instruments of the string family.

The best notice of all was for Mrs. Galpin's 'deft performance on the theorbo and lute'.

Another zealot for early music was Edward Dannreuther, whose book on ornamentation[16] was long regarded as a standard work on the subject. Despite being also a firm supporter of Wagner, his interest in the early composers led him to give chamber concerts in his own home as early as 1874, and he also lectured at the Royal Institution. Bach's music had received slightly more favour since the Bach Gesellschaft was formed in 1850, and following this date regular publications of his works took place: certainly a few authentic performances were given. But it was Mendelssohn who was responsible for the return of Bach's music to the concert platform; he was conducting performances of the major choral works as early as 1855. However, it is important to remember that modern instruments were used. In the *Musical Times* of August 1886, an editorial notes that Sir Arthur Sullivan has the intention to conduct the B minor Mass in the Leeds Festival using the original trumpets and other instruments.[17]

Not one of these men, however celebrated in their particular field, set out to take practical steps for the general re-establishment of early music on the instruments for which it was written. That their contribution as individuals was of the utmost importance is not disputed: and Dolmetsch, who was in close touch with his contemporaries and had not yet begun to fight with them, would be the first to agree, as his correspondence proves. Their performances were sporadic and mainly experimental; their approach was confined to the museum and they did not attempt to reach the people in the same way that Dolmetsch did. His great gift was that he possessed the intuition, the curiosity, the imagination and in addition the craftsmanship to take a museum piece and make it speak a language intelligible to the people of his time: not by making it contemporary but by translating it to 19th- and later 20th-century cars. Perhaps it was no accident that the meaning of Dolmetsch in the original German[18] is— 'interpreter'.

NOTES

1. Grove's *Dictionary of Music* 5, p. 825.
2. His grandmother owned sufficient land to be able to sell a plot for the building of one of the first motor-car factories in France, the celebrated firm of Leon Bollet. The old lady was said to have driven a hard bargain.
3. Playford, *A Brief Introduction to the Skill of Musick*, 1664, p. 82.
4. The composite name was formed from christian names of Victoria, Alice, Leopoldine, Ada, Laura.
5. At the dissolution of the Sacred Harmonic Society in 1882, the College acquired what was the finest collection of music and musical literature ever gathered together by a performing body in England. At the present time this has now been catalogued and forms part of the Collection in the Parry Room at the RCM.
6. One of Sir Hubert Parry's daughters married Arthur Augustus Ponsonby, later the first Lord Ponsonby: his grandson, The Right Hon. Lord Ponsonby of Shulbrede, is on the board of governors of both the RCM and the Dolmetsch Foundation.
7. The viola d'amore has a carved head instead of a scroll.
8. The viola d'amore is a direct descendant from the lyra viol, a 16th-century English instrument. About 1600 the acoustic principle of sympathetic strings was investigated by English scientists, resulting in Daniel Farrant (musician in Charles I's band) in applying it to the viol. The experiment was short-lived on account of the complicated mechanisms and the difficulty in keeping so many strings in tune. The two survivors of the 'lyras' are the baryton and the viola d'amore, both with viol-shaped bodies, the same size as the viola da gamba and the tenor viol respectively. The d'amore has six or seven sympathetic strings running under the fingerboard and six or seven strings that are played with the bow. The strings are always tuned to the key of the composition to be played: there are 27 known tunings, D and A (major and minor) being the most common.
9. The Society consisted of Van Waefelghem, Dolmetsch's friend from Brussels; Louis Diémer, the famous pianist; Jules Delsart, the celebrated violoncellist; and Laurent Grillet, conductor of the Nouveau Cirque in Paris.
10. A chest of viols is a set of six instruments, usually two trebles, one alto, one tenor and two basses: one bass was smaller than the full bass, but the trebles were uniform.
11. In the RCM Library.
12. The clavichord, one of the first made by Dolmetsch, bought by Sir George is in the RCM collection of musical instruments.

13. Some are in the Dolmetsch Library at Haslemere.
14. Grove's *Dictionary of Music* 5, p. 945.
15. The Galpin Society was formed in 1946 to promote the study and preservation of early instruments. Many public and private collections have been saved from dissolution through the good offices of this organisation.
16. Dannreuther, Edward, *Musical Ornamentation*, Novello Primer Series, two volumes.
17. The trumpets used at the Leeds Festival were not 'old German', as stated in the *Musical Times*. The first trumpeter, Walter Morrow, played a modern two-valve straight trumpet in high A, by or supplied by G. Silvani of London, which he designed himself following the bore-valve trumpet. The first occasion in this country when the trumpet and oboe d'amore parts were played as written was in the 1885 performance, not the 1886.
18. The family is of Eastern European origin in what is now USSR or Asia Minor. German etymologists cannot agree on the linguistic components and origins of the word 'Dolmetscher' (interpreter), some claiming it to be of Hungarian, Polish or Turkish (*dolme*-to change) origin: certainly the word came into German from the East. Dr. Hugo Dolmetsch of Zürich, who has spent many years compiling a genealogical table (Stammfolge), thinks that the word was derived from the family rather than *vice versa*. The first documentary evidence of the name is in South Western Germany *c.* 1350, which shows them to be among the oldest Swabian families on record. They were said to have acted as interpreters to the Turks when they overran Eastern Europe and in the 15th century a Philip von Dolmetscher was knighted by the Hapsburgs.

CHAPTER III

The 'Magpie Minstrels'

DOLMETSCH'S daughter, Hélène, was now 11 and an accomplished performer: her technique and interpretation were said to have astounded all who heard her, whilst her feats of memory were considered exceptional even compared with those of a mature adult. At the age of four she had shown signs of this extraordinary talent and her ear was so acute that she could sing a tune after one hearing. On several occasions, Dolmetsch had found her playing his violin 'cello-fashion and it was on this instrument that she had made her debut at the age of seven. Dolmetsch's adoration of this brilliant child was excessive: her quick intelligence responded to his own, and musically they breathed together. Her great capacity for learning enabled her to master the viola da gamba without the slightest difficulty and in a few months she was as facile on that instrument as she was on the 'cello.

Dolmetsch was less successful in teaching his wife—or so he said. The changing pattern of his musical life required more readjustment than Marie could countenance and the marriage had begun to show signs of strain. Bourgeoise and parochial to the bone, Marie cherished hopes of settling down eventually as the respectable wife of a violin teacher, but as research took more and more of her husband's time, she saw those hopes receding. Bewildered and disappointed, she reacted uncharitably towards his work—a fatal error of judgement. He was never easy at the best of times: in 11 years of marriage Dolmetsch had matured from an emotional boy into a man of temperament who knew exactly where he was going. An unashamed perfectionist, he was ruthless in the pursuit of an ideal and extremely impatient with those who did not instantly agree with him: a major flaw in his character which was to cause misunderstanding for the rest of his life.

In later years, when discussing his efforts to instruct his wife, he dismissed her as being totally 'unmusical', and therefore 'unteachable'. This seems a little unjust and perversely inaccurate, for there is proof that Marie learnt to play the tenor viol sufficiently well to join in the consort, for her name appears on several of the early programmes. It is nore likely to have been her keyboard technique that Dolmetsch criticised: many years of what he called 'nineteenth-century thumping' had probably made her heavy-handed: certainly when keyboard instruments were introduced, Dolmetsch would never allow her to touch the harpsichords. But in fairness to Marie it must be remembered that she was almost 40 when Dolmetsch made his first important discoveries and had begun to reshape his career: until this time she had supported him loyally in whatever new venture the prevailing mood dictated. She was no longer a match for a husband in his early thirties. Although round-shouldered and small of stature, Dolmetsch was darkly handsome, and he well knew how to use his personal magnetism to the best advantage.

* * *

Whilst the consort worked to improve their technique, Dolmetsch searched the museums for more literature. Soon, music by the Lawes brothers, Simpson, Ferrabosco and Martin Pierson in 3, 4, 5 and 6 parts was an established part of their repertoire, but he became increasingly aware that they were handicapped by the lack of an authentic keyboard continuo instrument. They had been making do with a square piano but it did not produce the right sound. Eventually, it was a little spinet found in a junk shop that led Dolmetsch to Messrs. Broadwood, where he first met A. J. Hipkins.

It was on the strength of his reputation that Dolmetsch had inquired whether Hipkins could restore the spinet for him. He was now so committed to his work on the viols that he had difficulty in finding time for his teaching, let alone restoration of a keyboard instrument. Unfortunately Hipkins could offer no practical assistance; he, too, was busy. Nevertheless, he showed a lively interest in all Dolmetsch had to say, and the two men discovered they had much in common. When Dolmetsch mentioned his own early training as a piano-maker, Hipkins asked if he had thought of restoring it himself? When he left Broadwood's that day, Dolmetsch vowed that in future he would restore all the instruments himself, as he had in fact done already with the square piano in Brussels. If he could not find time, he would make time: if he did not know the principles upon which an instrument worked, he would research until he had learned down to the last detail. From that day on, Dolmetsch was never known to take an instrument to a dealer unless he wanted to sell it.

The restoration of the spinet was a larger undertaking than Dolmetsch had visualised and its completion took some time. There was nowhere to work but on the kitchen table and this did not improve Marie's rebellious attitude. When at last it was finished, and the spinet's gentle voice could be heard adding a new sparkle to the consort, Dolmetsch was happy: he had finally achieved a truly Elizabethan sound. By the end of 1889 he had, in addition, restored a Kirkman double-manual harpsichord, a set of Italian virginals and a large clavichord.

He made careful notes of the measurements of every instrument that passed through his hands and, at the same time, continued to study the instructions set down by the best makers. The idea of making instruments himself was already taking shape in his mind, but he had to postpone the practical fulfilment of such notions to the future, to be put on what he termed the 'one day' list. At that particular period, time was the most valuable commodity in his life. Besides, he was now anxious to present his music to the general public, preferably in London.

It was his pupil the young Countess Valda Gleichen who found a sponsor for Dolmetsch's first but brief appearance at a London concert on 21 May 1890, when the 'Magpie Minstrels'[1] gave one of their bi-annual performances at the Princes' Hall. The Countess sang *Sweet Echo* from Milton's *Masque of Comus*, set to music by Henry Lawes and arranged by Dolmetsch, who also accompanied her on the viola d'amore, with Hélène playing the viola da gamba. The concert was well-received by everyone except Queen Victoria. It reached the Royal ears that the Countess was not only singing in public but had been taking private violin lessons from a Frenchman. Whilst her Gracious Majesty approved in general of concerts organised for charitable purposes, she did not welcome the idea of one of her nieces becoming a professional singer, or even worse, a musician. When Dolmetsch wrote again to the young lady asking her to sing at one of his concerts, the reply he received indicates that the Queen and the Countess had come to terms, but with a proviso which seems unnecessarily harsh today. The ironic reversal of today's meaning of the word 'Pop' is interesting:

(undated)   St. James's Palace

Dear Mr Dolmetsch,

It is too kind of you to make such a suggestion and at any other time there is nothing that I should have liked better than to sing at one of your interesting concerts, but the fact is this. I have only been allowed to sing professionally on the condition that I do not sing, for the present at any rate, at anything of the nature of an evening party, and I fear that a concert given at the New Gallery must come under this description. Of course a public concert would have been quite different. My plans are all very vague still, but I intend to sing under the name of Mlle. Gerda, and if Mr Chappell gives me the chance, I hope very much to sing at one of the 'Pops.'

Yours very sincerely,
Valda Gleichen

A third book of the Corelli sonatas was published in the spring of the same year and in the *Musical Times* of 1 June a reviewer notes that: 'The two books of sonatas which have already appeared have exercised no little influence in reviving an interest in old violin music.' Dolmetsch was delighted at this response, especially when two weeks later his pupils' concert also drew excellent coverage from the press. The *Daily Graphic* critic (13 June) confessed that although he did not find pupils' concerts the most exhilarating form of entertainment, he would certainly make an exception in favour of Mr. Arnold Dolmetsch's performance. The music was 'exceedingly interesting' and he praised the ensemble for its 'purity of tone and vigour of attack . . . attained in the instrumental music of the 2nd part of Purcell's *Fairy Queen*, the score of which has been restored by Mr Arnold Dolmetsch from an old set of parts'. He reminds his readers that Signor Piatti had introduced a set of divisions on a ground for viola da gamba by Christopher Simpson [on the 'cello] 'at one of last season's Popular Concerts', and that 'These had been played for the first time on the 'cello last June by Miss Dolmetsch at a Pupils' Concert'. This is an interesting pointer as to the time when Dolmetsch made the transition from 'cello to gamba. At the same concert we learn that 'another set of *divisions* of a more complicated nature' was introduced: 'Three six-part chords, which could not be played on the 'cello, and other features peculiar to the viola da gamba were played by Mr Dolmetsch's little daughter in highly creditable fashion.'

The rest of the press comment varied from a description of Purcell's *Fairy Queen* as 'quaint' or 'curious' to the Divisions as being 'monotonous'. But no one was left unimpressed: rather the reverse. The *Musical Standard* felt strongly that 'Mr. Dolmetsch deserves credit for his efforts to place before an audience of today these echoes from the past.' This same publication unwittingly excelled itself in the typesetting department for the final sentence reads: 'Messrs Broadwood's lent for the occasion their beautiful Shudi Sharpsichord.'

However, irrespective of the pitch of Broadwood's instrument, their representative Mr. Hipkins had attended the concert and wrote to Dolmetsch the same evening: 'I must congratulate you on the success of your delightful concert. . . . I got Piatti to attend. . . . It will gratify you that he was very much pleased with your daughter: at which I am not surprised.' The following morning Hipkins wrote again, enclosing cuttings from half a dozen papers and commenting on the high note of approval throughout. 'Frankly, I should recommend you to persevere with these old music concerts. You are the very man for it.'

The warm reception fanned Dolmetsch's natural optimism into a roaring fire: there was no holding him when he heard from a man of letters who had also enjoyed the concert. It was from Herbert Horne,[2] architect, minor poet and decorator of books. He enclosed a copy of *The Century Guild Hobby Horse*, a finely printed and somewhat precious magazine of which he was the editor. Dolmetsch replied immediately:

4, Alleyn Crescent,
West Dulwich.   June 19th 1890
Dear Sir,

   Your letter did me great pleasure. I am glad to find that my efforts to make the old English Classical music appreciated as it deserves, are so far successful. I am very much obliged for the copy of your most interesting magazine, which I had never seen, and which was for me a great pleasure to read as to look at.

   I hope to be able to call on you Saturday afternoon next about three, although I cannot promise for certain as I am exceedingly busy just now. But I will try . . .
                                                         Yours very faithfully . . .

   It can here be seen that Dolmetsch was no respecter of persons: the work always came first. However important the personage, if a caller interrupted him when he was engaged upon an intricate operation concerning the life of an instrument, they were asked to wait. It is not known if this particular appointment was kept, but certainly the two men became acquainted at about this time. Horne was later to play a significant role in assisting Dolmetsch to gain recognition among the 'Bloomsbury Set.'

*   *   *

   The story of how Dolmetsch acquired his first lute[3] is well known. It seems that he walked into one of the London salerooms when an auction was in progress and saw an exquisite ebony and ivory lute being offered. He had not a penny piece of his own at the time so bidding for himself was out of the question. But he admired the lute and was interested to see what would happen. Anxiously he waited as the auctioneer tempted the assembly, but stony silence prevailed. At last a timid voice could be heard from the back of the room asking 'Five pounds?' Dolmetsch was incensed: a pittance for such a work of art was an insult. 'Five pounds!' he roared. 'Imbecile! It's worth fifty!' The quiet-voiced man did not argue: neither did the auctioneer, quickly bringing down his gavel so as not to impede the progress of such generosity. Dolmetsch had become the owner of a 'very fine 16th-century Paduan lute' without sufficient money on him to pay for a catalogue.

   It was Marie Dolmetsch who eventually paid for the instrument, but this typical example of Dolmetsch's hot-headedness was not an isolated incident. The irresponsible buying of instruments was a constant strain on their resources, whilst the little that Dolmetsch earned from his teaching was quickly exhausted on the raw materials he needed for his restoration. Even when the work was completed it was seldom remunerative, for since he could not afford to buy all the instruments he would have liked, he would purchase them on behalf of his pupils, and, more often than not, restore them for nothing.

All repairs were now completed on the kitchen table. The lute, with its complex and delicate construction, set Dolmetsch an unusually long and difficult task, especially when he carried out his normal practice of taking down measurements for his 'one day' list. No doubt precipitated by the advent of the lute, the already chilly marital relationship took a turn for the worse. When a woman's own domain is invaded to the extent that she herself feels an intruder, the most patient wife is liable to turn revolutionary, and Marie must have been sorely tried if she had to remove tools and dismembered instruments before she could set about her own work. But provincial pride ran through her like a grain and even under these trying circumstances she struggled to restore order out of chaos, for she knew well enough that unless some sort of compromise could be effected, they had little hope of staying together. The main reason for their differences was that Marie had been inadequately endowed by nature to contend with marriage to an ever-erupting volcano. Inevitably the child suffered most. If Hélène derived her intelligence from her father, she inherited her mother's conventionality as well as her strong sense of duty. Deeply affected by the perpetual wrangling, she fought to reconcile her divided loyalties. Never a very robust child, she succumbed easily to the strain which the situation imposed upon her. Her health began to deteriorate, she became withdrawn, and turned to her music for consolation.

In the autumn of 1890 the Dolmetsches moved house to 60 Croxted Road, West Dulwich. The new house had more living accommodation, a sizeable garden, and for Marie an advantage that outweighed all the others: there was an attic that could be turned into a workroom.

NOTES

1. The Magpie Minstrels Madrigal Society—a body of singers gathered together by Alfred Scott-Gatty to sing for charity.
2. Horne was also a critic of art and literature and a student of the Caroline poets. With Mackmurdo he designed the Savoy Hotel and later migrated to Florence to write his great biography of Botticelli to which he gave years of intensive research. His home, a Trecento palace of the Burgess type, filled with his collection of works of art, is now a museum.
3. In Padova, Michielle Harton. 1598 M L.

CHAPTER IV

The Gresham Lectures

THE winter of 1890 found Dolmetsch with a new platform: Dr. Frederick Bridge, that popular and industrious man who was simultaneously a professor at the Royal College of Music, organist and choirmaster at Westminster Abbey, and music professor at Gresham College, had asked Dolmetsch to provide musical illustrations for two of his lectures. Dolmetsch was delighted. He realised the significance of having Bridge on his side and sought to make the most of the opportunity. We know that Dolmetsch was no orthodox scholar: his teachers were the great writers of the musical past and his practical experience had been gained at an age when memory cannot be isolated from the beginning of life itself: in addition, his thorough researching had made him equal to any of his academic contemporaries. Nevertheless, to the Establishment he was an amateur musicologist and as such could not be taken seriously. It is a curious fact that British hypocrisy, then at its most rampant, held the greatest respect for the gentleman, and therefore amateur, sportsman, whereas the same word applied to any form of creative accomplishment evoked howls of protest. To Dolmetsch, Dr. Bridge's invitation was the symbol of hierarchical approval.

The first lecture, on 19 November, was called 'Mozart as a Teacher' and concerned the MSS exercises of his pupil, Attwood, written in Vienna, 1785–87. In the section dealing with 'Mozart's succinct method of Thorough Bass', Dolmetsch, Hélène and some pupils supplied illustrations of canons, fugues, minuets and variations both by Mozart and his pupil, presumably on modern instruments.

It was at the last lecture, on 21 November, that Dolmetsch was given the real opportunity to display his knowledge; it is, in fact, the first record in modern times of music by Byrd, Dr. Bull, Jenkins, Simpson, Lawes, Locke and Purcell being played 'on the instruments for which it was written'.

So successful were the lectures that Dolmetsch was asked to illustrate a further series the following spring. He was in his element. The first subject was 'Thomas Morley, an old English musical worthy . . . his theoretical writings and instrumental compositions'. Dr. Bridge himself played the harpsichord and Dolmetsch and his daughter performed two fantasies for viola da gamba and viol.

In the last lecture, 'A second look at the viols', seven items were devoted to Dolmetsch and his pupils: they played music by Este,[1] Tomkins, Locke and Simpson: it is also more than likely that it was the first time that Ferrabosco's beautiful *Four-Note Pavin*—the piece with which Dolmetsch was later to become so closely identified—was heard in modern times.

In April there were more lectures: Dolmetsch had now restored and restrung his Paduan lute and had also taught himself to play it. The story of how he performed on it for Dr. Bridge, and so enchanted him that he asked Dolmetsch to use it at the next lecture, is recounted in many versions, coloured variously according to the imagination of the narrator. It is highly improbable that the decision was so dramatically well-timed, but apart from the isolated performance by Mrs. Galpin (see p. 25) it was the first time that the lute had been played in public in modern times and possibly the first time since the middle of the 17th century, when its popularity declined in favour of what Dolmetsch termed its 'degenerate offspring', the mandoline.

The lecture 'Shakespeare and his music' was held on 23 April to mark the anniversary of the poet's death, and two of the earliest settings of *Where the Bee Sucks* and *Full Fathom Five* were sung by the choristers of Westminster Abbey, with Dolmetsch playing the lute and Hélène the viola da gamba. At a second lecture, the following evening, further settings of the same songs were given, with the addition of some of the music for Purcell's *Fairy Queen*.

The chance acquisition of the lute and its subsequent restoration was in many respects one of Dolmetsch's most remarkable achievements. We know there were no professional lutenists and neither are there records of any serious amateurs being associated with the instrument. Dolmetsch had no one to consult. The books in his own library provided the information he needed concerning the construction of the instrument, but he had to supply strings of the right length and gauge in order to tune it properly—a formidable task in itself with 15 strings, or *courses*, 14 of which are tuned in pairs. The music, too, presented a further problem with its old lute tablature: until Dolmetsch had found the key he was unable to decipher a single note of it. As late as 1904 Dolmetsch wrote:[2]

> There are some lutes in museums: in Bologna, Brussels, Paris, and other places, and a few in private collections; but spurious *property* lutes manufactured by clever, if unscrupulous, Italians for the benefit of later-day collectors, are far more numerous than genuine specimens, even in public museums.

Dolmetsch was never a brilliant lutenist in the technical sense, but his tone was superb. As with any instrument he touched, his instinct some-how guided him to produce the right sound, the sound which reached the heart of those who heard him play. Many performers today have become more technically advanced than Dolmetsch at his best; Diana Poulton,[3] one of his first pupils and present-day authority on the instrument, admits that she has never been able to achieve the beauty of tone that Dolmetsch could coax from it without the slightest effort.

Dolmetsch was well aware that the Gresham lectures had prestige value, but he was intent on giving an independent concert. How he raised the necessary funds is a mystery, but on 27 April 1891 he booked the Princes Hall in Piccadilly for 'A Concert of Ancient Music of the XVI and XVII Centuries'. On the eve of the performance every seat had been sold. On the programme was a footnote in small print which reads:

> N.B. Owing to the delicate nature of the tone of the instruments, and the style of the Music, which requires concentration of mind to be thoroughly understood, the doors of the room will be kept closed during the performance of the pieces.

Dolmetsch had not only begun to attract audiences, he had started to educate them.

His programme ran into seven pages and included introductory notes which he used at subsequent concerts: informative and amusing, the notes were in fact essential if his music was to mean anything to people who were accustomed to vastly different harmonies and dynamics. The extracts which follow show that Dolmetsch was thoroughly familiar with his subject:

> There has been, of late years, a wonderful revival of old English Music. The Madrigals of Morley, Gibbons, Wilbye, etc., are now familiar to many. Some of the 'Virginal' pieces of Byrd, Dr. John Bull, etc., have been reprinted in various collections, and can occasionally be heard upon the Spinet, or Harpsichord; but amongst the thousands of pieces written for the Viols, in various combinations, almost nothing is known to the public, with the exception of what was played as illustrations to the recent Lectures given by Professor J. F. Bridge at the Gresham College, and by Mr A. J. Hipkins at The Society of Arts. Yet, these Viol Consorts were undoubtedly the highest form of secular music in England during the Six-teenth and Seventeenth Centuries. That they have been neglected so long is due to several causes.
>
> First—the music is difficult of access. The only pieces which can be easily pro-cured are the Fantasies of 3 parts of Orlando Gibbons, which were reprinted by the Musical Antiquarian Society in 1843. These, however, have done much more harm than good to the revival of this ancient music, which I have so much at heart. They were given to the world as the best specimens of these compositions;

probably on account of the great eminence of Gibbons as a composer of sacred music and madrigals, but they were decidedly unworthy of the honour.

Dolmetsch goes on to say that those looking into this music and finding it 'dry' naturally concluded that the rest of it would be even more so. He touches on a concourse of 'circumstances' which led him to make a thorough study of the subject, the result of which was to prove that many of the 'Consorts of Viols' are not only very interesting but extremely beautiful.

Then he covers the very important question of playing the music on the 'instruments for which it was written' and explains that the viols had become obsolete. To get a chest of viols in playing order was by no means easy. It is not that the instruments were so very rare—some of them, the *viola da gamba*, for example, being by no means difficult to find—but that some 150 years of neglect having passed over them, they were never to be found in proper condition. The gambas had been turned into 'cellos, the smaller viols into violas or violins, or altered otherwise in various ways. He bemoans the contemporary violin-dealers' lack of skill in fitting a viol to perfection, 'no doubt, some day, if this revival of the viols succeeds, as it ought to do, it will be as easy to get a viol put into playing order as it was 200 years ago. It is not so now, however.'

The remainder of the notes deal entirely with the music itself[4] and Dolmetsch goes on to quote from Thomas Mace's *Musick's Monument*, published in 1676;

> In my younger time we had musick most excellently choice and most eminently rare, both for its excellency in composition, rare fancy and sprightly ayres; as also for its proper and fit performances; even such, as if your young tender ears and fancies, were but truly tincture therewith, and especially if it possibly could but be cry'd up for the mode or new fashion, you would embrace for some divine thing. . . . We had for our grave musick Fancies of 3, 4, 5 and 6 parts, interposed, now and then, with some Pavins, Allmaines, solemn and sweet, delightful ayres, all of which were, as it were, so many pathetical stories, rhetorical and sublime discourses, subtil and acute argumentations, so suitable and agreeing to the inward secret, and intellectual faculties of the soul and mind, that to set them forth accordingly to their true praise, there are no words sufficient in language, yet what I can best speak of them shall be only to say, that they have been to myself, and many others, as divine raptures, powerfully captivating all our unruley faculties and affections for the time, and disposing us to solidity, gravity, and a good temper, making us capable of heavenly and divine influences. 'Tis great pity few men believe this much, but far greater that so few know it.

The audience was treated to 11 items of music by Morley, Ferrabosco, Simpson, Este, Pierson, Tomkins and Locke, played on the viols, lute and harpsichord with tenor and soprano singers for good measure. The analytical notes give the exact source of each MS and, where possible, further details about the history of the composition and its writer, such as the following on the suite for 6 viols and harpsichord by Martin Pierson: I Fantazie   II Allmaine   III Allmaine

> Very little is known about Martin Pierson. His name is not in Grove's Dictionary.[5] The only particular I have been able to discover about him is that he took his degree as a Bachelor of Music in 1613. I found the present *Suite* in the British Museum, in a MS of the early part of the XVII century. The music is very remarkable on account of the bold and effective way in which the numerous parts are treated. They often move together in masses in a manner more suggestive of Handel than of early XVII Century Music. Indeed the Allmaine II, with its clear-cut rhythm and simple melody, might very well pass for a March from some opera of Handel.

The success of this concert encouraged Dolmetsch to persevere with his work: when offered an engagement he accepted it regardless of whether the fee would cover his expenses. The result was that he found himself travelling a great deal, giving concerts in small halls in and around London, which included one at the Society of Arts Conversazione at the South Kensington Museum: the concert was in two parts, from 9.15 to 11.15, and the audience were requested to change in the interval.

In July, Dolmetsch gave his annual pupils' concert at the Portman Rooms, his young Valda Gleichen singing to Dr. Bridge's piano accompaniment: the professor also played in a concerto by John Stanley, the blind 18th-century organist.

Meanwhile, Herbert Horne and Dolmetsch had been meeting, frequently exploring their mutual interest in the ancients. When he was in Italy, Horne generously passed on every scrap of information he was able to unearth in the museums of Florence and Bologna. On 20 October 1891 Dolmetsch wrote to Horne:

> 60, Croxted Road,
West Dulwich
>
> I have just received your papers, which I find *exceedingly* interesting.
> They contain a good deal of matter quite new to me, and I can venture to say to all my brother 'musicians' I had been puzzled about the 'Gottire' without success. I am glad to identify him as Jacques Gaulthier.[6]

Dolmetsch tells Horne that he will have some seats kept for him at the next two Gresham lectures: admission was free and it is known that during Dr. Bridge's time at the College the attendance increased so greatly that it was necessary to arrive very early to avoid being turned away.

However, Horne's assistance was as yet confined to research: it was Dr. Parry who crusaded so loyally on Dolmetsch's behalf to find new opportunities to present his music to the public. In a letter to Dolmetsch on 24 October 1891 he discloses some interesting facts about the penurious condition under which he and his fellow professors worked:

> 17, Kensington Square,
> W.

> I had already spoken to Sir John Stainer about it [a concert] and proposed to him to bring you in at the Sheldonian in one of my regular University Lectures. But it strikes me you might prefer to go down and give a regular concert. I cannot tell you how much it would pay as Oxford is such an independable place, and people like going to things when they have to pay nothing. My lectures have to be given to people who don't pay a penny, and the University pays me £13 a year, which barely covers my travelling expenses. So I cannot afford to give you anything worthy to be called a fee to illustrate one of my lectures. The outside I could go to would be £10, which would be almost the whole of my yearly salary! But I will gladly go to that if you could come for that. Please tell me which you would prefer—to come to one of my lectures next month, for £10 to meet expenses, or risk a concert on your own account.

> C. Hubert Parry

Dolmetsch accepted the more concrete offer and on Sunday 15 November Parry went down to Dulwich to make arrangements and made an entry in his diary that evening:

> His house is the characteristic symbol of an enthusiast. The walls are covered with lutes, gambas, spinets, harpsichords, and are in perfect condition, tended with enthusiastic love. He and his daughter aged 12 played me some things very well on gambas and he played a little to me on the lute.[7]

On 24 November, Parry wrote telling Dolmetsch that all arrangements were now complete and that a conveyance would meet them at the station, whereupon they would all proceed to Sir John Stainer's house for lunch.

Dolmetsch had selected a programme similar to those of concerts given earlier in the year with the interesting addition of a composition by King Henry VIII, *If Love now Reigned* from a MS at the British Museum which had recently been published by the Plainsong and Mediaeval Music Society. The lecture was well-received and Dolmetsch was jubilant. For Dr. Parry the evening had not been such an exhilarating experience. From his diary we learn:

> Down to Oxford in morning—met Stainer at station and he brought up a bus to take down Dolmetsch and his folk and his instruments. Lunch at Stainer's and a deal of talking which exhausted me utterly. By the time I got to the theatre I was quite unfit to say a word but I got through. D. gave the audience a very complete dose of old viol music. Too much contrapuntal stuff and too little damn music! His daughter played Christopher Simpson last division wonderfully well.[8]

About two weeks prior to the Sheldonian Lecture, Dolmetsch embarked upon his first essay into musical journalism, and as a result became embroiled in a public controversy. He had been engaged by the *Musical News* to cover a demonstration concert at 40 Wigmore Street,[9] when a Dr. Stelzner was to introduce an instrument of his own invention called the Violotta. A number of distinguished musicians had been invited to witness the proceedings and Emil Kreuz, Dolmetsch's ex fellow-student from the Royal College, now a celebrated violinist, was to provide the musical illustrations. In the *Musical News* of November, under the heading 'New Era in Violin-making', Dolmetsch contributed a witty and informed deposition of the latest so-called improvement to the queen of instruments. A short extract suffices to illustrate not only Dolmetsch's excellent command of English but his practical knowledge of the subject. After a few cynical introductory comments on the recurrence of people who claim to have outmastered all the old masters—and failed—Dolmetsch writes:

> Dr. Stelzner's theories, although explained with plenty of scientific terms and a large amount of confidence, are deduced from totally wrong principle, and the practical results are not satisfactory. Many of the theories given by him as proved physical laws would bear discussion and several of his statements are incorrect. His main idea is that the violin should be constructed of true ellipses and parabolic curves, so that the vibrations of the strings should be reverberated upon 4 points situated, of course, inside the violin, and coincident with the focuses of the curves of the sides. There might be some truth in this theory if a violin was intended to receive sounds from the *outside*, and made them heard to a person concealed *inside* the instrument, but this is not the mission of the violin.

Dr. Stelzner was then reported to have presented his Violotta—'destined to fill the gap between the compass of the viola and the 'cello'. Dolmetsch points immediately to the real comparison, which is between the 'cello and the true tenor, 'tuned the same as Dr. Stelzner's instrument, but had, it is hoped, a better tone!' Of his friend Kreuz he writes: 'He is an admirable player . . . so the performance gave pleasure in spite of the instrument.' Dolmetsch delivers the punch-line with all the skill of the professional journalist: 'The happy possessors of fine old instruments need not discard them just yet in favour of Dr. Stelzner's experiments.'
Dolmetsch had indeed put the cat among the pigeons. The correspondence came in thick and fast: it involved all kinds of eminent supporters, including Herr David Popper, the German-born 'cellist and composer. Translated into both French and German the letters were published well into the New Year. Nonetheless, Grove's *Dictionary* makes no mention of Dr. Stelzner or his violotta, and the violin has survived in its original form. We can presume that Dolmetsch had exploded one more myth from the

many that surround the violin and will continue to do so as long as man is charmed by its voice and perplexed by its construction.

* * *

Herbert Horne had been trying for some time to persuade his friend to give his own concert lectures, but with uncharacteristic modesty Dolmetsch protested that his English was not good enough. Certainly his French accent remained very pronounced to the end of his days, but his fluency in the English language, as we have seen already, was quite remarkable. Usually not lacking in confidence in his ability to carry out anything to which he had set his mind, Dolmetsch's unaccustomed modesty on this occasion is interesting. It reveals the high esteem in which he held his work and the importance that he attached to the necessity for the message to be transported correctly.

When Horne finally convinced him a further problem arose: that of finding a suitable hall in which to lecture. Dolmetsch's lack of academic qualifications automatically prevented him from using any of the recognised learned institutions, so Horne solved the problem by arranging a concert lecture at 20 Fitzroy Street in the studio he shared with A. H. Mackmurdo, the architect.

Horne arranged everything and designed and printed beautiful notices that would catch the eye. He handled the advance publicity with such skill that on the night of the concert (19 December 1891) the studio was packed. The best-known progressives in London had turned out for the occasion—artists, poets, writers: they were fascinated by this little Frenchman whose very appearance was more pre-Raphaelite than the pre-Raphaelites themselves with velvet suit, lace ruffles and silver buckles on his shoes. His music recaptured for them the delights of a lost enchantment: the embodiment of all their aspirations. He was loved on sight and when the concert was over they applauded uproariously. At last Dolmetsch had found his audience.

The denizens of Bloomsbury may have accepted Dolmetsch but to his wife it was no signal for rejoicing: she frowned upon these Bohemians, who called uninvited at hours that were not 'respectable'. As Dolmetsch's circle of friends widened, the marriage dwindled into what was little more than a means of existence. Too busy lapping up his success to pay attention to his wife's disrupted conventions, Dolmetsch was like a man reborn: he threw himself into his work with twice the energy and four times the enthusiasm. With the growing hostility between her parents, Hélène's suffering became more acute: her playing was said to have taken on a new dimension of spiritual beauty, as is so often the case when physical or mental pain becomes unendurable. Now bitterly aware of the dubious blessings that attend the children of genius, she was the first Dolmetsch to carry the dynastic burden, but by no means the last.

NOTES

1. The spelling of Este is variable: the more usual form used today is, Easte.
2. *The Connoisseur*, April 1904, Vol. VIII, pp. 213–17.
3. Poulton, Diana, *John Dowland*, Faber and Faber, London, 1972.
4. Viol music may be broadly divided into two classes: the first comprises the 'In Nomines' and 'Fantasies' or Fancies, the style of which was such that no one part could be said to be an accompaniment to another, but were all of equal importance. The 'In Nomines' were written upon a 'Canto Fermo', generally the Gregorian Melody of the 'Introit', 'In Nomine Jesu' hence their name. The 'Canto Fermo', or 'Plaint-Song', was played in very slow notes by one of the Viols, whilst the others, 2, 3, 4, or 5 in number, made a most elaborate, and often remarkably beautiful, descant upon it. The 'Fantasies', as their name implies, did not bind the composer to any established form, but allowed him to follow the bent of his genius unfettered. 'In this sort of musick,' said Christopher Simpson, 'the composer doth employ all his art and invention solely about the bringing in, and carrying on of these fugues. . . . When he has tried all the several ways which he thinks fit to be used therein, he takes some other point, and does the like with it; or else, for variety, introduces chromatick notes with bindings and intermixture of discords; or falls into some lighter humour, like a Madrigal, or *what else his* fancy shall lead him to; but, still concluding with something that hath art and excellency in it.'
   The second class of viol music comprises the 'Ayres, Pavans, Allmaines, Corantos, Sarabandes, etc. etc.'. These were composed in strict form, being divided in rhythmic phrases, with double bars and repeats, much like an ordinary Minuet. They are absolute tunes, the accompaniments, although often elaborate enough, being always subordinate to the melody.

   > Extracts from Dolmetsch's programme notes
   > for the concert 27 April 1891, at the Princes Hall, Piccadilly.
5. In the current edition (the fifth, edited Eric Blom), 1954, of Grove's *Dictionary of Music*, there is over a page devoted to Martin Pierson, spelled Peerson.
6. A court lutenist in England 1617.
7. Parry Diaries, Shulbrede Priory.
8. ibid.
9. Now the Wigmore Hall.

CHAPTER V

'The Fitzroy Settlement'

SPURRED on by the overwhelming success of the December undertaking, Dolmetsch needed no persuasion to give a series of four more concerts of a similar kind. Early in January, advance notices, again beautifully printed by the Chiswick Press on fine quality paper, were sent out announcing performances on the lute as well as the harpsichord, the greater number of the compositions being taken from the works of those musicians who:

> once lent to the English School its great repute. This school of Music, which first flourished, and was truly native, under Elizabeth, and which became more learned and Italianate in the Caroline age, yielded at the death of Purcell, to a less fine and severe taste; or, at least, to a kind of art, in which English writers did not prove comparable to the foreign masters. . . . In like expressions, do Christopher Simpson, John Playford, and other writers of that time, regret the decline of this admirable school, and the neglect of its masters. To revive, after an interval of two hundred years, a due interest in the works of these composers is my great endeavour, as it is my privilege first, in recent times, to transcribe their compositions, and perform them upon the proper instruments.

In addition to concerted pieces for viols by these composers, Dolmetsch would be presenting some of their songs with the original accompaniments on the lute, viols or harpsichord. He promised not to neglect the foreign masters: three sonatas of Bach for viola da gamba and harpsichord and one for flute, viola d'amore and harpsichord would be included. From this programme we are given some indication of how Dolmetsch's personal library had grown, for he claims to possess the complete collection of Marin Marais' viola da gamba pieces: some of these, together with the trios of Rameau and Leclair, were also to be performed.

J. A. Fuller–Maitland,[1] *The Times* musical critic, himself a good pianist and harpsichordist, had shown considerable interest in Dolmetsch's concerts and did, in fact, take part in a number of the Fitzroy Street performances. In a letter to Horne (12 February 1892), Dolmetsch 'hopes [that] *The Times* will give us a fine criticism on Monday next'. He is also confident that the concert will be well patronised: 'I think I shall want 400 circulars. I shall send them rather broadcast to see how the public bites . . . we need not accept everybody.' But a fortnight later the buoyant mood had changed to one of despair. Dolmetsch bemoans:

24 Feb. 1892   60, Croxted Road,
                                                                                W. Dulwich

The subscriptions are a complete failure—only 7. The Royal College of Music will send 12 students, but pays nothing. I have sent a good many invitations, I expect about 30 people altogether; you might send as many invitations yourself.

However, despite the fact that guests outnumbered patrons, the first concert was in the end very well attended and saw the introduction of five *new* works: fantasies by Easte and John Jenkins, a pavan for two viols and lute by Dr. Coleman, a suite for four viols by Locke, and an unaccompanied suite for viola da gamba by Marais. *The Times* critic certainly appeared at this concert for the *Musical Times* reported that:

J. A. Fuller-Maitland played on the harpsichord with perfect taste and skill Bull's 'St. Thomas's Wake' from *Parthenia* and, in response to an encore, the same composer's 'King's Hunting Jigg'. (April 1892)

20 Fitzroy Street,[2] known popularly as the Fitzroy Settlement, was an Adam building dating from the 1790s and had been purchased by Mackmurdo in 1889. The ground floor was fitted out as a workroom for The Century Guild; Selwyn Image, Herbert Horne and the painter T. Hope McLachlan had studios on the first floor; and Lionel Johnson lived in two rooms on the top floor, 97 steps from the street:

Mackmurdo [had] enlivened its face by white paint on the woodwork of windows, door and fanlight, and a number and knocker in brass. . . . An entrant was greeted by a circular warm Della Robia relief let into a wall of the white tinted vestibule. An imposing Italian painting in fine colouring in [the] original frame overspread the width of the projecting breast above the mantel in the drawing office. . . . Two large rooms which could be thrown into one [were] on the first floor. . . . Dullness was absent, disposal of furniture was discriminating and airiness prevailed.[3]

The house was a hive of artistic activity over whose threshold almost every famous personage of the 'nineties had crossed at some time or other:

Sturge Moore, looking with his flowing beard like one of the apostles, reciting verse to a zither; [W.B.] Yeats declaiming, [Walter] Sickert, [Walter] Crane, Augustus John, William Rothenstein, [Edgar] Jepson, [Ernest] Rhys and [Oscar] Wilde.[4]

Dolmetsch fitted admirably into this setting, but not all the visitors who had been invited to his concerts found inspiration in them. Those two meticulous poetesses Katherine Bradley and her niece, Edith Cooper, who published jointly under the name of Michael Field and managed to dwell so successfully in two worlds—that of Victorian propriety on the one hand[5] and Bloomsbury on the other—wrote in their diary of being invited by Horne to attend a concert:

> The men achieve a ladies' cloakroom, but no adequate reception, the guests wander . . . at last we find a room where the harpsichord stands—the studio. A man with large hair and panther eyes moves about—it must be Dolmetsch. The discord, the untidy business of tuning up distresses the ear peculiarly and seems to take longer than usual. At last the six viols make the ancient novel music. How strange the tone of these old instruments—what a far-off tinkling of youthfulness. They cannot express the subtlety nor the volume of our modern emotion . . . they have a sunny gala thinness, or a quaint sorrow that scarcely swells into passion. Men must have been half crickets when this music satisfied them.[6]

The piece for solo viola da gamba is described by Michael Field as 'toothache calling unto toothache . . . physical torture . . . nothing divine in it'. Fortunately this was an isolated view for a rather different opinion was expressed by Alfred Piatti, the celebrated 'cellist, who writes: 'Bien de choses, à toute votre famille surtout à votre *talented* fille, votre devoué, Alfred Piatti.' (March 1892)

At the second Fitzroy Street concert, Dolmetsch introduced no fewer than ten works receiving their first modern performances music by Richard Deering, Dr. John Bull, J. S. Bach, the Lawes brothers, Locke, Jenkins and an unknown French composer, Jean Marie Leclair.

The *Musical Times* (1 April 1892) suggests that to connoisseurs Dolmetsch's work is already well known, but that in the interest of a wider circle it is well to mention that the repertoire of his concerts is drawn principally from the suites and fantasies which were the delight of our forefathers 'at a period when as a nation we were more truly musical than now, and that they are performed upon the instruments for which they were written'. He says that it is a rare opportunity for cultivating a knowledge of an unjustly neglected branch of a national art and reminds his readers that the instruments and music are 'more or less inaccessible to any but such enthusiasts as Mr. Dolmetsch'. Finally, he asks, 'If we are really a musical nation, why do we have the best works of our old masters unprinted?'

*   *   *

With his ever-increasing repertoire it was now a comparatively easy matter for Dolmetsch to find suitable material to illustrate musical lectures. Dr. Bridge recalled Dolmetsch to play music for one of his lectures at Gresham College on 'John Jenkins—an old English Musical *Worthy*'. The subject was close to Dolmetsch's heart and the occasion attracted, as usual, a crowded audience: 'the musical excerpts were cleverly played on viols and a viola da gamba by Mr. Dolmetsch and his pupils.' *Musical Times* (1 April 1892).

Dolmetsch was also becoming known outside the artistic and academic *coterie*, at the *soirée musicale*. Fashionable hostesses who usually preferred Mendelssohn and Liszt performed by singers or pianists who could be relied upon to 'render' the music in the approved manner, were growing bolder and began to look to this little Frenchman with his persuasive charm and his 'funny old instruments' for entertainment. One such hostess, Lady Ashburton, invited her friends to hear 'A Consort of Viols' at Kent House, her Knightsbridge home. Bewitched by the music of the Elizabethans, she writes:

> April 5th 1892   Kent House
>   Knightsbridge
> Thank you for the deliciously lovely concert you gave us—the sweet sounds still linger in my ears with gratitude in my heart.

The mutual ecstasy was doubtless more genuine on Dolmetsch's part; excitedly he writes to Horne the same evening:

> April 3rd 1892   60, Croxted Road,
>   W. Dulwich
>   S.E.
> Very distinguished audience and immense success! Many encores—the song 'Gather Your Rosebuds' very *well sung* by Mr. Avalon Collard with lute. We had to do it *four times*. Very fair pay also—20 guineas.

The letter is further concerned with Horne's research at the British Museum:

> The Campion songs are lovely—but I wish I had the other two, I cannot wait more for my programme—If you have not got them, we may *very well* keep them for the last concert!—I *cannot* get them myself, but I should be *exceedingly sorry* to give you any trouble on that account. It is *most kind* of you to have got me those two. The lute accompaniments are very fine.

In a postscript he adds:

> But if I can have the songs in time, I shall put them on the programme; only I must *study* them first—and I must not be late for my programme.

Dolmetsch's persistence won the day: all four songs were performed at a concert on 23 April at Fitzroy Street.

Horne and Dolmetsch were destined to enjoy a life-long friendship disrupted by only one serious quarrel which apparently disturbed Dolmetsch very much indeed. The tantalising lack of any record of the cause of the disagreement makes an assessment of the relationship exceedingly difficult. The surviving correspondence makes it quite clear that Dolmetsch had the highest opinion of Horne; he appears to have trusted him implicitly, writing frankly about a variety of personal matters ranging from his wife's ill-health and his disputes with the critics to his ever-recurring financial difficulties.

The other side of the relationship poses more of a problem and we must go more by inference than proof, for the few remaining letters from Horne to Dolmetsch are kindly but precise, dealing purely with the matter in hand. They confirm his support of Dolmetsch and his work and that the two men are closely linked by their common interest in the past; but the personal affinity remains an enigma.

It could have been the attraction of opposites. Dolmetsch was no sophisticated man of the world; in spite of his much-married state, or perhaps because of it, his attitude to women was simple and direct. He admired pretty women like any other healthy man, but there are no records of any extra-marital escapades. On the one occasion in which he set up house with a woman outside marriage, he did it openly until such time as they were free to marry. But on the whole his work was of paramount importance; the women in his life were there to run the home and give him encouragement, smooth out the wrinkles of mundaneness and, if possible, participate in his musical activities.

Horne was a far more complex character: a scholar with a taste for both sexes, he was continually struggling towards the recognition of the dual elements in his nature, the voluptuary and the precision, which were to be finally and fruitfully reconciled in the passionately accurate scholarship of his last years.

In addition to his own series of concerts, society engagements and lecture illustrations, Dolmetsch was playing in small halls up and down the country, and whatever the conditions he never refused an opportunity to make his work known. His seemingly inexhaustible supply of energy never failed to carry him through but he made little or no money out of these ventures. The cost of transporting his players and the instruments, particularly the harpsichord, invariably exceeded the fee he received from his patrons. His wife's income still provided the bread and butter; occasionally there was a little cake. In a letter to Horne he writes:

April 24th 1892   60, Croxted Road,
                                                   West Dulwich
                                                   S.E.

I enclose a cheque for £12, which I understand will cover your expenses—If you find it does not, kindly say so; I find I have made £30 now—allowing £3 for next concert—say £33—out of which I give you £12—I have to give one guinea each to . . . [performers]. It is not possible that the cost of printing and my other incidental expenses say altogether £15. 3s. should go to anything like the remaining £18, so there may be some little profit.

The next concert was indeed a financial success; it attracted a capacity audience and was extremely well received by the press. They

> . . . congratulate Mr. Dolmetsch on the service he renders by the reviving, for the instruction of musicians today, not only the music which delighted our ancestors but the instruments upon which it was played. The work was one which could have been undertaken by none but an enthusiast, and it has been accomplished with a completeness which could have been achieved only by a sound and learned musician . . . Mr. Dolmetsch may be said to have reinvented the viols, rediscovered the art of playing them, and rescued from oblivion the music written for them— all of which things had disappeared before the noisy and aggressive violin . . . Dolmetsch appears to possess a complete mastery of the whole family of viols, and his daughter, Miss Hélène Dolmetsch, showed in her rendering of a sonata by Bach, a quite remarkable command for her age [13] of the viol da gamba. *St. James's Gazette*, April 25th 1892.

The Times (26 April 1892), too, was unstinting in its praise, remarking on the increased attendance that it may be taken as:

> . . . a sign of a desire to become acquainted with some of the masterpieces of the composers of the fifteenth and sixteenth centuries, which, until now, there has practically been no opportunity of hearing.

Although the billow of Horne's encouragement carried Dolmetsch ever further, he was always punctilious in acknowledging the comfort it brought. In an exuberant letter of 15 May 1892 he writes to Horne, thanking him for:

60, Croxted Road,
West Dulwich,
S.E.

> . . . all the kindness you have shown me about these concerts. We have had five of them! And they have really given you an enormous amount of trouble. At all events, it is satisfactory to think that the result has been quite as valuable as we could possibly expect . . . I know that Mr. Fuller-Maitland was *very* pleased last night and also Mr. Watson of the St. James's Gazette—We may expect very good notices. I shall send you a list of all we get.

The Times 17 May confirmed Dolmetsch's hopes:

> Mr. Dolmetsch brought forth several interesting concerted works for viols— among them a beautiful 'Dovehouse Pavan' by Alfonso Ferrabosco the elder . . . He, Dolmetsch, played 3 lute solos from Mace's famous Treatise[7] the interest of the second, 'My Mistress' was greatly increased by the reading of a very amusing extract concerning its origin. Miss Dolmetsch displayed her remarkable skill on

Grandmère Guillouard

With his grandfather,
Armand Guillouard

Advertisement for Gouge-Guillouard, Le Mans,
after Marie Dolmetsch's remarriage

Arnold Dolmetsch's parents,
Rudolph and Marie

Arnold

Aged 14   Aged 17

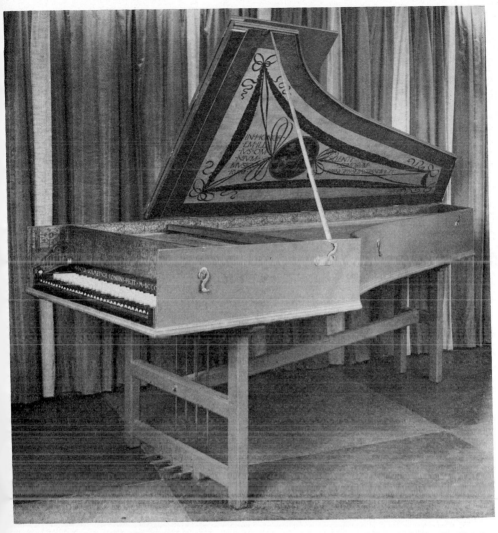

The 'Green' harpsichord made at William Morris's suggestion for the Arts and Crafts Exhibition, 1896, decorated by Helen Coombe with lettering by Selwyn Image. Design over the keyboard is by Herbert Horne

Hélène Dolmetsch
playing a bass viol
by Bergonzi

Dolmetsch in 1895

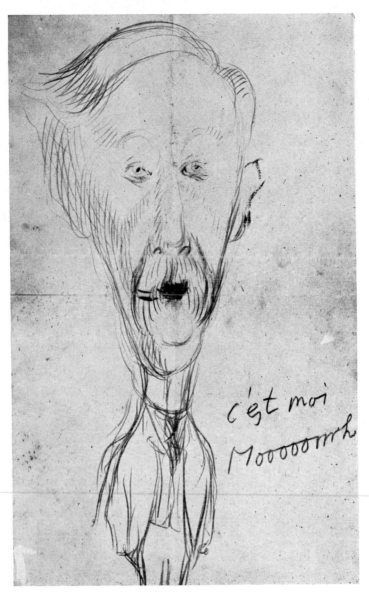

George Moore, a caricature
by William Rothenstein, *c.* 1897

Dolmetsch, a drawing by William Rothenstein;
signed 'To the lute-player, in admiration, Will Rothenstein,
May, 1897.'

Arnold with his first wife, Marie,
and their daughter Hélène.

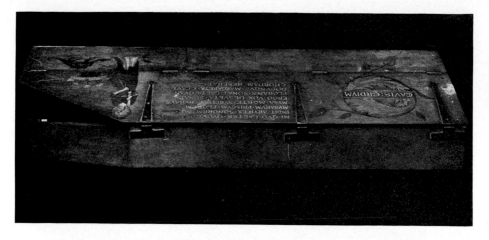

A clavichord made by Dolmetsch in 1897 and decorated by
Burne-Jones for his daughter, Margaret Mackail
(*above*) The lid, showing St Margaret upside down
(*below*) The sound board

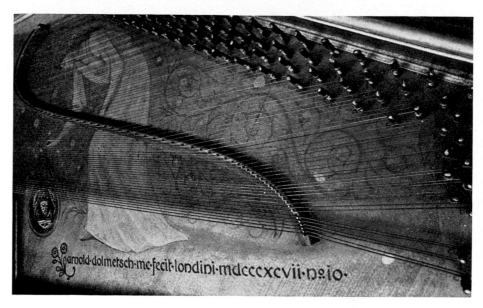

Photos: Denis Waugh

the viol da gamba in a long chaconne by Marin Marais, a composer of whose revival is entirely due to Mr. Dolmetsch.

*   *   *

It would be both wrong and foolish to suppose that no one besides Dolmetsch ever paid attention to early music or its performance. Mendelssohn's revival of Bach has already been acknowledged, likewise Dr. Bridge and the Gresham lectures on the English School: Bridge was always a strong advocate of early music. Edward Dannreuther, whose 'Musical Evenings' at his home at Orme Square[8] were reported in the press and celebrated for performances of Bach: Dannreuther himself once performed the *Goldberg Variations* on the piano. Professor Niecks, Reid Professor at Edinburgh University, gave a course of four lectures on 'The Early Development of the Forms of Instrumental Music' (7 March 1892) and selected examples of music going back to 1452 (*Ascensus simplex* from Conrad Paumann's *Fundamentum Organisandi*) and dance rhythms from 1530–51. But all the performers used modern instruments: organ, violins, violas and 'cellos.

The second lecture dealt with the 17th century and was treated in the same way. Under the heading 'Early English Music at Home and Abroad' the last lecture presented the music of Byrd, Bull, Tye, Morley, Holborn, Easte, Jenkins, Locke and Purcell, all performed on modern instruments, including the piano. Therefore, with the exception of Dr. Bridge, who invariably used Dolmetsch to illustrate his lectures, there would appear to be little evidence of any other musical bodies having employed instruments contemporary to the period. In consequence there was a corresponding dearth of knowledge, both of performing styles and terminology of the time. Musicians of the 'nineties, prompted more by apathy than modesty, preferred to keep their ignorance to themselves, but occasionally one of their number felt it incumbent upon himself to proclaim a discovery for the enlightenment of his fellow musicians. A perfect example exists in the findings of William Hayman Cummings,[9] the Victorian ideal of an 'upright worthy man' who adopted a patronising and didactic manner in both his writing and his speeches to the numerous musical societies to which he was affiliated. He had a finger in every conceivable musical pie but did not always pull out a plum.

In the *Daily Graphic* of 2 April, under the heading 'Musical Jottings', there appeared the following paragraph:

> The exact meaning of the term 'broken music' so frequently referred to in Shakespeare has recently been occupying the attention of musical *cognoscenti*; Mr. W.

H. Cummings in a communication to a musical contemporary, has been able to define the strict sense in which the term was used by musicians, by reference to 'a remarkable manuscript volume in the handwriting of the celebrated Matthew Locke'. This interesting book is a tall folio bound in calf with the Arms of King Charles II on the covers and contains compositions by Locke given by him to the King. The title in the composer's autograph is as follows—Compositions for Broken and Whole Consorts, of two, three, four, five and six parts, made by Matthew Locke, Composer in ordinary to His Majestye. A Consort consisted of six viols, usually kept in one case, and when the whole of the viols were played together, it was called a 'whole' consort; when less than the six it was called a 'broken' consort.

To ensure that he should be fully understood by his musical colleagues, Mr. Cummings expands and develops this remarkable piece of information in the *Musical Times* of 1 April 1892. He quotes several examples from the Shakespeare plays in which the term 'broken' occurs, such as 'Queen of all, Katharaine, break thy mind to me in broken English' (*Henry V*) and 'But is there anyone else who longs to see this broken music in his sides' (*As You Like It*). He relates this punning to the simple meaning of broken as being 'in parts or parts of a whole'. He refutes a statement by the late William Chappell that 'broken music meant the music of stringed instruments in contradistinction to those played by wind. . . . Mr. Chappell', asserts Cummings, 'subsequently changed his opinion and concluded that "broken music" meant the combination of stringed and wind instruments'. Sir George Macfarren apparently also adopted this view and quotes from an essay by Bacon in which the mixture of one consort with another is referred to as 'broken music'. Cummings will not have it: he accuses Sir George of having misread his Bacon and then proceeds himself to misquote from *Of Masques and Triumphs*.

But Cummings was not to have it all his own way: in the *Musical Times* of 1 May a correspondent expertly challenges him:

BROKEN MUSIC
Sir,

   Bacon's 'Sylva Sylvarum' (page 72 1628 ed.) says: All Concords and Discords of Musicke, are (no doubt) Sympathies, and Antipathies of Sounds. And so (likewise) in that Musicke, which we call Broken Musicke, or Consorts Musicke; Some Consorts of Instruments are sweeter than others: (a thing not sufficiently yet observed.)

The writer then draws comparison between instruments which do and do not agree, and suggests that it is this essay rather than *Of Masques and Triumphs* to which Sir George had referred. Cummings was allowed one bracketed protest at the foot of the printed letter, after which the matter was closed.

Fortunately the Locke MS is preserved in the British Museum[10] and shows simply that the compositions are for:

> Broken and Whole Consorts of two, three, four, five and six parts, and the "Little Consort' of three parts for Viols or violins 1657—containing Pavans, Airs, Corants and Sarabands for Viols or Violins. In two several varieties the first twenty are for Treble and Bass—The last twenty are for Treble, Tenor and Bass. To be performed either alone, or Theorbos and Harpsichord.

How Cummings arrived at his conclusion is a mystery, but it is ironic that the two gentlemen whom he takes to task are much nearer the correct meaning of the term.

There is no evidence that Dolmetsch entered into the argument. If he had something to say on the subject, certainly he would have lost no time in doing so, for Cummings never stood high in his esteem. But one fact emerges quite clearly: the almost total lack of knowledge among the musical *cognoscenti* of music before Purcell. Dolmetsch's work was only just being noticed: it is curious that in 1892 there should be two such displays of ignorance, both in realms where Dolmetsch was later to reign supreme—even if uncrowned.

In the November of that year Dolmetsch found himself back at the Sheldonian Theatre at Oxford; this time it was to supply illustrations to 'an erudite and interesting lecture entitled, "The Lute, the Viol and the Voice", given by Sir John Stainer.' Here, Dolmetsch introduced the complete *First Suite of Lessons for the Lute* by Mace, published in 1676, a praelude and sarabande by Reussner, works by Marais and anonymous composers, by which 'the value of the lecture was greatly enhanced' and 'excellently played on fine instruments by Mr. Dolmetsch and his family'. (*Musical Times*, 1 December 1892)

From Oxford, Dolmetsch made his way north for the first time, giving concerts and lectures in Liverpool, Chester and the surrounding district. The prime purpose of the tour was to illustrate a lecture, one of three given by Dr. Joseph Bridge (brother to Frederick) on 'Music of the Past'. It was the last of these, 'The Early Instrumental Writers of England', for which Dolmetsch had been engaged. But it was the first programme, entitled 'Ancient Minstrelsy' (at which Dolmetsch was not present: he was performing in Liverpool), which gives further proof of the prevailing lack of knowledge; in this instance it was the capabilities of early wind instruments.

All three programmes for the lectures were printed on the same double sheet so that Dolmetsch must have seen the heading, which read:

Part II

A few remarks on 'Recorders' or Ancient Flutes

(Musical illustrations will be given on a set of our 'Recorders'[11] belonging to and exhibited by kind permission of the Chester Archaeological Society.)

The Chester Chronicle (26 November 1892) writes:

> A most enjoyable programme concluded with a performance on a set of 4 'recorders' belonging to the Chester Archaeological Society of the 'Chester Round' and an equally ancient melody entitled, 'Chester Waits' being interpreted in a manner which perhaps appealed more to the love of the antique than to love of music.

The writer maintains that the success of the evening was due to Dr. Bridge being such an interesting lecturer, 'endowed with the power of communicating to his audience much of the enthusiastic appreciation of ancient music which he himself so strongly evinces'. Of the third and last lecture, in which Dolmetsch appeared, the same paper extols the competence of the performers:

> Mr. Dolmetsch was perhaps the only man in England who could play the lute, which was an extremely difficult instrument to manipulate, and especially to tune, an operation which required at least four or five hours, so that there was no wonder at it becoming obsolete. The spinet could also find no place in modern times, but the lecturer thought there was still a place for viols in our orchestras. . . . In the capable hands of Mr. and Miss Dolmetsch these instruments of bygone days were clothed with a beauty and grace such as we fail to reach on our ordinary concert platform, the sweetness of the lute being simply incomparable while the duets for viols, and viol and spinet were marvellously quaint.

Dr. Bridge concluded by saying that 'No one could dip into this old-world music without receiving benefit from the research, for the more one studied it, the more enthusiastic he became.' He also remarked that when the lectures had been repeated in Liverpool on the previous evening; a gathering of over 1,500 people, principally working men, exhibited an interest that was 'truly marvellous'.

On his return to London an enthusiastic Dolmetsch wrote to Horne:

Dec. 11th 1892

60, Croxted Road,
West Dulwich,
S.E.

> We had a very great success both at Liverpool and Chester. At Liverpool, in a hall which holds comfortably 1,000, no less than 1,642 people crammed in! There were quite 1,000 simple workmen amongst them. They were evidently greatly interested and gave us the most perfect silence. They cheered us tremendously and wanted to encore everything.
>
> The president of the Liverpool Music Club was there, and I am now negotiating with him about another concert at his club. Same thing in Chester, but a much

smaller audience in the refectory of the old Cathedral: a delightful old Gothic room, *excellent* for sound.

* * *

A glance at musical journalism throughout 1892 points to a feeling of unrest and near-revolt: no doubt a sign that the general dissatisfaction and questioning which marked the 'nineties as a period had now spread to music. Because of the enormous cost of mounting performances, music had always been more dependent upon popular taste than any of the visual arts. Popular taste in the 'nineties was suspect. Articles in musical journals posed questions in their titles; 'Are the English a Musical Nation?' or 'Musical Criticism—Does it *exist* in England', and many on similar themes, all symptomatic of underlying frustration. A light-hearted unsigned article in the *Musical Standard* on New Year's Eve, called 'Music out of the Doldrums', ironically sub-titled 'A Christmas Dream', tells of the adventures of a critic who bumped into the New Year, a young lady who has been allowed a week of liberty to change the order of things. Her sister, the Old Year, is deaf and despondent and lacks interest in any new schemes. The New Year reads from a scroll on which she has recorded all the changes she would like to make but is told by her other sister, 'Truth', that nobody will be very pleased with her ideas. She suggests that Madame Batti, a great singer who has been a favourite for thirty years, will, in accepting encores, absolutely refuse to sing either *The Last Rose of Summer* or *Home, Sweet Home*. She will sing operatic arias that have never been sung by her before in public and she will also vary her programme on the occasion of each public performance. Further suggestions are that no works should ever be performed without proper rehearsal and that the conductor should be the one to decide when this stage has been reached; if his masters do not intend to pay for two rehearsals they cannot expect him to rehearse the work properly.

Ballad concerts, that most popular form of musical entertainment of the time, would be reformed by persuading the publishers to give up paying the successful singers to sing stupid songs, which is what they have been doing in 'The Old Year's' time. Then the really *great*, instead of the most successful, singer should be engaged: the critic is then handed a list upon which the names of Schumann, Schubert, Handel, Grieg, Gounod, Goring Thomas, and Beethoven appear as being seldom-heard composers. Following on some ideas for re-organising a well-known string quartet, she further suggests that an 'innovation hitherto unthought of' will be the employment of native talent. She advocates the extension of the list of pianists and suggests that they should be allowed to play on the instrument of their choice without any suggestion from pianoforte makers.

On opera, the 'New Year' suggests that no 'stock' opera will be put up without at least five rehearsals with principals and no new work without three months' constant rehearsal. No new work will be accepted because a composer, a prima donna, or the friends of either are willing to pay the expenses, but only because the work is really good. She would bring all this about by forming a committee of good musicians and would abolish all critics except that of *The World*,[12] 'which is an honourable exception', but would leave the ordinary 'newspaper men' alone. The critic is suddenly aware that the 'New Year' has bundled up her papers and fled, and he awakes.

Doldrums or no, it was into such a sea that Dolmetsch guided his frail barque. All his energies were directed towards arranging his new series of concerts to be given at Fitzroy Street—by popular demand. He could look back on the year with some satisfaction: up to this date he had introduced no less than 130 compositions of early music either completely unknown or very rarely performed—certainly not on the instruments for which the music had been intended. Only a fraction of these were published, and even then had to be verified for authenticity: sometimes they were rare editions from the libraries of friends, but mostly they were in manuscript in the British Museum or the Royal College of Music Library, and every part had to be copied down by hand by Dolmetsch himself. In addition to this he was arranging concerts, teaching his pupils to play the early instruments, restoring them as he acquired them. This would have been more than enough to have occupied a man with a normal background based on love and security but Dolmetsch and his wife no longer inhabited the same world—a sad fact that neither would openly admit.

NOTES

1. J. A. Fuller-Maitland (1856–1936), scholar and author best known for his editing with Barclay Squire of *The Fitzwilliam Virginal Book*, 1899.
2. Destroyed in the 1939–1945 war.
3. Henry Sirr. Letter to Miss E. M. Pugh, 6 May 1942.
4. ibid.
5. 'We did not write to each other when our dear Queen died. We knew what was in each other's hearts; our early Victorian girlhood will always be very precious to us. What nice, good and pretty girls we were. I do not meet any girls half so nice and serious.' Field, Michael, *Works and Days*, John Murray 1933, p. 238.
6. ibid., p. 189.
7. *Musick's Monument*, 1676.
8. The Music Room at 12 Orme Square, Bayswater, was built by Edward Dannreuther

in 1873 to Philip Webb's design. A photograph of the room was taken about 1882 for a collection of houses in which Richard Wagner had stayed in England since his first visit in 1855. Wagner and his wife stayed at 12 Orme Square in 1877, during his last visit to England. It was in this room that the poem of Parsifal was read by Wagner for the first time to an assembly of famous musicians of the day. The room was 11 feet high—considered by Dannreuther to be the perfect height for chamber music; he had studied acoustics to the extent that he had made the platform of a semi-circular shape with the piano in a central position: he regarded this as the perfect position in which the instrument could be heard. Contemporary accounts all speak highly of its acoustical properties and it was often termed as being 'the best room in London for a concert'.

9. W. H. Cummings, born 1831, was an organist, tenor singer, musical scholar and composer, and professor of singing at the RAM 1879–96. In 1882 he was appointed chorus-master of The Sacred Harmonic Society, of which he subsequently became conductor: in 1896 he succeeded Barnby as principal of the GSM. In addition to these professional activities he filled several posts with the Philharmonic Society, The Musical Association and the ISM. Grove's *Dictionary of Music 3*.

10. British Museum Add. MS 17,801.

11. These instruments came to light in 1886, when the collection of antiquities belonging to the Chester Archaeological Society was removed to new quarters. The case which contained them was so worm-eaten when they were discovered that, with the exception of the green baize lining, it fell to pieces on being handled . . . They were sent for repair to a local music-seller, who had a new key made for the alto, and the tube for carrying the wind from the player's mouth to the top of the instrument added to the bass. In 1939 they were restored to playing condition, re-voiced and their tuning checked so that they could be played together as a consort. Before this time, one had been mute and the pitches did not agree. This work was carried out by Carl Dolmetsch.

A detailed description of the history of these instruments can be found in *Welch's Lectures on the Recorder*, Oxford (London, 1961) from which these extracts are taken.

12. George Bernard Shaw was then music critic of *The World*.

CHAPTER VI

Greek Meets Greek

By the beginning of 1893, Dolmetsch's audiences had outgrown Fitzroy Street: there concerts had enjoyed such unexpected success that the room was no longer large enough to contain them. By good fortune Dolmetsch secured the use of the hall at Barnard's Inn in Holborn—a fine panelled chamber with an open-timbered roof probably dating, in part, from the reign of King Henry VI. He announced a new series of concerts which would, he hoped, be given 'under circumstances more advantageous'. He was 'not unmindful of what an old master [Mace] has delivered upon this head. "The 1st. thing to be consider'd, as to the Advantage of Good Musicke, should be a convenient and Fit Place to perform it in; such I would call a Musicke Room; and is considerable in a 4-fold Respect, 1st in Respect of the Instruments, 2nd. the Musicke, 3rd the Actors, and 4th the Auditors." '[1] Dolmetsch continues:

> During the intervening period I have not been idle; but I have reviewed, with care, both my instruments and my practice. In especial, I have devoted much time to the study of the Lute and I have, also, added a few new instruments to those, which I formerly employed; and among which, I may mention the Spinet. My programmes will contain a selection of the more important pieces given in my former concerts; with additions. This repetition I have deemed advisable, on account of the present age, which will not always allow an ear unaccustomed to these early compositions, to appreciate them on the first occasion.
>
> My principal end in giving these performances, is to draw attention to the excellency of the English School of Music, during the 16th and 17th centuries; and to show how worthy it was to go in paragon with the incomparable literature of those ages. To illustrate this latter persuasion of mine, I shall give, upon each occasion, two or more of the most admired lyric poems in the language, with their original setting. Among these will be: 'Take, O take those lips away' by William Shakespeare; 'Gather Your Rosebuds' by Robert Herrick; 'Go, Lovely Rose' by Edmund Waller; with others by John Milton, Ben Johnson, Sir John Suckling and Thomas Carew; not to omit certain of the songs for which Thomas Campion wrote his beautiful airs.

Dolmetsch assured his patrons that he would repeat the great sonatas of Bach and works by French composers that had been performed at Fitzroy

Street. The subscription for the four concerts was one guinea and an additional comfort was to be the provision during the interval of tea and coffee, for which there would be no charge.

The series was well received by patrons and press alike: 'The ancient Hall made an appropriate setting . . . Musical antiquarians are deeply indebted to Mr. Dolmetsch for his energy in organising this concert' writes the *Musical Standard* (28 January 1893). The *Musical Times* (February 1893) captures something of the spell that Dolmetsch cast over his audience:

> As on former occasions, many charming and most interesting specimens of the musical spirit and skill of our forefathers were made to tell again their story in the same sweet expressive tones in which they first appealed for welcome and sympathy. Nor did Mr. Dolmetsch stop here, for he would have his audience 'admire with understanding' and so he had provided diagrams of two 'points' of contrapuntal complexity which occurred respectively in Martin Pearson's 'Fantazie' and a composition of like nature by 'Coperario', otherwise John Cooper. Over his explanation of the latter the concert-giver waxed enthusiastic, and said 'he was quite sure that no living composer could write such counterpart', naively adding 'he had tried to himself', a remark which caused much good-humoured laughter.

But the most vivid account appeared in the *Westminster Gazette* (15 February 1893)

> In the quaint old Hall belonging to Barnard's Inn, one of the few remaining Inns of Chancery, Mr. Dolmetsch gave last night one of his curious and interesting concerts of old English music for the viols, lute and harpsichord. It was like a sudden plunge from the 19th to the 17th century to turn out of Holborn under the narrow archway of the Inn and up a dimly lit passage to the gabled Hall, with its panelled walls and great fireplaces at either end. Above the low platform hung a goodly row of viols of all sizes and shapes, a fine harpsichord filled almost one side of the Hall, while the audience sat around in high-backed chairs which savoured of an age when music was taken more seriously than it is these days. Mr. Dolmetsch, though a foreigner, has devoted himself to the task of reviving old English music with an ardour and devotion which should win for him a lasting debt of gratitude. The madrigals of the Elizabethan Age are well known, but Mr. Dolmetsch's researches have shown that the men who wrote the ballets and the fa-las which are still heard with so much delight, were equally skilled as composers for the viols, virginals and lute. The earliest number in the programme last night was a grave and solemn air for 3 viols by no less a personage than Henry VIII.[2]

The writer extols the obvious merits of the piece and suggests that the King's other compositions, 'of which a goodly number are in existence', might be published as a companion volume to the works of Frederick the

Great of Prussia, and Ferdinand III, Leopold I and Joseph I of Austria, which have recently been printed by the German and Austrian governments.

There came also at this time a rare invitation for Dolmetsch to entertain his fellow musicians at the annual conference of the Incorporated Society of Musicians at the Grand Midland Hotel.[3] The occasion was more opportune than Dolmetsch realised for George Bernard Shaw was in the audience. Shaw had been attracting attention by his outspoken musical criticism, and his account of the conference[4] is hilarious. He suggests that, 'being rather short of subjects to confer about' the ISM have taken to listening to music—even the organ—to while away the time. He considers it a pity that there is no Incorporated Society of Critics: they might also amuse themselves by conferring together, 'with a strong police force to maintain order'.

On the part of the conference which he personally attended—the lecture on the spinet, harpsichord and clavichord by Mr. Hipkins and that on the lute and viols by Mr. Dolmetsch—Shaw claims that Mr. Hipkins' skill is well known and need not be dwelt upon, but he warns that 'any swaggering pianist who underrates that proficiency should try his hand on a clavichord and see what he can make of an instrument that depends upon the dexterity of the player for its "action"—not on the elaborate mechanism of Erard or any modification thereof'.

He also points out that the clavichord music is generally of the kind in which every wrong note or rough touch betrays itself at once, unlike the modern, thickly-harmonised pieces, 'in which one fistful of notes is as good as another when a grandiose chord is wanted'. He has no doubt that eventually the piano must succumb to the overwhelming objection that it can be heard next door. He reflects how much more pleasant it would be to live next door to Mr. Dolmetsch than to an ordinary string quartet. But should we return to playing the old instruments, Shaw foresees a difficulty: 'I suppose we should have to begin to make them again; and I wonder what would be the result of that.' And even if we did, Shaw asks if there is any reason to suppose that we should make good ones.

For him the question has already been answered since Mr. Hipkins, in addition to playing old keyboard instruments, also performed on 'a new harpsichord manufactured by a very eminent Parisian firm of pianoforte-makers: and not only did it prove itself a snarling abomination, with vices of tone that even a harmonium would have been ashamed of, but it had evidently been deliberately made so in order to meet the ordinary customer's notion of a powerful and brilliant instrument . . . Mr. Dolmetsch did not exhibit any modern lutes, perhaps because none have been made; but if our fiddle-makers were to attempt to revive them they would probably aim at the sort of "Power" of tones produced by those violins which ingenious street-players make out of empty Australian mutton tins and odd legs of stools'.

Finally, Shaw finds that Dolmetsch's concerts, 'apart from their historical interest, are highly enjoyable from the purely musical point of view, his own playing and that of his daughter (on the viol da gamba) being excellent'.

Shaw's witty account of the ISM conference had greatly amused Dolmetsch and he lost no time in inviting him to his second concert at Barnard's Inn. That first historic meeting must have been electrifying: Shaw, red-bearded and over six feet in height, Dolmetsch, volatile, dark and dwarf-like, with burning eyes that could challenge the devil himself. Some would have thought that meeting Shaw would not be a bad beginning. Here were two rebels each searching for an ideal in totally different fields. Both instantly recognised the affinity which was to bring them into a lasting friendship. They frequently disagreed but never quarrelled—unlike so many of Dolmetsch's other relationships, which started in a gust of enthusiasm and ended in storm.

On the day following their meeting, Shaw conscripted Dolmetsch into the front line of one of his favourite battles: he writes of having seized the opportunity to put in a protest on behalf of opera-goers against the use of the viola as opposed to the viola d'amore for the obbligato in the first act of Les Huguenots. He announces that Mr. Dolmetsch promises to bring a viola d'amore tuned for playing the obbligato to his next concert and he will also say something on the subject. Shaw hopes that the upshot will be to get the obbligato played at the opera as Meyerbeer intended it to be played. 'The difference to the singer, who would be coaxed into the dulcet style, instead of having his teeth set on edge with his worst shouting propensities stirred up, would be considerable, and the difference to the audience incalculable.'[5]

Dolmetsch, a match for Shaw, revelled in the opportunity to prove it. At the final concert in the series, Dolmetsch's manner was even more puckish than usual when he addressed his audience: he invited them to participate in a little drama in which the principal actor was his newest acquaintance. Shaw, sitting in the audience, unsuspecting, later recorded the story in his own words:

> At Mr. Dolmetsch's viol concert in Barnard's Inn yesterday week, I enjoyed the unexpected sensation of having one of my criticisms read aloud to the audience. 'This' added Mr. Dolmetsch with an air of conviction, 'is severe language; but it is true.' Whereat the audience—well, I had better say they smiled, but sniggered is the expression I should use in unrestricted private conversation. The precedent appears to me an excellent one. I am confident that the Philharmonic concerts and

those of the Bach Choir, nay, the very opera itself, could be most agreeably enlivened by a judicious selection from my articles.[6]

*   *   *

In announcing a summer series of concerts, Dolmetsch takes his first
step towards specialisation:

> The music of the first two concerts will severally be chosen from the compositions
> of the Italian and French composers of the Seventeenth and Eighteenth Centuries:
> whilst that of the third concert will be taken entirely from the works of J. S. Bach.[7]
> The Lute, Viols, Violins, Clavichord, Harpsichord, and Flute will be employed in
> the performance of these compositions, which will in every instance be performed
> upon the instruments for which they were originally written. The Violoncello
> Piccolo or Viola Pomposa, are instruments with five strings for which Bach has
> written some inimitable music, will be revived for the first time at the last concert.
> The music, which it is now proposed to give, is intended to form a complement to
> that of the concerts lately given by Mr. Dolmetsch, which was chiefly taken from
> the works of the English composers of the same period.

The all-Italian programme on 9 May brought names before the public
that were with a few exceptions virtually unknown at the time. They were
familiar to musical scholars from an historical aspect, but it is very doubtful whether they had actually heard music written by the lesser known of
these composers: Caroso, Picchi, Frescobaldi, Corelli, Marcello, Domenico
Scarlatti, Bononcini and Vivaldi. Shaw, who describes the concerts as
'gems of musical entertainment in their way', heard the last half of the
Italian one and was delighted by a sonata for the viola da gamba by
Marcello with 'a peculiar effect made by an interrupted cadence which
sounds as fresh now as it did when it was written. It was beautifully played
by Miss Hélène Dolmetsch.'

*   *   *

It was early in 1893 that Dolmetsch's first and only contribution to
Herbert Horne's *Century Guild Hobby Horse*[8] was published. Twelve
pages of lucid, live and scholarly writing were obviously from the pen of a
man who knew his subject from source material.[9] Quoting freely from
contemporary authors and detailed description from his own writing,
Dolmetsch proves that his knowledge of the subject was both genuine and
profound. He gives a brief history of each instrument of the viol family
and its evolution under three headings, 'The Consort Viol', 'The Viola
d'Amore' and 'The Viola da Gamba'. He discusses the different kinds of
music written for these instruments and the techniques employed in their

execution. An important point which Dolmetsch makes clear is the use of the outcurved bow as opposed to the Tourte, or modern bow. We know that at this time there was some speculation as to the correct way to hold the viols when playing: Dolmetsch has no doubts. He quotes Sympson on the viola da gamba:

> Being conveniently seated, place your viol directly betwixt your knees; so, that the lower end of it may rest upon the calves of your legs. Set the soles of your feet flat upon the floor, your Toes turn'd a little outward. Let the top of your Viol be erected towards your left shoulder; so, as it may rest in that posture, though you touch it not with your hand. Hold the bow betwixt the ends of your Thumb and two foremost forefingers, near to the nut. The Thumb and first finger fastened on the Stalk; and the second finger's end turn'd *in* shorter, against the Hairs therof; by which you may poise and keep up the point of the Bow. If the second finger have not strength enough, you may join the third finger in assistance to it; but in Playing Swift Division, two fingers and the Thumb is best. It will be seen from this description, that the proper method of holding the bow in playing upon this viol, as upon other viols, which are held between the knees, or resting on the ground, is, in its general principle, the same, which was used, until the beginning of the present century, in playing upon the violoncello, and which still survives in the bowing of the double-bass. In this position, the wrist is not brought over the bow, as in playing upon the violin and the viols, which are held under the chin, but is kept on the hair-side of it; as it is unnatural and unnecessary to bow the violoncello like a violin.

In his summing up Dolmetsch says that if he has shown that the viol is an instrument distinct from the violin, and that the one cannot be compared with the other since they were intended to produce wholly different effects, he will not have written in vain. He explains that the disuse of the viol was due partly to its ineffectiveness in the orchestra and partly to the tendency to increase the tone of every instrument: a tendency which began towards the close of the 17th century and has continued until the present time. Dolmetsch continues:

> Still it [the viol] remains among the most beautiful of chamber instruments. But let me be well understood; for by chamber music, I do not mean what, at the present time, ordinarily passes under that name in the concert room, but chamber music, in the strictest sense of the term, such as Roger North describes[10] and such as we constantly read of in the diaries of Pepys and Evelyn. Chamber music of this kind was in daily use, in most gentlemen's private houses, during the seventeenth century; and if we consider the secular work of that great school of music, which flourished in England, during the sixteenth and seventeenth centuries, we find that its masters were, without exception, writers of chamber music. Opera and the grand manner, as understood by the Italians, have never commended themselves to the English genius: and who knows, that, in the return to a good

tradition of Chamber music, another school of musicians may not arise in this country, worthy to go in paragon with musicians of the age of Milton?

The writing of the *Hobby Horse* article is evidence of Dolmetsch's fluent command of English: although words came as readily to his lips when speaking, they were so heavily accented that he was not always well understood. It is interesting, too, to note the prophetic underlining of his hopes for English music; even the deadliest of his Anglo-Saxon enemies would have had to admit that for a Franco-Swiss of Byzantine-Bohemian origin he put their case rather well.

All contemporary accounts of Dolmetsch's concerts show that his following was still mainly among the literary and art men of Bloomsbury. There is no direct evidence to suggest that either Parry or Bridge ever came to his concerts, although they both supported his work and certainly brought engagements his way whenever possible. Indeed, Dolmetsch skilfully balanced the tight-rope between Bloomsbury and the musical Establishment. His name was also becoming known abroad. At this time anything Teutonic was above criticism, so that a letter to Dolmetsch from the eminent German musical scholar Chrysander held a certain significance:

July 8th 1893
                                                        19 St. Mark's Crescent
                                                        Regent's Park,
                                                        N.W.

It is possible that I can get back to England [from Germany] in September but in any case I will sketch out a number of pieces for your forthcoming Handel concert, including entirely unknown compositions for the harpsichord[11] which I shall send you or bring over with me. Please keep the proofs of the Gamba-Sonata until I send you a complete print, and accept my best thanks for the musical treat you gave me on Tuesday.

Until 1893, Hipkins was probably the only person who regularly played the early keyboard instruments in public. As we know already, Dolmetsch had his wholehearted support, but following the publication of Volume I of Dannreuther's book on ornamentation,[12] he found in it a point of argument. It would appear that a meeting had taken place between Hipkins, Dannreuther and Dolmetsch and an argument had ensued: on 29 November 1893, Hipkins writes to Dolmetsch:

                                                        33, Great Pulteney Street,
                                                        London, W.

I am afraid you won't think me a high-minded man for I cannot agree with you and Dannreuther about rapid harpsichord playing. I know, of course, that one can play as fast, perhaps faster, on a harpsichord than you can on a pianoforte, but I have had a good many years experience of playing the harpsichord before audiences and maintain that pianoforte *tempo* will not hold them. I shall retain that opinion until Dannreuther has had a larger experience of the harpsichord. I hope he won't alter his book: if he does the responsibility will be his own.[13]

There is no record of Dolmetsch's reply, but he must have sent a note for on the following day Hipkins pursues his point:

November 30th 1893   33, Great Pulteney Street,
                                                                    London, W.

I don't think I ought, in fairness to you, let this little correspondence drop without reminding you that there is no appreciable 'accent' to be got from the harpsichord. The figuration has therefore to be made out like it is on the organ. Otherwise it is a blur. The clavichord is different, the accent carries the passage along, and, as with the piano, where accent tells with greater effect, it facilitates rapid playing. It is no question of unfamiliarity and even perfection of regulating cannot change what is inherent in the instrument. So you see I don't give way, but you must excuse me.[14]

The offending passage must have been the following:

If the ornaments throughout can be rendered truly and without curtailment, so as to chime with the text without any wrench or sense of effort, it is more than probable that the pace adopted for a movement will prove the right one in the end. In the writer's opinion a temptation to go wrong may lie in our taking too literally the words contained in the obituary notice which appeared in 1754: 'Bach took the Tempi of his compositions "sehr lebhaft" '—'in a very lively manner'; 'Which', adds Professor Spitta, the biographer *par excellence,* 'must have been particularly the case with regard to the clavier pieces in accordance with the nature of the harpsichord and the clavichord'.[15]

This is the first time that we learn of Dolmetsch paying attention to Bach's *tempi*: it is also the point where his own studies on the subject were to diverge from the ideas currently held by the musicological Establishment.

However, it was the lute, not keyboard instruments, which occupied so much of Dolmetsch's time during 1893. Unfortunately, there is no direct reference in his correspondence but we know that he completed his first lute at this time; he made it in the workroom of his Dulwich home and it is a particularly fine example of his craftsmanship.[16] It is typical of Dolmetsch that he should have set himself the discipline of attempting what he always maintained was the most difficult instrument he had ever undertaken; but it was also his best-loved, and for this reason he was determined to succeed in its reconstruction.

In the winter of 1893, Arnold and Marie Dolmetsch could no longer tolerate life together. The increasing success of Dolmetsch's concerts and his ever-widening circle of unconventional friends only drew their opposing worlds into stronger contrast. When ultimately faced with defeat they acted swiftly. Marie removed to a small house in Streatham, taking the fifteen-year-old Hélène with her. Meanwhile, Dolmetsch tackled every house agent in the district and, with his accustomed zeal, took very little time to secure exactly what he wanted.

NOTES

1. Mace, Thomas, *Musick's Monument*, 1676.
2. If Love Now Reigned, *c.* 1508.
3. 4 January 1893.
4. 11 January 1893.
5. Shaw, G. B., *Music in London*, Vol. II, pp. 247/8, Constable, London, 1932.
6. 22 February 1893.
7. This must surely be the first all-Bach chamber music programme at a public concert in modern times.
8. Holbrook Jackson in *The Eighteen-Nineties*. Jonathan Cape gives the demise of *The Hobby Horse* as 1892, but the date of Dolmetsch's contribution and another by Hipkins is clearly 1893.
9. The *Century Guild Hobby Horse*, No. 2., 1893. At William Morris House, E. 17.
10. ibid.
11. Performed 8 May 1894.
12. Dannreuther, Edward, *Musical Ornamentation*, Vol. I, Novello Primer Series March 1893.
   At a much later date (in the 1920s) Dolmetsch made the following comment:
      There are many mistakes in this work; but I respect Dannreuther as a man because, for one thing, he was always willing to acknowledge his errors and to correct them . . . Although he did not know the early instruments as a player, yet, he was honest minded.
   And to one of his American pupils, Jean Buchanan, he pointed out that in Dannreuther's work it is stated that the *mechanism* of the harpsichord in Bach's time did not permit of very quick playing. When Dolmetsch told him that this was a fallacy and proved it to him by playing some rapid music on the harpsichord (one that was similar to those of Bach's time), Dannreuther admitted the mistake and corrected it in his work.
13. Hipkins also mentions that Dannreuther has seen Dolmetsch's *Dom Bedos* MS. which he used later in his book *The Interpretation of the music of the 17th and 18th centuries*, Novello, London (1915).
14. Hipkins used a Kirckman harpsichord and it is true that these harpsichords, beautiful as they are in tone, do have a slightly slower action than the old French or Italian instruments. This might have coloured Hipkins' view.
15. Dannreuther, Edward *Musical Ornamentation*, Vol. I, Novello, Primer Series pp. 193–4.
16. Tenor lute. *Dolmetsch Collection of Instruments.* No. 14, 1893.

CHAPTER VII

'Dowland'

DOLMETSCH permitted his wife to take Hélène with her to Streatham on the strict understanding that she should be allowed to continue practising and performing with him as before. Consequently, the girl spent a miserable Proserpine-like existence flitting from one parent to another, her divided loyalties stretched to the utmost. For her mother the move meant a return to conventional living: but she was now 44 and a very lonely woman. Little is heard of Marie after the break except that she remained 'very French' and that she had a passion for order. She was known to take part in performances with Hélène and Dolmetsch even after the separation: when desperate, he was perfectly capable of asking, even commanding, her to play and it is to her credit that she obliged on these occasions without demur. For Dolmetsch the break was one of the more pleasant changes in a life prone to vicissitudes of a less agreeable kind and he intended to use this liberty to advantage. He was fortunate in finding a large villa at 172 Rosendale Road, West Dulwich, only a stone's throw from the house in which he had been living.

West Dulwich was just beginning to change from uninterrupted meadows and pastureland to the site of fashionable two storey yellow-brick villas of which 172 Rosendale Road was one. These particular houses were the result of a builder's experiment, and erected in the hope of attracting wealthy West-end business men and shopkeepers, but the houses did not sell, and when Dolmetsch approached the agents, they were willing to entertain all his proposals, which included extensive alterations and the acquisition of the lease at a greatly reduced rental. He called the house 'Dowland' after the Elizabethan composer. Partition walls which separated the two largest rooms on the ground floor were taken away to make a music room, and except for a small room at the back used as a dining room and kitchen combined, the remainder were converted into classrooms, with Dolmetsch's workshop on the first floor.

It was on his much-longed-for music room that Dolmetsch lavished most attention. He placed his beloved little 16th-century chamber organ in the centre of the raised platform extending from the front bay window, and stood the keyboard instruments round the sides of the room; the walls were hung with viols, violins and lutes, whilst highbacked chairs and candles in brass sconces completed the picture of the past come to life. At last he had found the perfect setting for his 'Home music' and the house-warming concert took place on 12 December 1893.

Printed invitations headed, 'Mr Dolmetsch moves to Dowland', were sent to the elite of Bloomsbury, leading musicians and critics. To ensure that his guests would not lose their way, a printed map was enclosed with every invitation, showing that his house was 'a few minutes walk from Dulwich Station on the London, Chatham and Dover Railway'. A train from St. Paul's at 8.15 or Victoria at 8.18 gave ample time to walk from the station and be seated for a concert beginning at 8.45.[1] For those who came by carriage, the distance from London was given as under four-and-a-half miles.

The *Musical Times* (1 January 1894) critic had obviously enjoyed the house-warming party and drew his readers' attention to an anthem *Quam pulcra es* by Henry VIII, sung to the original accompaniment of three viols and organ, remarking on the sweet tone of the latter instrument. It was, of course, the little 16th-century chamber organ of which Dolmetsch was so fond. He praised Dolmetsch's playing of 'an exceedingly elaborate fantasia for lute' and a setting of *Have you seen but a White Lily Grow* sung to lute accompaniment.[2]

An almost identical programme was to be repeated the following Saturday at 5 o'clock as the first of a series of subscription concerts: the critic hoped that this 'praiseworthy undertaking' would not suffer because Londoners would need to undertake a short railway journey.

The move to 'Dowland' marked the beginning of a new era for Dolmetsch: the list of subscribers to his concerts were no longer subject to domestic censorship so he celebrated his new freedom by arranging a series of eight. However, at the same time he continued to accept engagements outside, his patrons varying from the organisers of entertainment for the Constitutional Club to Eton College. To the latter audience he introduced several new items which he had recently added to his repertoire: *Symphonie*, *Jigg* and *Sarabande* from the suite for lute and 2 viols by William Lawes. Although other concerts are mentioned in that year, the *Eton College Chronicle* is regrettably silent on the effect of Mr. Dolmetsch and his music.[3]

Despite constant and enthusiastic comment from the press, Dolmetsch was not yet taken seriously by the musical establishment and society still regarded him as a curiosity. But the less conventional of his English brethren took the wider view. The artists and writers who were themselves struggling to rid society of Victorian ugliness were inevitably attracted to this volatile little Frenchman. It is true that Dolmetsch's illustrations for the Gresham lectures were appreciated, but it must also be remembered that Dr. Bridge was a popular man capable of attracting his own following by his eloquent and humorous delivery. Most people regarded the early music as the citizens of Chester had their recorders, 'Chiefly of antiquarian interest'. It had not yet occurred to them that this was music they could play themselves. 'Musical evenings' were then the most common form of home entertainment and it is ironic that although consorts employing up to six players excluding singers were ideal for the purpose, amateurs continued to hammer out Liszt and Chopin whilst singers warbled through endless ballads under the impression that they were making music.

Dolmetsch knew that he could not expect to arouse a desire in his audiences to play themselves unless the instruments were available. Junk shops and auction rooms yielded a certain number, which he acquired cheaply and restored for his pupils, but if his revival were to succeed, Dolmetsch knew that he would have to find another source of supply. He was fully aware that he must start sometime to build instruments himself, but he had work to occupy him for 30 hours a day as it was. However, the decision was taken out of his hands when his friend, the artist Edward Burne-Jones brought along William Morris to one of the concerts at 'Dowland'.[4] Morris was well known to be not musical so it surprised everyone, including himself, when he found that this early music stirred emotions which had hitherto not been aroused. It is also possible that he saw a parallel, in Dolmetsch's attempts to resuscitate the early music, to his own in painting and design. Morris, who had seen industrial development as a danger to art, still struggled to teach the common man to enjoy art as part of his daily life. But he was now an old man, reconciled to the fact that gentleness and revivalism do not marry well. Therefore he had sympathy with the younger man's passionate endeavour to succeed. Whatever other thoughts ran through his head at the time, he determined to help Dolmetsch to realise his ambitions. Morris, ignorant of music in a technical sense, could contribute little to that side, but when he learned that Dolmetsch had been trained as a craftsman, he did some constructive thinking. Here was a man who could not only make beautiful things, he could give them voice. Dolmetsch had gained another friend.

Shortly after this first meeting, Burne-Jones writes to Dolmetsch:

undated [1894]   The Grange,
                                                  49, North End Road,
                                                   West Kensington,
                                                          W.

I have been exceedingly excited about that British Museum MS you told me of, of the 300 ancient songs, and on Sunday morning when Mr. Morris came to me I fired him up on the subject too, and I want us, if possible, to meet, we three so as to take counsel together how such a godsend can be best used. You know he's the Kelmscott Press, and you may have even seen some of his late printed books which are the most beautiful that have been done for hundreds of years. I believe, if you edited the book, and he printed it, we should have a blissful old age amongst us. He comes to me every Sunday morning, staying till about one o'clock. I wonder if it would be possible for you to come so far any Sunday you like, but the sooner the better. If you reached here about twelve we should have time, before he goes, to discuss the matter thoroughly and you could stay to lunch with us, it would give us great pleasure.

Following the luncheon, Morris writes to Dolmetsch (8 January 1894) that he is 'much delighted at the prospect of the work' and that he can be expected on Thursday at the Museum. Dolmetsch's account appears in a letter to Horne, written the same day:

> Dowland,
> West Dulwich
> S.E.
>
> I had lunch with Burne-Jones and William Morris. They want to publish the Henry VIII MS. And also an album of songs, of course, edited by me—I am awfully pleased by the idea! They are both quite enthusiastic about it![5]

Dolmetsch bemoans the fact that the subscriptions to his concerts are coming in very slowly. But he closes with good news:

> Fuller-Maitland will *not* buy that spinet [unidentified]. He prefers to wait and have mine. I have a definite order from him for the clavichord.[6]

The first 'Dowland' series of concerts were held on Tuesday evenings and as an enticement to take out subscriptions, Dolmetsch now included permission to attend rehearsals held on the previous Saturday for an inclusive price of two-guineas; single tickets remained at 7s 6d each for either concert or rehearsal—at that time a high price.

The concerts were well-planned and of a more comprehensive nature than those in previous series. The first four were concerned only with English music.[7] The works of Bach, and indeed all the other composers, 'have not in living memory been heard upon the instruments for which they were written' and they were 'being performed according to the original intentions of the writer'. Inconceivable as it may seem today, in 1894 Dolmetsch's words were not only true, they were brave.

*   *   *

Although Dolmetsch was an independent thinker who made his decisions without being influenced by his contemporaries, he fitted in very well to the last decade of the century in which he was born. The 'nineties, with its abundance of creative genius and larger-than-life personalities, 'a renascent period, characteristed by much mental activity and a quickening of the imagination',[8] was a natural setting in which his ideas could flourish. In literature and the visual arts the movement towards freedom was in full swing: Shaw and H. G. Wells were using their plays and novels to criticise morality and teach newer social ideas, whilst in *The Yellow Book* and *The Savoy*, Aubrey Beardsley satirised and shocked with his brilliant and original designs.

In music, few progressive steps had been taken. The Royal College in Kensington remained aloof and unconcerned with change and the Royal Academy of Music was described as a 'cesspool of academic life . . . dominated by commercial men who, without shame, perpetrate feats of dishonesty'.[9] But outspoken critics were in the minority, and music as a whole remained virtually unshaken by any revolutionary ideas comparable to those affecting other spheres of art. Dolmetsch was music's natural embodiment of the spirit of the 'nineties. In many ways he was a direct link from Ruskin and Morris: the only difference was that Dolmetsch was quite unaware of this relationship. He wished only to share his discoveries with a public too long saturated with music that was large and loud, and who were also almost totally ignorant of their own heritage of music before Purcell. By resuscitating the past he began to initiate his audiences into appreciating music that was exactly the reverse of that composed in their own time. It was pure accident that he found more supporters among the *avant garde* than the Establishment: he liked them because they liked him and they liked his music. He would have loved a body of reactionaries or Patagonian savages equally well had they approved of what he was doing.

*   *   *

One of the outstanding literary figures who frequently visited 'Dowland' was George Moore, the 'Balzacian Irishman', born on the same date as Dolmetsch and six years his senior. His novel *Evelyn Innes*, published in 1898, was based on Dolmetsch's work, house and instruments. Moore's name is often mentioned in contemporary accounts of Dolmetsch's concerts but since Moore seldom dates his letters it is difficult to ascertain when they actually met for the first time, but we do know that it was Herbert Horne who introduced them. George Moore was born into a wealthy family of landowners: his father was an MP and his childhood companions the two Wilde boys, Willie and Oscar. Moore was passionately fond of racing, fine clothes, Zola and the poetry of Shelley: he was

'amusing, imperfectly educated, a bit of a cad, likeable but infuriating'.[10]
He went to Paris at the age of 21 to study painting but returned disillus-
sioned a year later. Despite this disappointing start, and further hampered
by a lack of education through backwardness in childhood, Moore
managed to turn from art to writing and eventually won for himself a
respected place among the novelists of the day. At 22 his punctuation and
spelling were appalling and his knowledge of the classics, nil: but through
punctilious effort and love of his subject he went through a process of
self-education which, though ridiculed by Wilde,[11] gained the respect of
more tolerant men. Moore was notorious for soliciting the help of his
friends to assimilate background and character:

> In one sense he had no pride, or, to put it better, his pride was that he refused no
> help that would improve his work. There are instances even in his later books of
> whole passages written by others at his request, and incorporated in some form or
> other in the narrative.[12]

Evelyn Innes is essentially a musical novel: almost pedantically so.
Selfconsciously it abounds in unnecessary attention to technical details
which are useless to the layman and superfluous to the musician. The story
tells of a Mr. Innes living in a house called 'Dowlands' in Dulwich[13] who
possesses a collection of early musical instruments which he restores and
plays. His late wife had been a professional singer and he had been responsible for the upbringing of his only daughter, Evelyn, who also aspires to
an operatic career. Mr. Innes has made of Evelyn 'a fine musician able to
write fugue and counterpoint'; nonetheless, she deserts her father and his
early music for Paris, where she takes some extensive training and
becomes the mistress of a baronet, Sir Owen Asher, who has '40 suits,
slight hips and a golden moustache: he affronts the town at mid-day in
patent leather boots with tan tops'[14] and presents his *prima donna* with
a pair of 'almost thoroughbred horses'. Evelyn becomes famous as a
Wagnerian singer and after sundry changes of heart and couch, she is
reunited with her father prior to betaking herself to a nunnery in Wimbledon.
   The first letter in which Moore professes to be interested in Dolmetsch
was written from his rooms at 8, King's Bench Walk, Temple, and dates
from early 1894:

> You talked to me a great deal about music and I was much impressed by your
> ideas. I have often thought of you since. The novel [sic] I am now composing has a
> great deal to do with music. I should like to introduce your ideas about early music,
> perhaps I should say I should like to suggest your ideas. To do this, I should
> require to see you, to talk at length. Can I do this? Any appointment you may find
> convenient to make in London or at your house will suit me or would you do me
> the pleasure of dining with me one evening this week? Any day will suit me.

Later, he writes:

> You say that you will probably be disengaged on Friday afternoon. I will come on
> Friday if I don't hear from you. If you find that you are engaged perhaps you will
> be so kind as to drop me a postcard and then I'll come on Saturday.
> I should of course like to see the instruments and to hear how you make them and
> how you got them. The music I hope to hear at your next concert. I should have
> gone to the last had I heard of it. But for the immediate purpose of the book I
> want to hear you talk about the music.

In the next letter Moore shows an interest in detail and also mentions a
specific date:

> 8, King's Bench Walk
> Temple
> I remember thinking that the viols were out of tune in a piece called *La My* played
> in your house in Dulwich on the 30th Jan 1894. You explained to me afterwards
> that the viols were not out of tune, but the piece was written in one of those early
> modes in which half the notes are wanting. I am not sure that my mistake occurred
> in *La My* or in the following piece, *Gentill Jhesu*. Both pieces were written in one
> of the early modes. Can you tell me the name of the mode?

In a postscript, Moore writes: 'I am getting on with my book. I hope I
shall see you one of these days.'

In *Evelyn Innes* a critic, discussing his review prior to sending it to
press, says he must consult Mr. Innes for:

> In the first piece, *La My*, the viols had seemed to him out of tune. Of course, this
> was not so—perhaps one of his players had played a wrong note; that might be the
> explanation. . . . 'From the 12th to the 15th century, writers', he [Mr. Innes]
> said, 'did not consider their music as moderns do. Now we watch the effect of a
> chord, a combination of notes heard at the same moment as the top note of which
> is the tune, but the older writers used their skill in divining musical phrases which
> could be followed simultaneously each one going logically its own way, irrespective
> of temporary clashing.'[15]

Edward Martyn, a close friend of Moore's, better educated than he and
devoted to both polyphonic music and Wagner, would seem the obvious
choice for Moore's researches, as indeed he was. The following letter was
forwarded to Dolmetsch, presumably after Martyn had either failed or
declined to answer satisfactorily:

> My dear Edward,
> The . . . [illegible] you sent me about the Missa Brevis is very abstract; it might
> apply to almost anything. This is what I want. I send you the literary skeleton and
> I want you to fill it in. If you can't fill it in let me know and I'll ask someone else
> but you ought to be able to do it.
> Listening Evelyn noticed that the trebles were the weakest part of the choir. The

leading treble a beautiful voice in a way was deficient in . . . [left open] and she
doubted his power to lead off effectively in the passage etc. The high B flat at the
end of the bar he would not be able to get except by a screach (*sic*) and to the others
it would prove still more trying. At the same moment the basses were (doing something or other) the tenors were singing (doing something else) and the whole effect
had depended upon the trebles which came in a little later. She knew the passage
perfectly and was sorely tempted to sing it. The B flat which would be so trying to
them she would sing without the slightest effort. But independent of the astonishment that her voice would produce amid the congregation she knew that the
sexual quality rendered it unfit for this music whose sound was like that of silver
bells.

She held her breath waiting for the boy to sing. The first notes (give the notes)
he sang well enough but the effect of the B flat was spoilt it came out thin and poor
on quality to her ear [did] not ring true it was a trifle sharp to her ear.

In the credo she especially admired the passage for the basses the effect of which
was got by . . . [left open] the tenors too were (something or other). But her interest
centred in the trebles, it represented her own voice only much more pure but thin
and crystal like . . . were so feeble. She remembered the men she had heard in the
Papal choir in Rome. Never had she heard a voice like (a celebrated singer) it was a
sharpness which was not of this earth. How it would sound in an opera she did not
know, but in a church where there is no sex it created the impression of an angel
standing by pale Benedictine Heavens lighted by stars where Jehovah listened on
His throne of gold.

The 'someone else' was Dolmetsch. However hard the pressure of work,
he could never refuse a cry for help. He sat down immediately and wrote
the following revision:

The Altos were weak: they disappointed her at the very beginning. She had been
eagerly expecting the wondrously beautiful phrase which opens the Kyrie and in
itself contains the whole of the first part of that movement. But, the Voices were
mostly trebles, singing in the lower register of their voices, and they were not quite
in tune. An ordinary musician, with ears spoiled by the coarse approximation to
intonation which modern keyboard instruments train us to, would have found
nothing to blame, but, she was longing for the sweet concord of a pure third, which,
when it came at the end of the first note of the Basses, sounded as sharp as that of
an ordinary piano.

It was a shock to her. She remembered the enormous pains her father had taken
to train his singers with the harpsichord to just intonation, and how untiringly he
had endeavoured to make them realize that most of the effect of that music
depends upon it, and that, at one time, he had almost obtained it. But apparently
the Corruptive influence of modern chromatic music had been too strong, and the
falling off from the ideal purity was very great.

The coarse intonation was still more painful in the Christe Eleison, sung by four
solo voices, than in the Kyrie which was for the full choir. The leading treble had
a hard unsympathetic voice which did not suit the ornate passages three times

recurring on the second syllable of 'eleison'. He almost hammered them out, instead of lovingly, caressingly singing them.

The Credo went better: it is more straightforward and easy to sing, and does not so much depend upon refinement of execution: the 'Et Incarnatus Est.' was, of course, quite spoiled: she quite expected that; it would require almost heavenly, not earthly voices to do justice to it. But, the Basses were undoubtedly the best part of the choir. Among them she recognised two of her father's oldest pupils: she had known them as boys singing alto, and she well remembered their beautiful voices. They had now deep men's voices, but as good as ever the boys were.

Of the two Agnus Dei, the second has been selected for performance that day: she was eagerly awaiting its beautiful melody, apparently so free, and yet contrived to contain its own descant and harmony within itself: for it is a strict 'Canon in unison' for two treble voices.

She had heard it performed by two men in the Papal Choir in Rome. Never had she dreamed of voices like these. Their strangeness was not of the earth! How they would sound in an opera she did not know, but in that music, they gave the impression of Angels singing near the Golden Throne of Jehovah.

She knew that the first treble was not capable of singing this canon properly. She felt an intense longing to somehow stop him, and take his place. The 2nd treble would have followed her lead, she thought. But this was impossible, for independent of the astonishment which the sexual quality of her voice would have caused to the congregation: she would not reveal herself.

She had to be content to listen, and how it can be explained, she was deeply moved, for her wonderfully fine musical organisation enabled her to correct, in her mind, the shortcomings of the performance.

A grateful George Moore writes from the Lake District:

(undated)
Derwentwater Hotel
Portinscale,
Keswick

It was most kind of you to write so careful a letter. I think I understand. But when I return to London I hope you will let me show you what I have written. I hope the book will do something towards the reformation of the music in Roman Catholic Churches which is really disgraceful and am convinced that it is as impossible to write religious music as it is to paint religious pictures. I heard a modern mass the other day—I remembered one of the pictures one sees in Paris Salons, Christ in Evening Clothes.

The book, published in 1898, shows that Moore used Dolmetsch's version with the minimum of alteration.[16]

Further passages throughout the book exploiting Dolmetsch's musical knowledge are too numerous to mention in detail. Moore consulted his tutor regularly during the time of writing the book; the final letter is dated 18 June [?] from 92 Victoria Street. It would indicate that Dolmetsch had been asked to read the book in its final draft:

> Your letter was a great pleasure to receive for no one's good opinion do I value as much as yours. For you are not one who has fatigued and blunted his taste with hundreds of volumes lightly read. To read a book is an event in your life as it is in mine.

Excepting that Mr. Innes is depicted as an old man whilst Dolmetsch was then in his middle thirties, and beguilingly handsome, Moore's description fits him perfectly: curiously prophetic, too, for no better pen-picture could have been drawn in later years, than:

> Iron-grey hair hung in thick locks over his forehead, and, shining through their shadows, his eyes drew attention from the rest of the face, so that none noticed at first the small firmly cut nose, nor the scanty growth of beard twisted to a point by a movement habitual to the weak, white hand. His face was in his eyes; they reflected the flame of faith and of mission; they were the eyes of one whom fate had thrown on an obscure wayside of dreams, the face of a dreamer and propagandist of old-time music and its instruments. . . .[17]
>
> The black frock coat which he wore on Sundays was too small for him. If he buttoned it, it wrinkled round the waist and came across the chest: if he left it open, its meagre width and the shortness of the skirts (they were in the fashion of more than ten years ago) made it seem ridiculous. At the elbows the cloth was shiny with long wear and the cuffs were frayed. His hat was as antiquated as his coat. It was a mere pulp, greasy inside and brown outside; the brim was too small, it was too low in the crown, and after the severest brushing it remained rough like a blanket. . . . But in spite of shabby coat and shabbier hat, Mr. Innes remained free from suspicion of vulgarity—the sad dignity of his grey face and the dreams that haunted his eyes saved him from that.[18]

Of the people who attended the concerts, Moore writes:

> Jesuits were not infrequently seen . . . Painters and men of letters were attracted by them; musicians seldom. Nor did Mr. Innes encourage their presence. Musicians were of no use to him. They were, he said, divided into two classes—those who came to scoff, and those who came to steal. He did not want either sort. . . . The rare music interested but a handful, and the audience that had come from London shivered in remembrance of the east wind that had accompanied their journey.[19]

In his biography of Moore, Joseph Hone (who admittedly confesses to know nothing about music) writes:

> Throughout the book, the musical background is convincing as few novels written by non-musicians ever have been. It is not only the almost complete absence of slips which is remarkable for Moore always took enormous pains over the background of his stories and was adept at picking the brains of others; but there are many passages which persuade the reader that he really understood something of his subject. Mr. Innes's Dolmetsch-like enthusiasm for the old music and Ulick Dean's [a character in the book thought by some to represent W. B. Yeats]

exposition for the ancient modes ring as true as that musical work which was the natural ambit of a social letter in the nineties.[20]

The use of the phrase 'Dolmetsch-like enthusiasm' as a comparison is a flagrant example of the way in which Dolmetsch's help went unacknowledged. Edouard Dujardin writes of Moore:

> I don't think he had any ear, and it always seemed to me that his interest in Wagner, on whom we had endless conversations, was mainly literary. His brother, Colonel Moore, said that 'the members of our family were all unmusical, George no better than the rest. He could not hum a tune correctly and what he wrote about music was what he heard others say. Perhaps he had some taste, but he had no ear.'[21]

Obviously Hone's researches did not take him to the Dolmetsch archives, where he would have found the letters from Moore; but this was largely Moore's fault, for when the book was published[22] he dedicated it to Arthur Symons and W. B. Yeats, both Dolmetsch's close friends and frequently to be seen at his concerts. It is therefore significant that several decades later, when Dolmetsch was celebrating his 80th birthday, he recollected living in a 'sort of informal club . . .' containing all the poets and creative geniuses then alive: the long list of names does not include that of George Moore.

Only two people have, to date, made any effort to identify Dolmetsch's contribution to Moore: the first was Dr. H. H. Noyes in 1938,[23] and, more recently, Professor Sarah Watson who writes: 'The importance and true significance of the friendship between Moore and Dolmetsch have been overlooked.' She goes on to quote a number of musical parallels which have so far been ignored by Moore's biographers and other writers of the period. Of *Evelyn Innes*, Professor Watson says; 'This novel is significant because it is one of the earliest musical novels in English; because it demonstrates the truth of the adage that a body of explicit detail creates realism; because it, together with Shaw's musical reviews, helped to spread the work of Arnold Dolmetsch and contributed to the revival of Renaissance and Baroque music, its instruments and composers.'[24]

NOTES

1. A revealing comparison with present-day time-tables.
2. Later known to be Dolmetsch's own: published by Boosey and Hawkes. Vol. I, 1896, *Collected Songs and Dialogues* arr. and ed. A. Dolmetsch. Vol II pub. 1912. Both volumes are still in print.
3. An interesting sequel to this is that Professor Edward Dent was at this time, a schoolboy at Eton. He later told Carl Dolmetsch that it was Arnold Dolmetsch's

concert that influenced his decision to become a musicologist specializing in early music.

4. Most probably the house-warming concert on 19 December 1893.

5. Unfortunately this plan did not materialise.

6. This is the first indication that we have of Dolmetsch actually *making* a clavichord (we know that William Morris had suggested that he should make a harpsichord); the firm order he received from Fuller-Maitland would appear to be the first.

7. The first concert with music of the 16th century, devoted entirely to the Lawes brothers: the third was selected from the works of John Jenkins and Christopher Simpson, including an unpublished set of *Divisions* by Simpson being played for the first time. The music of Matthew Locke and Henry Purcell (in whom it was then supposed that the great schools of English music had its close) and contemporary music for viols and violins played side by side were to be introduced at the fourth concert. The remaining concerts were to be devoted to music by foreign composers.

8. Jackson, Holbrook, *The Eighteen Nineties*, Jonathan Cape, 1913, p. 118.

9. Scholes, P. A., *Concise Dictionary of Music*, Oxford, 1912, p. 499.

10. Hone, Joseph, *George Moore*, Victor Gollancz, 1936, p. 465.

11. Wilde is reputed to have said that Moore took seven years to discover grammar, that he then discovered the paragraph, etc . . . shouting his discoveries from the housetops.

12. Hone, Joseph, *George Moore*, Victor Gollancz, 1936, p. 114.

13. 'The name was no indication that Dowland was the name of Henry VIII's favourite lute player, and there was nothing in the smug masonry to suggest an aestheticism of any kind. The dulcimers, lutes and virginals surprised the visitor coming in from the street and he stayed his steps as he might on the threshold of a fairyland' *Evelyn Innes*, p. 29.

14. When Oscar Wilde's attention was drawn to the dreadful sartorial solecism, he said: 'Next time Moore will get it right. He conducts his education in public.' Robert Ross, who was present, replied: 'Well, the public pays for it. They have a right to know how he is getting on.'

15. Moore, George, *Evelyn Innes*, T. Fisher Unwin, 1898, p. 16.

16. ibid., pp. 227/8.

17. ibid., p. 1.

18. ibid., pp. 22/3.

19. ibid., p. 11.

20. Hone, Joseph, *George Moore*, Victor Gollancz, 1936, pp. 131/2.

21. ibid., p. 131.

22. In *The New Age* of 30 June 1898, the critic holds that 'the musical preferences of Mr. Innes have been described rather more minutely than the necessities of the novel require'. Two weeks later *The New Age* returns to the subject and devotes a long article to it: 'There is much novel music in Mr. George Moore's musical novel' writes the musical critic. 'A careful perusal of the book, solely from the musician's standpoint, fills the reader with a certain admiration, not unmixed with awe, for the evident industry with which the musical colours have been mixed and laid on . . . .Writings of the professional realistic school frequently make a spacious

impression of reality and accurate detail upon the general reader, while they irritate the specialist. . . . One hardly knows whether to regard the alleged art theories in *Evelyn Innes* seriously. It is easy to make the rejoinder that they are not those of the author, but of his puppets, and besides, there is not sufficient evidence in the book of ability or equipment to theorize to any purpose.' The critic quotes numerous errors: viz, Moore's description of an instrument which is 'a cross between a harpsichord and a virginal'. The reader is invited to imagine an instrument tuned in the bass to one system and in the treble another.

23. Noyes, Dr. H. H., *The Novels of George Moore*. A thesis, 1938, University of London, Library.
24. *English Literature in Transition*, Vol. VI. (1963), Professor Sarah Watson, Fenn College, USA.

CHAPTER VIII

'The Harmonious Blacksmith'

SINCE the average concert-goer of 1894 was prompted more by popular than personal taste, it is remarkable that Dolmetsch's concerts were so well-attended. Sir Joseph Barnby, speaking at the annual conference of the Incorporated Society of Musicians on 'The Position of Music in England', puts us in the picture very well. It appears that in 1869 only one elementary school in the kingdom claimed a grant of 4 shillings offered two years previously for having music taught. The next year 43 of the 12,000 obtained the grant, and from this meagre beginning the increase had been rapid and extensive until in 1894 nearly four million children, principally under the age of 14, had been instructed at a cost to the body politic of about £165,000 annually and correspondingly.

The efficiency of the teachers had been greatly increased since the establishment of the training schools. The public schools fared less well, for 25 years earlier there had been no music master at Eton: if a boy wanted to learn music, he had to take lessons in Windsor during play-hours. But from the time 18 years before that Sir Joseph himself had attended this famous school he declared that 'never a year passed when the captain of the boat and the captain of the eleven—names to be spoken with great reverence—were not members of the Musical Society'.

It was fashionable at this time to finish one's musical studies abroad, despite the fact that there were perfectly good schools and professors in this country. Sir Joseph considered that audiences 'need educating very much at the present time'. He regretted the scarcity of concerts even in the larger towns, but at the same time he blamed the public for their lack of catholic taste in preferring oratorios to other music.

Meanwhile, George Bernard Shaw was inviting the public to hear music of a very different style. 'There has been a general clearing out from the hall of Barnard's Inn, The Artworkers' Guild betaking themselves to Clifford's Inn, and their whilom tenant, Mr. Arnold Dolmetsch, falling back with his viols and virginals on Dowland, his own house at Dulwich.'

Shaw attended most of the concerts and his observations are invaluable today. Although he hopes that Dolmetsch 'will dig up plenty of genuine

medieval music for us', he also points out the dangers of reviving medio-
crities of the past which have no merit but age: 'Once my bare historical
curiosity has been satisfied,' he writes, 'I do not value the commonplace of
circa 1600 a bit more than the common place of circa 1900. . . . The quality
of the performances, which has always been surprisingly good considering
the strangeness of the instruments, continues to improve.'

He marvels at Dolmetsch's increasing command of the lute, but is not
impressed with Fuller-Maitland's playing on the virginals: it is the vocal
music which Shaw sees as presenting the greatest difficulty, mainly
because singers have their heads full of modern 'effects' and 'shew but a
feeble sense of the accuracy of intonation and tenderness required by the
pure vocal harmonies of the old school'.[1]

Despite having to make the journey to Dulwich, the press covered all
the concerts and wrote at length, mostly appreciative notices. The *Musical
Times* (1 March 1894) cynically refers to the intended publication of
Henry VIII's music by Dolmetsch, Burne-Jones and Hollis [Morris]:
apart from their experiencing pecuniary difficulties, the writer foresees
further problems when deciding the 'Precise locality where Henry VIII
begins and his music-master leaves off'. At the concert devoted to the
music of the Lawes brothers, in which Dolmetsch introduced no fewer
than 14 items which were new to his audience, *The Times* (18 February
1894) thought it 'delightful': *The Royal Consort* was described as 'a
beautiful suite which occupied a prominent position in the first part [of
the programme] and in which the treatment of the parts is always interesting and not seldom effective, even to ears unaccustomed to the later
developments of chamber music'. Writing on the same concert, a *Musical
Times* (1 March 1894) critic becomes bold enough to suggest that although
Dolmetsch and his pupils evince considerable command over the respective bygone instruments, 'the music would acquire greater charm if more
variety and warmth of expression were infused into the renderings'.

Of the third concert, devoted to Jenkins and Simpson, *The Times*
(2 March 1894) recognises that 'The music of these great men, though
ancient in age, is by no means antiquated in spirit; and when played as at
these concerts, on fine specimens of contemporary instruments, no close
observer can fail to remark not only on the wonderful knowledge of effect
possessed by the writers, but also how comparatively short has been the
advance in the last two hundred years of skill in interweaving melodies.'
The *Musical Times* (1 April 1894) critic thought the performance was:

> . . . a surprising revelation of the remarkable musical abilities of our ancestors and
> that we should be indebted to the enthusiasm of a foreigner for our due apprecia-
> tion of the talents of our own countrymen afford[s] another proof of the existence

of a peculiar and regrettable form of national modesty which frequently causes us
to underrate and ignore that of which it is our duty to be proud.

Shaw not only attended every concert but found plenty to say about
them. One of his particular dislikes was late-19th-century piano technique,
which he describes as 'springing along like a pole-jumper', as opposed to
the older method of 'walking' on the keys. He draws our attention to an
article in which a well-known critic had claimed to have arrived at the
early method unaided. Shaw consulted Dolmetsch, who procured in time
for his next concert a copy of a suite for harpsichord by Matthew Locke
with the fingering marked: Dolmetsch described the 17th-century keyboard technique as the wing-like movements we see painted in old pictures
of St. Cecelia and other celestial musicians.

Shaw confesses that he especially enjoyed hearing the chamber music
of Matthew Locke, 'the last English musician who composed for the viols
and founder of my school of musical criticism. His denunciation of the
academic professors of his day is quite in my best manner.' He points out
that Dolmetsch has taken up an altogether un-English position by acknowledging Purcell as a great musician; therefore we should perform some of
his works. The English musicians also appreciate Purcell's worth but
continue to perform Mendelssohn's *Elijah* over and over again—a
conclusion which he deems even more intolerable than Christopher
Sly's 'Tis a very excellent piece of work: would t'were over'. According
to Shaw, this is what most people say to themselves at performances of
the Ninth Symphony. 'Mr. Dolmetsch gave us *The Golden Sonata*, some
harpsichord lessons and several songs, one of which, *Winter*, created
quite a burst of enthusiasm by the beauty of its harmony which Brahms
himself, in his very different way, could not have surpassed for richness,
much less for eloquence.' Shaw apologises 'for having devoted so much
space to a concert of English music given by a foreigner, when I have in
hand plenty of concerts of foreign music given by Englishmen'. He
suggests that up to the time of Purcell, nobody ever supposed that the
English were less musical than other people, but that since then they have
been 'blotted out of the musical map of Europe'. He is curious to know
'whether any change occurred in the construction of the English ear at the
end of the 17th century?' He declares that 'What broke up English music
was opera' and discusses his reasons for this view: 'It was when opera,
providentially, began to die of its own absurdity, that music showed signs
of reviving.' He is convinced that in this revival the old music must serve
as a starting point, just as 13th-century work has served in modern re-
vivals of the other arts: 'That is why I attach such importance to these
concerts of Mr. Dolmetsch, which are, besides, highly enjoyable, both to

experts in music and to the ordinary Englishman who, with every respect for "classical music", has deep down in his breast a rooted belief (which I rather share) that three quarters of an hour is too long for any one instrumental composition to last.' Shaw ends[2] with a few praiseworthy remarks on the forthcoming publication of the *Fitzwilliam Virginal Book* and recommends it not only to musicians but to those who are in the habit of buying three new waltzes every month and are feeling the need of some music they have never heard before.

The fifth concert in the series devoted itself to the Italian school of the 16th, 17th and 18th centuries and Dolmetsch introduced a long list of composers whose work was new to his audiences, but which would need no explanation today: Frescobaldi, Cesti, Corelli, Vivaldi, Picchi, Caroso, Caccini and the two Scarlattis. The notices were encouraging, as usual, one critic remarking especially upon the beauty of the concerto by Vivaldi for viola d'amore and lute, accompanied by muted violins: it was a work which Dolmetsch claimed as being the only concerto in which the lute was known to have been introduced (*Musical Times*, 1 May 1894).

The next concert was concerned with the music of unknown or, more correctly, unplayed French composers of the same period: Adrien le Roy, Nicolas Valet, De la Barre, Marin Marais, Rameau, Charles Riviere, Du Fresny and Couperin. *The Times* noted the performance of two works by Marais, 'a very important composer of the 18th century, the credit of whose discovery is entirely due to Mr. Dolmetsch'.

The Handel concert which followed brought forth six items which had not been heard in modern times. 'Handel is known to so many people only as a composer of oratorio that there is an element of novelty in a programme which includes none but his instrumental works', writes *The Times* (11 May 1894). The same writer refers to a fine sonata, played by Hélène, for the viola da gamba which was 'absolutely unknown to Tuesday's audience, since it has not yet been published in Dr. Chrysander's edition of Handel's works'.[3] The Bach evening includes six items which had not been given a modern hearing. The *Musical Times* (1 June 1894) acknowledges that:

> Great credit is due to Mr. Dolmetsch for having so successfully aroused interest in so much that is good to remember. The performances must have been a revelation to many and even for those for whom the old music possessed but little musical charm must have been impressed with the great skill of our forefathers who, with such comparatively small means, accomplished so much.

*   *   *

Exactly how Dolmetsch managed domestically following the separation from his wife is open to conjecture, but he was known to be an excellent cook. However, it would seem that he was missing Marie's organisation, for in a letter to Horne, recently removed to Florence, he writes:

4th March 1894   Dowland,
                                                     West Dulwich,
                                                     S.E.

I was awfully sorry not to be able to see you before your departure. You would not believe in what an awful mess of work and bother I was then! It is a little better now; but not good yet. . . . The concerts are *very* successful. They don't pay much. Did I tell you I have got Lord Dysart's Ruckers?[4] for repair and restoration. It is a fine instrument—I know another one for sale—much better still, *covered* with paintings outside and inside—*very* cheap. £350;[5] but I need not tell you it is too dear for me!

I am going to accompany the recitatives of Bach's St. Matthew Passion upon the harpsichord at the Queen's Hall on the 15th.[6] Hélène will play the famous obbligato for the viola da gamba, and Joachim the violin. We tried the harpsichord—in the Hall – Stanford says the full tone is *too* powerful for the singer. I am to use only one quill, and the leather, for a change. You would not believe how well it sounds in that room!

'This business of restoring harpsichords is thriving' writes Dolmetsch to Horne later (3 July 1894). Instrument-building, too, seemed to be flourishing for the little clavichord on which Dolmetsch had been working for some months was now finished and soon to be heard at 'Dowland'. He writes to Horne: 'Have you seen today's *World* about the Handel Festival and my clavichord? It is *well* worth 6d!'

Induced by the warm July weather to open his windows, Shaw found his ear more acutely aware of the noises inflicted upon him by his neighbours. His fancy led him to a contemplation of the Handel Festival at the Crystal Palace with thousands of singers and hundreds of instrumentalists employing themselves simultaneously and with dire effect in 'renderings' of *Israel in Egypt* or *Messiah* to a spellbound audience of equally gargantuan proportions. In the *World* (4 July 1894), Shaw writes of the people who already make enough noise out of their iron-framed pianos to bring them under police regulation in Germany and to make them impossible neighbours in London. He compares the present age of loudness to the earlier days when we played the viols instead of the violin and virginals instead of the piano. He has practical advice to offer on the subject:

A first-rate clavichord from the hands of an artist-craftsman who, always learning something, makes no two instruments exactly alike, and turns out each as an individual work of art, marked with his name and stamped with his style, can be made and sold for £40 or less, the price of a fourth-rate piano (no. 5768 from Messrs.

So-and-so's factory) which you can hardly sell for £15 the day after you have bought it. Above all, you can play Bach's two famous sets of fugues and preludes, not to mention the rest of a great mass of beautiful old music, on your clavichord, which you cannot do without a great alteration of character and loss of charm on the piano.

These observations have been provoked by the startlingly successful result of an experiment made by the students of the R.C.M. They, having their ears and minds opened by Mr. Dolmetsch's demonstration to the beauty of our old instruments and our old music, took the very practical step of asking him to make them a clavichord. It was rather a strange request to a collector and connoisseur; but Mr. Dolmetsch, in the spirit of the Irishman who was invited to play the fiddle, had a try; and after some months work he has actually turned out a little masterpiece, excellent as a musical instrument and pleasant to look at, which seems to me likely to begin such a revolution in domestic instruments as William Morris's work made in domestic furniture and decoration, or Philip Webb's in domestic architecture. I therefore estimate the birth of this little clavichord as, on a modern computation, about forty thousand times as important as the Handel Festival.[7]

In the *Saturday Review* of 15 December 1894, we learn from an unsigned article called 'Bach and the Harpsichord' that this instrument, 'although obsolete and, for the ordinary purposes of music, rightly consigned to the taciturn seclusion of the museum', has some charm and quality of its own and has occasionally figured in the concert-rooms of Paris and London during the last few years. Although the recently constructed Pleyel *clavecin* is reputed to be an instrument upon which it is possible to play with a certain speed and semblance of expression, the writer points out that Dolmetsch had succeeded in restoring a two-manual harpsichord by Kirkman sufficiently well 'to show that a fine harpsichord in its original condition must have been as much superior to Messrs. Pleyel's harpsichords as that instrument was to the spinets and harpsichords which from time to time have been exhibited to our credulous generation as excellent examples of their kind, but which in reality were but the chattering ghosts of their former selves'.

In the writer's opinion, Pleyel's harpsichord suggests more of the piano than the harpsichord, especially as certain contrivances have been introduced which serve no other end than to bring the two instruments into a kind of competition. Since they have only their own experience as pianoforte makers to guide them this is not surprising: 'Such attempts can only be counted as part and parcel of the old fallacy that the piano has been developed from the harpsichord and has surpassed it. Yet the one is no more the development of the other, than the harmonium is a development of the organ. The piano has not surpassed, but superseded the harpsichord.'

He goes on to say that it was not until Lord Dysart's harpsichord, by

Andreas Ruckers, was heard at Dulwich, after it had been put into playing order by Mr. Dolmetsch, that 'a fine instrument, by a great maker, existed, which possessed all its original beauty and character of tone. For the first time within living memory the harpsichord was heard to perfection; and the reputation which the instruments by the Ruckers retained until almost the close of the last century (a reputation which can only be compared to the reputation of a Stradivarius at the present day) was at last understandable. The experience of many years of research and experiment had enabled Mr. Dolmetsch to obtain an extraordinary brilliancy and pureness of tone, which the pianoforte makers who had previously attempted the restoration of old harpsichords never suspected the instrument to be capable of producing.'

The writer then deals firmly with 'those theorists who argued that the compositions of Bach and his predecessors were intended to be played more slowly than they are now performed, since it was impossible to play effectively on the harpsichord with any degree of speed, were proved to be wholly mistaken, for not only can the mechanism of the harpsichord respond to the swiftest sequences which the hand is capable of executing, but the most elaborate ornaments can be performed with a rapidity, precision, and clearness not attainable on the piano'.[8]

The critic then reviews Dolmetsch's concert at Clifford's Inn on 6 December in which there is yet another opportunity to judge the value of Bach performed on the harpsichord. In Fuller-Maitland's playing of the Concerto in D minor the writer finds the contrasting tone of the two manuals of the harpsichord far more effective in colour than the single keyboard of the piano, which is 'painfully monotonous'. He also commends a performance of Bach's *Cantate Burlesque*, another of Dolmetsch's undertakings of which there was no parallel in modern times.

In the beginning of 1895, Dolmetsch was engaged for four West-End concerts under the management of Daniel Mayer: two at the Salle Erard and the others at Queen's Hall. Dolmetsch's performances now received regular comment in the press, although the occasional reaction to both music and instruments is interesting. One critic thought the lute 'a poor and feeble instrument at its best' and that 'Mr. Fuller-Maitland did all that was possible with six pieces from the *Fitzwilliam Virginal Book* but they are wanting in character and interest'. The same writer found that 'the rich, full tone of the viols like a beautiful male voice was pleasant to the ear' and 'the Suite of 3 pieces for four viols and harpsichord by William Lawes, in many ways the most interesting composition in the programme. How very modern it sounded!' (The *Musical Standard*, 19 January 1895). But the same critic has very different feelings about another concert in the series:

Have we sympathy with the honest amateur when he bluntly declares that the modern pianoforte—a development in itself—is a more beautiful instrument than the harpsichord? Well, of course it is; no one wishes to return to the coarse, confused tone of the latter instrument.

He goes on to agree with Dolmetsch in his assumption that works written for the harpsichord are best rendered on that instrument, but insists that Bach, 'so prophetic in his modernity, is really more beautiful on the pianoforte . . . Are we to suppose that Bach was satisfied with the musical effect of the popular instrument of his day? Would he not have admired the purity and sustained musical tone of the common pianoforte?' (The *Musical Standard*, 2 February 1895)

The *Saturday Review* soon began to devote several columns to Dolmetsch's activities; although the articles are unsigned they were surely from the pen of Shaw's successor. On 31 January, Shaw writes to Dolmetsch:

> 29, Fitzroy Square,
> W.
>
> Now that I have taken to dramatic criticism I find that the theatre keeps me away from concerts almost as completely as the concerts used to keep me away from the theatre. I was quite unable to get to the Salle Erard on either of your evenings.
>
> My chief regret at the discontinuance of my musical work is that I lose my power to help you to make your work known quickly. My successor on the *World*, Mr. R. S. Hichens, seems a clever and sympathetic critic: if you do not already know him, he might respond to perhaps maintain the interest which the *World* musical column has so often shewn in the revival of the clavichord and the old chamber instruments generally. My musical colleague on the *Saturday Review* is a very, very able young man, enormously interested in Purcell, named J. F. Runciman. He is a skilled professional musician and a slashing journalist; and he could be of more use to you on the *Saturday* than even Mr. Horne, who does not deal with concerts. Now I have a suggestion to make. You once asked me to call on you some afternoon and see your workshop. Shall I avail myself of the invitation, and try to persuade Runciman to come with me? Or do you know him already?[9]

In the light of Shaw's letter, we can compare Runciman's criticism to that of the *Musical Standard* (p. 84):

> Mr. Maitland scurried through the selection from the *Fitzwilliam Virginal Book* at such a pace, and with so small a show of interest in even the technical structure of the pieces, so weak a sense of the subtleties of rhythm that count for such much in this old music, that its meaning, and even the old-world quality, were wholly lost.

Dolmetsch's ever-increasing participation in musical activities put a greater strain on his domestic arrangements than ever before. Finally, he sent a call to Zürich and in prompt answer there arrived his father's youngest sister, Aline. A typical product from the family mould, she was tiny, busy and imperious, 'imbued with an old-fashioned Swiss code of politeness. On entering a shop, for example, she would always, before coming to business, drop a formal curtsey to a shopkeeper'.[10] Although willing to help out for a while she had no intention of becoming a permanent housekeeper, so she sent to France for Elodie Desirée, the beautiful, talented and recently divorced wife of Edgard, one of Dolmetsch's younger brothers. Dolmetsch liked the idea for a trial period; but was a little apprehensive when he met her at Dover and found her laden with her entire worldly possessions, together with a fresh cheese and a bunch of dead fowls. But Elodie was an instant success: musically outstanding and a brilliant keyboard player: 'There was an extraordinary charm and fluent grace in her playing. Her light touch, acquired through frequent use of a small square piano in the convent where she had been educated, enabled her rapidly to adjust herself to the more ancient keyboard instruments. She was able to master pieces of considerable difficulty in a few days and play them by heart.'[11]

To have gained such a performer within the family suited Dolmetsch admirably for he no longer needed outside assistance at his concerts. He could, and often did, play the harpsichord himself but he preferred to perform upon the stringed instruments: his first love, the violin, his second, the viola d'amore, and then the instrument for which he had developed an insatiable passion—the lute.

It is probable that at this time the combination of Dolmetsch, Hélène and Elodie was as nearly a virtuoso group as was ever achieved in those early concerts. However, Dolmetsch's love affairs were not wholly confined to his lutes and his fiddles. Elodie, in addition to her musical ability, was a woman of great physical attraction with a lamentably weak stomach—an irresistible combination never known to fail in gaining the attention of the opposite sex. She captivated Arnold from the outset and he resolved to marry her as soon as he was free to do so. Divorce proceedings were already in progress but repeated delays, either through technicalities of domicile or lack of money, slowed them down to walking pace. Eventually, when the case was about to be heard, Dolmetsch mentioned his intended remarriage: he was then told that since Elodie was his sister-in-law such a union was not permitted under English law. So they started all over again, transferring the proceedings to Zürich. Meanwhile, Elodie, using her legal name, lived with Dolmetsch quite openly. The gossips were thus satisfied, whilst audiences and press alike called her 'Mrs. Dolmetsch', blissfully ignorant of her true spouse's identity. Her name first appeared on the programme of a concert of ancient Venetian music at the New Gallery on 3 March 1895.

In early April, Dolmetsch gained a foothold in a new and important field: he was engaged to give a series of lectures at the Royal Institution on 'Music and Musical Instruments of the 16th, 17th and 18th centuries'. The *Musical News* announced the event with the assurance that 'Mr. Dolmetsch is now well known and recognised to be one of our most enthusiastic and thorough students of the period. . . . His lectures are always interesting for the amount of careful research they exhibit'. John Runciman, as enthusiastic as his predecessor, Shaw, devoted almost a column to Dolmetsch in the *Saturday Review* (11 May 1895) and warns: 'Really, unless Mr. Dolmetsch takes the greatest care he will presently become a popular man. Quite recently he gave some concerts of old music, with literary explanations, at the Salle Erard and Queen's Hall; now he is giving a series of lectures with musical illustrations at the Royal Institution; and the unmusical—or rather, non-musical—audience that flocks to the lectures is even more enthusiastic than the section of the musical public that crowded to Queen's Hall and the Salle Erard.'

The audiences, usually more interested in 'argon and the temperament of the amoeba', were sitting wide-eyed and open-mouthed as Dolmetsch speculated, theorised and generally stated his case concerning the old instruments, as if these had been brought to them from another planet. Runciman suggests that if Dolmetsch can so stir up these scientific folk there is no saying what he may do with 'ordinary people who are not pre-occupied with the amoeba'. He hopes to find the small Queen's Hall packed to the ceiling at Mr. Dolmetsch's next concert. The Royal Institution lectures are not very different from the Queen's Hall concerts, says Runciman: 'At the one Mr. Dolmetsch talks and plays, at the other he plays and talks'. He takes his audience charmingly, irresistibly, into his confidence about his rare old music books and is prettily scornful of the 'Authorities' who declare that no one can do upon the harpsichord what Mr. Dolmetsch immediately sits down at the harpsichord and does.

Here we also find the first approval of Elodie's performance: 'Mrs. Elodie Dolmetsch played some harpsichord pieces by Couperin with daintiness of colour, piquancy of rhythm, and quite remarkable freedom from the nervous scrambling that ruined the playing of some of Dolmetsch's previous harpsichordists. [J. A. Fuller-Maitland] The only fear we have now is that there may be a craze for these old instruments. Mr. Dolmetsch's price for a clavichord is, we believe, only one quarter the price of a piano of equal quality, and now that his workshop is conveniently situated on the classic ground of Queen Square[12] we are much afraid that every West-End dame with the smallest pretensions to culture will run thither to complete the furnishing of her drawing-room.'

On 22 May (1895) Dolmetsch provided a concert of music at a *conversazione* at the Royal Institute of Painters in Water Colours in Piccadilly, given by the Huguenot Society of London. The programme, printed on luxury paper, ran into several pages with crests and motifs surmounting every item: words, music and history of each song was written in full and, for the first time, included a description of the instruments.[13]

It so happened that the Huguenot concert was instrumental in bringing Dolmetsch into the front-line of a battle which raged for several months in the *Musical News*. On 1 June 1895, there appeared in its correspondence columns a letter from Cummings:

> Sir,—At the Conversazione of the 'Huguenot Society of London' on the 22nd, a selection of music was performed presumably all of French origin, one of the pieces was Clement Marot's *Plus ne suis ce que j'ai eté*. The book of words contained the music, which proved to be an adaption of Handel's Suite, so well known under the absurd title of *The Harmonious Blacksmith*. Immediately before the song was sung, Mr. Dolmetsch in a most authoritative manner announced that the piece about to be performed was usually ascribed to Handel, but was in fact, as printed in the book, an old French song, music and words by Clement Marot. Mr. Dolmetsch ought to have been better informed, and in order to prevent the repetition of such a flagrant mistake, I ask you to insert this note. Mr. Wekerlin, in his *Echos du temps passé*, has included the song above referred to with Marot's name attached, and when asked for an explanation, he replied in writing, stating that he had taken it from the *Choix de Chansons* by Moncrif, and adds, 'The Collection of Moncrif' (one volume in 12 mo., printed in 1757) is exceeding rare. I only know two copies of it; one of which is in the library of the Rue Richelieu, and the other in a private collection. It is beyond a doubt that the theme of *Plus ne suis* is borrowed from the *Pièces de Clavecin* by Handel, and that Moncrif committed a fault in not affixing the name of the author. Perhaps he was himself ignorant of it; for he was not very well acquainted with music. I only made this discovery after publication of my book otherwise I should not have failed to mention it in my notes.
>
> Let me add that Handel's volume containing the air was published by him in 1720: doubtless in the course of 37 years the air with its variations had become popular and travelled to Paris, where it tickled the ears and captivated the fancy of Moncrif.

In the issue of 22 June 1895, Dolmetsch takes up the challenge:

> Sir,—I have just chanced to see in your issue of the 1st instant a letter reflecting upon some remarks of mine at a concert of old French music which I gave before the Huguenot Society. In that letter, Mr. Cummings, the writer, says that I was not only misinformed, but that I delivered myself 'in a most authoritative manner' of a statement which was not correct. Now, Sir, it was the writer of that letter, not I, who, to use his own phrase, 'ought to have been better informed', for he puts

into my mouth a statement which I never made. It is he who speaks 'in an authoritative manner'. In the first place he says that I attributed to Clement Marot 'music and words' of the song, *Plus ne suis ce que j'ai été*, the tune of which is nearly the same as the air known by the name of *The Harmonious Blacksmith*. That is a statement which I never made; what I said was, that the tune of the song was the traditional music to these words, and that it was not Handel's.

The writer of the letter in question then proceeds to conclude in an arbitrary manner that the air of *Plus ne suis* is borrowed from Handel's *Suite de Pièces*. I am sorry that Mr. Cummings, who is in possession of so much information on that abstruse subject, has not given his authority to this conclusion, but since he has neglected to do so, and the subject is an interesting one, it may perhaps amuse your readers to know my own conclusion in the matter.

The tune of *Plus ne suis* is, I held, and still hold, very strong evidence against Handel's authorship, for it is not only written in a manner entirely unlike his own, but it is especially unlike in style the other themes which he elsewhere uses for variations. It has all the character of a *song*, written to words, and it apparently belongs to a period earlier than the time of Handel; to the 17th, I do not say the 16th, century.

In the *Choix de Chansons* mentioned by Mr. Cummings, and in the *Anthologie Française*, published in 1765, which is a more accurate work, the music is given as the traditional tune to the words *Plus ne suis* which are ascribed to Clement Marot and it is given among other early songs, the authenticity of which is not disputed. But I can bring another curious fact to bear on the subject. In a last-century manuscript in my possession, among pieces by Purcell, Dr. Pepusch, Dr. Green, Handel, etc. . . etc. . . , there is a *Lesson with variations by.* . . . Here a name has been scratched out, and the words, *Mr. Handel* substituted in a later hand. The tune runs as given here.

The variations which follow are quite childish, they contain nothing of Handel, and it is difficult to believe that they were written by one who was acquainted with his famous variations. Can this be the *Lesson* by Wagenseil, which is mentioned by William Chappell in his searching article in Groves' Dictionary of Music on the *Harmonious Blacksmith*? But Mr. Cummings will doubtless be able to inform you on that point.

Arnold Dolmetsch

An editorial note explains:- (As Mr. Dolmetsch's letter was crowded out last week, we submitted it to Mr. Cummings in order to save time.) Cummings is quite ready to accept that the tune of this song was 'the traditional music to the words and that it was not Handel's'. But after having read the article in Grove's, he still finds the authorship of the words doubtful: the piece cannot be found in any of the collections of Marot's poems so Cummings is therefore convinced that the name Clement Marot is an assumed one. He then pursues at great length the claim for Wagenseil as the composer of the tune.

However, not content even with his own reply, on 13 July Mr. Cummings continues:

Then as regards the words; French writers are agreed that they are not Marot's, but were probably written about the time of their first publication, 1765: this again would be 45 years after Handel published the tune: what folly then to talk of the 'traditional' music to the words!

On 20 July, Dolmetsch replies:

Should Mr. Cummings be able to prove that the words of *Plus ne suis ce que j'ai été* were written as late as 1765, it would no doubt be strong evidence against my belief that the air is earlier than Handel's time. But this mere assertion will not suffice. The style of the air too clearly indicates a 17th-century origin to make another opinion admissible without proof.

The battle rages and another voice is heard, that of a correspondent, E. J. D. [Edward J. Dent]:

Sir,—I do not wish to separate such combatants as Mr. Dolmetsch and Mr. Cummings, but I feel rather disappointed at the prevalence of statements regarding the *use* of the notorious tune, by various persons. From the arguments adduced one is almost left to suppose that the origin of both the tune and the words in question is a never-to-be-fathomed-mystery.

He then goes into great detail to make his case and sums up with the following points:

> The *words*—'French writers' may be 'agreed', but it is not theirs to 'agree' 1765 with 1565.
> The *tune* of the 'Harmonious Blacksmith' is of a date prior to 1565, i.e. at least 120 years prior to Handel's birth.
> The *variations* are by Handel.
>
> E. J. D. [Edward J. Dent]

Cummings will not let the matter go and another long letter appears on 27 July in which he refutes every one of E. J. D.'s statements. Dolmetsch makes no attempt at further argument but Sir George Grove has the last word:

Sir:-

> A good deal has been said of late in the *Musical News* on the subject of the 'Harmonious Blacksmith', but I do not remember to have seen any notice of one curious fact, namely, that Beethoven wrote a two-part fugue upon the tune; certainly it can be no other.

> though the allusion ceases after the first few bars. The fugue bears the date of 1783, and therefore belongs to the time when Beethoven was 13 years old, and under Neefe's tuition at Bonn, and is 95 bars long. It is said to have been written as his examination-piece for the post of second court organist to the Elector, and is printed at the end of the Supplemental Volume 1st to the great edition of Messrs. Breitkopf and Härtel.
>
> Yours truly,
George Grove

NOTES

1. Shaw, George Bernard, *Music in London*, 7 February 1894. Constable, Vol. III, pp. 147/8.
2. ibid., 14 March 1894, Vol. III, pp. 171/6.
3. See p. 62.
4. Now in the Victoria and Albert Museum.
5. Unidentified.
6. Description of this hall when it was first built can be seen in the *Musical Times*, 1 December 1893.
7. Shaw, George Bernard, *Music in London*, Constable, Vol. III, 4 July 1894, pp. 257/8.
8. See pp. 62–3.
9. Shaw and John Runciman visited Dolmetsch in his studio in West Dulwich on 6 February 1895. The *Collected Letters*, *Bernard Shaw*, Laurence, Dan, p. 481, London 1965.
10. Dolmetsch, Mabel, *Personal Recollections of Arnold Dolmetsch*, Routledge & Kegan Paul, p. 14.
11. ibid., pp. 14/15.
12. Dolmetsch had a workshop at 6, Queen Square before it was taken over by The Artworkers' Guild.
13. Lute, made in Venice by Magno Stegher about 1560. [15 strings].
    Viola d'amore, made in Milan by Carlo Antonio Testore in 1736 [seven principal strings and seven sympathetic strings. Peg-box terminated by the head of a cupid, beautifully carved.]
    Tenor viol made probably by Simpson in London about 1710.
    Viola da gamba, made in Cremona in 1720 by Carlo Bergonzi [seven principal and seven sympathetic strings].
    Harpsichord, made in London by Jacobus Kirkman in 1738 . . . two keyboards and five stops.
    [There were included many further details unnecessary today about the capabilities of the instruments.]

CHAPTER IX

The 'Green Harpsichord'

IN the summer of 1895, Dolmetsch made his debut in the theatre. He had recently met William Poel, whose work in the drama could be compared with Dolmetsch's own efforts to resuscitate the old music. Poel was later to revive and establish the principles of Elizabethan stage production: he 'consistently refused to work within the framework of the modern "picture stage" '[1] and built platforms out over the stalls in order to reproduce as nearly as possible conditions as they existed in the 16th-century theatre.

The Elizabethan Stage Society was constituted in 1895, and for their first production, *Twelfth Night*, at Burlington Hall, Savile Row, Arnold Dolmetsch provided the music. He and his players were also in costume and, born actor that he was, he entered into the spirit of the thing with enthusiasm, quite frequently joining in the action of the play with a few lines of dialogue that had certainly never been written by Shakespeare.

Concert engagements, theatrical performances and teaching, together with the restoration and building of instruments, made Dolmetsch a very busy man. The first step he took toward relieving the pressure was to pass on some of his teaching to Hélène and a few advanced pupils: the next was to make the move to Bloomsbury, where most of his friends resided. He was fortunate in renting a large house at 6 Keppel Street ideally suited to his purpose. There was ample space on the ground floor for a workroom and French-style kitchen and dining-room combined; on the first floor there were two drawing-rooms with communicating doors which, when fully opened, provided an excellent concert room. With Elodie to take care of the domestic side of things, Dolmetsch's zeal was unabated; he settled down at once and sent out the customary announcements that a series of autumn concerts would be held at his new address.

One of the first letters Dolmetsch received at Keppel Street was from Antoinette Sterling, a famous singer of the day. She writes:

(undated)   125, Ashley Gardens,
[October 1895]   S.W.
It will be a great pleasure to have you and hear you at my concert and it will be a great advertisement for you, which also pleases me very much.

She signs herself, 'sincerely your sister in music and in truth'.
A jubilant Dolmetsch writes to Horne:

29th October 1895   6 Keppel Street
                                                          W.C.

We have been suddenly and unexpectedly engaged to play at Mdm. Sterling's
Concert at Queen's Hall on Friday! It's extraordinary! Perhaps Patti or Sims
Reeves will want us next. However, she pays, and it is an opportunity of trying
our wares upon 'the Masses' and I am glad of the experiment.

The concert was billed as a 'Complimentary Farewell to Madame
Sterling', and Dolmetsch, Hélène and Elodie contributed an abundance
of Scarlatti, Rameau, Jenkins, Marais and Couperin, played on the old
instruments: it must have contrasted strangely to the audience, who also
heard, *Salve! Dimora casta e pura*, the ballad to Tennyson's poem
Crossing the Bar, Liszt's *Liebestraum* and the terzetto from *Elijah*, *Lift
Thine Eyes*, together with other succulent morsels from the typical
Victorian feast.

*   *   *

Frederick Niecks, Reid Professor of Music at Edinburgh University,
had given a number of his famous 'Historical Concerts' since taking the
Chair in 1891. He had approached Dolmetsch asking him to prepare a
programme for the forthcoming 1896 series, and although we have no
record of Dolmetsch's reply, it is evident he had been laying down the law
in characteristic fashion. However, the German professor was not to be
intimidated. On the 2nd October he writes:

                                          University Music Class Room,
                                                     Park Place,
                                                     Edinburgh

Dear Sir,
    Well, let it be Wednesday, the 29th January, and the programme one of Italian
music.
    I thought I had made it clear that my wish for as much music and as little
speaking as possible was not suggested by any distrust in the interest and value of
your remarks. It was dictated by the object of our Historical *Concerts*, which is to
supplement the historical lectures by practical examples. To increase the number
of examples, and to concentrate the attention of the audience, I have myself given
up making *viva voce* remarks. I did not impose this self-denying ordination on you,
did not ask you to abstain from speaking altogether; but only pointed out that
these performances are concerts, not lectures with musical illustrations, and that
speaking therefore (ought) to be reduced to a minimum.
    Don't you think it was a little rough on a serious student of musical history,

especially on one who has paid particular attention to the history of instrumental music to write: 'I have something to say, and I assure you it is *not* anything like what has been said in the lectures.' You seem to confound me with the generality of musicians who derive their knowledge of musical history from text-books or Grove's Dictionary.

However, don't misunderstand my foregoing remarks. They are purely explanatory. I am not offended (thanks to a very thick skin). But be careful when you write to other historians, their skins might be thinner.

Looking forward to your programme and the songs,

I am,

Yours very truly,

Fr. Niecks

Dolmetsch's reaction to Niecks' request is a perfect example of his irresponsible condemnation of anyone who crossed his musical path. Ironically, it came at a time when he was beginning to be better known and, although he was not making a great deal of money, leading concert promoters and society hostesses were asking for him. This was not enough: unless people agreed with him wholeheartedly, he would dismiss them out of hand. Undoubtedly it was from this particular human weakness that he created the stumbling block which was to hamper him for most of his life.

However, Dolmetsch was accustomed to academic reprimand and the warning would probably have gone unheeded. In any case, he was arranging his first series of concerts at Keppel Street and when in the throes of optimism he was indefatigable.

The first concert took place on 15 November 1895 and he had produced a variety of unfamiliar music to celebrate the occasion. There were four pieces for the lute from the *Straloch MS.*, a Fantazie by Coperario, an Allman for virginals by Pierson, a set of Divisions by Daniel Norcombe and three unpublished sonatas by Scarlatti. The latter pieces were executed with great skill by Elodie, who also played the Prelude and Fugue No. III in C sharp minor by Bach, on the clavichord further items included for the first time in a Dolmetsch programme.

A pair of newcomers, Horne's sister, Beatrice, played the viol at this concert and Lucy Broadwood sang to Dolmetsch's lute accompaniment. The usual crowd of artists and writers were much in evidence: John Sargent, the painter, enjoyed the evening so much that he wrote immediately asking for tickets for the next one, to which he would be bringing 'a French composer, M. Gabriel Fauré'.

In December, Dolmetsch again joined William Poel and his Elizabethan Stage Society in a performance of *The Comedy of Errors* at Gray's Inn Hall: the play had first been presented there in 1594 and the present revival was designed to recall that first performance before the Treasurer and Masters of the Bench of the Honourable Society of Gray's Inn and their guests at a banquet in their Hall: On the tercentenary of this occasion, 'The Benchers and their guests sat in their usual places at the long tables, and the actors appeared through the Tudor doors at the lower end of the hall and played on the same level as their audience.'[2]

The play was given without an interval, and whilst the company were having supper the Dolmetsch ensemble entertained them to music of the period. This was described by Shaw as a 'delectable entertainment which defies all description by the pen' and in the same article he awarded the Elizabethan Stage Society the season's palm for 'a delightful, as distinguished from a commercially promising, first night. . .'[3] Shaw adds that he has never in the past underrated the importance of the amateur but is now beginning to cling to him as the saviour of theatrical art.

Dolmetsch had by now become an interesting and entertaining lecturer: his English, spoken at lightning speed, was not always easy to follow but he knew his subject: such was his genius for communication that he had not the slightest difficulty in keeping his audience's attention. At the Royal Institution on 12 December, Dolmetsch's lecture inspired the *Musical Times* critic (1 January 1896) to devote a long article to the occasion. The writer goes into great detail as to how Dolmetsch describes the instruments and their capabilities, remarking on the particular interest shown in 'a fine-toned virginal, dated Venice 1550, upon which was played some of the music contained in the *Fitzwilliam Virginal Book*'.

* * *

'We reverence his name, and refuse tacitly to have anything to do with him. He is our greatest musician, we say, and therefore, well, we will occasionally consent to endure the hearing of one of his little songs. . . . Very kind of us, is it not?' We, the British, then discover that Purcell has been dead for 200 years and 'the merit of this proceeding strikes us forcibly. . . . Forthwith, for two or three days we prostrate ourselves before his shrine.' The music critic of the *World* has much to say on the feeble attempts of the British to pay homage to otherwise neglected musicians who are brought out occasionally and deified to celebrate an anniversary. The writer suggests that the shade of the dead master must have been smiling ironically at the 'Purcell Week' which caused so many people to 'read up' all about the composer or tell their friends that they had for years been paying him homage, and then inspired them to drown themselves in his 'long-neglected and well nigh forgotten music'. The shade might have ceased to smile though if it had heard 'the stolid echoes of *The*

Golden Sonata as performed on two modern grand pianofortes, with full orchestra! . . . But we must advance, mustn't we? It does not do to stand still and become obsolete.'

He suggests that we must dress up poor Purcell, as no doubt future generations will dress up Wagner, to 'disguise the leanness of his genius'. The *Golden Sonata*, performed on two violins, a 'cello and a spinet, may have been adequate in an age when there were no railways, but would not be fit for the present generation of music-lovers. 'We want more "body" and the Philharmonic Society kindly gives it to us at the expense of the spirit.'[4]

As we know, Dolmetsch had been paying Purcell homage for many years: his own contribution to the bicentenary was held at the Portman Rooms on 20 December. *The Times* critic, presumably Fuller-Maitland, writes (21 December):

> The concert of Purcell's music given last night . . . was a worthy sequel to the recent Festival in the composer's honour, and not the least artistic part of it. The most important feature of the programme was the series of specimens from the concerted works for strings, enabling an instructive comparison to be made between the master's work before and after he came under Italian influence.

The writer singles out the Fantasia upon one note for five viols, dating from a period shortly before 1682 as being a composition of wonderful ingenuity and *The Golden Sonata*, 'played, of course, on the instruments for which Purcell wrote it, and therefore [was] most effective'. Of the fifth harpsichord suite, 'The Saraband . . . was taken at a pace that seems unduly rapid even taking into consideration the evidence of the time-signatures as explained in the preface of the "Choice Lessons" '.

This criticism of Elodie's tempo was no dispassionate judgement: now redundant in his capacity of harpsichordist at the concerts, Fuller-Maitland was, in Dolmetsch's opinion, clearly jealous of Elodie's dexterity. Objectivity was never one of Dolmetsch's virtues and he was notorious for blaming others when things went wrong, but it would seem that in this particular instance his remarks were justified. Fuller-Maitland's own performances were never written about with enthusiasm, except by Barclay Squire, his collaborator and brother-in-law. The hostility caused Dolmetsch some concern and in a letter to Horne he brings up the matter:

December 29th 1895   6, Keppel Street,
                                                       W.C.

I have been waiting and waiting, in hope that something unexpected would turn up to get me out of trouble, but nothing comes, and it is too late now! Alas! I shall not go to Florence[5] I am nearly crying for it. But I have got *no money*. I have had awfully bad luck. First, Mdm. Sterling has gone to America without paying me. 2nd the extraordinarily stupid mistake in the date which made me miss my Wimbledon lecture (£12. 12s.); 3rd the Gray's Inn people don't pay me; 4th the Tollemache harpsichord I have not been able to finish yet. I am working day and night to it: that means £35—5th the Birmingham Series of concerts has fallen through.

Yet I am tired, and unwell, I *must* have some change and rest. I shall go to Brussels in 2 or 3 days for a week. Ah! I was forgetting: my Purcell Concert results in a loss of £2 or £3!

It was fine though: and we had great success! Some harpsichord pieces were enthusiastically received, and encored.

I am afraid war with Maitland *and* Barclay Squire is getting unavoidable. M. is sho[c]kingly jealous of Melody.[6] He does *not even mention her name* in his notices, although he mentions everybody else. B.S. the other day gave the most absurd praise to Maitland's performance of 3 Scarlattis at Bispham's[7] Concert which were not well played. He says that Melody's technique is deficient although she accompanies well. The fact is she played her solos, the toccata, etc., extremely well, but was not so successful in her accompaniments. Then both say she played the Saraband of the Suite much too fast . . . she played it, if anything, *slower* than I . . . have played it before. I wrote to *The Times* explaining, explaining that the Sarabande *was the quickest* of all dances, at the time of Purcell. My letter was good, correct, and with two or three good kicks to Maitland. . . . The Editor sent it back after a week, during which he evidently sent it to Maitland, saying he does not see sufficient cause for its insertion. What will happen next? I don't know. I have a headache and am going to bed. How lucky you are. I am getting envious.

A Happy New Year to you *all*.

Dolmetsch appears to have recovered sufficiently to travel north with his family at the end of January to give two concerts in Edinburgh. One was held in the Masonic Hall for the Edinburgh Bach Society and the other, the cause of the contretemps between Niecks and Dolmetsch, at the University. Both were well received and for the 'Historical' concert Dolmetsch produced two 'new' pieces of early music: *Pur Dicesti*, a song by Lotti with harpsichord accompaniment, and a suite for viola da gamba by Marin Marais.[8]

In February, Dolmetsch gave a lecture recital at Wimbledon in a series known as 'Wimbledon Nine o'clocks' and three concerts at Keppel Street. At the first of these he presented music by Bach, Handel and Telemann which had not been performed previously before the public of that time; at the second, he excelled himself by giving a programme in which eight pieces were new to his repertoire. The most original, *The Bible Sonata* (*David and Goliath*) by Kuhnau, was for harpsichord. Fuller-Maitland writes in *The Times* (19 February 1896):

It must be many years since one of Kuhnau's *Bible Sonatas* was last heard in public, if, indeed, any of them has ever been heard before. Mr. Dolmetsch brought forward the first of the set of six at his concert in. . . . The set is entitled 'Musical Representation of some Bible Stories' and if not the earliest examples of programme music, the sonatas are almost undeniably the finest specimens composed before the beginning of the 18th century or even later . . . the music itself is full of a quaint dignity and a character all its own.[9] . . . [other works on the programme] were all played by Mrs. Elodie Dolmetsch and Mr. and Miss Dolmetsch.

At the third concert at Keppel Street, Dolmetsch brought forth more 'new' music: three pieces for lute from the Straloch MS, *Spagnioletta for the Virginals* from the *Fitzwilliam Virginal Book, Divisions on a Ground* by Norcombe, music by Purcell, Marais and Bach, and the second in the set of 'Bible Sonatas' by Kuhnau. *The Times* next day was unstinting in its praise, even of Elodie.

Shaw had missed the last concert at Keppel Street and wrote explaining the reasons for his absence. He goes on to say that he has had 'a passage of arms' with Finck [an eminent Austrian critic] over Dolmetsch's work. He [Finck] ridiculed Shaw's praise of the old instruments and 'demanded loftily whether I had ever heard a Steinway Grand! I spilt as much of his blood as possible by way of advertising the clavichord in very red letters.'[10] Unfortunately no letters from Dolmetsch to Shaw are extant: it would have been interesting to have read his response to such a boost.

Throughout April, Dolmetsch was either giving concerts or lecturing in London and the provinces, but May, free of engagements, he devoted to instrument-making, which was now becoming of ever-increasing importance. At the end of the month he announced a further series of concerts at Keppel Street which would be 'as interesting as any yet arranged by Mr. Dolmetsch. Special attention is called to the Cantata by Bach . . . it is delightfully light and comic in character, and will doubtless prove very attractive.' *The Times* critic (15 June 1896) was, for once, in accord with Mr. Dolmetsch for he thought the most interesting feature was 'the funny little libretto in praise of coffee at a time when it was a new-fangled beverage in Germany', and draws comparison between the merits of it and its companion work, the *Peasants' Cantata.*

The rest of the concert is merely reported: Fuller-Maitland was subtly continuing the war by ignoring Elodie's technique and interpretation. However, Dolmetsch had recently gained an ally in John Runciman on the *Saturday Review*. He had criticised the performance of the *Coffee Cantata*, but to Dolmetsch this was but a pin-prick compared to the stab-wound inflicted upon Fuller-Maitland's pride: he took a childish delight in these little affrays. Runciman claims that the last two concerts had differed widely in artistic value as well as in the degree of artistic skill brought to the playing of it. He had thought the Handel sonata for flute, violin, 'cello and harpsichord 'superb' but that the *Coffee Cantata* only 'came off fairly well' and that the fineness of interpretation was frequently broken by patches where uncertainty, lack of grip and unfairly balanced playing took away from the beauty of the music. He does concede that when such works are attempted under present conditions this is bound to be the result. He bemoans the fact that out of the five million people in London, not more than ten in each million have 'intelligence and love enough of beauty to support Mr. Dolmetsch in reproducing some of the loveliest music that ever was or will be written'. Runciman admits that there is an advance on the time when there were only one in each million and for that advance, next to Mr. Dolmetsch, the credit goes perhaps equally to the critic of *The Times* and the late critic of the *World*. Runciman is aware that Mr. Fuller-Maitland's friends are fond of pointing out his mistakes[11] and by way of 'keeping the war in the enemy's country' he occasionally points out one of the real errors into which Maitland, 'like every critic', has fallen. But Mr. Maitland's articles in *The Times* and helping Mr. Dolmetsch at the harpsichord, 'an amusement of which he appears to have grown a little shy', have done much to spread an appreciation of the old music. Nevertheless, 'there are still too few who have not bowed the knee to Baal to permit Mr. Dolmetsch to go to the expense of rehearsing difficult and unfamiliar works as they should be rehearsed if irreproachable performances are to be given'.

*   *   *

It is not known exactly when Dolmetsch started work on the harpsichord that he intended to display at the Arts and Crafts Exhibition Society's Show at the New Gallery in October, but the fact that it was started at all was due to William Morris, who had suggested that he should complete it for the exhibition. By the middle of July the work was well enough in advance for the decorative paintings to be made on the inside of the lid and for this Dolmetsch engaged the artist Helen Coombe. Following her own designs she worked in tempera to produce some exquisite decoration on what was already a truly beautiful example of Dolmetsch's craftmanship. She was then engaged to Roger Fry and in a letter to him from Ham House, presumably at the rehearsal on 17 July, she writes:

> Working . . . family life at the D's is too lovely for anything. They are going to play at Ham House on Sunday.[12] Melodie and Hélène do nothing but recount the strawberries they will eat and the tea and ices—while D puts in words of wisdom rather in the manner of the Vicar of Wakefield to his daughters. In fact that is

rather his general attitude all day; he has to be coaxed to give them money for frivolities and then he turns his purse inside out to show that he has none.

A few days later she writes again:

> 6 Keppel Street,
> W.C.
>
> I stayed at Dolmetsch's. He tries to keep me prisoner until the harpsichord is finished, in the manner of the Italian Popes (there was a French Pope, you know) and I am only let out by the hour: however, I ran away yesterday while they gave the concert at Ham House. . . . Besides that, although it is charming to sit on the leads of Keppel Street while Dolmetsch serenades us—I weary a little of the many intricacies of Melodie's *éstomac*—it's really as complicated and perverse as my own temperament. D comes tonight and I'm not finished.

The harpsichord decoration was never finished. Helen Coombe's work was completed, Selwyn Image did the lettering and Herbert Horne executed the design above the keyboard, but owing to the shortage of time before the opening date of the Arts and Crafts Exhibition, the outside was coated in green lacquer ready for further painting at some future date. It was nicknamed 'The Green Harpsichord'[13] and has remained unadorned until the present day.

Dolmetsch was now so busy that he firmly refused to take on new pupils. But in June 1896 he received a letter from a Miss Mabel Johnston and promptly broke his own rule. There was no particular reason why he should have suggested that the young girl should come for an interview, but he did and she came. It was a decision he never regretted.

Mabel Johnston was from nearby Denmark Hill but she had never actually encountered Dolmetsch when they were both living in the same district. Her letter had been addressed to 'Dowland' and was forwarded to Keppel Street. After Dolmetsch's death, when she had been married to him for 37 years, she recalled that first meeting:

> I was led upstairs to a large and pleasant room, actually composed of two, divided by folding doors. In the larger portion, rows of Artworkers' Guild chairs had been set out, looking artistically suited to their surroundings, the inner room being reserved as a sanctum for the artists and their instruments. Here we found Arnold himself tuning a fine Kirkman harpsichord. . . . Though unable to attend [a concert which had been arranged] at such short notice, I straight away booked three seats for the second concert in the series. The extra two were for a musical sister and the indispensable chaperone![14]

It was Lucy Carr Shaw, G. B. S's sister, who assumed this role. When Mabel asked her friend to accompany them to the concerts, Lucy had exclaimed, 'What! You mean Dolmetsch? Of *course* I will! George is crazy about him!' Mabel's impression of the room on the evening of the concert remained undimmed:

> The concert room, tinted a diaphanous green, was entirely illuminated by wax candles, set around the walls in handbeaten brass sconces, and interspersed with rare lutes and viols, suspended from hooks. The inner half, with its varied assortment of instruments and players, formed a picturesque *mise en scène* that focused the rapt attention of the audience. . . . One's attention was drawn away from the neutral clothing to his [Dolmetsch's] brilliantly expressive eyes, which Lucy Shaw characterised as 'Lamps of genius'.[15]

The atmosphere of these concerts was pleasantly informal and in the interlude, coffee and *petits fours* were handed round. Mabel Johnston was struck by the 'unusual nature of the audience'. Prominent on this occasion was the famous Violet Gordon Woodhouse, 'then a sparkling bride', Margaret Mackail, 'fragile and fair like the etherealized pictorial creations of her father, Sir Edward Burne-Jones, the beautiful Miss Kingsley with William Rothenstein whom she later married'.

There were many more personalities whom Mabel recognised when coming to know them later: Laurence Binyon, the poet and scholar, Mrs. Patrick Campbell, 'who inevitably drew all eyes to herself as she glided into her place', George Moore, 'exchanging brisk badinage with Lucy, they having been neighbours over in Ireland'. Side by side with these were many members of the Artworkers' Guild, Walter Crane and Cobden Sanderson, 'who in his latter years threw his printing press into the sea so that it should never fall into the hands of some unworthy successor'.[16]

Herbert Horne was, of course, a familiar figure, likewise Arthur Symons and subsequently Robert Steele, the consummate scholar and authority on mediaeval French literature and early English music printing. It seems that he and Dolmetsch developed an unshakable friendship wherein they could say anything they pleased to each other with impunity: quite a feat where Dolmetsch was concerned.

Mabel Johnston, 13th child in a family of 14, was the daughter of a well-to-do Scottish insurance broker who had settled south of the border. They lived in a large house in Denmark Hill, set in its own grounds with lawns, fountains and all the accompanying luxuries synonymous with late Victorian middle-class prosperity. Perhaps because their father was a Scot, largely responsible for his own further education, he saw to it that his children received the best possible academic and cultural training, which naturally included the study of foreign languages. Mabel's fluency both in French and Italian gave her a distinct advantage with Dolmetsch, but proved an impediment to the Johnston family. When Mabel was taken on, not only as a pupil for the violin but as an apprentice for musical instrument-making, which necessitated living in the same house as Dolmetsch, there was howl of protest all round. Culture was one thing but music quite another. The 'rogue and vagabond' image still persisted in those days, and Dolmetsch, separated as he was from his wife and living with his sister-in-law, had little to commend him to the worthy Johnstons. Mabel's mother had died when she was still an infant and her father only recently, but despite the pleading of her numerous relatives she insisted on following her own inclinations. She adored Dolmetsch from the minute she set eyes on him: it could not have been long before she fell in love with him—a seemingly hopeless position. But Mabel had youth on her side and was also patient in the extreme: she possessed an unflagging belief (which she held to the end of her days) in the hand of fate to move mountains; this quality gave her a quiet strength to carry on where another would have abandoned hope.

However, romance did not enter into the early part of Mabel's apprenticeship: the main task on hand was that of getting the harpsichord finished for the Arts and Crafts Exhibition[17] in October. Mabel's nimble fingers were soon given work to do even on this important instrument: she was responsible for the shaping on the fronts of the keys. On 24 September 1896, 'The Green Harpsichord'[18] was delivered to the New Gallery,[19] where the Exhibition was being held. In a letter from Helen Coombe to Roger Fry on 3 October we learn of the difficulties which beset them at the last moment:

> I will only tell you of the harpsichord, 'our child' as Frances Dodge[20] now calls it. I rushed off to the Arts and Crafts and found Dolmetsch performing on it. He jumped up and exclaimed, 'Here comes the artist who painted it'. Tableau and amusing throng. Met at Paddington by announcement of Morris's death. . . . D. came in the afternoon and quite believed the board had cracked on its own: but he has carried the big one off as I have to finish it in the instrument as they would crack with their own weight in this heat. We carried it together to Keppel Street. The small one has gone still further. Gave a loud report while D was still here: they can be mended all right.[21]

William Morris, who died on 3 October, never lived to see the opening of the exhibition. But Dolmetsch was possibly one of the last people to see him alive. Morris' condition had worsened and, knowing he had not long to live, he called for Dolmetsch so that he might hear the virginals for the last time. Sadly Dolmetsch took his little Italian instrument in a hansom cab to Kelmscott House. There, in the bedroom already inhabited by death, he sat down and softly played the tune that Morris loved so well: *The Earle of Salisbury's Pavin*. It was a moving experience for them both: Morris, who had found orchestral concerts and piano recitals 'too noisy' and through his friend had come to love the sound of the viols and the virginals: and for Dolmetsch it was one of the few direct tributes that he ever received.

On 29 October 1896 the exhibition opened with a concert and the harpsichord was given pride of place: it took the form of a 'Discourse on the Harpsichord' given by Dolmetsch with Elodie as the performer. Dolmetsch joined her in a muzette for harpsichord and viola d'amore by Couperin, which had not been previously performed in public in modern times. Hélène, Dolmetsch and Elodie rounded off the programme by the introduction of yet another 'new' work, the *Sixième Concert* by Rameau.

*   *   *

On 1 November 1896 the *Musical Times* announced that the Purcell Society, which was founded in 1876, had only published two works in its ten years of existence, and since 1882 had shown no signs of life at all. The difficulty in finding editors had been solved by the employment of W. H. Cummings, who had now agreed to undertake the sole labour of preparing Purcell's works for publication: 'no light undertaking when it is remembered that at least 27 odes and 45 operas, besides an immense amount of church music, remain to be published. The success of the undertaking now rests solely with the public, and there ought to be no difficulty in obtaining a sufficient number of subscribers who are willing to pay a guinea a year for the honour of England's reputation as a musical country.' Here were words that Dolmetsch understood only too well. He disliked Cummings, but he would probably have approved of the project even if he had criticised the final editing,[22] as any effort in presenting early music to the public would have been welcome.

*   *   *

In November, Dolmetsch travelled to the north of England with Elodie, Hélène and three singers: the largest group he had taken any distance as yet. They took part in a series of four concerts in and around Liverpool and Birkenhead in what were termed 'Winter Evening Entertainments'. The programme, 'Old World Night', was repeated at all four concerts and the performers appeared in Elizabethan costume.

Audiences behaved much as they liked in those days: but not when Dolmetsch was in charge. A printed notice in two places on the programme informed the auditors that if they were not in their places so that the performance could begin at 8 o'clock promptly, they would have to wait until after the first item had finished, as the doors would be closed until the end of that piece. Dolmetsch also made provision for the early leavers: 'Ladies and gentlemen wishing to leave the hall before the conclusion of the concert will kindly do so prior to the commencement of the last item on the programme.'

These restrictions do not seem to have curtailed the audience's enjoyment. The *Liverpool Daily Post* (20 November 1896) gives a vivid account of the 'old world' atmosphere that pervaded the Philharmonic Hall and devotes half a column to details of the instruments and music. The musicians, dressed in Elizabethan costume, 'indeed had clothed themselves in the right frame of mind. The ladies were as pleasant and *debonnaire* as e'er a mediaeval of them all' and so manly and modestly swaggering were the gentlemen that the audience's approval leads the writer to believe that they would have liked to 'forswear all modern cuts and addict themselves to slashes, puffs and trunks'. Dolmetsch, during one of his 'charming little explanations', asked 'Does anyone here dare to say that his evening suit is more beautiful than the one I wear?'

Dolmetsch took pains to prove that the modern piano offers very little comparison to the harpsichord 'beautifully' played by Mrs. Dolmetsch and which was 'a revelation to those who thought it was merely a pleasant old toy, and the player showed what delight could now be had from a now obsolete source'. The writer closes convinced that 'Mr. Dolmetsch is deserving the thanks of all musicians and students for his series of such entertainments.'

On the way south the players stayed for a night in Birmingham, where Dolmetsch had to deliver a lecture. In December he was northbound again: this time to Scotland, where he was again taking part in two of Niecks' Historical Concerts. A third engagement brought him before the Philosophical Institution, where he lectured on the music of Shakespeare. The *Evening Dispatch* (9 December 1896) devoted considerable space to the content of the lecture, in which Dolmetsch gave a detailed description of the dances of Shakespeare's time. The musical examples he gave had been taken from an old music book in the Advocate's Library in Edinburgh, which he believed to be the earliest record of Scottish music and which had never been properly studied by anyone: 'The entertainment was essentially musical . . . listened to with the closest interest by a crowded audience who expressed their hearty appreciation in warm applause.'

*　　*　　*

When living in an age of great musical development and tolerance, it is difficult to appreciate the full importance of Dolmetsch's efforts to present, authentically, the music of the past. The piano had been his arch-enemy since childhood, and in late-Victorian England his foe reigned supreme: and as with any successful commercial commodity, perpetual improvements in design or tone were being thrust upon the market. Of the latest 'resonator' by Schreiber, John Runciman writes in the *Saturday Review* (7 November 1896):

> No house is now complete until it is furnished with a piano, and no piano is complete until it is heaped with a matter of 3 dozen books, a score of ugly orna-ments, 3 or 4 heavy flower-pots, and a number of other nick-nacks for which places cannot be found elsewhere. Further it should stand on a thick carpet and if a rug can be shoved in between the carpet and the piano so much the better. All this spells ruination for the piano: it chokes the tone at once. Schreiber's resonator is now introduced: it is fitted to any piano and works wonders to give the piano a fuller, richer tone.

In the *Monthly Musical Record* (1 December 1896) Runciman writes more about the resonator, quite favourably, but at the same time points out that whereas this is purely a commercial venture, Dolmetsch's harpsichord[23] is not: for although he makes a harpsichord for those who can pay for it, his instruments are no more 'on the market' than Whistler's pictures. Mr. Dolmetsch carries on his harpsichord-making more as an art than as a trade and Runciman doubts if there will be a large demand for such instruments for at least another century to come, 'if, indeed, the world has learnt by then that the old music should be played on the instruments for which it was written'. He bemoans that no one seems to have grasped the fact that to play the '48' on the piano gives the listener no more idea of Bach's intention than he has of Wagner's intention if he hears the overture to *The Flying Dutchman* played on a church organ. Mr. Dolmetsch 'is doing his best to teach us the great truth' and an early visit to Keppel Street is suggested. Dolmetsch also advocates 'the use of the harpsichord instead of the piano at performances of Bach's "Passions" and other choral works; and he has constructed an instrument we are about to describe specially for that purpose'. Runciman extols the merits of the 'Green Harpsichord', whose 'tone is singularly pure and sweet, and quite free from the unpleasant twang one associates with the harpsichord, and it is quite loud enough to fill a large hall'.

Runciman goes on to write about the contrivance[24] which is the new feature of Dolmetsch's harpsichord, enabling the player to control his dynamics at will:

> Until now no one has hit upon a method of getting graduations of tone otherwise than with Venetian shutters, as in an organ. But Mr. Dolmetsch has at last devised a piece of mechanism of which neither Ruckers nor any of the great harpsichord

makers need have felt ashamed. We cannot, without the aid of diagrams, describe it in detail. But anyone can understand that if the vibrating wire is caught merely by the tip of the quill the sound will not be so loud as when it is caught by the thicker portion nearer the middle; for in the latter case the string has to be pulled much more to one side before the quill can get free of it. This is the principle of Mr. Dolmetsch's invention. When you wish to play soft you simply play away, and only when you press a knee movement you move the quills a little to one side, so that more of the quill catches the wire in passing. The wire is thus plucked more violently, and gives out the desired louder sound. The movement may be held at any place, and thus any degree of sound between *pianissimo* and *fortissimo* can easily be obtained.

Runciman concludes by saying that there is no longer any excuse for playing the music of Bach and Handel, and indeed all their contemporaries, upon instruments which they never dreamed of and for which their music is not at all suited: above all, we may now hear Bach's splendid vocal music with something of the instrumental colour that Bach intended us to hear.

* * *

On December 16th Dolmetsch writes to Horne:

6, Keppel Street,
W.C.

We have just returned from Scotland, and I am quite astonished at our success. Large rooms, 2,000 and more packed full! And most pieces encored! Surely these people are more intelligent than London people. Everywhere, they speak of having us again, and many concerts are as good as settled—tonight I lecture at the Society of Arts[25] on Purcell and Bach and this is the last before Florence.
Don't fear that I shall change my mind, everything is arranged, we shall leave London, Mme. Melodie and myself on *Christmas Day* and follow all your directions about the journey.
I shall bring the Venetian Dance Book. I am *sure* this will be a *real success* in Florence, as there would be no difficulty in finding willing dancers, and they could easily understand the directions.
You may arrange everything, settle dates, etc., I know what you do will be right. Between January 1st and 15th seem to me the best time.

This is the first mention of any arrangements for the proposed trip to Florence. Dolmetsch was always keen to perform in Italy but was unable to afford such a trip on his own account. Horne, as usual, came to the rescue and used his influence to obtain a sponsor, but nowhere is the benefactor named. Although Dolmetsch was scrupulous in limiting his spending to the musical requirements of an undertaking, he was blissfully unconcerned as to the source of the funds so provided. All that occupied his thoughts at the moment was that at last he would be going to Italy— the land where culture pervaded everything and the very speech was music.

NOTES

1. Speaight, Robert, *William Poel and the Elizabethan Revival*, Heinemann, London, 1954, p. 43.

2. ibid., pp. 109–10.

3. The *Saturday Review*, 14 December 1895, reprinted in *Our Theatres in the Nineties*, 1932, Vol. II, pp. 269 seq.

4. *The World*, 27 November 1895, pp. 24/5.

5. Horne was trying to arrange an Italian tour for Dolmetsch.

6. Dolmetsch altered the spelling of Elodie to Melody or Melodie.

7. David Bispham, celebrated American Quaker singer, and friend of Dolmetsch.

8. The date of this work is given as 1700, but as Dolmetsch was variable with his dates, it is possible that it had been performed previously.

9. Novello and Ewer Ltd., 1 February 1896.

10. There is also a long and amusing exchange of letters in *The Musical Courier*, published New York, in which Shaw states the case for Dolmetsch's clavichord as opposed to the grand piano.

11. In a previous article, Runciman made an ironical statement about Bach having written the first prelude of the '48' as an accompaniment to a melody by Gounod. In answer to the reader to whom he refers in this passage, Runciman writes: 'My warmest thanks to the correspondent who wrote to say that Bach did not write the first prelude of *The well-tempered Clavichord* as an accompaniment to Gounod's well-known melody. Such correction is always acceptable.'

12. No record exists of such a concert but no doubt it took place and Lord Dysart's harpsichord would have been the instrument used.

13. Now in the Dolmetsch collection of musical instruments.

14. Dolmetsch, Mabel, *Personal Recollections of Arnold Dolmetsch*, Routledge & Kegan Paul, London, 1958, pp. 17/19.

15. ibid., pp. 17/19.

16. ibid., p. 19.

17. The immediate function of art as understood by the Arts and Crafts movement was stated by T. J. Cobden-Sanderson in a lecture at the Arts and Crafts Exhibition in 1896 as the power of doing things in the spirit of an artist and in reference to the whole of life. 'Art implies a certain lofty environment and that can be done by mankind within it.' Jackson, Holbrook, *The Eighteen Nineties*, Jonathan Cape and Capricorn Books, New York (introduction by Karl Beckson, 1966) p. 253.

18. It has three pedals, one produced 'harp' tone and a contrivance to shift pitch up or down a semitone. This instrument was finally sold and Dolmetsch, who had a strong affection for it, missed it greatly. After 30 years, through the kindness of a friend, Mr. Gerald Cooper, it was returned to him.

19. 'A Harpsichord designed and constructed by Arnold Dolmetsch, assisted by W. H. Nearn: the decorative paintings, in tempera, invented and executed by Helen Coombe.' This delivery note of 24 September 1896 shows that Dolmetsch was already employing help in his workshop. Nearn was his first full-time employee.

20. Young American pupil of Dolmetsch.
21. There are no further reports of any mishaps with the wood giving trouble, so presumably Dolmetsch made the necessary adjustments before the exhibition opened.
22. Cummings' editing is today regarded as unreliable.
23. The Green Harpsichord.
24. In an article in the *Saturday Review*, 13 February 1897, Runciman writes: 'Everyone should observe how ingeniously Mr. Dolmetsch has solved a problem that baffled the great 17th- and 18th-century harpsichord makers.'
25. Under the auspices of the Society of Arts, Dolmetsch gave on 16 December 1896 a musical illustrated lecture on the chamber music of Purcell, Handel and Bach. 'These composers represented the highest standard attained in this branch of the art from about the last quarter of the 17th to the first half of the 18th century. Modern music might be considered to commence with the immediate successors of Handel and Bach, who saw the harpsichord go out of fashion and the pianoforte replace it. The style of music did not change very materially from Purcell to Handel and Bach, but there was a great gulf between Bach and the very earliest efforts of Haydn, although the gulf was filled by a number of minor composers.' Dolmetsch then talks about the instruments used then and now and thought it folly to play this music upon modern instruments. He denied that the old instruments were inferior to the new: 'The tone of the harpsichord blended perfectly with the stringed instruments. The piano never could agree with anything else: its tone in concerted music invariably stood out from the other music, which frequently becomes inaudible. The whole effect intended by the old masters was lost when the balance of tone was thus destroyed.'
    Although some of Dolmetsch's deadliest enemies (certainly Cummings) were in the audience, when the lecture was over not a single question was asked and the meeting closed without discussion. Dolmetsch had been anticipating criticism: the perverseness of his nature probably resented the lack of it as much as he would have enjoyed rejecting their refutation.

CHAPTER X

War With 'The Times'

ON their first evening in Italy the Dolmetsches were serenaded at their open windows by a group of musicians who also offered them bouquets, which they accepted, delighted with the unexpected and charming compliment. But their gratification diminished when, a few days later, they were presented with the bill. However, the rest of the tour was without setback. The highly successful concert in Rome was attended by Queen Margherita and members of her court. After the performance, when the players were presented, the Queen, in appreciation of the ancient music she had so enjoyed, asked Dolmetsch what she could give him as a memento of the occasion: 'Nothing, thank you, Madame,' he replied. Dolmetsch was no courtier.

Horne delighted in piloting his friend around the churches and museums, from which Dolmetsch had difficulty in tearing himself away. The Library of Bologna was one of his most fruitful sources of discovery and many profitable hours were spent there. His greatest treasure was acquired unexpectedly whilst visiting the Marchese Torrigiani, who owned a reputed Amati violin in which Dolmetsch was interested. Whilst bantering with the nobleman as to the value of the instrument, Dolmetsch noticed a curious-looking manuscript lying on the floor. He picked it up and found it to be 'a collection of 15th- and 16th-century music written in lute tablature and that the first page was stamped with three balls, the device of the Medici'.[1] The owner appeared quite impervious as to its value and Dolmetsch, suppressing his excitement with difficulty, was able to pocket the manuscript for a ridiculously low price. A discovery in reverse happened when Dolmetsch was taken to see the Browning's clavichord[2] and found it to be a square piano.

Dolmetsch was always interested in food and needed no encouragement to accompany Horne, also something of a gourmet, to some of his favourite restaurants. At one of these, Dolmetsch noticed an item on the menu called 'Irish Stev': out of curiosity he ordered a portion and found it to be a savoury curry. The waiter, when reprimanded on the misleading title, simply asked if it had tasted good and when reassured on this point, shrugged his shoulders and retorted, 'Va bene!'

Back in London, Dolmetsch writes to Horne thanking him for purchasing the violin from Torrigiani and acknowledges that the price of 2,500 lire is a good one: he hopes that he will sell it again and they will make some profit. He writes also that he 'is in an awful press of work, having practically 7 performances in 6 days . . . for the dress rehearsal of *Twelfth Night* is as good as a performance. . . .' His letter continued in buoyant mood:

February 6th 1897   6, Keppel Street,
                                                       W.C.

> Since I left you in Bologna I have not been unwell a single minute: no rheumatism, no headache, no liver, no cold, nothing! I had not been so well for years.
>
> Long live Florence, and you to have made me come to it . . . Melodie is better too, but not so well as I. She did not have enough of it.
>
> Kindly tell your sister that the music has arrived safely,[3] that I shall use two of her songs at my *next* concert, and that I am much obliged to her to have sent it so soon. She need not hurry to do the rest.
>
> At my concert here yesterday night, I played one of these violin pieces she copied down for me last winter; one with the title page lost, 'Inventione Sesta', it proved a *magnificent* thing, and was as successful as possible; it is a regular discovery.[4]
>
> Melodie played the Scarlatti fugue very well, and the Fantasia Chromatic and Fugue upon a new and indeed quite unfinished clavichord of mine which has an extraordinarily powerful and beautiful tone. Maitland was there, and he is as good as possible—He even smiled sweetly at Melodie! But, then he wants me to lend him my virginals on Tuesday, and to tune his clavichord in time for a lecture of his.

This reference suggests a lull in hostilities with Fuller-Maitland, who, following the next concerts, wrote favourably in *The Times* (8 February 1897):

> A set of Divisions on a Ground for Viola da Gamba by Daniel Norcombe, a harpsichord suite of Lulli and two sonatas of Bach's for viola da gamba and violin respectively, were most important features; a very fine violin sonata of uncertain authorship, and dating from the near end of the 17th century . . . a new clavichord of remarkably fine tone was used for the Chromatic Fantasia of Bach.

However, John Runciman, writing about the same concert, offered some criticism:

> The great violin sonata in A, long romped through by Sarasate, was played by Mr. Dolmetsch with expression enough, but with technique so lame and stiff as to show that Mr. Dolmetsch needs practice. As for the composition for two virginals by

Giles Farnaby, it was no better than Daniel Norcombe's Divisions on a Ground; and both pieces served to remind us that music is not necessarily good, as Mr. Dolmetsch appears to think, because it is old. . . . We are all apt to take too exclusively a literary interest in old music, and after warning Mr. Dolmetsch not to let his audience do it, I must warn him not to do it himself, for, of course, from the literary point of view it matters little whether a composition is fine or not so long as it is redolent of the century from which it comes. But in spite of such little lapses his concerts are most wonderful entertainments, and no one who would be thought genuinely musical can afford not to hear the Caccini[5] songs sung there . . . on 19th February.

The anonymous *Inventione 'Sesta'* discovered by Dolmetsch in Florence and the suite by Lulli he thought were 'delightfully fresh', containing 'passages of real loveliness'.

Dolmetsch's pleading to Horne that he was busy was no exaggeration: in addition to his own concerts he took part in William Poel's *Twelfth Night* production at the Hall of the Middle Temple, where the play had been performed in 1601. A very distinguished audience were gathered together, among them the Prince of Wales, sitting as a Bencher of the Inn, Princess Louise and the Duke of Teck.

In the middle of that month, Dolmetsch found himself appearing in a very unlikely setting—one of the ever-popular ballad concerts at Queen's Hall. It ran the gamut of every possible sentiment set to music: there was the *Bridal Chorus* from *Lohengrin*, and *Golden Slumbers* sung by Mr. Eaton Faning's Select Choir; the singers—Plunket Greene, Ada Crossley and others equally well known—rendered a great variety of songs by Mendelssohn, F. H. Cowen and Maud Valérie White, with excerpts from *Abu Hassan* thrown in for good measure, accompanied on a Blüthner grand pianoforte. Dolmetsch occupied the entire second part of the programme and, as with the Antoinette Sterling 'Farewell Concert', it would have been interesting to have had some account of audience reaction to the virginals and the viols after the excesses of the first half of the performance. At any rate, Dolmetsch was satisfied. His next letter to Horne is jubilant:

                                                      6, Keppel Street,
17th February 1897   W.C.

I am in a desperate hurry: Yet must tell you a brief summary of good news—Had great success in the big Queen's Hall last Saturday. Still better at Darwin last night: we are practically engaged again for next year—Same thing at the London Institution last Thursday—room *crammed*; they want me again.

I have just had a cheque form Harris[6] for £25 on account! I understand he does not care to spend much on the decorations so I am doing it *plain*; he can do what he likes with it afterwards.—All seats sold for my concert on Friday; I have had to refuse people: so you see, things are looking better just now.

Dolmetsch is also anxious to see the violin. On 24 March, after he had received the instrument, he writes again:

> 6, Keppel Street,
> W.C.

The violin came this evening about 7.30. It is now nearly 12. I have been looking at it, playing upon it, cleaning it here and there, and I have arrived at the very same conclusion as before: that the violin is unquestionably genuine in all its parts; it is a Nicholas Amati, of the very best period, of *quite* full size (The Amatis are often too small), as fine as possible, and in the most excellent preservation. Hill's or anybody else's opinion need not be feared, the instrument is above suspicion— You may therefore tell Torrigiani that I keep it.

I don't know what I shall do with it, but that there will be a substantial profit out of it may be considered granted. The tone is excellent, one cannot judge exactly, as it is not really in playing order—Yet its G string is *better* than my Guarnerius, although the three higher strings are not quite so brilliant. But that will likely be different, when all is right.

I shall go to Hill's tomorrow morning and sound him. It is a delicate business, as the violin must not be plainly *offered* to him. But, I *know* him!

I was most anxious to receive the violin. I wrote to the agent last night, they had not received it this morning: they sent a special messenger to the railway in the afternoon, and *just* got it. It has been a very long time to come: I paid £2. 9s. 5d.— a lot, but we can afford that. The bow is worthless.

About King's Bench Walk[7] I have been turning the idea in my head over and over again and I have come to the conclusion that I could not possibly find room for all my instruments there so as to be able to use them in any way. Even now I don't know how I shall be able to arrange. There are difficulties in my way, financial and otherwise, which will not easily be got over, when are you coming back? I should awfully like to *talk* it over with you.

I keep in fairly good health, although not as good as before, and I am frightfully pressed for work . . . I have given up my lessons in Dulwich: it wasted so much time; this is a great relief. I have given some of my pupils to Boxall and some to Hélène . . . Both are very pleased.

Two weeks later, Dolmetsch is less hopeful:

> 6, Keppel Street,
> W.C.

11th April 1897

I have nothing definite to tell you [Horne] about the violin. I put new strings on it the next day, and a new bridge which happened to fit it, and I got it to sound extremely well. I really prefer it in every way to mine. I showed it to Hill, who did not care much for it. He said the Amatis were not in vogue, they were not powerful, etc. . . I asked him which he thought could sell best of the two, the Amati or mine. He liked mine best. But, when I asked him for his best offer for my violin, I had a most unpleasant surprise. He said £150! Yet, he has *new* copies of it for sale! He has any amount of reasons to give: 'If it were a Stradivarius, in that condition, it would be worth anything between £1,000 and £1,500. But the name of Peter Guarnerius is a bad one; there is a prejudice against it: it is mostly a matter of fashion, but they cannot help it: he would not dare to ask more than £250 for it, and then there would most probably be at least £25 to some professional and he could not make less than £25 himself etc. etc.

He is right to a certain extent, still, I know that violin is worth more, but what can I do? I might have to wait for years, before I find a buyer. I think I shall get £200 out of him, and I shall let it go for that price. I asked him to name a price for the Amati: he said £100. I daresay one could get more; but that does not really matter, since *I* prefer to keep it. The point is what can I get for the other. I think we may reckon on £200.

I am repairing the Amati and getting on very well with it, it will be very soon ready. I have no violin to play now, for Hill took my violin away. . . .

You see my harpsichord was a real success at the Queen's Hall; it was plenty loud enough. I was to play it, but owing to a regular conspiracy between Stanford and Maitland, I had to give my place to M. at the last minute. The thing is a perfect shame: I shall tell you all, it is very long and almost incredible, had I not proof![8]

Early in March, Shaw wrote to Dolmetsch asking permission to attend a certain rehearsal[9] in order to form and deliver an opinion on the harpsichord. No further mention is made of this proposed meeting but it is possibly to this broken appointment that Shaw refers in a letter written a month later on 10 April 1897:

29, Fitzroy Square,
W.

Not until this morning, when I saw the Bach article[10] in the *Saturday Review*, did I realise how unpardonably I have behaved to you. I am somewhat comforted to see that the harpsichord triumphed; but I am none the less deeply ashamed of myself.

Shaw explains that the real culprit is the law of copyright. He appears to have experienced difficulties over a play of his being performed in New York. Shaw's critics are fond of stressing both his meanness and high-handedness: neither trait would seem to be evident in his dealings with Dolmetsch.

In the article by Runciman, 'Another Bach Festival', the event was described as a 'sacred orgy' which opened with a 'selection from the *Matthew Passion*'. However, The Bach Choir, 'stodgy and suburban though it is; inartistic as all its schemes are', in Runciman's view still seemed preferable to the Philharmonic Society, which 'now exists mainly to advertise gentlemen whose claims to be distinguished musicians have never been satisfactorily proved'. Although support is asked for it on the grounds that it works for the public benefit, no accounts are published. The Bach Choir apparently exists primarily 'for its own amusement and edification' and gives concerts irrespective of whether the public attends. Very few committee members are musicians and consequently are not to be seen running up and down the platform steps 'in the manner made classic by certain directors of the Phil.'. It gives no medals to prima donnas, neither does it cheapen itself by inviting tenth-rate foreign conductors to come here and be lionized. Runciman adds that within its limitations it endeavours to give adequate renderings of some of the masterpieces of choral music. It is therefore distressing to find 'that its light is dull and flickering' and 'that its intentions are often carried out in a way calculated to rouse the ire of even so placid a critic as myself. . . .' He concludes: 'The one first-rate point was Mr. Dolmetsch's new harpsichord which was, by the way, adequately played by Mr. Fuller-Maitland. If I cannot say more than this, Mr. Maitland will bear in mind that owing to the misfortune of my being a trained professional musician, I am always disposed to be a little suspicious of amateurs. But in justice, it must be said that for an amateur Mr. Maitland distinguished himself.' Runciman's attack would certainly have angered Maitland but nevertheless he went on reviewing Dolmetsch's concerts with objectivity: in his later years Maitland was described as 'a rather stuffy old trout, but kind and helpful'.

Dolmetsch continued with his series of concerts at Keppel Street, consistently introducing newly discovered works. Each series was preceded by printed notices in which he discoursed, usually at length, upon the forthcoming delights. He assured his patrons that 'great care had been bestowed upon the programme' and that, 'the room being small, it is necessary, in order to secure seats, to apply at once'. This was not a publicity carrot: the demand for seats increased with every performance and it was impossible to buy a seat if left to the last day. Players and patrons alike were extraordinarily loyal to Dolmetsch, despite his violent temper when crossed. There must have been some incentive where his players were concerned: it was certainly not money that attracted them. Beatrice Horne and Philippa Strachey admittedly had small private incomes and W. A. (Will) Boxall, the ex-Dulwich schoolboy who owed everything to his old master, was now a professional performer in his own right. Agreed, they shared a common interest in the early music, but it was Dolmetsch's personality that permeated everything; he exercised such charm with every stroke of the whiplash that they found him irresistible. 'He was a very rude man', recollected Philippa Strachey, when in her nineties. 'I never really *liked* him, but he was fascinating. . . . He got what he wanted every time . . . we used to have terrible fights.' Nonetheless, Miss Strachey, like all the others, played for him and continued to take lessons from him throughout the nineties.

With the May concerts behind him, Dolmetsch made another appearance with the Elizabethan Stage Society, this time in a reading of *The Tempest* at the Steinway Hall:

> In front of dark drapery, forming a species of screen, sat about a dozen ladies and gentlemen in nineteenth century evening attire who, representing the characters in the play, rose at their respective cues and delivered the lines allotted to them, the majority with books in their hands. Below the platform sat Arnold Dolmetsch and three lady assistants, who played the incidental music upon instruments of Shakespeare's time. . . . It was delightful to hear again the ancient instruments again giving life to the music composed for them, the 'Shapes' who offered the banquet to the King and his companions dancing (in weird costume) to a pavane and a galliard composed by William Byrd.

The Daily Chronicle
June 5th 1897

*   *   *

In the *London Musical Courier* of 10 June there appeared an account of two invitation concerts given by the 'Société des Instruments Anciens' at the Salle Erard in London. Formed in 1895, this group had enjoyed considerable success by its performances in the French-speaking countries. Louis Diémer, pianist and professor at the Paris Conservatoire, performed on the harpsichord, Louis van Waefelghem, violinist and viola player who had been Dolmetsch's friend and contemporary at Brussels, played the viola d'amore, and Jules Delsart, 'cellist and professor at the Paris Conservatoire, the viola da gamba. The fourth member of their group was Laurent Grillet, conductor at the Nouveau Cirque in Paris: his unique contribution was that of the vielle or hurdy-gurdy, his father having been a virtuoso on that instrument.

Their two concerts of music, similar to that which Dolmetsch had been presenting for some time, attracted large, enthusiastic audiences and this rare occurrence inspired E. Van der Straeten to devote a whole column in the same journal (1 July 1897) to a history of the Society and its members and its instruments. He writes: 'As there is, and has been for some time, a movement on foot, both in London and elsewhere, for the revival of the instruments of a bygone time, it may interest our readers to obtain a little more information on the subject. . . . The viola d'amore and the viola da gamba are less unfamiliar [than the vielle] to London concert goers, as they have been repeatedly brought forward by Messrs G. and H. St. George, Mr. F. L. Schneider, the Dolmetsch family and the present writer.'

During the summer Keppel Street became due for demolition as it came into the area commissioned for building an extension to the British

Museum. Dolmetsch, fortunate as always in quickly finding new premises, moved to 7 Bayley Street, just off Bedford Square. The new house was more spacious than the previous one and had an excellent workshop built on to the back. There was a good basement kitchen with an adjacent front room which was used as a dining-room and it was here that the Bohemians of the day would congregate. Mabel Dolmetsch recalls one occasion when Will Rothenstein was dining with them: 'George Moore entered, and thenceforth the conversation degenerated into a monologue concerning Moore's gallant adventures when he used to live in the Latin Quarter of Paris. Meantime William Rothenstein, at the other end of the table, was mutely fiddling with a blue pencil, a candle end and a stub of sealing wax. When Moore had departed, Rothenstein produced a lifelike caricature made with these unusual implements, and bearing the explanatory footnote, "C'est moi! Mooooorr!"'[11]

House-moving never disrupted the flow of Dolmetsch's musical output. Throughout the summer he was playing at society soirées in Mayfair and Knightsbridge and in June he was invited to provide a concert to mark the opening of a 'Conversazione' held by University College, London.

The October Birmingham Triennial Musical Festival was an important event, with its principal performers drawn from the top-ranking singers of the day: Madame Albani, Ada Crossley, Ben Davies, Plunket Greene, David Bispham and many others, under the baton of Hans Richter. It was the performance of Purcell's *King Arthur* (as specially edited by J. A. Fuller-Maitland for the festival), that necessitated the employment of two harpsichords, and for this both Dolmetsch and Elodie were engaged. Presumably the arrangement had been made before relations had deteriorated between Fuller-Maitland and Dolmetsch. A major battle must have taken place during the festival and a brief glance at the press criticism of Maitland's score points clearly to the motive. Runciman, never a supporter of Maitland, devotes two-and-a-half columns to the subject in the *Saturday Review* (2 October 1897): 'With your permission Mr. Maitland', said Hans Richter at the semi-public band-rehearsal . . . on Wednesday afternoon 'we will play *forte* where you have marked *piano*, and *piano* where you have marked *forte*'.

Richter, a sincere, straight-spoken man would not tolerate such a hash being made of Purcell's score: later in the day he told the orchestra that the whole of Maitland's score would be revised before the next rehearsal and proper marks of expression would be inserted. Runciman, obviously in agreement with Richter's deposition, writes: 'A more incompetent piece of work it has never been my fate to set eyes upon . . . a mere travesty of Purcell, concocted by a gentleman wholly ignorant of the elementary rules of harmony and of the art of filling in accompaniments from a figured-bass.' [Runciman quotes almost a page of errors with accompanying justifications.] He goes further: he considers that if Richter had compared Maitland's edition with any trustworthy score, he would have been wiser to have taken *King Arthur* out of the programme altogether. He advises Boosey's to 'withdraw at once this deplorable exhibition of bad taste and entire lack of musicianship' on the assumption that a firm of Boosey's high reputation must inevitably lose something by having their name on the covers of so 'barbaric' an achievement. It will be a scandal if copies are allowed to get abroad, thus giving foreigners the idea that it is representative of English musicianship.

The real sting is in the tail of the article. He points out that Maitland is the critic of *The Times*, and for the honour of his profession he does not wish it to be too widely known that the critic of our great daily cannot work out a simple bit of harmony without coming to grief. He confesses that the critics have long known about Mr. Maitland but he fears to let the general public into the secret, and would prefer the edition to be withdrawn and the whole matter hushed up.

On 9 October John Runciman lashes out again in the *Saturday Review*; this time at the festival organisers. He gives an almost Shavian account of being given tickets in the gallery which entitled him to take his seat five minutes before the performances started. It seems that as his seat was already occupied he was 'given permission to stand throughout the performance, and that in the event of there being no standing room I had full permission to go home'. He fully understands that if this 'considerate treatment' had been extended to him alone, he would have regarded it as just award for the rudeness in which he had indulged in moments of wrath with artistic sinners. But this was not the case. Many of his professional brethren, 'the kindliest and politest of men, incapable of a harsh word to the vainest prima donna or the silliest tenor, were in precisely the same plight'. Runciman's reaction was to return his tickets and travel on the night train to London.

Of the *King Arthur* performance he criticises Richter's final cuts in the score and challenges him to do the work in a complete form before he can pardon him his offence. The two harpsichord parts 'were excellently played by Mr. Dolmetsch and Mrs. Elodie Dolmetsch'. It appears that 'a good many unintelligent musical people have complimented Mr. Maitland on these parts; but I may take this opportunity of saying that Mr. Maitland's parts were discarded for some reason and entirely new ones written by Mr. Dolmetsch'.

The correspondent of the *London Musical Courier* (14 October) plainly states that he will not enter into the controversy regarding the score but mentions the playing of the two harpsichords. 'Some folk laughed at the

antique tone of these instruments, but they cut their way through everything, and were distinctly audible even when the full chorus of 350 was
going. I was rather disgusted, though, to find they were of mere modern
make, and not the genuine old specimens; but that was because I possess
a very fine Tschudi and Broadwood harpsichord.'

Dolmetsch, writing to Horne on 2 November, mentions another visit
to Florence which seems to be 'more certain than ever'. The performance
of *The Tempest* at the Mansion House has been postponed until 5 November
because of the death of the Duchess of Teck and in turn Dolmetsch's
own concert date has been changed. 'But that will do no harm, rather some
good, as I have obtained invitations to Mansion House for all my subscribers, and that has been paragraphed in the press (not *The Times*!).
I have got 30 subscribers now. So that is not so bad.

7, Bayley Street,
W.C.

I sent an invitation to *The Times*. J-A-F-M sent it back himself, without comment.
So, now it is open war. But, I am not anxious.

The performance of *The Tempest*, before the Lord Mayor, was in the
Egyptian Hall and produced by William Poel, who had erected an Elizabethan stage for the occasion. The music had been arranged by Dolmetsch
from composers of the period, and the dresses worn by Ariel and the
'Shapes' taken from prints of a masque found in the British Museum:
when they brought in the banquet they danced a masque by Giles Farnaby
and went out to a coranto, whilst the Nymphs and Reapers danced *La
Volta* to the music of Thomas Morley.

For Shaw, writing in the *Saturday Review*, 'the performance went without a hitch. Mr. Dolmetsch looked after the music.' He suggests that if
Sir Henry Irving were to put on the same play at the Lyceum next season
he would do nought but multiply the expenditure and spoil the illusion.
He would substitute the 'screaming violin' for the 'harmonious viol', with
characteristic music scored for woodwind and percussion by Edward
German instead of Dolmetsch's pipe and tabor. He would produce an
expensive and absurd stage ship, 'and some windless, airless, changeless,
soundless, electric-lit wooden floored mockeries of the haunts of Ariel'.

On 10 November, Dolmetsch, 'awfully tired and disquieted with
overwork', writes to Horne, 'longing for Florence'.

7, Bayley Street,
W.C.

My concert went very well last night. Melodie quite distinguished herself, and a
sister of Bernard Shaw Lucy Carr Shaw sang delightfully. Sir Purcell Taylor[12]
came and began by asking me whether I was one of the ennemy [*sic*] and ended by

placing himself and all his scores at my disposal! He stopped until about 12.30—
But Symmons [*sic*][13] did not go before 1 o'cl. and yet, by the *first post* this morning,
I got a charming poem on Rameau.[14] He must have spent all night on it.

In the final series of Dolmetsch's concerts that year, the one on 19
November caused John Runciman to write almost two columns in its
praise in the *Saturday Review* (27 November 1897); he thought it 'one
of the most perfectly enjoyable chamber concerts given for a long time'.
A concerto of Handel in F major for organ and strings, he claims to be one
of this composer's 'most entrancingly lovely things, and exactly adapted
to Mr. Dolmetsch's little chamber organ and set of string players'. He
fears that most of his readers will associate a Handel concerto with the
Handel Festival and the 'huge wild beast' of an organ at the Crystal Palace.
He admits that certain Handel concertos gain by being played on a full-
sized instrument. But this little one 'is a dainty bit of almost miniature
workmanship and charmingly played as it was by Mrs. Elodie Dolmetsch,
the effect was exquisite. The literary flavour, intensified by the old-world
room and lit by candles in ancient brass sconces, carries one irresistibly
back into the 18th century, indeed for Runciman, 'a picture of Handel
playing just such music on just such an organ in the music room of
Thomas Britton, the musical coalman.'[15]

But the most stimulating item of the evening turned out to be a romance
for harpsichord by Claude Balbastre, 'less on its own account than because
of an extraordinary discovery made by Mr. Dolmetsch in connection
with it'. According to Runciman this discovery bears out all that he has
been saying about the old music during the last three years in his columns
of the *Saturday Review*. It seems that when an unfamiliar pianist has tried
to infuse 'a certain amount of feeling into a Mozart sonata', he has been
told by the daily press 'that such liberties with the tempo are not justified
in the works of any composer earlier than Beethoven (it is generally
Beethoven)'. Classical music must always be played in the classical
manner, that is to say 'the interpreter must not interpret, but must rush
through the piece with the unrelenting hardness and exactness of a
barrel-organ'. He suggests that they have always been instructed that the
classical composers always played their music in precisely this manner,
and that is how the phrase-playing in the 'classical tradition' arose. He
asks how can tradition have come through men who were 'non-conductors
of all the fine qualities that were fine in the old composer's playing?'

Runciman had always preferred to take the evidence of the music rather
than that of men who proved how little they understood the music and
who therefore may be assumed to have understood equally little of the
manner in which the music was played. He goes on to Dolmetsch's

discovery: 'A man called Don [sic] Bedos de Celles,[16] a Benedictine, wrote a treatise on Organ Building in 1766. . . .' Dom Bedos not only described the instrument in minute detail but told how music could be prepared to be played on 'that wholly diabolical instrument, the barrel-organ'. The piece he chose was that of Balbastre's *Romance*, then very popular. 'But', said Don [sic] Bedos de Celles, 'no true musician ever plays in exact time,[17] the music would sound absurd if he did.' So he got M. Balbastre to play the *Romance* over to him many times, which M. Balbastre, was possibly, very glad to do; he noted down the precise number of beats, or proportions of fractions of beats, each note got, and he mapped the thing out so clearly that it is practicable, with care, to play the piece as precisely as Monsieur Balbastre played it 150 years ago. And what do we find? That though the 'license' permitted to the player was not so wide as that granted to a modern Chopin-player, still there was a very considerable license indeed. Runciman concludes by saying that this diagram of Dom Bedos 'sweeps clean out of existence the "classical" mode of rendering the older music, and "traditions"' and 'the rest of those withered hoary, Academic bugaboos'. Runciman is celebrating as his enemy, the Academic, the pedant, is driven from his last stronghold. 'He will not love Dolmetsch the more; but what does that matter so long as the only truth flourishes?'

The two closing phrases in Runciman's bold article probably come nearer to the real essence of Dolmetsch's character than other eulogies occupying several pages in later years. The uncanny way in which Dolmetsch's genius for discovery and interpretation seemed to spring from his very breathing was a perpetual irritant to the majority of the musical Academics, who worked 'by the book' and could neither comprehend nor countenance how he arrived at his conclusions. The plain fact was that Dolmetsch had already spent more than half a lifetime studying the old music. With one good academic record at school and two at musical train-ing institutions, he was as well fitted to argue as the musical *cognoscenti* who had encompassed the whole spectrum of musical history in a general sense, and who probably knew as little about performing the old music as Dolmetsch did about the new: probably less. Throughout history, honest men in public life tend not to manage very well in their lifetime, but after death are invariably elevated to a kind of—secular sainthood. Unfortunately, Dolmetsch is still remembered for his steely tongue, which made him enemies unnecessarily. Even his supporters found it hard to reconcile his treatment of them with his passionate search for truth. Dolmetsch's congenital weakness was that he was a man to be 'understood' before any real relationship could be established; and even then one needed both tolerance and stamina if the friendship was to survive. Herbert

Horne was one of the few who fell into this category. He worked unceasingly to interest his friends and colleagues especially those with money and influence, in Dolmetsch's work. It was on Horne's advice that Dolmetsch invited Mr. Ludwig Mond (later Dr. and Chairman of ICI) to one of his concerts. The effect was far-reaching. A very excited Dolmetsch writes to Horne from The Grand Hotel, Birmingham:

> December 8th 1897
>
> It is the last concert that did it. Mrs. Mond *and* Mr. Ludwig Mond were so struck by the music and specially by the Bachs, that they offered to do anything for me in Italy. Everybody was in the highest enthusiasm especially Symons who remained with me until ab. 2 o'clock. Devising the means of raising some guarantee fund for taking my Harpsichord and Hélène to Italy. *He* volunteered to ask Mr. Ludwig Mond to be guarantor, and talked to him on Sunday. I went, on Mr. Mond's request to see him on Monday, and after talking the matter over, he simply wrote me a cheque for £40, to be returned to him upon the profits, *if any*, of the Rome concert, or concerts—nothing to do with Florence—I shall have letters of introduction to the queen, and everybody of importance in Rome—Mr. Mond *can dispose* of the Rome Bach Society—the day after my arrival in Florence, I shall go to Rome, for one day, where I shall meet the Monds, see everybody and settle all details. My harpsichord will leave for *Florence* by Grande Vitesse on Saturday—Hélène will come to Florence a day or two before the concert and we will all go to Rome together with the instruments. Then, I think straight back to Manchester, Newcastle, Edinburgh, London, where concerts will follow every evening. . . .

At the close of this letter Dolmetsch refers to some decoration executed by Burne-Jones: he 'has made an *awful hash* of the clavichord. I would not have it for nothing! It made me quite sick to see it on Monday, and I cannot give vent to my feelings!'

The instrument had been made for Burne-Jones' daughter, Margaret Mackail. The top of the case, ornamented with a representation of St. Margaret, depicted with her customary emblem, a dragon, the figure standing out strikingly against the rich red of the body of the case. The inside of the clavichord was painted with delicate floral sprays with a female figure in light robes on the sounding-board. Beautiful though the work may be, Burne-Jones' ignorance of the construction of a musical instrument caused him to place the female form so that the bridge of the clavichord broke right through it and the lid, painted so that 'when folded, it mutilates the figures and when opened makes them stand on their heads'.[18]

*　　*　　*

Dolmetsch and his family derived much pleasure and very little financial reward from the Italian tour, so that it is unlikely that Ludwig

Mond ever again saw the colour of his money. The only account in existence is one in the *Musical News* of 26 March 1898:

> The excellent peformance of the well selected and interesting programmes pleased the audience very much, but it was a pity that, Mr. Dolmetsch not having advertised his concerts beforehand, many who take deep interest in the history of music were unable to attend them.

Mabel Johnston had now become an accepted part of the Dolmetsch *ménage*. She was an efficient and willing assistant in the workshop and her placid temperament ideally suited to an unpredictable man like Dolmetsch: whatever her inner feelings were, his rages appeared to glance off her, leaving her patient and smiling like a female Job. But beneath this demureness was a very resolute nature. In her eyes, Dolmetsch could do no wrong: she determined to provide whatever he needed and for the rest of her days she never fell short of this aim.

She tells a delightful story of how she approached Dolmetsch about violin lessons (the instrument upon which she had originally been taught and upon which she had hoped to be instructed when she was first accepted as a pupil). Dolmetsch characteristically snapped his reply, 'Violin! I've plenty of them among my pupils! *Good* ones at that! If you want to do something *useful* then learn to play the viola da gamba!' And so, from Hélène, she learnt to play the viola da gamba. With the same blind obedience she later tried her hand with the violone and from thenceforth this instrument became her speciality.

The series of concerts at Bayley Street were given without a break and at this time continued to be well-patronised. Often the room was more than filled and the audience would overflow on to the landing and stairs. Occasionally a stray visitor from the world of music could be found among the artists and writers: one of these, Madame Marchesi, the famous singer and teacher, attended a concert. She is reputed to have applauded with such gusto that the slender 'Art Workers' Guild' chair, built no doubt to support a leaner aesthetic frame, collapsed beneath her.

Dolmetsch often worked far into the night repairing and making instruments, for he was now being asked to perform more and more in the provinces. In January he went to Tyneside for the first time and gave two very successful lectures before 'crowded and highly demonstrative audiences'. The critic in the *Musical Courier* (3 February 1898) wrote that it had been a long time since they had heard any musical lecture so full of historical interest and musical charm. Should Mr. Dolmetsch decide to come again to visit them, he could safely predict 'a crowded audience and a hearty welcome'.

John Runciman's writings in the *Saturday Review* are invaluable today for not only do they give a musician's opinion but his descriptions are so vivid that the events come alive against a background of prevailing taste in a remarkable way. He thought this last 'Lent' series, 'quite the most delightful he [Dolmetsch] has yet given'. Runciman bemoans the smallness of the audience. He admits that the wintry weather might be partly responsible but he asks: 'Is London, under the genial and inspiring patronage of the Academics, really getting behind the provinces in enthusiasm and musical culture?' He contrasts the interest which Dolmetsch's concerts arouse in the great manufacturing towns of the north, where he can count his audiences by the thousands and the newspapers report and criticise at length. In London nowadays his audiences are small and the daily newspapers pay no attention whatsoever to him. *The Times* used to be an 'honourable exception'. 'But in an unlucky hour', writes Runciman, 'I told the truth about Mr. Maitland's perversion of Purcell's *King Arthur*, and I am afraid Mr. Dolmetsch must also have let slip the fact that the part written for him by Mr. Maitland was so bad, so utterly unplayable— it contained notes that never were on any harpsichord—that Richter authorized Mr. Dolmetsch to rewrite it. Since then *The Times* has been silent about the Dolmetsch concerts: when Mr. Dolmetsch and his party appeared at the Ballad Concerts they were contemptuously called "some performers".'

However, it seem that Dolmetsch is not 'a halfpenny the worse' for he cheerfully proceeds with the building of his instruments, and his concerts draw a sufficient number of the elect to enable the work to go on. Runciman insists that we cannot do without Mr. Dolmetsch and a knowledge of the old music is as essential to a musician as a knowledge of the poetry before Shelley and Keats is to a literary man. When lacking this knowledge they are apt to talk, as do some of the critics and professors in the music schools, of music beginning with Bach or even Haydn. By reconstructing the old instruments and playing the old music as it was intended, Dolmetsch has shown us to be ignorant of musical history, 'and if only in the interests of truth, should be supported by those whose business it is to educate the young idea'. Runciman acidly points out that if Dolmetsch were in Germany he would long ago have been appointed a professor or lecturer in one of the big music-schools, but here in England, owing to the desire to preserve a simple faith in Burney, Macfarren, Hullah and 'all the old gang', he is offered nothing, 'though it is possible that one would quickly be offered if he would give an undertaking not to discredit the gods of English music'.

Runciman has some withering comment on the reverence that the academics hold for Bach: 'So anxious are they that the rising generation shall know how this music should sound that a clavichord made by Mr.

Dolmetsch for the Royal College of Music stands in a kind of museum there, unplayed, untuned, unremembered.'

The remainder of the article deals with the ever-recurring divergence of opinion as to whether Bach should be played on the piano or the harpsichord. He makes the valid point that wrong assumptions passed from teacher to pupil *ad infinitum* inevitably become inherited traditions of wrong thinking. He protests that it is in this way the great *cause* of music prospers in England. By never admitting we were wrong thus we prove how right we always were. He maintains that to understand the old music it is not sufficient to read it or to fancy how it sounded on an instrument one has never heard. The music of both Handel and Purcell and most of the old dances, he claims, when played on viols and spinet, 'sound as different from what one might expect as English music sounds from Chinese'. He compares this music played on the piano to a Chinese translation of English verse, which therefore explains its lack of meaning.

*   *   *

Although he never earned more than a five-pound note for his trouble, Dolmetsch always enjoyed participating in William Poel's stage productions. On 5 April 1898, he was again summoned to provide music for the Middleton and Rowley comedy *The Spanish Gypsy* at St. George's Hall. It had last been peformed in 1624 and Poel had made considerable effort to present his revival as near to the 17th-century production as possible: Swinburne wrote a prologue especially for the occasion which was read by Edmund Gosse. Since none of the original music had survived, Dolmetsch composed new music exactly in the style of the time of the play; this was then wedded to dances by William Byrd and airs by some Italian composers. It was at this production that, when accompanying the song *O that I were a bee* on the lute, Dolmetsch 'interpolated ribald rejoinders between the stanzas'[19] much to the amusement of the audience, though doubtless less popular with the singer.

*   *   *

On 29 June there appeared an unsigned article in *The Sketch*, copiously illustrated and spread over two pages, devoted entirely to 'The Music of Yesteryear; and what Mr. Dolmetsch has done to revive it'. It acknowledges that George Moore, in his novel *Evelyn Innes*, bases his character on Arnold Dolmetsch, who 'has done more, perhaps, to reconstruct the musical atmosphere of yesteryear than anybody else!' The writer discusses Shakespeare's idea of music as being the lute, viols and virginals; but that the present-day understanding, meant 'the clash of an overweighted orchestra, the strident blare of a military band, the level monotony of the ubiquitous suburban piano'. He points to the 'kindly moderns' who are inclined to pity their ancestors because they were ignorant of the musical instruments of today: he advises them to conserve their pity for a more genuine need as musical instruments are not one of the things that are made better in modern times. He considers that the old instruments far surpass their usurpers, both as objects of beauty and creators of melody. South Kensington Museum will demonstrate the superiority in beauty and Dolmetsch's music room in Bayley Street, the pre-eminence in melody.

At South Kensington there are innumerable specimens of these instruments, but 'the hand of time is heavy upon them, their glory of ornament is dim, and they are as mute as the voices which once mingled with their tones'.

At Bayley Street there is an equally fine collection of these old instruments: 'but there, they are as rich in colour and as firm in outline as when they left their maker's hands, and living fingers and voices waken again the strains of such melody as Shakespere [sic] meant by music. South Kensington looks upon virginals, harpsichord, clavichord, lute as articles of vertu or curiosity; Mr. Arnold Dolmetsch looks upon them as musical instruments which have been ignorantly deposed from their sovereignty over the emotions.'

The writer continues with a mention of Dolmetsch's 'Green' harpsichord, manufactured because there was 'no old harpsichord of sufficient power to be effective in a large concert hall.' This instrument had been used by Dolmetsch at the Royal Opera [Covent Garden] for the last two years and 'its effectiveness in that huge building will be fresh in the memory of all lovers of music'.[20]

In alarming contrast, a journalist in the *Musical News* (11 June 1898) bemoans that the Summer Festival at the Crystal Palace is advertising its mammoth programme: namely the Handel Festival, with choir of 3,000, orchestra of 500, and with Patti and Clara Butt included among the soloists. Since the programme is commemorating the 60th anniversary of Queen Victoria's reign, the writer considers it a pity that the directors could find no more British music than *God Save the Queen*, *Rule Britannia* and Sullivan's *Imperial March* from *The Golden Legend*, and a couple of Irish ballads. Otherwise, Handel, Mendelssohn, Wagner, Mozart, Berlioz and Gounod occupy the lion's share!

The journalist is outspoken on the non-support of native music and musicians by the Royal family and the aristocracy, 'which simply follows the fashions set by the Queen and her immediate circle'. He condemns the increasing number of foreign bands which come over every season and usurp the places at society functions which ought to be occupied by our own players. 'The daily papers' he writes, 'are simply teeming with advertisements of these combinations': no less than seven appeared in a recent issue of *The Times*. Our military bands, 'supported by the officers at great personal cost', are losing engagements daily in favour of foreigners. It seems that the only form of serious music receiving any support from the upper classes is the opera, and that is only during 'the season', chiefly for social and display purposes. It is the middle classes who support the best concerts: those where the programmes are well chosen and varied. It is a pitiable state of things which, in the writer's opinion, will not change until the upper classes cease to be dominated by fashion. 'Truly, if English music is worth nothing, let us put it aside at once, and confess ourselves a nation of shopkeepers, "sunk in the mire of commercialism" as we are continually being told. But if English music is really worth something, if its composers are worthy of a knighthood, surely it and they deserve some encouragement. Virtually a man is told though not in words, "You are a splendid bandsman and your comrades are the best in the world; but when we give receptions, balls, garden-parties, we would rather have Hungarians, their names are so much more picturesque!" Or, (to a composer) "You work very hard and are most useful in various ways. We will make you a knight, but don't let us hear any of your music".'

Despite the fact that Dolmetsch was himself a 'foreigner', he endorsed these views wholeheartedly. Admittedly, he was free to choose and present his own programmes, but they were seldom financially rewarding. He never doubted that he was on the right course and although he suffered from sporadic fits of depression his innate optimism survived remarkably well. And 1898 was no worse than any others, it was just that the problems were different.

NOTES

1. Dolmetsch, Mabel, *Personal Recollections of Arnold Dolmetsch*, Routledge & Kegan Paul, London, 1958, p. 27.
2. This instrument was said to have inspired the poet to write the lyric, *A Toccata of Galuppi's* containing the lines: 'While you sat and played Toccatas, stately at the clavichord'.
3. Caccini songs.
4. We now know the composer to have been Nicola Matteis. Arnold Dolmetsch later obtained the original edition of the *Inventioni* which is now in the Dolmetsch Library.
5. Caccini songs mentioned in Dolmetsch's letter to Horne, 6 February 1897.

6. Frank Harris ordered an instrument from Dolmetsch. Dolmetsch later had difficulty in obtaining a final settlement, but nothing more specific.

7. Horne had offered Dolmetsch the use of rooms in King's Bench Walk.

8. Unfortunately the story ends here and no 'proof' is extant.

9. Probably the Bach Festival in which 'Selections from St. Matthew Passion' were given, with Dolmetsch at the harpsichord.

10. 'Another Bach Festival' by John Runciman in the *Saturday Review*, 10 April 1897, see p. 114.

11. A drawing of this caricature is at Jesses.

12. This could have been W. H. Cummings, at this time editing the publication of all Purcell's works. The 'Taylor' reference would have been to Edward Taylor, 1748–1863, bass singer, Gresham Professor of Music and one of the originators of the Vocal Society of the Musical Antiquarian Society (for which he edited Purcell's *King Arthur*) and of the Purcell Club.

13. Arthur Symons, close friend and supporter of Dolmetsch and his work: 'Poet of the music hall, the café and the demi-monde, literary impressionist of towns, penetrating critic of the writers and ideas of the decadence in France and in England.' Jackson, Holbrook, *The Eighteen Nineties*, Jonathan Cape, 1913, p. 42.

14. *An Air of Rameau to Arnold Dolmetsch*

A melancholy desire of ancient things
Floats like a faded perfume out of the wires;
Pallid lovers, what unforgotten desires
Whispered once, are re-told in these whisperings?

Roses, roses and lilies with hearts of gold,
These you plucked for her, these she wore in her breast;
Only Rameau's music remembers the rest,

How the heart that was warm for you withered cold.
But these sighs? Can ghosts then sign from the tomb?
Life then wept for you, sighed for you, chillled your breath?
It is the melancholy of ancient death
The harpsichord dreams of sighing in the room.

Arthur Symons

15. Thomas Britton (1644–1714), a 'small-coal' (charcoal) merchant who made a considerable contribution to the musical world of his time. He made a thorough study of the theory and practice of music and acquired a fine library of books and manuscripts. In 1678 he established weekly concerts over his shop in Clerkenwell: Handel, Pepusch and many other leading musicians and professors were among the performers. At first the concerts were free, but later Britton charged a subscription of 10s a year. He also served coffee at a penny a dish.

16. The acquisition of this MS is mentioned in a letter to Dolmetsch from A. J. Hipkins. 29 November 1893, see p. 62.[13]

17. This, five years after the acquisition of the MS, is the first intimation we have of Dolmetsch discussing variances of tempo.

18. *The Easter Art Annual*, 1900, p. 26, illustrations plate opp. p. 24 and Fig. 36.

19. Dolmetsch, Mabel, *Personal Recollections of Arnold Dolmetsch*, Routledge & Kegan Paul, London, 1958, p. 22.
20. The 'Green' harpsichord was played by Dolmetsch at a performance of Mozart's *Don Giovanni* on 19 July 1897, conducted by Mancinelli. Dolmetsch also played for Hans Richter at Covent Garden, using the same instrument.

CHAPTER XI

In The 'Courts'

In his late thirties Dolmetsch was showing signs of the hypochondria[1] which became so pronounced in his later years: his letters frequently refer to his feeling better or not so well as yesterday. The state of his liver seems to have been a constant source of perplexity both to himself and the folk around him. Nonetheless, when a performance was imminent all disability vanished and an impending tour abroad never failed in its therapeutic effect. His struggles to make money stretch far beyond its limits, combined with the effort to do at least three people's work, must have affected his general health, but despite these difficulties he managed to keep going surprisingly well.

However, in the summer of 1898, although the nature of the illness is not known, Dolmetsch found himself in the hands of the surgeons. This setback prompted Shaw to write commiserating upon the amount of money it will take for both treatment and the employment of nurses: he suggests that as Dolmetsch is not an opera singer but 'an artist, the value of whose work is . . . understood by very few people', it is unlikely that he has sufficient funds in hand to meet the cost. Shaw, having more money lying about in the bank than he wanted that year, offers to transfer £50 to Dolmetsch's credit until he should sell his next harpsichord or get in his next season's harvest. Shaw, so often accredited with being mean, once again gives proof of his generosity towards his friends. It is not known if Dolmetsch accepted the offer but it is more than likely that he did.

It was well into the autumn before Dolmetsch resumed his musical activities. There were a few performances in London, followed by a week in Scotland, where he had been engaged to give the first in the new season of 'Historical Concerts' at Edinburgh University: the remainder were in and around Glasgow and Greenock.

In December the first volume of Dolmetsch's *Songs and Dialogues*, published by Boosey, were reviewed by John Runciman very favourably. He is afraid only that they will become popular both at what are—often mistakenly—called high-class concerts and at the vulgar 'smoker'. *I am confirmed*, with its refrain, 'For hang me, ladies at your doore', and *Of thee kind boy* were obviously meant for the latter.

Runciman goes into raptures about Elodie's brilliant playing of the Purcell Toccata and of Hélène's in the 3rd sonata by Bach for the harpsichord and viola da gamba. He speaks of two novelties introduced by Dolmetsch: one, the lyra viol being played for the first time and the other, of making Mrs. Dolmetsch play a passage again because she had 'made a hash of it'. Runciman chides Dolmetsch for this action as he is certain that few would have noticed it had their attention not been called to it. He attributes it to a 'slight and merely temporary stiffness of the left hand following on Mrs. Dolmetsch's recent serious illness'.[2]

Ill health was not the only distraction that bedevilled Dolmetsch at this time: he was fully occupied with two major though contrasting developments: one, the completion of the first Beethoven piano, on which he had been working for some time, and the other, divorce proceedings.

There is in existence a long and pitiful document written in German, running into several pages, telling of the difficulties which beset Dolmetsch and his wife throughout their turbulent marriage. It is a tale of incompatability, resentment and insult: Marie's disadvantage in years inevitably outweighed the benefit Dolmetsch derived from her money and it is probable that they would have parted earlier if he had had to support her. In fairness to Dolmetsch, however, it must also be mentioned that he is said to have stayed with her because he feared the effect a break would have on Hélène. Whatever the real reason may have been, the tone of the prayer for divorce is essentially human, the most characteristic touch being that Dolmetsch, in his own petition, admitted to having an inclination towards his girl pupils and that he often insulted his wife both at home and in society. The *decree nisi* was granted at Zürich on 20 December 1898.

A few days later, in a long letter to Horne, Dolmetsch makes no mention of the divorce: he is concerned mainly with this Beethoven piano[3] and discusses in detail the moulding and the inscriptions which Selwyn Image will paint on the gold of the front. 'I have the piano, lid and all, here in my room. It looks most beautiful, and effective, and Bessant's[4] work is very well done; only I don't like his french polish; it is greasy and cloudy, and very mean compared with the soundboard varnish; but it is as good as average french polish, so there is nothing to say. I like the paintings on the soundboard very much. If the "voice" is as good as the "looks" it will be a success indeed.'

He writes also that Runciman is trying to fix up a series of concerts for him in Monaco and if this plan materialises, another trip to Florence could be arranged: it might also be possible to give a concert in Rome.

However, Dolmetsch does not want to risk a failure like the last trip. He needs to cover all travelling expenses and accommodation for Hélène, Melodie and himself: otherwise, he will not go.

The business of the Torrigiani violin is still unsettled. Dolmetsch finds himself in a fix since he had promised Horne £30 profit on the sale; and he hoped to give him £10 or £15 on account before the end of January, with the rest following shortly afterwards. But the situation has changed:

December 28th 1898   7, Bayley Street,
                                                          W.C.

The violin I bought in Florence is only worth what I gave for it. Under the best circumstances I could not sell it for more than £100. The mistake I have made about it is unpleasant to acknowledge, but it must be faced.

This disappointment made me over anxious to settle my liabilities with you: I unwisely accepted the very inadequate offer from Hill for £190 for my Guarnerius violin. It is worth quite double that sum, and only a few days afterwards (I almost cried for it) I could have got the full value for it . . . far from making any profit . . . I am very much the worst for it. The profit we had agreed to divide does not exist. Don't you think that under the circumstances it would be fair to abandon the 'share' principle and to consider that you lent me the £100 for a month or so, that your expenses amounted to £5, or what, and the interest £3 or so? You may logically say that you are not the cause of my having been so stupid and that you expect me to fulfil my promise. If so, I shall pay the £30 as I said before, and we shall be quit.

However, Dolmetsch's optimism prevails; he tells Horne that his lectures have been more successful than ever and that he has a number of good paying engagements in view. 'If I have been able to do little more than make both ends meet, this year, I am confident of finding myself well out of all financial difficulties during the next.'

The spring season of concerts attracted, as usual, the artistic elite. An account by Robert Hichens (*The World*, 22 May 1899) captures the atmosphere well:

A young lady dressed in white met me with a serene smile of welcome and ushered me into a most characteristic *sanctum* in an abode that is evidently dedicated entirely to music. The walls . . . are tinted a dark and restful green, and are decorated with a few pictures and prints and with a great many musical instruments . . . Wax candles shed a gentle light on a dark-haired man, with enthusiastic eyes, who is leaning over a harpsichord . . . The Dolmetsches are enthusiasts. . . . And their delight . . . is generally shared by those who come under the spell of their happy influence. Mr. Dolmetsch himself is sincerely learned, and has the most charming habit of assuming that all those around him share his erudition. In his whimsical speeches he informs, and explains, but he does so rather as one who discusses with his equals than as one who instructs the bruthishly ignorant.

but he is also convinced that:

> Mr. Dolmetsch would . . . as soon knock a baby on the head as behave badly to a virginal, and his delicacy with a lute is something to marvel at.

It is this very warmth of personality and the affection for his instruments that William Rothenstein captured so well in some delightful drawings that he made in May of that year.[5] In his memoirs the artist remembers well the struggles that Dolmetsch experienced in his efforts to present concerts with little or no money at his command.[6]

This perpetual state of impecunity was, as we know, partly due to Dolmetsch's inability to refuse engagements which brought little or no profit—especially where friends were concerned. A typical example was that of one of William Poel's more ambitious productions in July of that year. It was the Kálidasá 6th-century Hindhu classic *Śakuntalá*, in the translation by Sir William Jones. Poel had chosen the Conservatory of the Botanical Gardens in Regent's Park as the eminently suitable venue and had gathered together some Indian actors for the performance. When they moved about in the tropical fiolage the effect was truly lifelike: 'But the horses of the car of India, the stuffed tiger and antelope provoked the hilarity of the audience.' The music, 'which never quite lost its Eliza-bethan idiom', was composed by Dolmetsch. Even if his music sounded English, his appearance was not. Colourfully attired in appropriate costume, he and Elodie entered into the spirit of the thing, much to the delight of their oriental colleagues, who declared Arnold to be indistin-guishable from a Moslem musician from Kashmir.

At the end of July Dolmetsch received news that his decree absolute had been granted and he writes to Horne (20 July 1899) that, having finally obtained a settlement, he will shortly be going to Zürich, where he and Elodie will be married. He explains that although the divorce is perfectly legal, they cannot be married in this country for according to English law they are still brother and sister-in-law. However, since they are both Swiss nationals, the same law does not bother itself with the legality of the marriage once the ceremony is over. Printed accouncements in French were sent out to friends on 15 September announcing that the marriage had taken place in Zürich, 'leur pays d'origine', four days earlier.

Shaw acknowledges his note from the *SS Lusitania* on 25 September, offering his 'shocked congratulations', adding that had he known Elodie was not married, he would have proposed to her himself, years ago. If Shaw was ignorant of the domestic arrangements prior to the wedding, it seems more than likely that others shared this assumption. Bearing in mind the standards of moral behaviour consistent with 'respectability' at the time, it was a considerable achievement that they had kept their secret so well.

The young Mabel Johnston could not have welcomed the marriage: she was now a permanent part of the menage, an asset to Dolmetsch in the workshop and a useful, though not outstanding, performer at concerts. However, there is no indication that any postnuptial changes took place. Mabel continued to worship her idol and Dolmetsch ruled over his little kingdom as before. If sacrifices had to be made from time to time, they were offered in the cause of music: and to Dolmetsch there could be none better.

Dolmetsch was seldom approached by anyone as knowledgeable as himself, either in the study of early music or instrument-making, so it was for him an unexpected pleasure to receive a letter from August Tolbecque,[7] the well-known musician and musical-instrument maker who wrote introducing himself as a writer on musical instruments played with a bow. He asks if Dolmetsch knows of his name from a catalogue.[8]

Tolbecque had recently finished his very important work on the making of instruments[9] and needed to research on several points before giving it to the printers. He had seen in Liepmannssohn's catalogue a copy of *Observations sur la construction des instruments à archets* by Bottée de Toulmon, but when he tried to purchase the book he was informed that it had already been sold to Dolmetsch. He writes therefore to ask if he may borrow it in order to complete his researches. Dolmetsch immediately sent the book with a covering letter: he never hesitated in such matters. Apparently Dolmetsch had written some details about himself and his family, for in the next letter from Niort[10], Tolbecque tells Dolmetsch that he also comes from a family of artists, musicians and luthiers and that his two daughters play the piano and the violin.

Tolbecque has been in retirement for some 15 years but he still spends most of his time making or restoring musical instruments and writing about them. He recalls memories of his time at the Paris Conservatoire, where he took the Premier Prix in 1849, but although he knows that Dolmetsch was at the Conservatoire in Brussels, he makes no mention of having been there himself. This is rather curious for, by a strange coincidence, it was he, in 1878, who played the Boccherini Minuet (see p. 9) on the viola da gamba and caused Dolmetsch, then a member of the audience, to wonder why it did not sound right. Although Tolbecque knew a great deal about instruments of the early period, his technique was presumably incorrect so that even as a student Dolmetsch's keen ear had detected something amiss.[11] There then follows a very interesting passage: in which he tells Dolmetsch that he had the good fortune to have bought from Tarisio,[12] a marvellous viola da gamba, and from this time he began the groundwork of his studies on the earlier musical instruments. He had as yet, never found anyone with the same tastes as himself, except his friend, M. Cavaillé-Coll, the organ-builder. Tolbecque goes on to say that even when surrounded by people who are indifferent to art, one must still have faith to follow one's ideals.

It is a great pity that no letters from Dolmetsch to Tolbecque have as yet come to light, for the correspondence as a whole might have been of considerable value. There is no doubt that the two had much in common. The letter ends with a firm desire to, 'strengthen the links of friendship they have forged together'.

On 9 October, Tolbecque responds to a request from Dolmetsch to copy some pieces by Forqueray, telling him he may borrow the pieces with pleasure, but he adds a proviso which indicates the lack of knowledge, even among the enthusiasts of early music:

> Vous savez que les doigtés sont souvent fautifs pour nous autres modernes. Cela vient naturellement de ce que nous jouons la viole sans sillets mobiles en cordes, et que nous sommes obligés de mettre les doigts à leurs place rigoureuses.[13]

From a letter written on 16 December we have an amusing insight into the jealousies which bedevil artists and craftsmen and which Dolmetsch was to experience himself many times. Tolbecque had come up against M. Paul de Wit[14] in an experience which he terms 'ridiculous'; 'le plus fort de tous'. It seems that Tolbecque and de Wit had known each other for many years and Tolbecque had acquired a very fine bass viol for his friend. Although he knew very little about it, de Wit was very keen to play the instrument. This particular viol had been converted into a 'cello and Tolbecque had sent all the information de Wit would need to restore the instrument to its original state: quite a major undertaking. It appears that de Wit duly finished the work and came to Paris to play at the Salle Erard. Tolbecque, sitting in the audience, was disgusted when he heard de Wit announce that it was his own unaided work that had brought this beautiful instrument to light after centuries of neglect and had restored it to its present perfection. He then told his audience he would play some music most suitable for that instrument: namely, a melody by Mendelssohn!

> ... et personne n'a protesté contre cette bouffonnerie. Et que pensez-vous de cette fameuse pièce *pseudo-ancienne* pour basse de viole, clavecin, viole et vielle que ces Messieurs promènent partout et qui obtient tant de succès?[15] Eh bien, personne ne proteste et ces quatre blagueurs doivent bien rire quand ils rentrent dans la coulisse. Qu'en pensez-vous?[16]

*　　*　　*

As the century turned its back on the 'nineties, Dolmetsch's activities increased. He was now giving concerts at St. James's Hall in London and in leading and small halls throughout the country. He provided music for a scene from Congreve's *Way of the World* at a charity matinée, for Isadora Duncan's *Dance Idylls* at the New Gallery, and for the first performance in England of Milton's *Samson Agonistes*, produced by William Poel in the Lecture Theatre of the Victoria and Albert Museum.

Dolmetsch had now been giving concerts for nine years and had gained a small following of devotees but in general the attitude to early music was still very detached. In the press, writers stress the novelty rather than the influence of both music and instruments of the period: 'The music of the lute is far too thin and delicate for modern use, you have to preserve solemn silence to hear it properly, whereas in the present day the sound of instrumental music gives the signal for tongues to wag' (*Paddington, Kensington and Bayswater Chronicle*, 9 December 1899), and, 'Once the ear has become accustomed to the comparatively feeble tone of these instruments, there is something very soothing in their low sweet voices.' (*Musical Times*, 1 July 1900). A letter to the editor in the same journal regrets, as had Shaw some years previously (see p. 59), that the viola d'amore and viola da gamba 'are now considered obsolete'. Besides echoing Shaw's example of the obbligato by Meyerbeer in *Les Huguenots*, and also in the *St. Matthew Passion* by Bach, he quotes Berlioz as having pleaded the cause of the d'amore in particular, expressing incredulity that this and other instruments have 'fallen into disuse, especially as the great masters have used them so successfully'. He then suggests that one of the best methods of re-introducing them into the orchestra is that they should be taught along with other orchestral instruments in our colleges of music.

Whilst the critics were speculating on the future of early music, Dolmetsch was preparing his summer series of concerts at Bayley Street. He informs his patrons that these will be the 71st, 72nd and 73rd of the concerts personally sponsored by himself, and begun in 1891 'in the hope that they would bring to light some long-forgotten composers, English and Continental, and present their works as originally conceived by their authors. How far this hope has been realised may be seen from the fact that 280 English, 125 French, 107 German and 87 Italian works have been performed. Of these only a very small proportion have been heard elsewhere in our times, even in the mutilated condition in which ancient music is presented by modern musicians.'

Even the sternest critics of Dolmetsch's performances do not deny the excellence of his craftsmanship. The consummate skill apparent in every instrument to which he turned his hand was the subject of an article in *The Studio* (Vol. 19, 1900). Dolmetsch's 'thorough and first-hand knowledge of the old keyboard instruments has kept him constantly in touch with the historic styles of decoration. . . . He has seen his knowledge tested experimentally by the artists who have painted his own clavichords and harpsichords.' As an expert he has expressed the opinion that an ornament should be 'sufficiently flat in treatment to seem part of the wood itself'.

To the inquisitive who wish to know the way in which a musical instrument is designed, Mr. Dolmetsch gives very little encouragement, having no recipe of designs to offer. He says with enthusiasm, 'Musical instruments design themselves', meaning by this that the beauty of their constructional parts and lines has its origin in certain fixed mechanical rules and practical needs that govern a master craftsman throughout the whole course of his constructional work. He goes on to describe how the curve of the bridge of the clavichord is determined 'not by somebody's unfettered inventiveness, but by the required length of the strings; while the length of each string is plainly dependent on the tone you wish it to give you. For these reasons, and many others, Mr. Dolmetsch arrived at the art of design by being submissively obedient to the science of construction.'

The writer passes on to one of the most important of Dolmetsch's dictums—one that he never abandoned;[17] that he 'to the regret of cabinet-makers, refuses to touch any wood with glasspaper, the effect of the minute particles of wood-dust penetrate into the grained surface and destroy the brilliancy. The smooth cut of a well-sharpened tool is a thousand times better than rubbing with glasspaper, so Mr. Dolmetsch never interferes with the lively quality of surface to be obtained by planing. This method of work was obligatory among the great old makers of violins, it survives here and there, as in the best ecclesiastical woodwork, and those who have tried it know that Mr. Dolmetsch is right in his high estimation of its worth in decoration.'

The writer is not so sure about Dolmetsch's employment of a thick transparent varnish and points out that whereas some admirers of good work find pleasure in carefully varnished woods, others do not, the writer being amongst them. They think regretfully of the time when the finished surfaces, after being darkened by exposure to the light, were vigorously polished with beeswax and plenty of elbow grease.

* * *

Charming though the Bayley Street house was, the expansion of Dolmetsch's work in the last few years, combined with the need for a larger concert room, had forced him to look for larger premises. On 16 January 1901 he sent out notices, prefaced as always with a quotation from Mace's

Musick's Monument, that 'The first thing to be considered, as to the advantage of Good Musicke, should be a convenient and Fit place to perform it in.' He explains that he had not, until now, been fortunate in finding a room spacious enough in a house not too large for him to live in, situated in an easily accessible part of London. 'Such a one I am at last going to have at No. 85, Charlotte Street, Fitzroy Square, W. It will be roomy, airy, quiet, and well lighted, and is now being fitted in the manner which experience has taught me to be the best for a "Musick Room".'

Dolmetsch had sub-let the Bayley Street house to an Italian who intended opening it as a music club, and in February they took up residence in Charlotte Street with only one casualty: a beautiful ebony and ivory arch-lute was lost or stolen during the move and never recovered.

The new house was gaunt and gloomy on the outside but it had, as promised, a spacious and well-appointed interior. The fine studio was in the ideal proportions of a double square with a raised platform at one end. The smaller rooms served as workshops; Mabel Johnston was highly delighted when given one of these for herself.

Dolmetsch's resilience was remarkable. Barely ten days after the move he was giving the first of three Lent concerts, to serve as 'a consecration of the room and devoted to English music of the 16th and 17th centuries'. Of particular interest was the anthem for five voices and five viols by Orlando Gibbons: 'This is the Record of John'. Dolmetsch claimed that since they (the Dolmetsches) had revived the classical method of singing, it was now possible to perform such works, and the excellent acoustics of the new Music Room provided an encouragement to the singers.

Violet Gordon Woodhouse, Van Waefelghem, Henry J. Wood with his Russian wife, W. B. Yeats and Florence Farr were among the many distinguished people who frequented the Dolmetsch concerts. It was here at Charlotte Street in 1901 that the first modern psaltery was made for Florence Farr, who used it to accompany herself reciting Yeats' poems.[18] On hearing the instrument played, Mrs. Patrick Campbell promptly ordered three: she and two others had been engaged to play the parts of the Rhinemaidens in a production of *Das Rheingold*. She had the psalteries specially tuned so that their singing could be accompanied with sweeping strokes across the strings.

The last of the three Beethoven pianos was also completed at Charlotte Street,[19] and is mentioned in a letter from Elodie to William Rothenstein (24 March 1901) letting him know that the instrument was on view for two afternoons a week.

The value of Dolmetsch's unique work was now being noticed by publishers, several of whom had approached him on the possibility of writing a book on the results of his research and practical experience. The

Connoisseur magazine had asked for some articles on mediaeval music or ancient instruments and would welcome his suggestions as to illustrations. They leave the choice of subjects and order of publication entirely to Dolmetsch. A note at the foot of their letter in Dolmetsch's own hand shows that he has offered to write 10 articles, 2,500 to 4,500 words long, at two guineas per 1,000, and reserving the right to publish in book form. Dolmetsch wisely seeks advice from Shaw. That seasoned dramatist knew a great deal about copyright and contributed some valuable suggestions. He considers it would be well worth Dolmetsch's while to have a book published in addition to the 2 guineas per 1,000 words from the *Connoisseur*, otherwise, as Shaw points out, they can prevent Dolmetsch from re-publishing the articles for 23 years. He advises that in dealing with Bell, the publisher, Dolmetsch should 'stand out for a limit to the agreement; as to whether he takes the 5s royalty with an advance of £50 or take £150 down for everything, depends on the pressure of his circumstances'. In either case, Dolmetsch should not let the book go for ever. Shaw advises an agreement for a term of years, or better still, an edition, and finishes in characteristic vein: 'Later on he [the publisher] may go bankrupt or sell his business or die or be imprisoned for Humanitarianism with your copyright tied up on his shelf, useless to him and inaccessible to you, unless you provide a definite terminable period or edition limit. So take care to guard yourself. *He* won't mind: no publisher ever believes that a book will be of any value to him after eighteen months'.[20]

To have gained a foot in yet another field would indicate that things were going well. But 1901, the year that had begun with such promise, turned out to be disastrous. The Italian tenant had been running the Bayley Street house as a brothel and Dolmetsch, who held the lease, was served with a writ. When the Italian was finally brought to trial and convicted, Dolmetsch, also being a foreigner, was cited as an accomplice. Had he behaved diplomatically he might have convinced the court of his innocence; but his enraged protestations, delivered in his arrogant best, antagonised everyone concerned, with the result that his lease was confiscated and he was heavily fined.

Dolmetsch never had much money in reserve and payment of the fine drained his meagre resources. In August, acting upon the suggestion of Shaw and others who, at the time were unaware of the far-reaching consequences of such advice, Dolmetsch filed a petition for bankruptcy. The Public Examination took place two months later. Shaw writes to Dolmetsch (24 August) telling him to use his own discretion regarding the personal debt owed to him and if a friendly creditor is useful then Dolmetsch should by all means put him down, adding that, in England, the more one owes, the more one is respected.

Shaw, though convinced that Dolmetsch will ultimately receive an honourable discharge, is concerned with the fate of the instruments. He asks if Dolmetsch has raised money on them or sold them, foreseeing the danger that they may be sold as second hand, much under their value. 'Can anything be done?' he asks, 'a subscription, or anything of that sort? What is the sum total of your indebtedness?' He apologises for asking such 'indelicate' questions but points out that it is his only means of finding out. Here again, Shaw shows a deep concern for Dolmetsch's plight. Unfortunately there is no further mention of the offer being taken up, but the bankruptcy proceedings certainly took their unrelenting course and all Dolmetsch's effects were seized by the bailiffs. Naturally they were forced to leave the house in Charlotte Street but as always when a crisis occurred, some kind benefactor stepped in to ease the pain.

Their patron on this occasion was a wealthy pupil of Elodie's. She owned six 15th-century cottages at Boveney, five miles out of Windsor, reached through winding lanes and three miles by river. The crossing was effected in a little boat called 'The Hermit'. Three cottages were sufficient for Dolmetsch's own needs and this included his workshop. The others were divided between Mabel Johnston, Beatrice Horne, who was now a part of the menage, and a local woman, an accomplished 'bonne à tout faire'. The cottages, surrounded by large gardens, were built on high ground so that they survived the spring floods common in these parts. An excellent resident gardener produced all the fruit and vegetables they could eat. In many ways it was a regenerative period for Dolmetsch: the boating and fishing evoked childhood memories of Le Mans: his affinity with the soil and the countryside had always been very strong and many years had passed since he had possessed a stretch of his own ground.

The late summer at Boveney proved only a temporary alleviation of Dolmetsch's worries. In the autumn came the stark reality. The sale by Puttick and Simpson of his library and instruments took place on 29 and 30th October at the Sir Joshua Reynolds Auction Galleries in Leicester Square. There were 40 musical instruments and over 400 volumes, portfolios and parcels of books, music and manuscripts, together with a dozen paintings, prints and lithographs. A short account in the *Musical News* (2 November 1901) regretted, as would their readers, that 'the collection . . . formed with such patience' should have been brought under the hammer. Nevertheless they were gratified to record that 'the bulk of the lots became the property of one lady, a most spirited bidder'.[21]

The report goes on to give a sample of the prices gained: 'An Italian theorbo—1550—in playing order and richly inlaid with mother of pearl and ivory fetched £14, an old English viola da gamba by Richard Meares 1669, £5 and an old German lute, in original condition—£5, also another by Arnold Dolmetsch for the same price. The harpsichord made by Mr. Dolmetsch with Mrs. Helen Fry's (neé Helen Coombe, now the wife of Roger Fry) part decoration exhibited in the Arts and Crafts Exhibition 1897 was the object of much interest and compliment and realised £89. An old square piano by Zumpe fetched 9s. and an old square virginal, 27s. 6d., whilst a chamber pipe organ by Gray and Davison with 6 stops and pedals in solid mahogany case went for 7s.' In addition to this, another old square pianoforte went for 3s. and 4 volumes of Grove's *Dictionary* for 2s.[22]

Barely six weeks after the auction, on 12 December 1901, Dolmetsch sent out a notice calling attention to the 'interest attaching to the performance of Bach's famous *Goldberg Variations* at my forthcoming concert. This work has been rightly acknowledged one of the most important pieces of music ever written. It may be considered, besides, as resuming the whole art of harpsichord playing in its most advanced state of development.' He points out that several attempts have been made to perform it upon the pianoforte, but that many of the variations, when executed incorrectly, become quite incomprehensible to any except the performer, when played upon that instrument. Moreover, 'one would always lack the wonderful and practically inexhaustible changes of colour in the tone which can be produced upon a first-rate Harpsichord by a thorough master of its resources'. He adds: 'The work might perhaps prove long to impatient and frivolous hearers; but to understanders, i.e. lovers of that kind of music, it must be a pleasure of the rarest and most delicate kind.'

These variations were played by Elodie and acclaimed by the press. This concert was also memorable for a sadder reason. There is on the programme a note in Dolmetsch's hand correcting the preceding item. There was to have been a performance of Porpora's Concerto for violoncello accompanied by strings and harpsichord but it was replaced by Bach's Concerto in A Minor for violin, string quartet, violone and harpsichord. All the familiar names are there, including Mabel Johnston, but Hélène's name has disappeared. She was never again to play at a Dolmetsch concert. As the result of a quarrel they were estranged for over 20 years and were only briefly reconciled before Hélène's death in 1924.

There has been much speculation[23] as to the real cause of this disagreement but no reliable evidence has been established. An unpleasant outcome was that the trustee in Dolmetsch's bankruptcy case brought Hélène to court for the return of her viola da gamba, claiming that it was not her personal property. The unfortunate girl was compelled to face her father in court and swear that the instrument had been a gift to her in 1893; she further insisted that although it had been kept at her father's house, she always retained the key. Dolmetsch denied this, protesting that her key was a duplicate supplied for convenience. Dolmetsch's professional enemy, W. H. Cummings, was called as a witness for Hélène, a move which would have caused Dolmetsch considerable spleen. Cummings said that he had often heard Mr. Dolmetsch talk of how his daughter played upon 'her viola da gamba' or 'her instrument'. Judgement was awarded against the trustee. However, when his temper had cooled, Dolmetsch wrote to Hélène but the letter went astray. She also had tried to get in touch with him but misinformed gossips had told her that her father would never again receive her. Since both shared the same dominant pride, neither would give way. But it was a decision Dolmetsch regretted for the rest of his life.

Some weeks after the sale of his instruments Dolmetsch moved from Boveney to a house in Seymour Place, just off the Edgware Road. It is not known how he managed to pay for this further change of residence but it seemed to have been accomplished without much difficulty. As he continued to give concerts at the Hall of Clifford's Inn it was evident that the Artworkers' Guild were still ready to support him.

*　　*　　*

Friendship with Dolmetsch was not difficult to achieve but to maintain that state was quite another matter. W. B. Yeats was one who came to know Dolmetsch well and who kept in touch throughout the years. Fellow visionaries working in closely related fields, each recognised and respected the other's ideals: 'Behind the solemn mask of the mystic there was a rare imagination and, what was less often suspected, shrewd wisdom.'[24] Dolmetsch was not much interested in mysticism but imagination and shrewd wisdom were certainly attributes that they shared. Unfortunately, little correspondence survives, but in a letter dated 3 June 1902, Yeats clearly shows that in asking Dolmetsch to chair[25] a lecture he is soon to give, he would sooner have him than anyone else: 'You are the only one, I suppose, in the world now, who knows anything about the old music that was half speech, and I need hardly say that neither Miss Farr nor myself, could have done anything in this matter of speaking to notes without your help.' This confidence is reflected in a letter from Frank Fay to Yeats when discussing a stage production in Dublin: 'What a pity there is not here someone like Dolmetsch, who would do for our old music what he has done for other old music.'

*　　*　　*

It took Dolmetsch the best part of 1902 to recover from his losses of the previous year but by Christmas he was looking forward to an entirely new venture. For some time it had been in his mind to take his players to the United States of America. Through an introduction to Sam Franko, a European-born violinist who had emigrated to that country as a soloist and later turned impresario, a tour was arranged. On 27 December, an odd trio set out to cross the Atlantic: Dolmetsch, his wife and young Mabel Johnston, the girl who was to become his bride within the year.

NOTES

1. This would appear to be a family trait. Much later letters from Albert Dolmetsch to his brother, Arnold, are almost totally concerned with their respective illnesses. Although no letters to Albert from Arnold have been traced by the writer, the impression one gets is that they vie with each other as to whom is the greatest sufferer.

2. Elodie's complaint is not specified in any extant correspondence, but her name disappears from programmes for some time that year. Janet Dodge, an American pupil of Dolmetsch's, often deputised for her.

3. The first of the Beethoven pianos was made for the Rev. Stewart Headlam. The second for Mrs. Violet Gordon Woodhouse: after passing through several hands it was restored to working order and is now in the Raymond Russell Collection in Edinburgh.

4. Bessant, a craftsman occasionally employed by Dolmetsch.

5. Now at Jesses, Haslemere.

6. Rothenstein, William, *Men and Memories* (1872–1900), Faber & Faber, London, 1931, pp. 212–13.

7. Auguste Tolbecque (1830–1919), French 'cellist, composer, writer and instrument restorer.

8. Letter dated 28 July 1899.

9. *L'Art du Luthier*, Niort (1903).

10. 10 September 1899.

11. In later years Dolmetsch was said to have claimed that he heard someone playing the top string only (of the gamba) on this occasion, but there is no written evidence to substantiate this assumption.

12. Luigi Tarisio, b.? Milan. A carpenter who collected old violins from the Italian peasantry, restored and re-sold them for profit. His flair for detecting the work of the masters amounted to genius and over a period of twenty years he travelled to London and Paris trading with the most famous dealers in both capitals. When he died in 1854 he left over 200 valuable stringed-instruments which were sold for a profit of 300,000 lire. One of these instruments was the celebrated 'Messiah' Stradivari violin, now in the Hill Collection: Ashmolean Museum, Oxford.

13. You know that the fingering is often faulty for us moderns: this comes as the natural result of our playing the viol without frets and our having to put our fingers

strictly in their set places. (This is conclusive evidence that Tolbecque played the viol without frets.)

14. Paul de Wit, Dutch virtuoso 'cellist (1852–1925). His collections of musical instruments were sold to the Hochschule in Berlin and the W. Heyer Museum at Cologne. Despite Tolbecque's story, de Wit did much to bring the playing of the viola da gamba back into favour.

15. 'The Société des Instruments Anciens'. They enjoyed a certain success for a few years but finally disbanded and were never re-formed (see p. 116).

17. In the present Arnold Dolmetsch Ltd., no glass-paper is used.

16. No one protested against this buffoonery. And what is your opinion of this famous pseudo-ancient music for gamba, harpsichord, viols and vielle [hurdy-gurdy] that they so successfully display everywhere? Nobody protests about these four humbugs who must have a good laugh when they go off the platform. What do you think?

18. In a letter to Joseph Hone, 9 January 1940, Mabel Dolmetsch recalls having heard Florence Farr (in 1899) reciting 'accompanying herself upon the psaltery. The thrilling tones of her low voice . . . left a lasting impression on me . . . I think her trouble was that she was not an executive musician; and so could not detach herself from the physical action of plucking the right notes when, carried away by excitement, she had changed the pitch of her voice.'
In January 1940, one month before his death, Dolmetsch wrote:
'I tried to revive the Art of reciting to well defined musical tones, and I made a "Psaltery" to accompany the voice, as was done in the early days of Celtic and Greek Art. The point was to find the "tune" to which the poet recited his own verse. I spent a whole night listening to Yeats reciting but I came to the conclusion that he did not realize the inflexions of his own voice. In fact, he had a short phrase of fairly indistinct tones which he employed to recite any of his poems. This did not interfere with the expression of his readings, which were very beautiful; but it was useless from my point of view.'
Dolmetsch then confirms the opinions expressed by Mabel Dolmetsch that Florence Farr raised the pitch of her voice and was not able to follow it on the psaltery. The first of many public performances of Florence Farr reciting to her own accompaniment on the psaltery was at the Hall of Clifford's Inn, Fleet Street, on 10 June 1902.

19. The third Beethoven piano was made for Cecil Rhodes and is now at Groote Schuur in South Africa. It is erroneously described as a spinet in *Groote Schuur, Residence of South Africa's Prime Minister*, Pretoria, Republic of South Africa, 1970, and also in an article by Paul Loeb Van Zuilenburg, '*Cecil Rhodes's "Spinet"* ', together with several dubious speculations in the *Galpin Society Journal*, May 1973, pp. 138–40.

20. G.B.S. to Dolmetsch, 29 September 1901.

21. Beatrice Horne.

22. Many MSS, books and instruments have now been returned to the Dolmetsch Library and Collection at Haslemere.

23. Some say that Elodie drove Hélène out: others that she was jealous of her father's

affection for Mabel. If the latter be true, it is ironic that Mabel should have finally brough about a reconciliation.

24. William Rothenstein, op. cit., p. 282.
25. *Letters of W. B. Yeats*, Wade Edition, Rupert Hart-Davis, London, 1954.

CHAPTER XII

New York

THE American tour, though highly successful from the musical point of view, suffered sporadic domestic eruptions. Such a curious *ménage à trois* must have been very difficult to handle. Only a man like Dolmetsch would have been sufficiently naïve to believe that a wife and a bride-elect could combine happily united only in the cause of music. It was also probably the one time in Dolmetsch's life when his own perverseness was outdone.

Nonetheless, on the evening after their arrival there was a little light relief. A band of musicians called on Dolmetsch to welcome him to New York and straightway escorted him around the town, stopping frequently for some liquid refreshment. Of habit a wine-drinking man, Dolmetsch was unprepared for the effects of strong concoctions such as the 'Eye-opener' or 'Corpse-reviver'. The cocktail had not yet crossed the Atlantic. Dolmetsch confessed next morning that for the first time in his life he had tottered home feeling decidedly unsteady. On the afternoon following this all-male party, Dolmetsch and his ladies attended a more sober reception in their honour where they met many of New York's leading musicians, including the then famous Kneisel Quartet.

The first concert in New York on 6 January was held in a packed Daly's Theatre at 3.30 in the afternoon—then a fashionable time for concert-giving. The trio appeared in period costume and Dolmetsch plied every trick of his inimitable showmanship with asides and comments that sent the audience into raptures.

The concert caused considerable comment from the press: most reviewers had enjoyed the unusual experience of hearing the early music played on contemporary instruments, and all recognised the historical significance of such a performance: 'Yesterday's concert afforded an altogether exceptional opportunity . . . in that it brought before the public for the first time some of the most characteristic of the old-time instruments in the performance of the music that was written for them. . . . The harpsichord sounded at first, to ears attuned to the resonance of the modern pianoforte, like a far-away tinkling. But it soon took its place in the right perspective and compelled admiration and liking for beauty and qualities of tone all its own. . . . The Bach Concerto [for harpsichord, flute and violin with string accompaniment] was of a loveliness and a dignity that may have seemed small in scale to modern listeners, but that was almost like a glimpse into another world of beauty. . . . The playing of these pieces can scarcely be judged by any standards to which we are accustomed; but the rectitude of style, the fluency of technique and the lovely enthusiasm of the three performers were always clear.'[1]

The critic from the *Evening Post* held a more equivocal view, 'Undoubtedly modern instruments are vastly superior . . . and yet the harpsichord and the viola da gamba . . . are more than curiosities . . . they have a genuine musical interest not only to students but to all amateurs.'

The *Commercial Advertiser* had no doubts as to the place in which their critic put this music: 'It would be going too far to say that the old music played on the old instruments can give unlimited pleasure to the ear that has been educated by the full-voiced richly coloured instruments of today, but that the interest excited by the performance was unquestionable. While Daly's Theatre is not at all well suited to such music—to any music—in fact, Mr. Dolmetsch was able to give the audience a very clear idea of what pleased our ancestors of two centuries ago. In fact, the chief interest in the performance . . . rose from the revelation of how completely impossible it will be to revive more than an interest of curiosity in music of this kind. Faddists will prate of its pure beauties and will rhapsodize over the joy of having the sensations that contemporaries of Bach and Handel had, but they are as likely to rhapsodize over Chinese music. . . . The viola d'amore and the lute are enjoying a revival—but the viola da gamba, the violone and the harpsichord are past resuscitation, except for such semi-educational purposes as inspire Mr. Dolmetsch. The reason is obvious. They have served their purpose. They represent the highest achievement of their time and were used by the old musicians for lack of better instruments. Primitive, naïve and interesting they certainly are, but it is just as certain that the music which was written for them sounds better on the superior instruments of today.'

The *Evening Sun* plainly mocked: 'Bowed with the weight of centuries he stands—does Dolmetsch about five feet in his stockings. But then there is his hair: the iron-grey crowning glory is the hair and it hangs like a wreath about his deep eyes and brow. A diminutive beard hides the rest of the face. To know what he looked like, take a portrait of Daudet . . . forget it for at least 10 years and then recall its outlines . . . the daguerreotype style is enforced with a mode of dress that avoids everything modern or conventional. . . . It might have been in his studio jacket that the man made his bow to the public here . . . the instruments [were] not heard . . . the audience smiled nobly . . . the instruments [were] tired after their

Atlantic crossing with a cabin to themselves . . . it was easy to see why music written for it [the harpsichord] had strict limitations, which modern taste could not tolerate for long . . . the lute . . . looks like an overgrown mandoline and sounds like a glorified banjo.'

The critic from the *Morning Telegraph* had been infused with the real spirit of the thing and wrote warmly of his appreciation of having heard settings never before heard on 'this side of the Atlantic'. He explained that proper analysis of these compositions would probably not be very enlightening to any one who had not heard them: 'Suffice it to say that they are marked by a quaintness, naivete, freshness and exuberance or pathos, as the movement may demand, quite delightful to the modern ear, used to heavier orchestration and wearied by the laboured efforts of the composers who attempt to express reality or abstruseness in harmonic sound. The old composers had no purpose but to arrange a concordance of sweet sounds. They succeeded to a point almost impossible at the present moment.'

From New York City the Dolmetsches went on to give some 14 concerts in New York State and one at the Steinert Hall in Boston. Here again the large audience was clearly delighted and the critics enthusiastic. A writer in the *Boston Journal* (29 January 1903) claimed that Dolmetsch had succeeded in making him feel that 'the music is as though it were written solely for you and perhaps one other. There is necessarily close relationship between player or singer and the hearer. And then the emotion is in the player and hearer as well as in the sonata or the song. . . . They [the audience] now know that music is not a thing of purely modern invention: and that there were musical instruments before the day of gigantic orchestras and ingenious contrivances.'

Besides the public concerts the Dolmetsches had been engaged to play at a number of soirées in the private houses of New York society. One of these, held in honour of the famous Mrs. Jacob Astor, was at the home of a newly-married grand-daughter. For the occasion, the entrance hall and corridor were profusely decorated with masses of long-stemmed crimson roses which, according to Dolmetsch's agent, cost a dollar apiece. The musicians duly settled in the corner appointed to them and commenced their programme with a couple of ensemble pieces. Then, as Elodie began to play the opening notes of a Scarlatti sonata, the sound was completely swallowed up by a burst of melody from a Hungarian string quartet installed in the opposite corner. The rest of the evening's entertainment resulted in a series of strange musical contrasts, with considerable mis-understanding as to whom should play and for how long: a procedure unaided by the fact that it was conducted almost entirely in Hungarian.

The Dolmetsches sailed home on the *Mauretania* on 7 February, armed with many promises of further engagements in the USA. News of their success had evidently reached England, for in the *Musical Times* it was reported that 'strange to say, the Dolmetsches have caught on in America'.

On 24 February, Dolmetsch's 45th birthday, Mabel Johnston presented him with a copy of Couperin's *L'Art de Toucher le Clavecin* that she had picked up in a second-hand bookshop. This was one of his most important literary acquistitions since he had chanced upon the viol MSS in the Royal College of Music Library. The book now led him to new fields of exploration: not only was it concerned with harpsichord technique, it was the sound guide to interpretation which was to place Dolmetsch in such a strong position when he began writing his own book many years later. At this date not one of his contemporaries had researched into this side of keyboard music.

Soon after the return from America, the internal disturbances of the Dolmetsches' domestic life became so obvious to everyone that they could no longer be ignored and the uneasy situation that had prevailed for some time was finally recognised. With incompatability as his plea, Dolmetsch went off once more to Zürich in search of his second divorce. Meanwhile, Elodie moved from Seymour Place and busied herself with playing and teaching, at which she achieved considerable success. After the decree was made absolute, she sent out notices in withering rejection of Dolmetsch's teaching: she 'begs to announce that she has ceased to play the Virginals etc . . . and to sing the old songs at the so-called "Arnold Dolmetsch Concerts", and that she will have, therefore, no connection with them.

'She will give at Caxton Hall . . . with the help of competant and delicate artistes . . . three Concerts of Old music played upon the instruments for which it was written. . . . A beautiful grand piano, made by Broadwood in 1800, which can produce exquisite effects and sweetness of tone, will be introduced.' The notice (printed by Horne at the Chiswick Press) was sent out from Eton Cottage, Eton Wick, a small property Arnold had bought when the cottages at Boveney had served their purpose and been returned to the owner.

Under Swiss law, division of property following a divorce was recognised procedure, in sad contrast to the lack of machinery under which a divorced wife could claim anything at all in Victorian England. The other item that Dolmetsch was forced to part with to his former wife was the Kirkman harpsichord and this caused him great pain. Elodie later returned to France, where for a short while she achieved considerable fame as a harpsichordist, but at a fairly early age she retired to live on the Riviera.

When Dolmetsch wrote to Shaw telling him of the divorce, he received a typical reply:

Strachur,
28th Sep. 1903   Argyllshire

What is the use of going to all that trouble? In another month you will be snapped
up again: and the chances are that the new one will be possessed of seven devils
for every one that possessed the other. Much better marry Elodie again: she was
no worse than any other woman.

G. Bernard Shaw

But Shaw was wrong. Arnold married Mabel Johnston at Marylebone
Town Hall on 23 September 1903, four days after the decree was
made absolute. The girl from Dulwich had finally achieved her desire and
this marriage, which was to last for 36 years, turned out to be ideal. There
is no doubt whatsoever that Dolmetsch's later achievements and partial
recognition of his work by the musical world, would never have taken
place but for his wife's patience, understanding and almost superhuman
ability to remove obstacles when they impeded her husband's work. She
managed to run a home on a pittance and brought up a family under the
greatest difficulties: but her calm was absolute and her optimism indefatigable. Whatever Arnold wanted she would provide, if it were humanly
possible. They never had a serious disagreement. Mabel could see no
fault in her lord and master and therefore never criticised him: it may have
suited Dolmetsch down to the ground but it did not help in his human
relationships in general; all through his life he lost the support of some
of his greatest admirers because of his inability to forgive other people's
shortcomings whilst remaining in childish oblivion to his own.

*   *   *

Elodie's removal from the ensemble caused a sad musical loss and
Dolmetsch had to set about finding a substitute. This was no easy matter. It
was impossible to advertise for a harpsichordist as such: there were probably
no more than a handful of people who knew anything about the instrument,
and those were gifted amateurs like Hipkins and Fuller-Maitland, whose
main professional occupation lay in related fields. According to Dolmetsch
there were only pianists and 'high-wristed thumpers' at that. But after
hearing a number of these he decided upon a young woman called Kathleen Salmon, whose touch was considerably lighter than most. She had a
pleasant little singing voice and knew how to use it; she was also small in
stature—always an asset where Dolmetsch was concerned.

At the age of 85 she recalled vividly her first meeting with Dolmetsch:
'I had called to see him and was rather taken aback by his appearance at
first. I told him I had just taken my LRAM but he wasn't a bit interested
in qualifications. He asked: "Have you ever played the harpsichord?"

When I said no I hadn't, he retorted, "You must have learnt some Bach?" I remember saying "Good Lord, yes! Plenty of Bach." This seemed to please him and he pointed to the instrument in front of us. "Sit down and play some Bach on that harpsichord!" So I did. I can't remember what I played but I can remember that it sounded so different from the piano. I knew immediately that this was the only way to play Bach. Dolmetsch seemed satisfied. "That's all right. . . . Do you like playing the harpsichord?" I answered quickly, "Yes, I do, very much." The next minute, I was *in*! I enjoyed being with them . . . the concerts were very successful . . . always lots of applause . . . there were so many engagements and we worked very hard . . . Dolmetsch knew exactly what he wanted and he knew how to get it—he couldn't be played up.' Kathleen Salmon was one of the few people who remembers Dolmetsch playing the solo violin: 'He was then still a very fine performer and it was a joy to accompany him.'

Evidently Kathleen Salmon was an apt pupil, for after a few weeks of intensive study with Dolmetsch, and much private practising on her part, she was by the autumn being given equal prominence on the programme with Dolmetsch, Beatrice Horne and Mabel Johnston, who still used her maiden name. The success of their united efforts may be measured by a report following a concert at Clifford's Inn on 19 November, when the critic of the *St. James's Gazette* wrote: 'She [Kathleen Salmon] played a Bach prelude and fugue on the clavichord with a nice clean touch and appreciation for the beauties of part-playing.'

A notice in the following February announced that she was playing a Couchet[2] harpsichord recently restored by Dolmetsch: this was proof that she had reached Dolmetsch's required standards, otherwise he would never have allowed her to touch the instrument.

On 16 December, *Punch* satirised an activity in which Dolmetsch was concerned. Florence Farr was acting as secretary for a newly-formed fellowship known as 'The Dancers', a body whose aim was to 'fight the high and powerful devil, solemnity'. In a poem entitled *L'Allegro up to date*, the final stanza is devoted to Dolmetsch:

> The old forgotten dancing-lore,
> The steps we cannot understand,
> DOLMETSCH agrees to take in hand,
> These on the well-trod stage anon,
> When next our learned sock is on,
> We'll show, while ARNOLD, Fancy's child,
> Tootles his native wood-wind wild.

This verse is curiously prophetic for Dolmetsch had not yet introduced the recorder into his concerts, although he occasionally included a flute.

Dolmetsch did know something of the steps of the old dances but it was his wife who later researched the subject most thoroughly and wrote two books on the subject.

In the early part of 1904 Dolmetsch provided the music for seven performances of *Much Ado About Nothing* with the Elizabethan Stage Society directed by his old friend, William Poel, and arranged by Ben Greet. Experimental performances given at town halls in the East End and at Hammersmith, these were part of a scheme sponsored by the London School Board to provide students of the Evening Continuation Schools (which later became Evening Classes) with some knowledge of Shakespeare and drama in general. At the age of 96 Sir Lewis Casson, then a young actor playing the part of Don Pedro, recalled: 'a vivid picture of Dolmetsch sitting on a stool with a great lute on his knees, playing the music of those times . . . a beautiful figure in Elizabethan costume.' Of one of these performances *The Times* wrote: 'It did not need his [Dolmetsch's] Elizabethan hat to make him the most charming piece of archaism of all.'

In the spring of 1904 the Dolmetsches' first child was born, and they named her Cécile after the patron saint of music. Mabel moved out to Dorking, staying at a farmhouse, whilst Arnold continued to live and work at Seymour Place, joining his family at weekends. It was during this time that he took to his habit of sleeping in a hammock hooked up across the room that served as a workshop during the day.

In June and July 1904 the Worshipful Company of Musicians held their famous Loan Exhibition of Musical Instruments at the Fishmongers' Hall. Some 500 instruments, 448 rare books, and 633 pictures, drawings, manuscripts and photographs had been gathered together on loan from members of the Company and a number of other notable collections. A special feature of the exhibition was a series of 17 lectures given each afternoon in the beautiful Court-room adjoining the Hall.

The main idea of the exhibition was to show the development of musical instruments, and the advance that has taken place in the art during the past 300 years, especially in England. In addition to displaying the exhibits it was decided that some musical education for the visitor should be provided: lectures were given daily, either on the progressive improvements in the instruments themselves or on some historical development of the art.

Until this time no similar attempt had ever been made to bring so much before the public at the same time: the lectures were illustrated with musical examples, and every afternoon the lecture hall was filled with visitors who came in from the exhibition to listen to the discourses. All the leading names in the musical world were to be seen on the programme:

T. L. Southgate, W. H. Cummings, Sir Frederick Bridge, the Rev. F. W. Galpin, Henry Watson and many others, mainly members of the Company. But not that of Arnold Dolmetsch.

Despite the trouble that had been taken to mount this superb exhibition, which consisted mainly of old instruments, the general attitude of the lecturers was patronising; a sample appears in a preface written by T. L. Southgate when the text of the lectures was published in book form in 1906:[3]

> Not a few of the pieces given revealed a realm of beautiful old English music which is known only to the musical historian and a few cultivated amateurs. In many instances, instruments in use in bygone periods were brought into requisition, and afforded an intellectual treat.

When Novello published a limited edition of a splendid illustrated and detailed catalogue in 1905, they asked Arthur Hill to write a preface: he continued the practice of ignoring Dolmetsch's efforts. After dwelling upon the uniqueness of the exhibition and marvelling at the expertise with which T. L. Southgate had carried out the idea, he deals with the relative value of previous attempts to present early music from an educational point of view.

A peformance of 16th-century music on contemporary instruments was given in 1845 at the request of the late Prince Consort: he then recalls the delightful concert of old music played on ancient instruments given at the South Kensington Exhibition in 1885 by musicians who came from Brussels and Amsterdam expressly for the purpose. He admits that, although we no longer have to seek such players abroad, 'as yet, we have no society or regular body of professional players who devote themselves solely to the study and mastery of the many instruments that are no longer heard, except on rare occasions. Owing to this fact, and to the craze for "big effects" begotten of the modern orchestra, the charm possessed by much perfect and delightful music written by composers of the sixteenth and seventeenth centuries is practically lost to the world.' He goes on to suggest that this exhibition, by instituting lectures with musical illustrations, had 'served to open up a practically unexplored region of most beautiful music which, notwithstanding all that has hitherto been done, is known only to the musical historian and to a very small number of zealous amateurs'.

Perhaps here, in the last two words, Dolmetsch attains anonymous recognition. It is therefore not surprising that nowhere in the 540 pages of the 1906 publication does the name of Arnold Dolmetsch appear; his daughter, Hélène, played at the lecture on early English viols, but that is all.

Fortunately, Dolmetsch, then living in London, wrote to his wife regularly and the letters have been preserved. He makes passing references to the antipathy that obviously existed: 'Cummings saw me—seemed much annoyed. Looked very red and nervous—perfectly contemptible lecture which he read out of a book making "our English Songs" begin *after* Purcell. He sang with a cracked flat voice, accompanying himself on a piano with wooden fumbling fingers.' Indeed, Cummings, whose pompous writings and conceited utterings make one automatically sympathetic to Dolmetsch's opinions, said at this lecture:

> Purcell seems to have been the first English composer who produced song and recitative in perfection, with a just balance of sound and sense, in which expression, rhythm, melody and harmony are all in good keeping.

He seems to have been quite carried away by stirring pieces like *Rule Britannia* and *God Save the King* and hastens on to the 19th-century composers, with their sentimental ballads, whilst Henry Lawes and John Dowland are mentioned only *en passant*. But at the same lecture, Dolmetsch writes: 'Several people spoke to me . . . very amiable all.'

This antipathetic attitude continues throughout the lectures. Even Dolmetsch's erstwhile supporters like Dr. Bridge seem to have forsaken him, for in the lecture conducted by him on 'Music in the Year 1604' he passes over Dolmetsch's discoveries as though they had never existed. He tells his assembly that he will let them hear a piece arranged from Morley's Consort Lessons and explains that he has found the various parts, published in six different books, some of which were, no doubt destroyed in the Great Fire. He mentions that the one part left was that of the viol in the Sacred Harmonic Society Collection[4] and the flute part (recorder) was found at the British Museum. At the Bodleian Library at Oxford, he and Sir John Stainer researched further and came across the citterne part. He goes on to say that through the news of the exhibition becoming known, the pandora part turned up, so that they now have four of them and the piece will be played that afternoon. The lute part has yet to be supplied, 'but strictly speaking, we have got the real thing, which has not been played for two or three hundred years until it was played before their Royal Highnesses the Prince and Princess of Wales the other day.'

He next introduced a piece, *O Mistris Myne*, first played by the band and then by one of his 'boys'.[5] The professor had certainly gained a precious manuscript but no mention is made of Dolmetsch, who had been presenting such works to the public since the early 1890s and whose first performances had been those illustrating Dr. Bridge's own lectures at Gresham College.

The omission becomes even more pointed in a later part of the lecture

when he asks whether 'home music' is as much practised now as in 1604:—
especially concerted music. 'Where are now the "Sets of Recorders" or the
"Chest of Viols" once found in not a few English houses in Elizabethan
and Jacobean times? Will you find families able to play upon the strings
the "Fancies" our composers put forth?. . . In what present day houses
can the Madrigal books be placed upon the table, and the members of the
family display their skill in singing this delightful music? I know of none!'
Dr. Bridge tells his audience that there was a time in which every educated
lady played the spinet and accompanied her songs on the lute: it was
expected that a cultured gentleman ought to show his skill on the recorder
or the viola da gamba. 'Certainly we have gained something in this last
three hundred years, but I fear we have also lost one of the delights of the
united home circle.'⁶ This was exactly the theme of so many of Dolmetsch's
own lectures expressed in almost the same words, 'Home Music'.

However, it was at the lecture on 'The Early English Viols and their
Music' by Dr. Henry Watson that Dolmetsch must have felt the most
indignant. At the onset the lecturer took an arch attitude to his subject
with apologies for it being 'trite'; therefore his audience would find it
uninteresting; and that in coming from Manchester to London he is
bringing 'coals to Newcastle . . . for in these last musical days nothing new
can be said about old instruments in general or about the viol in particular.
Its history has all been told, and its secrets, if ever it had any, are all out . . .
every darkened cellar, every dusty closet, every chest rusty of hinge has
been rummaged and ransacked, and the occupation is all but gone of even
such ingenious enthusiasts as the Rev. Mr. Galpin, Mr. T. L. Southgate
and Mr. W. T. Taphouse.'

He purports that the enlightened people of 1904 'smile at the reverence
with which the earlier composers bowed down before the rules of primitive
counterpoint and took for gospel the deliverances of their arbitrary
decalogue. We wonder sometimes why they did not discover the narrow-
ness of their restraint, and why they did not sooner and more daringly
break through them. But we must not lose sight of the fact that *it was
limitation of resource, rather than of courage* that delayed the English
composer of those days in their experiments and researches.'

Dr. Watson then has something to say on the shape and construction of
the viols, inferring that the viol is an inferior instrument to the violin. He
points out that at the present time it is common practice to alter the five-
and six-stringed viols and so 'add insult to injury by endeavouring to
convert them to the form and character of that younger branch of the
family to whom their own ruin is due'—the violin. He bemoans the practice
of cutting down and narrowing finger-boards, especially as, in his opinion,
the final result is that 'although it may be the neck of the 'cello the voice

remains that of the viol'. He does not, however, object to a temporary change in the stringing of the viols so that the instruments can be tuned and played as an ordinary violin or 'cello, for this is a thing he has done himself. It would have been interesting to note Dolmetsch's reaction to the assumption that:

> Few players would care to give the necessary practice in order to learn a system of fingering that is obsolete and of no practical value.

He defends the frets as being the 'very marks of their antiquity' and condemns those who would lay 'unhallowed hands' upon them. He proudly announces that the viols he uses himself, with one exception (the viola da gamba), have been strung as modern instruments and he himself can detect no noticeable change in the quality of the tone, although 'some eminent authorities are of the opinion that the character of the instrument is changed'. Dr. Watson considered that the violin finally superseded the viol in the time of Purcell and that Purcell's use of the former instruments in many ways sounded the death-knell. He quotes an epigram of 1670:

> In former days we had the viol in
> Ere the true instruments had come about,
> But now we say since this all ears doth win,
> The violin hath put the viol out.

He praises the fuller and brighter tone of the violin, its higher capabilities of nimble expression and confesses that we must now 'smile a little at the ingenious advocacy of the weaker instrument by Mace in "Musick's Monument" and Playford's "Introduction to the Skill of Musick" and other teachers of the viol and lute indulged in at the time'. He also compares the differences in the style of music written for viols and violins, the one the viol 'bound by the limitations of rigid law; the other, the violin, knowing no restrictions to its resourcefulness of tone and expression', other than those placed upon it by the composer and the performer.

In a patronising summing up, Dr. Watson says that we must not forget that the style of playing necessary and appropriate to the viol was quite in keeping with the musical requirements of 300 years ago, when Thomas Britton, the musical small-coal man gave concerts in the narrow room over his shop and the 'daring outline for a music room six yards square by Thomas Mace had not taken shape' and all music was domestic. But time works wonders and it has worked on the once-condemned fiddle. Originally a despised outcast assigned to the wandering ballad-monger, it was fated to supersede the viols which now 'lay ensconced in their green-baize luxury'. He considers that the difficulties of playing an unfretted instrument ceased to be insurmountable, though John Playford in his once-famous 'Introduction' recommends beginners to fret their violins. The round-backed violin it seems has cheated the flat-backed viol and has left for this Ancient and Honourable Company of musicians only a pleasant and interesting memory. But the audience have a treat in store since the memory has not robbed them of the means of recalling sounds with which it 'delighted our musical ancestors, and excited the wonder of those simple souls who thought as they listened that the perfected end of all things musical had been reached'. There then followed musical illustrations in what Dolmetsch described as a 'very tame programme'. It must have been hard for him to see the daughter in whom he once had such high hopes collaborating with his musical enemies.

Unfortunately there is no record of the cause of the blatant snub that Dolmetsch received throughout this exhibition and the later publications connected with it: Cummings was never a favourite of Dolmetsch's so a conflict between those two would have been expected. But the high-handed attitude of Watson and Bridge entirely ignoring his work, must have cut deep into Dolmetsch's pride. The chip on his shoulder was becoming noticeably heavier each year. But in fairness it must have been exasperating to see so much attention being paid to work that he had pioneered, even if much of the prejudice had been engendered by misplaced sincerity and sharp tongue.

It was this same directness that prompted Dolmetsch to write an unresponsive letter to James Joyce when the latter, full of enthusiasm, wrote to Dolmetsch asking him to make him a lute. Joyce had previously written to his friend Gogarty on 3 June 1904:[7]

> 60 Shelbourne Road,
> Dublin
>
> My idea for July and August is this—to get Dolmetsch to make me a lute and to coast the South of England from Falmouth to Margate singing old English songs.

Clearly Joyce had no idea of how long it would take to make a lute and he was evidently over-confident of his ability to master the instrument in a few weeks. Dolmetsch's reply was not encouraging:[8]

> July 17th 1904   2, Seymour Place
>   W.
>
> Dear Sir,
>   Lutes are extremely rare. I have not heard of any for sale for years. You should read my articles on this subject in *The Connoisseur* for April and May. I have made one lute, some years ago, but it is doubtful whether I shall make any others. It would certainly be very expensive, and I could hardly say when it would be finished. The lute is moreover extremely difficult to play, and very troublesome to keep in order.

A spinet or some simple kind of harpsichord, or even a very early piano, would be far more practicable.

I could get you one of these fairly easily—£30 to £60 would get one.

Yours faithfully,

Arnold Dolmetsch[9]

Joyce read the recommended copies of *The Connoisseur* and though his 'dream of minstrelsy was abandoned . . . he made capital of the acquired information, from Dolmetsch.[10] 'The modern painter who wishes to introduce a lute into one of his works, a fashionable thing nowadays, has every chance of reproducing some impossible model, perhaps a complete forgery.'[11] Thus: 'The resonant voice of the Hungarian was about to prevail in ridicule of the spurious lutes of the romantic painters.'[12]

In *Ulysses*, the purchase of a lute is under discussion between Stephen and Bloom: 'an instrument he was contemplating purchasing from Mr. Arnold Dolmetsch, whom Bloom did not quite recall, though the name certainly sounded familiar, for sixty-five guineas'.[13]

Joyce had possibly heard about Dolmetsch making a psaltery for Florence Farr, but Dolmetsch probably knew next to nothing about Joyce. He might have been surprised to learn that Joyce stemmed from several generations of Irish tenors, and indeed possessed a pleasant tenor voice himself. In his youth he had been given singing lessons by Vincent O'Brien, alongside another Dublin lad, John McCormack. When John took the Gold Medal in the *Feis Ceoil*, the annual Irish music festival, Joyce was given third place; on another occasion the two appeared together on the stage in a Grand Irish Concert at the Antient Concert Rooms in Dublin.

No doubt Dolmetsch dismissed Joyce as yet another wandering Irish Minstrel—an unaccomplished one at that. In any case he had more important things on his mind. By late summer, plans for a second American tour were being discussed. The New York agent wrote suggesting that they should arrive early in November in order to give a few concerts in that city before taking to the road. The advice 'extra lady unwise' would refer presumably to Beatrice Horne or Janet Dodge. The suggestion was evidently accepted by Dolmetsch for it was the trio as it stood, with Mabel and Kathleen Salmon, who sailed from Liverpool on 29 October, arriving just in time for their first concert at the Manhattan Theatre on 9 November.

NOTES

1. Aldrich, Richard, *Concert Life in New York* (1902–1904), Putnam, New York, 1941, pp. 17–19.
2. Now in Raymond Russell Collection at Edinburgh.

3. Worshipful Company of Musicians, *English Music*, The Walter Scott Publishing Co. Ltd., London, 1906.
4. Royal College of Music Library, now Parry Room (1973).
5. Choirboys from Westminster Abbey, where Sir Frederick Bridge was organist and choirmaster.
6. Worshipful Company of Musicians, *English Music*, The Walter Scott Publishing Co. Ltd., London, 1906, p. 189.
7. *Letters of James Joyce*, Vol. I, p. 54, ed. Stuart Gilbert, Faber and Faber Ltd., London.
8. In 1924, Dolmetsch also refused Andre Segovia's request to make him a guitar. He personally visited Dolmetsch at his home to try to persuade him, but Dolmetsch said he was 'too busy'.
9. Ellman, Richard, *James Joyce*, Oxford, 1959, p. 161.
10. Ruff, Lillian, 'James Joyce and Arnold Dolmetsch', *James Joyce Quarterly*, Vol. 6, No. 3, Spring 1969, p. 227.
11. Dolmetsch, Arnold, 'The Lute', *The Connoisseur*, April 1904, pp. 213–17.
12. Joyce, James, 'After the Race', Guild Books, 1914, *Dubliners*.
13. Joyce, James, *Ulysses*, Shakespeare & Co., Paris, 1924, p. 615.

CHAPTER XIII

'A Fine Specimen'

As before, Mr. Dolmetsch emerged in velvet knee breeches and the ladies in 'robes and furred gowns of picturesque descriptions' recalls Richard Aldrich[1] but he admonishes Dolmetsch for insisting that modern music is noise and only the old music and its instruments are good. 'Statements like this', says Aldrich, 'go to discredit Mr. Dolmetsch's soundness of judgement; but like all enthusiasts he must not be taken too literally. So much of what he offers is so charming and is so nearly unique in the musical life of today, that much exaggeration may be pardoned him. There is a singular suggestiveness in all this music and its performance that does more than can be done in any other way to bring out the historical background and to show how far the art of music has travel(l)ed in three centuries.'

Aldrich goes on to discuss Mr. Dolmetsch's reputation in London, which is, no doubt, 'based less on his proficiency as a player than on his work in restoring the old instruments to practicability and re-establishing the methods of playing them—matters indeed, deserving of high appreciation. He points out that the lute is an instrument of great difficulty and that the art of manipulating its 19 strings is one that cannot be learned today, 'for there is none to teach it. Yet for centuries it was the most popular instrument cultivated by everyone.' Aldrich then comments on the playing of all three upon the harpsichord which, as executants, cannot be compared with the lady 'who bore Mr. D's name two years ago and who played at his concerts in such a strikingly beautiful and temperamental manner'. It is obvious from this and other contemporary comment that in losing both Hélène and Elodie, Dolmetsch's performances suffered and probably never regained, in his lifetime, the overall high standard attained in what was a period of outstanding talent.[2]

The second concert, at the Mendelssohn Hall, again attracted only a small audience 'but [which] made up in eager attentiveness and appreciation for what it lacked in numbers'. Apparently Dolmetsch, for once, discarded his velvet knee breeches and appeared in 'the conventional clawhammer coat and stovepipe trousers of modern times'. The ladies, however, still wore their period costume. The *New York Times* 'doubted if modern ears sympathised as much with the music as they do with some of that of later date, but it was none the less interesting and delightful to listen to, though Mr. Dolmetsch's enthusiasm be not entirely shared'.

Undeterred by this luke-warm start the Dolmetsches played in and around Boston and New York, with concerts in Springfield, Holyoke, Northampton, Providence and then on to Baltimore, Pittsburgh, Indianapolis, Ann Arbor, Chicago. After a concert at the Steinert Hall, Boston, one writer said that the audience was appreciative but the performance deserved a larger attendance. Another critic thought the entertainment pleasanter than that offered by Mr. Dolmetsch two seasons ago, when the concert was evidently transformed into a lecture. Dolmetsch's epigrams were always good for journalistic quotation: the Boston critic selects 'In music, the survival of the loudest has been the law of the past hundred years'. The same writer does not love the lute any more than he did two years before; it 'still sounded like a banjo with two pennies under the bridge'. However, he liked Mabel's gamba solo, *Heartsease*, and praised Kathleen Salmon's brilliant performance of Handel's *Harmonious Black-smith*. Nonetheless, for him the whole occasion was weird: 'a view still held by many today largely due to the "cult" breed of early music fanciers'. His description is so graphic that it is worth recording:

> While Mr. Dolmetsch talks in praise of bygone days, the ladies, in their flowing robes, with faces as impassive as those of the Aeginetan marbles, tread stealthily about the stage, as though fearful of making a sound, taking Botticellian looking instruments from queer boxes, and putting them in place. One wonders who and what these people may be? Where do they come from, and where are they going? How came those mysterious boxes in Steinert Hall? Surely no common express-man brought them? Are these strange people actually alive? To keep alive, must they eat? If so, what is their diet? One cannot picture them sitting down to a beefsteak.
>
> *Boston Transcript*, November 23rd 1904

The tour had originally been planned for seven weeks but it was continually being extended. The later concerts were a great success, especially with the less sophisticated audiences outside the big cities.

It was at this time too that Dolmetsch met Ben Greet for the first time and was engaged to provide the music for a festival of Shakespeare plays. This was the beginning of a long association in which this gifted pair combined their respective talents to such effect. As further requests for concerts poured in from music clubs throughout the country, Dolmetsch decided with some misgiving to settle in the States for good. He had recently quarrelled with his agent and he writes to W. B. Yeats of his plans for the future:

2nd April 1905   The Virginia Hotel,
                                                     Chicago, Ill.

I have been loosing [*sic*] a lot of money in the beginning of my tour, through very bad management. But, I am my own manager now: I have not only made good all the loss, but some profit is in hand, and I see more coming. I shall not come back [to England] and will only stay . . . a few weeks. I shall return to America for an indefinite period alas! They are willing to support me here, whilst in England they let me starve . . . I am now doing a Shakespeare Festival here with Ben Greet. . . .

The Dolmetsches' temporary home for the last few months had been in Chicago, where they rented an apartment at 242 E.57th Street: so once firm plans had been made, Dolmetsch left his wife there while he returned to England to fetch Cécile, who had been boarded with friends in Dorking. He also intended selling up their home effects so as to bring only what was strictly necessary and inexpensive to transport by sea. The sum total of his financial assets at this point was $1,045, the profit from the American tour.

On 18 May, Dolmetsch writes from the *Twentieth Century Ltd.*,[3] that his heart is heavy but his work is not impeded by the fact. He nearly always writes to Mabel in French: only when he wants to explain something idiomatically does he use English: sometimes it is an engaging mixture of both. The letters are very revealing: all the impatience and intolerance is there in abundance, but so is the naïveté and sincerity, showing sadly how his foolish zeal could be misjudged.

Dolmetsch was now happy beyond measure in his new marriage and his adoration of his young wife is touching. It was a devotion that lasted through to old age, for even when he was taking cures in the South of France, those last letters are full of the most tender affection.

At the end of May, Dolmetsch and Kathleen Salmon sailed for England together. Despite a successful professional association that had lasted well over a year, Dolmetsch had no great personal admiration for the little harpsichordist. He writes gleefully of her being put in a small cabin with a very fat woman. 'Difficulté!' He tells how the fat one is removed to another cabin and that now, all alone, she will have no one to argue with. She infuriates Dolmetsch by staying in her cabin all day reading and as the days go by he finds her increasingly tiresome. His feelings about the boat are mixed. It is an English boat and quite good but all the windows are open and it is freezing: 'puis le café est abominable!' But apart from the rather too frequent serving of roast beef, the food is excellent. He writes of a brush with the ship's doctor: 'C'est un idiot!' who will not prescribe the right treatment for his ear-ache; a ship's concert, in which he did not take part, he describes with withering comment. The entire voyage seems to have been fated, for in addition to the minor irritations, Dolmetsch had travelled without sufficient money. A cable to the bank in England to wire money to Liverpool went astray and it was the Cunard Shipping Line who eventually gave them two first-class tickets to London. But even then they were unable to take a meal on the train for between them they possessed only 1s. 6d. In consequence, Dolmetsch had nothing but a 1d. madeira cake and a cup of tea to sustain him all the way to Dorking.

However, hunger pains vanished when Dolmetsch saw his baby daughter for the first time after several months' separation and his delight at the reunion is expressed on every page of his letters. We also see that in typical fashion Dolmetsch was preparing himself for the American way of life. He begins to view the English in a different light, for, seeing all the men going to work in the city, he was 'struck by the general look of dullness, stupidity and carelessness of most of them. Very different from the Americans. The women are good-looking but never seem to look straight ahead.'

The next few weeks in London were spent in feverish activity. There were half-finished instruments which must be completed, restorations to be delivered and money for both to be collected: the household effects had to be sold. In between he paid flying visits to Dorking to marvel at the 'prettiest . . . most intelligent' child ever born.

He slept in his hammock at Seymour Place and usually kept to a frugal daily diet of 'Pain 1d., milk and butter 5½d.' with a necessary 'Bain 7d.[4]' at wider spaced intervals. Occasionally he would allow himself a meal at the 'Montblanc' restaurant in Soho, where he was sure to find some of his Bloomsbury friends, but he is constantly worried about money. He mentions having written to France to enquire about his inheritance[5]; the lawyer tells him that he is able to get 3,000 fr. in 15 days, which after conversion will not amount to more than £200. Dolmetsch, in an effort to reassure his wife, still hopes that if all goes well they will not have to touch it.

Dolmetsch often worked far into the night in order to lessen the time when he could be reunited with his 'Babette'[6] and as soon as he could see the end of his work in sight he booked their passages on the *Minnehaha* sailing on 1 July. He would be taking a nurse for Cécile and they would have a cabin to themselves next door to him. The 2½ fares cost £40.

Convinced that he would not be returning to England, Dolmetsch tried to find time to take leave of some of his friends of long standing: one of these was William Poel, now an old man, disillusioned and suffering a loss of £1,300 on his recent tour. Shortly after this setback, Poel sold up his company and retired to the country to live on a very small income.

On 6 June, in a letter to Mabel, we see a reference to what may have been the first meeting between Landowska and Dolmetsch. The legendary encounter must have been much later.[7]

> A Mme Somethingska, piano player and Pleyel harpsichord player told her [Janet Dodge] that a friend of hers was engaged by Mrs. Elodie Lelong [Elodie's maiden name] for a concert in the South of France. It was arranged but at the last minute E. L. disappeared and concert did not happen. I shall meet Mrs. Smska at Mrs. Wilkinson if I can spare time and hear more perhaps.

In the same letter he tells Mabel that he also went to the preview of the sale at Sotheby's in the Strand to see the instruments belonging to the late Mr. Taphouse of Oxford. He says there is 'beaucoup de rubbish' but also a pretty ottavina, a one-octave clavichord which is too small—at four octaves it would be useful; also an Italian harpsichord which he restored himself in 1894. According to how the money from France works out, he will see what he can buy. He knows that if he can get anything at all he will easily sell it in America. He had to go to St. Margaret's-on-Thames[8] on the day of the sale and was worried in case he would not return in time; but it seems that he did attend, at least for some part of the time, and recorded details of some of the instruments and the prices they fetched:

> 7th June 1905
>
> Virginals £12, trop cher—Clavichord £15 trop cher, Clavicembalo £15—trop cher pour moi—Pipe and tabor ab. £5—trop cher tout. . . . .[9]

And then there is the sentence which must surely be the understatement of the century:

> Enfin, vers la fin j'ai acheté pour £2 un beau old English recorder 1630 boxwood and ivory. Perfect preservation. Sweet tone. . . . Cela me sera très utile.[10]

The Sotheby Catalogue lists three recorder lots:

> 61. RECORDER or Flute à Bec, English, ivory, about 1730, *in leather case, a fine specimen.*
>   The buyer was Thompson and the price £5. 2s. 6d.
> 62. RECORDER cocoa-wood and ivory; and another in ivory.
>   The buyer was Milner and the price £2. 4s. 0d.
> 63. RECORDER, Ivory by *Schobart* [Schuchart?] about 1700, *a fine specimen, in good condition.*
>   The buyer was Fenton and the price £3. 5s. 0d.

However, there seems no doubt that the recorder Dolmetsch bought was the one in leather case and dated about 1730. Dolmetsch's '1630' must have been a slip of the pen. But the identity of the purchaser is a mystery. Perhaps Dolmetsch, not knowing for certain if he could catch the train from St. Margaret's, had delegated a friend or colleague to bid for him:

or he might still have been an undischarged bankrupt, although this is unlikely since he was about to travel to the States. If he had still owed money there would have been some difficulty in leaving the country. He also writes to his wife that he bought it for £2. This could be a purely domestic deception in that he did not wish her to know that he was spending £5. 2s. 6d. on a recorder when they needed all the money they had for sheer survival. We know that he was at the same time trying to sell various pieces from their home that had been in store for the past year, and he writes to tell her every time a piece was sold and the price it fetched.

Apart from the rather painful encounter with the recorder in his student days in Brussels (see p. 12) he had not experimented with any of the early wind instruments. To the musical historians the recorder was yet another anachronism: they loved to talk about it and listened carefully to any account of its evolution. One notable occasion was the 24th Session of the *Musical Association*, at which Mr. C. Welch[11] read a paper on 'The Recorder', discussing its history from its origins in the South Seas to Egyptian flutes and the zenith of its popularity, about 1512. In an account in the *Musical Times* of 1 July 1898, Mr. Welch makes it quite clear that, in his opinion, the recorder is dead:

> Just as the harpsichord gave way to the pianoforte, so the Recorder yielded to the German flute, the greater command over sustained notes and the power of influencing intonation possessed by the lip flute proved too strong to be resisted, and an indication that the career of the Recorder was drawing near to a close was to be found in its name undergoing another change. The German flute was called 'the flute' and the Recorder was called, 'the common flute'. Its knell was now about to sound; with the harpsichord it scarcely survived the eighteenth century.

Certainly it remained so, until Arnold Dolmetsch attended the Sotheby's sale with a few pounds in his pocket intent on buying a set of virginals.

The next almost sleepless weeks were spent in preparation for the trip. Every letter is concerned with selling off their possessions, trying to finish making the instruments that were outstanding, and paying various debts. This naturally affected Dolmetsch's health and he writes of feeling too ill to manage the journey. But change, as always, works wonders for his infirmities: at all events he appears to have arrived safely at Tilbury on the Friday evening of 30 June, complete with Cécile, the nurse and 41 cases weighing about 3,500 lbs.

After a few days at sea his letters are full of hope for the future and the small pleasures of the voyage itself. Apparently there were some cows aboard and it did not take Dolmetsch long to make a satisfactory deal with the steward in charge of them. For the rest of the trip he took Cécile twice daily to collect a supply of fresh milk in a jug: no doubt to the amusement of the other passengers.

If Dolmetsch's spirits were flagging when he boarded the ship, they were sharply revived by the success of a concert lecture he gave to his fellow voyagers. According to Dolmetsch, all who attended were delighted with a programme which included some Shakespeare songs, the *Earle of Salisbury's Pavan* and *Galliard*, with music by Purcell, Scarlatti and Bach thrown in for good measure: all played on the harpsichord which he took into the dining saloon. But Dolmetsch's new love was the boxwood and ivory recorder and he practised each evening in his cabin after Cécile had gone to bed. Until this time he had thought that flute fingering would be a natural choice for the recorder, but he soon realised his mistake—a conclusion due to Dolmetsch's acquisition of *The Compleat Flutemaster*[12] from Taphouse in exchange for an instrument from his own collection. He does not mention the tutor in his letters but in his diary of 26th and 27th June he writes: 'Taphouse books'. To Dolmetsch the recorder was a delightful new toy: he had not the slightest inkling that he had started a revolution which by the middle of the century would make the *flute à bec* one of the most popular instruments in the world.

NOTES

1. Aldrich, Richard, *Concert Life in New York*, pp. 75–6.
2. However, by the late 1930s, the individual performances by Rudolph and Carl Dolmetsch were certainly responsible for much improvement in the standards of playing at the Haslemere Festival.
3. The 20th Century Ltd., was the crack New York-Chicago express rather like the Brighton Belle.
4. Dolmetsch's diaries (now at Jesses) contain detailed accounts of his daily expenses.
5. Inheritance was probably from his grandmother, but the exact details are not available.
6. 'Babette' was Dolmetsch's pet name for his wife: sometimes he called her the more usual 'Mab'.
7. There are various accounts of the meeting between Landowska and Dolmetsch: some say that Dolmetsch gave Landowska the idea of playing the harpsichord and that she fell at his feet when they met, calling him 'Maestro!'. Dolmetsch claimed that she asked him to make her an instrument for nothing—as did Pleyel—because she was a great artist. Dolmetsch is reputed to have refused saying she knew nothing about harpsichord-playing and that he never 'gave away' his instruments. From Landowska's point of view the story is told in reverse but neither source can be relied upon. Carl Dolmetsch claims that he was present when Landowska and some of her pupils visited his father at Haslemere in 1927 and that she addressed Dol-

metsch as 'Le Maître' and admired his latest instrument. She told him that she had taken up the harpsichord at her late husband's suggestion after they had heard him playing at a concert in Paris. However, it is interesting to note that on 15 November 1905, Landowska played in one of Niecks' 'Historical Concerts' at Edinburgh, called 'J. S. Bach and his Contemporaries'. She used both harpsichord and piano, as follows:

> Bach and Couperin—harpsichord
> Zipoli, Durante, Domenico Scarlatti,
> Handel, Matthewson, Telemann, Clerambault
> and Daquin—piano.

8. The home of a Mrs. Woolridge, a once-famous ballerina. She bought the forte-piano for Stewart Headlam (see p. 143). Fifty years later, when she was ninety-six, she gave this instrument to Carl Dolmetsch and it is now played regularly in the Haslemere Festival.

9. Virginals £12, too dear—clavichord, £15, too dear—harpsichord, £15, too dear for me—pipe and tabor ab. £5 all too— dear.

10. Finally, just before the end, I bought for £2 a beautiful old English recorder 1630 . . . It will be very useful to me.

11. The first of *Six Lectures on the Recorder and other Flutes in relation to Literature*, published in 1911 and more recently by Oxford University Press in 1961 with a new introduction by Edgar Hunt.

12. *The Compleat Flutemaster*, Dolmetsch Library, Jesses, Haslemere.

CHAPTER XIV

Dolmetsch At The White House

SHORTLY after Dolmetsch's return to the States, Mabel gave birth to a second daughter, Nathalie, an event which seems to have done little to disrupt the ever-increasing number of concerts in which she took part. In November of the same year, Dolmetsch was again asked to provide music for a Ben Greet season in New York—an engagement that brought about his first meeting with two young actors on their first American tour, Sybil Thorndike and her brother, Russell. In her eighties, Dame Sybil recalled that association with affection:

'He looked as if he had jumped out of an Elizabethan picture . . . dressed in a mole coloured velvet suit . . . he looked charming . . . a wonderful musician too . . . but we used to have terrible arguments . . . he would say, "Why do you bother with such a hateful instrument as the piano? . . ." I told him I loved it . . . the feel . . . and the sort of velvet sound you can get out of the piano that you can't get out of an instrument that is just strings. The battles were not confined to harpsichord v. piano. My goodness he would argue! . . . He'd argue the toss about every mortal thing . . . and always got his own way with Ben Greet . . . *always*! Whatever Greet wanted . . . Arnold wanted something different, and Arnold won! But we loved touring with them . . . they looked enchanting in their costumes . . . I think they looked more enchanting than the players sometimes!'

Dame Sybil recalled the occasion when she had to play Katharine in *Henry V* at a moment's notice. The Dutch-French actress originally engaged for the part had lost her temper with Greet and had been asked to leave. 'So I went on . . . The Dolmetsches were so sweet and kind . . . they gave me some lovely little music for my entrance and did everything they could to help. . . . They were always so *a propos* with everything . . . absolutely authentic.' Dame Sybil is often reminded of these days when she hears modern settings of Shakespeare's songs. 'I never quite get away from it . . . I think to myself, Oh *no*! That's not a bit what Dolmetsch would have liked!'

During the winter of 1905 Dolmetsch signed a contract with Chickering's of Boston, America's leading firm of piano makers, to open a department for the manufacture of early keyboard instruments, viols and lutes. Here he would be his own master, completely in charge of staff and the selection of materials. It is not known exactly how much he earned, but there are still visible signs of the prosperity that the family enjoyed at this, the only time in their lives when they were truly free from financial worry. It is interesting to note that the theory of artists producing their best work under conditions of poverty and stress does not appear to have applied to Dolmetsch; for him it was quite the opposite. There is no question that some of his best work was produced in the Chickering factory[1] during the six years of his association with the firm.

One of the first to write congratulating Dolmetsch on his new venture was Bernard Shaw.[2] He can no longer bear to hear pianists struggling with their fingers, and has come to the conclusion that the human hand is too mechanical for music. With the advent of pneumatic suction he contends that there is no difficulty with fingering, besides which it 'allows much more poetry and individuality' One can readily imagine the twinkle in those famous eyes as he wrote: 'Have you ever studied the pianola? A pianola that will play the clavichord is indispensable if the clavichord is to be a success.' It is a pity that Dolmetsch's reply is not available.

Early in the new year, Dolmetsch brought his family to Boston and in April they moved out to the little town of Cambridge, taking a house at 16 Arlington Street. Situated on the Charles river and bordered by green fields, Cambridge was a quiet and pleasant spot in which to live; it had an added charm for Dolmetsch for the red-brick, English-style buildings of Harvard University reminded him of the country he had been so reluctant to leave. There was also no difficulty in reaching the factory since the trams were then running from Harvard Square right into the centre of Boston.

Once Dolmetsch's fame had reached the ears of the more artistically inclined members of Boston society, they were eager to make his acquaintance, to have such a distinguished European in their midst was indeed an acquisition. Dolmetsch, in addition to having achieved financial security, was also now accepted in society, his wife being called upon by the town's leading hostesses. This had never happened in England, so it is not surprising that Dolmetsch warmed to his new surroundings. None the less he could still deal effectively with those who infringed upon his self-imposed rules for audience behaviour. One afternoon, when asked to perform at the fashionable Boston Arts Club, he arrived on the platform to find the ladies still engrossed in conversation to the accompaniment of rattling teacups, as was their habit, ignoring him completely. Dolmetsch waited for some acknowledgement but none came. He tapped sharply on the lid of the clavichord with his knuckles and the noise ceased immediately. With a bemused expression on his face he addressed the sea of frozen bonnets whilst their owners sat open-mouthed at this unaccustomed treatment. 'Ladies! If you do not stop talking, I cannot play!' said Dolmetsch. 'The voice of this instrument is like that of the mosquito: it cannot be heard above a noise, so until you stop I will not play!' A lady who had been present remarked later that it was the first time anyone had called Boston's élite to order, but they responded without a murmur and he had their rapt attention for the rest of the afternoon.

There was no shortage of pupils who wanted to learn the viols, and Dolmetsch did not take long to seek out the most talented to form a consort; soon he was able to give *intimes* in his own home, run on the same lines as they had been in London, with coffee and Mabel's home-made *petits fours* served in the interval. These evenings usually attracted a few notables such as the Longfellows or the notorious Mrs. Jack Gardner,[3] but they also tempted an occasional member of the Boston Symphony Orchestra.

One particular family, the Kelseys, were closely associated with the Dolmetsches throughout their stay in Cambridge. There were three children, Laura, Alice and Paul, all musical and eager to learn about the early music. From Alice Kelsey's[4] diary in 1906, when she was fourteen, we learn some interesting sidelights on the Dolmetsch approach. In the beginning, she was taken on by Mabel and on arriving for her first lesson she was shown a painting by Ter Borch so that she could see how to hold the bow. After she had made sufficient progress she was permitted to meet the master himself, 'a most fascinating man and a pure musician'. The entries show how strong an influence Dolmetsch exercised over his pupils. Hardly a day passes without mention of the name. 'Hurried to the Dolmetsches . . . D showed us some old pictures before we went home. Looked over . . . Ben Greet programmes . . . found . . . the . . . music . . . arranged and played by Mr. Dolmetsch . . . Tomorrow I shall learn to play the treble viol. I hope I shall not be stupid . . . Mrs. D says I have a good wrist . . . Mr. D says my tone is good.'

The speed with which pupils were brought into performance cannot be judged in retrospect for these may not have been anything more than practise concerts, but Alice was given her first lesson on the treble viol on 19 October and had a lesson almost daily, some 'good', others 'rotten'. On 3 November she writes: 'My pavin went very well and I am to play in the quartette, Sunday.' This apparently went well, as did Dolmetsch's playing of the viola d'amore, which 'has a soft, rich dreamy tone so beautiful that it makes me shiver'.

Perhaps because of her extreme youth, Alice Kelsey did not remember being afraid of Dolmetsch, whom she found was 'mostly wrapped up in business'. She recalls that he was sometimes very caustic with his wife, which she [Alice Kelsey] disliked, but she does not remember him being particularly harsh with her—if she made an honest mistake. However, she recollects most vividly that when she told Dolmetsch that she was going on to Radcliffe instead of taking up music full-time, he stormed at her, telling her she was making a terrible mistake.

In September 1906, Wm. B. White, editor of the technical column of *The Music Trade Review* (Sept. 1906), takes a look at the progress being made in Dolmetsch's department at Chickering's. We learn that the business is thriving; many old instruments have been restored and a number of new instruments made in response to the demand by private customers. The writer discusses the differences between the piano and the plucked stringed keyboard instruments and the suitability of their being played for the early music. He supports this thesis by comparing the differences in the harmony of the two periods: the 'vertical' of the contemporary music and the 'linear' of the polyphonic era: no wonder the latter sounds weak on a modern piano when this instrument cannot supply the separate voice of each instrumental compass required by such music. He presents a sound and logical case for the ancient instruments and further explains in detail how the keyboard instruments work and the various kinds of touch are obtained.

He is in no doubt as to why Bach preferred the clavichord to the piano, 'even though the first crude and feeble hammer-harpsichord of his day possessed far greater dynamic resources as regards mere volume than did the clavichord, for, indeed, the player of the clavichord was enabled to express his feelings upon it in a manner that cannot be duplicated on the piano. So we find ourselves, in considering this instrument, face to face, with a realm of tone production at present entirely unfamiliar to the greater part of the musical world.'

In order to publicize his work at Chickering's and also to keep his name before the public, Dolmetsch would go on an occasional tour of the eastern and middle-western states, safe in the knowledge that his skilled workmen were capable of carrying on in his absence. These concerts were generally received with enthusiasm and the press often devoted several columns to the description of both instruments and costumes—clearly an excellent advertisement:

> The pathos, beauty, true musical quality of their performance will long linger in the memory. When the Chickerings send out their harpsichords and clavichords they will find welcome in many homes.
>
> *Wisconsin State Journal, Madison*
> Feb. 22nd 1906

Another platform that offered Dolmetsch the opportunity to demonstrate his instruments was that of the Chickering Concert Hall on Huntingdon Avenue. Built in 1901, it was then in the very latest design with neo-classical pillars, art nouveau decor and an abundance of red plush. The acoustics were excellent and a large audience could be seated in comfort. The first series of Dolmetsch concerts was given there in February 1907; tickets for the three cost $5.00, a single seat $2, with a special reduction for students.

A critic in the *Boston Transcript* on 23 February gives a whole column to his impressions of the first concert, dealing in particular with Dolmetsch's study of the tempi and ornamentation of harpsichord playing, together with the sources of his research. The reviewer mentions the Couperin *Methode de l'art de toucher le clavecin*, 'a book which had a palpable influence upon Sebastian Bach', as being frequently consulted by Dolmetsch, since it contained full and accurate information of the important question of the interpretation of the embellishments.

Another well-consulted book is the Emmanuel Bach *Versuch, über die wahre Art das Klavier zu spielen*, dating from 1780 and which gives indispensable material for the execution of works by his father, the great Johann Sebastian, in the principles of fingering and execution of ornaments:

> The striking feature of his performances, and of others under his direction, is the ardent sympathy displayed with the spirit of this bygone age. One of his strongest convictions is that musical art in all times is but the mirror of the habits of thought, and the personal habits of its musicians.'

Since Dolmetsch was convinced that this was true of his contemporaries, it seemed logical to suppose this to be so regarding the earlier period. He is quoted on his view that 'The time has come when cultivated people must acknowledge that they should know the old music and judge it for themselves, instead of accepting what ill-informed and prejudiced writers say on the subject.'

As always, there were conflicting opinions and one writer declared that it was the group of players on the stage who were the counterfeits in this performance. He qualifies his assumption by saying that the audience of 1907, as children of their time, are attuned to the music of the same period. He did not hold high hopes for Mr. Dolmetsch's efforts to change people's natural reactions. (*Boston Transcript*, 28 February 1907)

Another doubtful voice is that of Philip Hales in the *Boston Herald*. 28 March 1907. Although at first he finds the performances charming and interesting, after a while the combination of timbres blends so intimately that they become aggressively monotonous. 'A little of this music played after the ancient manner is delightful. A concert devoted to the music of Bach and performed in the historical manner is well nigh intolerable.' As to the harpsichord, 'for a few minutes [it] is piquant: it interests, it amuses, and then its acidity and coldness fret the nerves which have been accustomed to a more sensuous tone. Mr. D. would say that too much importance is put on fullness and sensuousness of tone. Aesthetically, he may be right, but it would be necessary for him to educate the public taste backward (chronologically) if he wishes it to share honestly his enthusiasm.'

However, Edward Burlingham Hill, in the *New Music Review*,[5] seems to have captured the very essence of Dolmetsch's aims:

> In considering Mr. D's personality as displayed in his manifold activities, as performer, lecturer, or artist-artisan, one dominating trait detaches itself at the very outset, his unswerving fidelity throughout to the traditions and sentiments of the epoch with which he deals, his total absorption in scrupulous reconstruction as far as possible of conditions then existing. No compromise or deviation is permitted from the exact intelligible guidance furnished by authorities whose standing was deemed irreproachable by their own contemporaries; this consistent adherence to genuine sources of tradition constitutes Mr. D's strength and pervading sense of his authenticity which is the distinguishing feature of all that he attempts.

We learn also from this writing that Dolmetsch's library appears to have been considerably restored since its depletion in 1901. Several manuscripts are mentioned by name. Ariosti; 6 Lessons for Viola d'Amore, Corelli; complete works, Frescobaldi; harpsichord works (1657), Handel; all instrumental and many vocal works and suites for violin with figured bass and Nicola Matteis; sonatas for violin and harpsichord, Marais; *Pièces de viole* in 8 books, Lulli; operas *Atys*, *Armide*, *Rolando*, *Achilles et Polyxène*, *Bellerophon*: works by Senaille, Leclair, Vivaldi, Albinoni and many others. Since this article also mentions manuscript copies of music made under his supervision of some 4,000 songs, it is more than likely that Dolmetsch had managed to hold back his hand-copied viol music when the bailiffs had seized everything. There is no proof that he did so, but the possession of such a large amount of manuscript only a few years afterwards would point to some kind of an attempt to preserve a substantial part of it. Finally the writer discusses several aspects of Dolmetsch's work in detail drawing some interesting comparisons. His summing up is Dolmetsch to perfection: 'That we forget the archaeologist and are conscious only of the artist is perhaps his greatest triumph.'

* * *

In November 1906 the Dolmetsches' third child was born; at last they had the son they so eagerly awaited. Both the girls were blonde but

Rudolph inherited from his Italian forebears an olive-skin and black curly hair. Within a year Dolmetsch recognised his son's phenomenal musical ear and he began to plan his future with as much care as a monarch arranges his heir's betrothal.

With a growing family and a well-filled purse, Dolmetsch decided to build a house to his own design, and in the autumn of 1907 he sketched the outline. Finished in the following spring it was deemed 'un-American' for a variety of reasons. Instead of being built on Elmwood Avenue, along-side the other houses, no. 11[6] was situated at the end of a long drive backing on to other houses and gardens, well concealed from the road. Dolmetsch wanted seclusion and this was the only way to achieve it. The 30-foot music-room[7] ran the length of the house and was fitted with soundproof French windows. The large dining-room, divided from the music-room by folding doors, opened on to a piazza almost as large as itself where the family would take their meals in summer. There was a fine bathroom with an 'automatic, instantaneous water-warmer',[8] five bedrooms, an upstairs sitting-room and a large room in the attic, complete with window and running water, that Dolmetsch used for a workroom. All the floors were beautifully laid in strips of beech and pine, and the staircase was designed with four steps and a landing throughout so that the children should not hurt themselves if they fell.

The most typical Dolmetsch touch was to be seen in the bannister rails made of flat strips of pine in which the shapes of instruments and treble and bass clefs were cut out, each landing marked with a 'pause' sign.

The garden planning received as much attention from Dolmetsch as if he had been making an instrument. The espaliers he planted caused considerable interest among the natives since the only fruit trees they knew grew in a straight line. Vegetables and flowers received the same devotion from this man who could never truthfully decide between music and horticulture. His vigilance occasionally shocked early-risers who were privileged to behold Dolmetsch performing some gardening task at five o'clock in the morning, barefoot and clad only in pyjamas.

The neatly printed notices which were an indispensable part of Dol-metsch's concert-giving were sent out in October and announced that the series would take place at Elmwood Avenue and, it was hoped, would prove 'an intellectual treat of a high order'. Dolmetsch does not excuse the comparatively high price for admission as 'musicians must receive some recompense for their labours'. Artfully he reminds his patrons that in the 17th and 18th centuries it was usual to charge a guinea a seat for such performances, a sum equalling 15 dollars at the present time. None the less, he is aware that 'those who can appreciate refined and delicate things do not always possess a well-stocked purse'; he therefore offers tickets at

$4 per concert or $10 as a subscription to all three, the number of places being limited to 30. However, he informs his prospective audience that the music will begin at 8.30 punctually and it is expected that no one will arrive late or leave early and that there should be no disturbance during the evening. The music will last not more than one hour and twenty minutes, which, with an interval for refreshments and conversation, should bring the evening to a close at ten minutes to ten.

The Johnston family were a tenacious breed, and this quality was not lacking in the quiet-voiced Mabel. Whenever an opportunity arose to further the cause of her husband's work, she took advantage of it to the utmost. In the winter of 1908 there came the chance to promote interest both in Dolmetsch and her own family. Her brother Sir Harry Johnston, the explorer,[9] was about to make his first visit to the USA and Mabel wrote to inform the President of this fact. Theodore Roosevelt's interest in big-game hunting was well known and he replied promptly, showing eagerness to meet 'her distinguished brother'. He straightway invited him to dine at the White House for he wished to discuss many things, from big-game hunting to the condition of Liberia. Eventually the celebrated Sir Harry stayed at the White House and, as a result, Dolmetsch himself wrote to the President. On 14 December he received the following reply:

The White House

My dear Mr. Dolmetsch,

Indeed it would give Mrs. Roosevelt and myself great pleasure if you could come to the White House on Wednesday, at 2.30, and let us hear the clavichord. It is most kind of you to make the offer. I heard much of you thru Sir Harry Johnston, and of course entirely independently know about your work in introducing the harpsichord and clavichord, at least to the American world of music.

Sincerely yours,
Theodore Roosevelt

Despite the counter-attraction of election campaigning, the visit took place as planned on 17 December. Whether the President enjoyed the experience or not is open to question, but the publicity derived from the occasion benefited Dolmetsch considerably.

Another distinguished meeting which took place some two years later was with the pianist and composer Ferruccio Busoni, who in a letter to his wife[10] describes a visit to Mr. Dolmetsch at his home in Cambridge:

12 April 1910   Boston

He [Dolmetsch] looks like a little faun, with a handsome head, and lives in the past. He builds pianos, clavecins and clavichords. The clavecin (the English harpsichord) is magnificent. I made capital out of it at once, first of all, brought the instrument into the Brautwahl[11] . . . and secondly, begged for one to be sent to Berlin. They are beautiful outside too.

Busoni subsequently took harpsichord lessons from Dolmetsch: from a letter to his wife we learn:

30 April 1910   Hotel Astor
                                                                  New York

Busoni a eu une bonne leçon hier—Encore une ce matin. Il est très intelligent et très enthousiaste—. . . Il [Busoni] m'a dit 'Êtes vous content de votre élève?' J'ai dit, 'Il doit y avoir longtemps que vous ne prenez plus de leçons.' Il répond 'Personne ne m'a jamais rien enseigné—J'ai appris tout seul!' J'ai repondu 'on ne peut rien enseigner à *personne*.' Il a dit '*C'est Vrai*! Mais alors les élèves? Il en faut des élèves . . .'[12]

*   *   *

Life at Elmwood Avenue continued to be happy and uneventful. Dolmetsch worked under ideal conditions with a reliable and competent staff: his right-hand man, an immigrant Swede who had originally trained as a violin-maker, had now become a highly skilled maker of viols and lutes. In a household augmented by a French governess, a cook and a parlourmaid, Mabel had time to teach, entertain and accompany her husband on concert tours. They had holidays in the Catskill mountains, like most of their neighbours, and lacked very little in material comforts. It was probably as near a conventional existence as was possible for the Dolmetsches either before or after this time. But American living has always been subject to flux, even in that first decade of the 20th century. The Dolmetsches had enjoyed their new house for less than two years when the tide of prosperity began to turn.

NOTES

1. There is a comprehensive list of instruments completed at this time in the archives of Chickering and Sons, Rochester, N.Y. This includes the instrument made for Busoni, now in possession of Ralph Kirkpatrick, no. 60, dated 1909.

2. Laurence, Dan H., *Shaw Collected Letters*, 26 January 1906, Doheny Library, Calif.

3. A wealthy patroness of the arts. She built an Italian-style palace in Boston and filled it with 14th- and 15th-century paintings and sculpture: it is now the Gardner Museum.

4. Alice Kelsey, now Mrs. John Dunn of Ann Arbor, Mich.

5. *New Music Review*, Sep. 1907, No. 70, Vol. 6.

6. When the streets were renumbered, 11 Elmwood Avenue became 192 Brattle Street. The April 1912 *The House Beautiful and American Shrubs* (New York), pp. 135/6, has a story and pictures of the Brattle Street House. The article is entitled 'A Small Plaster House—Luquer and Godfrey, Architects'.

7. This room is today virtually the same as when owned by Dolmetsch: only white paint has replaced the brown. No structural alterations have been made. Simon Marks, who bought the house from Dolmetsch in 1911, inserted a codicil in the deeds preserving the staircase in its original condition.

8. Letter from Alex Johnston to his sister congratulating her on 'this wonderful modern invention' which seemed 'too good to be true!' 15 December 1907.

9. Sir Harry Johnston achieved considerable fame through discovering the okapi (Lat. *okapia johnstoni*) in 1901 in the Semliki forest (then) Belgian Congo.

10. Ferruccio Busoni, *Letters to his Wife*, translated by Rosamond Ley, Arnold, London, 1938, p. 172. Original in *Briefe an seine Frau*, ed. Friedrich Schnapp (Zürich & Leipzig, 1935).

11. Busoni's opera *Die Brautwahl*, first performed at Hamburg in 1912.

12. Busoni had a good lesson yesterday and another one this morning. He is very intelligent and very enthusiastic. . . . He [Busoni] asked me, 'Are you happy with your pupil?' I said that he needs to have more lessons. He replied 'No one has ever given me lessons. I have learnt everything myself.' I replied 'One is not able to teach anything to anybody.' He said, 'This is true, but what about the pupils? One needs the pupils.'

CHAPTER XV

Dolmetsch The Conductor

THE trade recession of 1910 was crippling commerce all over the USA, and Chickering's began to doubt the wisdom of maintaining Dolmetsch's luxury department when orders for their mass-produced pianos were steadily declining. Reluctantly the directors told him that they could not renew his contract when it expired the following year. It seems that they had offered him some alternative employment but since it would have inevitably concerned piano-making, Dolmetsch refused. Chickering's trustee, writing the following year, considers Dolmetsch's decision to leave 'a wise move . . . for a while, until matters are in a more settled condition [in the USA]'.

The prospect of yet another fresh start at the age of 52, this time with a wife and children to support, would have daunted most men. But Dolmetsch generated resilience and soon a batch of letters despatched to London and Paris set new ideas into motion. In a letter congratulating his old friend, Selwyn Image, for having been elected Slade Professor, he writes:

> August 24 1910   11, Elmwood Avenue,
> Cambridge.
>
> Don't come to America. There are advantages but they are not sufficient to compensate all the fine things one loses. There are lots of learned people—experts on every subject. But all their knowledge seems to be artificially acquired. It never seems to penetrate them! . . . But I am *at last* going to Europe, in October. I shall be in London on my way to Paris for concerts about October 20. And what a delight to go to the old 20 Fitzroy Street and ring your bell!! I hope you will be there. . . . We have prospered well. We have three delightful children and a nice house, good garden, brilliant birds and lots of butterflies the size of this paper.

Image hastened to remind Dolmetsch that if he came he would find London noisier, for the taxi-cabs, cars and motor buses were now fitted with infernal horns 'which blow up on every side of us . . . with raucous noises like pandemonium let loose!' However, this time Dolmetsch was looking further than London. The Parisian musical instrument-making industry was increasing in importance and all three major houses had responded warmly to Dolmetsch's inquiries. So even though his future was at stake, Dolmetsch sailed from New York in late September as eager as a young man seeking his fortune.

His extraordinary gift for reorientation exudes from the letters to his wife, written during the voyage. The boat, the *Ivernia*, was British and English cooking, for which he had never previously shown any preference, now becomes a gastronomic miracle: grouse, pheasant, plum pudding, boiled mutton and 'delicious' tea are talked of as if they were part of a Lucullan banquet, whilst lunch served on the train between Liverpool and London receives underlinings worthy of Queen Victoria. '*Damson Tart*, REAL, Delicious!'

At his London hotel the mood persists: 'Could not think of French . . . too happy to be in old England.' He delights in seeing familiar streets still unchanged, and at the Artworkers' Guild everything down to the 'old plain wooden-white scrubbed round table' has endured in his absence. There are two noteworthy exceptions, 'automobiles and large hats', but he concedes that the latter are not as enormous as those worn by American women, and less ugly.

It is surprising that he had time to notice things like female headgear, for his three weeks in London were packed with activity. He gave one highly successful concert at Clifford's Inn and a few at private houses. All the old friends turned up in force: the Mackails, the Rothensteins, Violet Gordon Woodhouse, John Todhunter, Neville Lytton, Norman Wilkinson, and W. B. Yeats with Florence Farr. Dolmetsch is particularly happy with the results of the Clifford's Inn concert, from which, with '63 tickets paid for' and his expenses at only £7, he will have 'quite a little profit'. The clavichord, as always, seemed to triumph. 'I never played better!' On this high note of confidence Dolmetsch leaves for Paris.

Writing from Montmartre, Dolmetsch is 'full of hope'. He has just seen M. Gaveau, who has admired his instruments 'enormously' and has promised to see him again on the following Sunday. Tired but excited after the interview, he writes to say that he has received a definite offer from Gaveau which may not be a fortune but on which one or even five would not starve: 500 frs. ($100) a month, fixed salary, freedom to give concerts and keep all profits, and in addition half the profit on all instruments sold. Gaveau were also willing to give 5 or 6,000 francs to help with their cost of moving. But Dolmetsch was leaving the offer open whilst he collected some 'real figures' as to the cost of living, which, on the face of things, appeared to be immeasurably lower than in the USA.

Dolmetsch was also playing for time: as yet he had seen neither Pleyel nor Erard, the two other Parisian manufacturers. Pleyel had agreed to attend a concert demonstration arranged by *S.I.M.*[1] the following day at the Bibliothèque Nationale, and Erard, whom he usually deemed un-approachable, were cordially prepared to come and see him and his instruments at any time convenient to him.

Dolmetsch's genius for self-deception was engendered more by enthusiasm than fantasy: he could don the mantle of the moment without difficulty and in the final paragraph of his letter he has, for the occasion, put on his 'French' coat:

> Sunday night   51, rue de Clichy,
> [31 October 1910]   Paris
> *This* is the *best* place in the world—People have more taste, knowledge, and less prejudice than in England—They *all* say I am wanted in Paris—They seem to discover it by instinct—And they say; 'Vous êtes *Frr*ançais [sic] n'est ce pas? Et je dis, oui, naturellement!

A few days later, still in high spirits, he is triumphant at having 'tamed' a 'cellist into playing the viola da gamba for some later performances. The concert demonstration at the Bibliothèque Nationale appears to have been a 'Succès de premier ordre. Gens très interessants là qui m'ont fait une vrai ovation'. With his natural lack of modesty Dolmetsch declares that he 'spoke admirably and played [the clavichord] very well . . . the lute also'. He goes on to say that the French singer Madeleine Bonnard sang *Que vous contez cher mon coeur* with the utmost perfection, Ecorcheville, the director of *S.I.M.*, having remarked that by comparison to her previous performances her ornamentation was greatly improved.

By 9 November, although trying not to transmit his anxiety to Mabel, Dolmetsch is feeling apprehensive. 'This is the worst time to go through . . only two more days and nothing settled . . . of course there is plenty of hope. . . .' There appears now to be some uncertainty about the Gaveau offer, since they have a lawsuit pending and Dolmetsch's job depends largely on the outcome. The head of the firm of Erard had come to his concert and had 'raved about his instruments and his playing', but they were now out of the running. 'This' writes Dolmetsch, 'is *quite* as much, and more, than could have been expected from a fossil house like that one.' He still believes his best hope is with Pleyel although, owing to a general strike at the factory, their director could not come to his concert. The following day, after the interview with Pleyel, Dolmetsch writes again that he prefers Gaveau's terms, but since they must await the result of the lawsuit it is well to nurse the other 'so that they have something to fall back upon'. He is convinced that 'it will end all right'. Dolmetsch's confidence was well founded, for, although no decision had been made when he returned to Boston in November, in the following spring Gaveau's legal difficulties were smoothed out and the contract signed.

It was fitting that Dolmetsch's final engagement of importance in the States should have taken place at Harvard University, for which he had made a number of instruments which had been in use for some time. He was asked to give a series of 12 lectures in the old Fogg Museum on 'Early Music and its Instruments'. The subjects were already familiar to the Dolmetsch-orientated students: Music at the Court of King Henry VIII, Elizabethan music, and on to Purcell right through to the Italian, French, Spanish and German composers of the 16th to the 18th centuries, bringing the study full circle with the music of J. S. Bach and the transition between Bach and Haydn. The lectures attracted large audiences which included members of the general public as well as students. Richard Appel,[2] then a freshman at the university, recalled having attended all 12; for him the lectures had opened up a completely new world and it was from this initiation that a life-long study developed.

As soon as the lectures were over, the family began organising themselves for the transatlantic crossing. They sailed for France on 29 March with all their possessions, including a store of seasoned wood that Dolmetsch had collected over the years and which had automatically become part of their luggage. Some of these were prize pieces of maple and sycamore that he had reserved for his 'One day' list for making violins. Even the patient Mabel sometimes protested at the eternal transport of a package of such bulk, but Dolmetsch would sooner have parted with his best suit than leave behind his precious timber. So alongside the cases, holdalls, trunks and wicker baskets went the wood, packed as carefully as if it were a set of Dresden china. According to Mademoiselle Gaisser, the French governess, the entire move went without a hitch, Mrs. Dolmetsch remaining cheerful and calm throughout: quite an achievement for a woman with three small children at her skirts and another on the way.

The Gaveau factory was situated at Fontenay-sous-bois, a village of some 10,000 inhabitants only three miles outside the fortifications of Paris and barely 15 minutes by train from the Gare de Vincennes. Flanked as it was by woods and fields, it seemed to Dolmetsch to be a hundred miles from the city. They took to their new surroundings very quickly: on 29 June 1911, Dolmetsch wrote to Simon Marks, the man who had bought his house in Cambridge:

3, Rue de l'Audience,
Fontenay-sous-Bois
Seine.

We are now settled in a nice old house, with walled garden, in a pretty old village a few miles out of Paris.

The music room is too small, but the rent is only $240 a year, plus about $40 for taxes and water! You see, one can afford to make a little less money under such circumstances.

I enclose the list of plants in your garden. I hope you will be able to make something of it. I have not found any simple book on the pruning of trees in espalier. But I shall look again. We miss our old house very much. However, we are quite happy here, we find that it is quite possible to do without electric light, bathroom, and ice cream, or even plain ice. We get over it some other way!

From the artistic point of view, the surroundings are incomparably more congenial here than in America. I am one among a number of people who work on lines similar with mine, whilst in America I was alone, preaching in the desert!

If Paris stimulated Dolmetsch's craving for renewed contact with European culture, it did little to promote the great revival in early music that he had anticipated. In many ways it was a disappointing period: although he made some fine instruments during this time and completed a number of important restorations, he was continually frustrated by the restrictions placed upon him. Working conditions were far from ideal and Gaveau were not prepared to spend money on his department. He was fortunate in that Nils Ericsson, his right-hand man from Boston, gave up his job at Chickerings to join him in Paris. Ericsson worked for considerably lower wages, but stayed with the firm until Dolmetsch moved on. In time, the contract with Gaveau also revealed its flaws, when the agreed percentage system turned out to be unrealistic in terms of pure income.

It is a curious and sad reflection that Dolmetsch now felt alien amongst his own people: that is except for a small group of personal friends such as Gabriele d'Annunzio, the poet whom Dolmetsch had first met when he gave a concert in Rome in 1897: the two had since become friends. They were in the habit of going for long country walks together and d'Annunzio was a constant visitor to the Dolmetsches' house at Fontenay-sous-Bois. On one occasion they had all met accidentally at a concert and d'Annunzio insisted upon driving the entire family home, announcing at the same time that he would like to dine with them. As he was a vegetarian, Mabel had to make a few hasty purchases en route. The main part of that evening and half the next morning were spent making plans for the production of a play of d'Annunzio's at a Paris theatre in which the heroine would play the viol; all the music would be played on stage, using Dolmetsch and his instruments. These ideas were followed up by letters and telegrams as and when the poet had new inspiration, but the collaboration never materialised. Though the play *La Pisanelle* or *Perfumed Death*, was put on, Dolmetsch was not engaged; the instruments were stage properties handled by supers, and a hidden orchestra played the music off-stage. This was said to have come about because when Dolmetsch was introduced to the lady who had promised to finance the effort, he, with typical tactlessness, had made some derogatory remarks about her pet monkeys.

*   *   *

Carl Frédéric, the Dolmetsches' second son, was born on 23 August at Fontenay-sous-Bois. They now had a full family consort and Dolmetsch looked forward eagerly to the time when his 'Home music' could be performed by a true 'Dolmetsch' ensemble .The two girls were now playing both recorder and viols under their father's instruction and a little notebook has survived in which he recorded the progress of his pupils. His comments ranged typically from 'Très bien', 'Mieux', 'Pas mal' to 'Mal!', 'Très stupide' and '7 fautes!' If his daughters did not always come up to his expectations, he had a son in whom he had high hopes. Rudolph at the age of five was showing the same precocity as had his daughter Hélène some 30 years before: he could play simple pieces by Bach and had developed an extraordinary gift for improvisation. On the crossing from the USA to France, he had amused the other passengers by playing his psaltery and composing his own tunes as he went along.

*   *   *

If there was anything Dolmetsch enjoyed more than selling a harpsichord to replace a family piano, it was the conversion of a pianist to the clavichord. In Paris, in the autumn of 1911, he met a 30-year-old pianist and made the conversion of his career. Dorothy Swainson had received a 'sound musical education' in the accepted standards of her time: she had studied in Dresden with Paul Roth, a pupil of Liszt, and had completed her training in Paris under Thérèse Chaigneau. She made her debut in that city in 1906 and had been appearing as a soloist in Paris, London and other European capitals ever since. She specialised in playing the music of Mussorgsky and Debussy at a time when their work was seldom heard, being considered too *avant garde*. She had never attended a Dolmetsch concert but when asked to prepare a programme of 18th-century French music she was recommended to this legendary expert for advice on ornamentation and style. So it was as an experienced and successful professional that she set out for her first meeting, armed with Rameau's harpsichord pieces, gavotte and variations well prepared. They spent an hour and a half on the gavotte but never reached the variations. In one afternoon this young pianist received her initiation. As soon as she entered the room Dolmetsch threw aside her modern copy with the retort, 'Never accept anything at second-hand: always consult the original'.

Many years later she said: 'He then explained the old signs: not simple directions as to which notes must be played but *why* the ornaments were there at all, what their expressive meaning was, and how incomplete the music was without them.' Having been taught like everyone else at that time to play the music exactly as it was written, Dorothy Swainson was stunned by this revelation. Today this might seem an exaggeration, but we must remember that in 1911 no one had offered clear and precise directions that the layman could understand. This was mainly because the musicians themselves were not overconcerned with the true interpretation of the early music. Since most compositions were transcribed for the piano, there was little hope of a pupil getting authentic assistance from anything but source material, and even then it needed to be interpreted.

Dorothy Swainson's first and most lasting impression was of Dolmetsch's 'flair' for the right interpretation of any piece of music: 'because his musical instinct told him how it should go and how it should sound . . . he sought confirmation *afterwards* in the old books, not the other way round'.

At that first meeting Dolmetsch had played the clavichord, an instrument with which Dorothy Swainson was totally unfamiliar. She was so enchanted with the sound that she decided instantly to have one for herself. When it was finally delivered, she practised diligently for many hours but to her dismay found the instrument getting more and more out of tune. She wrote to Dolmetsch complaining, but he replied tersely by return of post telling her that it was she, not the instrument that was out of tune. He also suggested that unless she could rectify this fault she need not come for her next lesson. Although she finally managed to overcome the difficulty, she admitted later that it had been quite a new problem for a pianist to tackle. However, once these initial misunderstandings had been straightened out, Dorothy Swainson and Dolmetsch enjoyed a lifelong friendship. His most celebrated pupil, she eventually became the first professional clavichordist. [3]

It was at her house that Dolmetsch first met Paul Brunold, teacher at the Schola Cantorum and organist at the Church of St. Gervais, [4] where the Couperin family had played for eight generations. Describing the encounter in later years, she said that they were delighted to meet each other, 'these two small (but great) men, both with a stoop and shocks of grey hair and luminous eyes . . . talking ten to the dozen'. It seems that after Dolmetsch had been telling Brunold about his work, Brunold exclaimed rather sadly that such achievements were only possible when one had the means. Dolmetsch nearly jumped out of his skin: 'The means!' he said, 'Did you say, the means? But I have *never* had the means! Yet I have managed to do what I have wanted to.' Perhaps he should have added that, owing to a tolerant and devoted wife, he had been helped to find 'ways' even if he did not always have the means.

On 4 November, Maison Gaveau held a reception to introduce the 'Epinette' number one made by Dolmetsch: it was much admired and a number of orders were taken. The first clavichord followed on 26 November, whilst the building of harpsichords and virginals was well under way by the end of the year: a charming little catalogue with line illustrations appeared in early 1912.

However occupied Dolmetsch appeared to be in the factory that first winter, he still managed to fulfill a variety of concert engagements. He appeared at the Salle Gaveau with 'Les Chanteurs de la Renaissance', a society which had been founded in 1907 by Henry Expert, their director and conductor, with the aim of reviving the music of the 15th and 16th centuries by living performance. Although they specialised in vocal music, on this occasion they interspersed their programme with two groups of pieces performed by Dolmetsch: Purcell, Rameau and Bach on the harpsichord and more Bach from the '48' on the clavichord. Press notices praised Dolmetsch's musicianship and style and as always acknowledged the debt that was due to him for bringing these delights before the public.

Another notable engagement was that of a soirée known as 'Le Five o'clock du *Figaro*', sponsored by France's most famous right-wing newspaper. At a fashionable salon in the rue Frouet, the élite of Parisian society flocked to this, the first important function of the 'season'. An account in *Le Figaro* of 30 December 1911 lists almost a column of distinguished patrons. Dolmetsch, Mabel and a young pupil, Marie Thérèse de Lens, opened the programme with a fantasie by John Jenkins and three preludes for the clavichord by Bach: among the most notable of the other performers were the famous Italian bass Titta Ruffo, and the darlings of the Paris Opera, the incomporable Nijinsky and Karsarvina, who brought down the final curtain to tumultuous applause after dancing one of the *valses* from *Les Sylphides*.

It was some time since Dolmetsch had taken part in a musical argument and when the opportunity arose to challenge his old enemy, J. A. Fuller-Maitland, he seized it with both hands: Maitland had never forgiven Dolmetsch for his part in the Purcell *King Arthur* affair (see pp. 117–19, 195) and Dolmetsch in turn smarted from the memory of Maitland's boycott of his concerts in the 1890s. A paper read by Maitland at the International Musical Congress in June 1911 was printed in the *Musical Times* (1 October 1911) and Dolmetsch replied in the *S.I.M. Revue Musicale* on 15 February 1912 with an article entitled *Un Cas d'orne-mentation chez Bach*.[5] Maitland advocates Daniel Gottlieb Türk as being the best authority on the practice of the epoch of Bach, although he admits his *Klavierschule oder Anweisung zum Klavierspielen für Lehrer und Lernende, mit kritischen Ammerkungen* did not appear until 1789, nearly 40 years after Bach's death. He maintains also that C.P.E. Bach was too close to the epoch of his father to explain quite clearly the signs in use at that time since everyone understood them. He considers that Türk combines the practice of Bach's time with that of more recent composers and gives the clearest idea of what was common usage a little before him. His [Türk's] explanation of the long appogiatura is admirably clear, although he concedes that Dannreuther[6] is right when he says that Türk's explanations 'cannot be strictly applied to compositions anterior to the time of C. P. E. Bach'. All this Dolmetsch summarises briefly and comprehensively, in contrast to Maitland's long-winded and involved account. He proceeds:

> Il serait [Maitland's article] bon que ceux de nos virtuoses et chefs d'orchestre qui s'intéressent, ou veulent nous intéresser, à la musique ancienne lisent et relisent cet article. Il est rempli de renseignement utiles et d'excellentes suggestions.
>
> La phrase suivante, par exemple, devrait être répétée matin et soir par nos interprètes de Händel et Bach jusqu'à ce que le voile de préjugés et d'ignorance qui s'interpose entre eux et la musique commence à se trouer. 'But if editors and others would approach the older music without their present conviction that the written note is to be interpreted as it would in the present day, we should get a far more flowing effect in many things by Bach and other masters.'

While Dolmetsch agrees that 'C'est absolument vrai et formerait un excellent point de départ pour une réforme urgente',[7] he goes on to say that Maitland is less happy in his practical application of these suggestions, complaining that this reasoning lacks logic:

> 'Quelle raison pouvait avoir C.P.E.Bach d'écrire son livre si chacun en comprenait le contenu?' he asks. Et pourquoi se baser sur 'Türk'; puisqu'il admet que ses préceptes ne peuvent strictement s'appliquer etc. Après cela on ne s'étonnera peut-être pas outre-mesure que l'interprétation de M. Fuller Maitland soit discutable.[8]

Dolmetsch points out further inaccuracies and finally presents his own answer:

> En fait, on pourrait se fier à 'Türk' pour la plupart des ornements de J. S. Bach; mais il est préférable d'étudier d'Anglebert, Couperin, Rameau, Quantz, C. P. E. Bach et avant tout J. S. Bach lui-même qui a noté des explications fort claires sur ses ornements dans le petit livre qu'il écrivit en 1720 pour l'instruction de son fils aîné.[9] M. Fuller-Maitland aurait trouvé là une solution toute simple à ses plus grosses difficultés.

Dolmetsch completes his explanation by illustrating 32 bars of the excerpt

from *The Goldberg Variations* as quoted by Maitland, with his own interpretation, together with the original Bach. The bars reproduced will
suffice to show that Dolmetsch's interpretation unconsciously reveals his
instinctive understanding of the development: the example is in 3/4 time.

a. In bar *1*. The correct interpretation of ornaments where Dolmetsch
   has taken a cue from the pointé rhythm of the bass to 'manner' the
   right hand accordingly.
b. In bar *2*. The phrasing and length of notes shows Dolmetsch's more
   acute attention to details of phrasing.
c. In bar *3*. A compendium of the two opposing attitudes: one flowers
   naturally from a knowledge of d'Anglebert whilst the other represents
   a backward look from Beethoven.

It is significant that no counter-claims from Maitland are to be found in
print.

While the French musical *cognoscenti* were reading his denunciation of
Fuller-Maitland, Dolmetsch and his wife were in England fulfilling a
number of concert engagements: this time they had taken their eldest
daughter, who joined them in an occasional piece, playing the treble viol.
At the first concert at Clifford's Inn on 15 February, although only eight
years old, 'Miss Cécile earned warm praise as a promising executant in a
little *Musette* by d'Hervelois and two *Minuets* by Marais.' Between the
two London concerts they toured Scotland, where they were all three well
received by both press and public. However, the critic from *The Times* on

27 February writing after the second concert at Clifford's Inn, is more interested in the introduction of a novelty than Cécile's youthful prowess:

> The concert began with a few tunes on the recorder which had no place assigned to them in the programme. Mr. Dolmetsch apologized, needlessly, for having scant skill on that particular instrument; the fact is that he scrapes up something more than a speaking acquaintance with any instrument which is a few centuries old quicker than most people; he seems to divine its character, what will suit it and what will not, and, above all, he plays it in tune.[10]

*   *   *

Dolmetsch's instinctive contempt for the baton may have given him a few misgivings, but it did not prevent him from accepting the post of director and conductor of 'Les Chanteurs de la Renaissance'[11] when it was offered him in October 1912. When Henry Expert retired, the committee voted unanimously in favour of the post being offered to Dolmetsch. Unanimous approval was something that Dolmetsch could not resist, especially when he learned that, in return for conducting the singers, he would have the chance to promote opportunities for his own instruments to be played. A number of successful concerts were given and the press praised Dolmetsch and his music, although they were not always kind to the singers. One critic made the curious statement that since Dolmetsch speaks French with difficulty, it detracted from the explanations. It is odd that he should have been accused of mis-pronouncing his mother-tongue: ironic when we know that his English was fluent but overlaid with a heavy French accent.

However, accent or no, if music was the main concern, whether they be speakers, singers, actors or dancers, Dolmetsch could provide it, and with almost uncanny understanding of the mood so required. In November he appeared in a number of stage performances with Loïe Fuller and her young dancers in Paris and made a short tour of the provinces. Loïe Fuller specialised in presenting her dancers barefoot, whilst their twirling chiffons were dramatised by ingenious lighting effects. One critic writes that 'ces jeunes filles renouvellent la grâce, le rhythme, la beauté libre et harmonieuse des danses antiques'. He finds that Dolmetsch fits admirably into the picture, as well he might. His musical 'taste' and 'suitability' are mentioned in almost every review. Remarkably, Dolmetsch conducted a small orchestra playing airs by Mouret, Mozart, Purcell[12] and Handel. But:

> Cet orchestre, dirigé par M. Arnold Dolmetsch, qui, à certains moments, quitte le bâton pour exécuter au clavecin une délicieuse sonate, est composé d'anciens

instruments de musique, auxquels se joignent des violons, des flûtes et des violoncelles.[13]

When we consider Dolmetsch's output at this time, it is difficult to realise that he was still imposing the strict discipline of working fully stretched all day and every day, in the same way as he had as a young man. The instruments were sent out from Gaveau perfect in every detail,[14] and his concerts and lectures were undertaken with the same attention as if he had no other occupation but the event in hand. He had gained a number of pupils in Paris, several, like Dorothy Swainson, professionals who would later bring him credit. In his free time he lovingly tended his garden and could grow anything he set his mind to.

In addition to all this he was setting down on paper his own theories on the interpretation of music of the 17th and 18th centuries. He had been working on this manuscript since the turn of the century with the idea of getting it published, and it was now nearing completion. One curious point arises in that he started writing in English and even when living and working in Paris continued to do so. Was it his prophetic instinct at work again, or just coincidence, that his diary seemed to be accumulating a number of engagements to play on the other side of the Channel?

NOTES

1. *S.I.M.*, a monthly journal containing scholarly articles on music and musicians, published by the Société Française des Amis de la Musique.
2. Richard Appel, Head of Music Department, Boston Public Library, from 1922–1954.
3. Dorothy Swainson (1882–1959) 'long occupied a unique place in the musical revival inaugurated by her master, Arnold Dolmetsch, among whose pupils she was the one who, in style and conception, most nearly approached her own great teacher. On the clavichord she displayed a combination of interpretative insight with technical skill given to very few.' *The Times*. Dorothy Swainson also contributed to BBC *History in Sound of European Music*, and to Vol. 6 and 7 of the ensuing *History of Music in Sound*, HMV (1953). She also made a complete translation of Dolmetsch's book *The Interpretation of the Music of the XVII and XVIII Centuries* into French, but it has never been published in that language.
4. Paul Brunold (also curator of the musical instruments of the *Conservatoire National Supérieur de la Musique* in Paris wrote a book about the organ at St. Gervais. He asked Dolmetsch to examine the instrument as plans were afoot for its modernisation and electrification. In a letter to Dorothy Swainson (25 August 1928) Dolmetsch writes: 'I examined the organ in 1913, I protested strongly against the project then planned to have the instrument "destroyed" . . . at a cost of 60,000 francs.' The plan was never carried out.

5. *S.I.M.*, Paris, 15 February 1912, pp. 24–30.
6. Dannreuther, Edward, *Musical Ornamentation*, Parts I and II, Novello Primer Series, 1893.
7. It would be good if the virtuosi and conductors who are interested in, or who want to interest us in, the old music would read and re-read this article. It is full of useful information and excellent suggestions. The following sentence, for instance, should be repeated day and night by interpreters of Handel and Bach until the veil of prejudice and ignorance which comes between them and the music, is lifted.
It is absolutely true, and would form an excellent starting point for urgent reform.
8. What reason could C. P. E. Bach have for writing his book if everyone understood the contents? And why base his book on Türk since he admits that his theories cannot be strictly applied? As a result of this [après cela' sarcasm] one will not perhaps be surprised to any great extent that Fuller-Maitland's interpretation is disputable.
9. In fact, one could have confidence in Türk for the greater part of Bach's ornaments but it is better to study d'Anglebert, Couperin, Rameau, Quantz, C. P. E. Bach and above all, J. S. Bach himself who noted down very clear explanation of his ornaments in the little book which he wrote for the education of his eldest son. Mr. Fuller-Maitland would have found them a very simple solution to his greatest difficulties.
10. This is the first recorded instance of Dolmetsch having played the recorder at a public concert, though he claimed to have played it in America, and to have attempted to teach it to flautists in Boston.
11. *Les Chanteurs de la Renaissance*, a band of 40–50 singers under their founder and director, M. Henry Expert (founded 1907) whose aim it was to give concerts of the vocal music of the period.
12. There is an amusing typesetter's error in an account in *Le Gaulois*, 6 November 1912: 'Nous aurons la primeur d'un opera de Purcell: *Dioclesian*', *la primeur* meaning 'fresh or early spring vegetables'.
13. That orchestra, directed by M. Arnold Dolmetsch, who at certain moments leaves the baton in order to perform at the harpsichord, is composed of ancient instruments joined by violins, flutes and 'cellos.
14. There are a number of instruments extant from this time. The Epinette number one is at Maison Gaveau in Paris. Madeau Stewart has a harpsichord dating from this period.

CHAPTER XVI

A Family Workshop

AFTER three months' leave of absence giving concerts in England, Dolmetsch returned with his family to Paris in March 1913. About this time he must have been considering the possibilities of making a permanent home in London; certainly the increasing number of engagements that he accepted indicates that he had given it some thought. Since there were no pianoforte-makers whom Dolmetsch could approach with a view to opening a department for early keyboard instruments, he knew that if he chose to live in London it would mean starting again on his own account. He was well aware of the risks attending such a decision.

However, in the spring of 1913 his contract with Gaveau had still some time to run, and on his return Dolmetsch was concerned only with the unrelenting demands of work that had accumulated in his absence. His main job now was to finish his book, and every evening was spent writing, often into the early hours of the morning. Refreshed by a minimal amount of sleep he would still put in a full day at the factory. In addition he had a few special pupils whom he preferred to teach personally; there were also concerts.

It was in his garden that Dolmetsch sought relaxation: somehow he always had time to tend his little patch, with its neat rows of vegetables framed by flower beds: here was his peace. But Dolmetsch also had a phenomenally robust constitution: even into old age he could adjust the seemingly frail body to accept conditions that would have handicapped a healthy younger man. That year in Paris was proof of his indestructability.

An undated account in the *Daily Telegraph* from this period tells how Dolmetsch gave a concert to the workmen and workwomen, with some sprinkling even of Apaches, of the 'Popular University' who for 5d. a month were given musical entertainment in the Faubourg St. Antoine. According to Dolmetsch, although an 'uncultivated audience [they] showed extraordinary appreciation and approved exactly where they ought to have approved'. Dolmetsch always enjoyed playing to the proletariat.

An important concert-lecture to an entirely different kind of audience

was given at the Sorbonne consisting of a programme of music performed comparatively on the modern piano, the clavichord and the harpsichord. Dolmetsch himself played on the early instruments, and Dorothy
Swainson the piano. This experiment, with music by Scarlatti, Rameau
and Bach, was interesting enough to prove the point but, in Dolmetsch's
opinion, 'not quite fair' since Dorothy Swainson had already become
accustomed to the old instruments: he thought that 'the piano would have
appeared at greater disadvantage if played by the average (good) pianist
who had never played the clavichord or harpsichord'.

December brought Dolmetsch back to the British Isles again with an
extensive tour of Scotland and three concerts at Clifford's Inn. This time
he had brought his three eldest children to take part and in the third
concert his pupil Mrs. Violet Gordon Woodhouse was to play the harpsichord: at the same performance the Hon. Neville Lytton[1] showed his skill
on the 18th-century flute. Dolmetsch had become acquainted with Lytton
through their common interest in the past and had obtained a fine ivory
18th-century flute for him.

Dolmetsch's old friend, John Runciman, devotes a great deal of space
to the Clifford's Inn concerts in the *Saturday Review* (13 December 1913).
He writes that some years ago he never tired of insisting on the value of
Dolmetsch's work: 'His concerts of old music were an unfailing sense of
joy; his little concert room was always crowded,' but the concerts did not
pay, so Mr. Dolmetsch had to betake himself abroad. He is therefore
delighted to see that the small hall of Clifford's Inn is full at each of his
concerts and that Dolmetsch is now lecturing to audiences of two to three
thousand in the provinces. All this is excellent but Runciman offers a
warning: 'His [Dolmetsch's] three children are exceptionally gifted; but,
to speak vulgarly, it is hardly good enough to charge half a guinea to hear
them play and sing the old music. The fault of these concerts always was
their casual, amateurish character . . . and this defect was rather accentu-
ated than otherwise on Tuesday evening of last week.' He maintains that,
as Mr. Dolmetsch knows, 'the old stuff . . . is very difficult; the most
consummate musicianship, insight, mature understanding, are required
for its interpretation' and therefore much of the music did not make its
effect owing to the immaturity of the little artists. 'In a word, the affair was
too little of a concert and too much of a baby-show. I do not say this in an
unkind spirit. I want these concerts to prosper . . . it seems to me that people
will not attend them regularly unless the finest and ripest artists available
take part in them.'

Paternal pride would never have allowed Dolmetsch to agree with such
a view. In general he respected Runciman's judgement and there is no
evidence of any violent reaction on this occasion, but the children con-

tinued to appear at the rest of the London concerts. However, the Scottish audiences were spared the young performers. A Dundee paper tells us that 'attired in velvet jacket and breeches' he held the audience spellbound in a lecture on 'The Original Music of Shakespeare's Plays'. The *Aberdeen Free Press* of 12 December 1913 described a lecture at the Aberdeen Art Gallery as one of the finest musical treats people had had for many a day.

The mounting tension during the oppressive year that was to bring Europe into war before the summer was over had nothing to do with Dolmetsch's final decision to quit Paris and settle in London: it was simply another case of the Fates watching over his interests. Only one thought was uppermost in his mind: how to finish the book in time. Ernest Newman was editing the manuscript for Novello's and on 1 February 1914, Dolmetsch writes to let him know that he has the first part finished and the second well advanced. He bemoans the scarcity of time he can devote to writing since his days are so filled with concerts and lectures. He tells Newman that he is coming to London in February and after fulfilling one concert engagement will be going to a village in Kent where he intends to 'stay until the whole work is finished', which will be about five weeks. Eleven days later he sends two-thirds of the MS to Newman and makes various suggestions as to how to make the musical examples easy to read. On 2 March he sends another batch, saying that he doubts if he can finish before the end of the month as promised. His main worry is the presentation of the musical examples and he asks Newman if it might be a sensible idea to print a separate appendix. He has also just come across a book of harpsichord pieces *c.* 1705 by Dandrieu, 'which are fingered throughout for teaching by the composer. They are charming. A few of them would fill up nicely if need be.'[2]

However, by 14 June, Dolmetsch had not only finished the book but had returned and corrected the first batch of proofs to Novello's. 'I have attended to all your queries,' which were right in almost every case. I like the type and the size of the pages very much, it will make a nice book to read—the music types are very poor. It is strange, when there are so many beautiful models available, that such clefs, rests, etc., should still be tolerated.'

Newman answers a few days later hoping that Dolmetsch 'will soon become reconciled to the music type when the volume appears'. It had not struck Newman as being objectionable, 'but that may be because I am used to it'. He suggests that Dolmetsch might raise the question of the kind of type he wants for the Appendix and that a short summary of his investigations and conclusions would add to the book's usefulness. Dolmetsch replies on 3 September that he can 'derive it from the short chapter I am just writing about the musical instruments of that period', and adds that he has also made arrangements for the Appendix to be published separately.

Then follows a typical Dolmetsch enthusiastic overflow: 'Mr. Coburn, the wonderful photographer you know probably, has made some *extraordinarily beautiful* portraits of me. He knows of my book, for he is very fond of my music; and he suggested to me yesterday that one of these portraits should preface the book. What do you think of this?' A tactful response from Newman rejects the idea as it is 'not usual . . . it would create a precedent and . . . bring a heap of correspondence on my head if any controversy arises . . .'

Shaw was another who resisted Dolmetsch's suggestions: in his case that he should write a preface to the book. Shaw refused on the pretext that he did not know enough on the subject to write a really good one, and if he were to write a bad one, the book would be lost. He warns Dolmetsch that his last preface delayed the publication of the book several months and cost him 'untold gold' through the delay. Shaw cunningly alleviates the pain of refusal by his assurance that Dolmetsch is the only man alive capable of writing to any purpose about the old music.

*   *   *

Dolmetsch's powers of concentration were such that he could isolate in his mind a particular task, such as the completion of his manuscript, without allowing the mundaneness of daily life to intrude. The correspondence with Newman and contemporary accounts of concert activities[4] show that the family uprooted themselves from Fontenay-sous-Bois and moved to London without undue disruption: due, almost certainly, to Mabel's inexhaustible patience and resignation to a nomadic existence. From his Kentish retreat, Dolmetsch writes to Dorothy Swainson in Moscow (she had asked for a spinet) on 14 March 1914:

Falcon Farm
Badlesmere
near Faversham,
Kent.

I have left Gaveau[5] whom I *don't* regret; I have also left Paris, with a different feeling. We are all here in the country, whilst the house I have taken at 4 Tanza Road Hampstead is being fitted. . . . It is charming and quite close to Hampstead Heath, which the children will appreciate. I shall make all instruments myself; no more Gaveaus! but, until the workshop is ready, and things well settled, which will take perhaps a year, no spinet can be had . . . I have one here I could let you have . . . Needless to say, there will be no more instruments worth having from

Gaveau, for nobody there knows anything about them! The price of the spinet is £60, net, here in London.

As we know, no details as to the cause of the rift in the friendship between Herbert Horne and Dolmetsch have ever been disclosed. However, Horne's sister, Beatrice, had remained a close friend of the Dolmetsches throughout the years and had played at their concerts with unfailing regularity. It is evident that some kind of reconciliation between the two men had been effected for on 3 May 1914 Horne writes to her:

> 8, Lung'arno Archibusieri,
> Florence

> You can tell Dolmetsch, if you think fit, that a dealer here has a 16th cent. Italian clavichord for sale. Dolmetsch used to say that Italian clavichords were of the greatest rarity and that he would much like to find one. This is the first that I have come across in all these years. It is made on a wholly different plan from that D. made for me. It is shaped somewhat like a spinette; but with the keyboard to the left, and the soundboard to the right. The mechanism, however, is very complicated, with a second set of tangents working cross-wise. The instrument has no outer case. It is well, but very plainly made. No painting or decoration, except a little moulding or two. The soundboard is cracked in two places, and one or two keys are missing. Otherwise it is still pretty sound, and as far as I can judge could easily be restored. The dealer only asks lire 300. I think I could get it *packed* for Lire 250, but not less. As prices go here, now [Florence] this is very little. For that, D would have to pay carriage.

On 8 May, Dolmetsch writes to Horne that he is 'much interested in the Italian clavichord'[6] and confirms that they are very rare. He has seen only a few himself, and never one for sale. He asks Horne to make the best bargain he can and he will send his cheque as soon as the deal has been settled. He tells Horne that they are back in London making 'good music.   I play the clavichord and harpsichord very much better than it has ever been played by anybody in recent times, though far from that perfection which I, at any rate, will never reach. But I have a marvellously gifted boy, age 7, and *he* will do it.' In Rudolph's case this prophecy turned out to be accurate, but Dolmetsch's characteristic close to the letter that the other children 'are very clever too, and beautiful, and I have pupils and associates much more efficient than in former times' was typical of the rosy view that the present always had for Dolmetsch.

Another letter from Horne, on 13 May, confirms that he has managed to procure the clavichord (which is bigger than he thought—over two metres long), packed, for 250 lire. He finds on looking at it again that it never had an outer case but a removable lid which is lost and worked on sliding hinges. He notes also that 'there is a curious framed piece, attached, which appears to belong to the instrument', but which is past his comprehension. He thinks he has sent Dolmetsch a puzzle which he hopes will prove interesting musically. The clavichord duly arrives and Dolmetsch writes to Horne (6 June) that it did so in good condition:

> 4, Tanza Road,
> Hampstead, N.W.
>
> It is very interesting—The movements you did not understand are a very clever contrivance to get two notes on each string in the bass, which could not be done in the usual 'gebunden' way on account of the length of the semitone—The whole construction of the instrument is reversed: it is like the English Spinet where the bass strings are at the back instead of at the front as in the Italian instruments. I had never seen of [sic] heard of a clavichord made on that plan. I will restore it, and it might have an extraordinary quality of tone.

*   *   *

By the beginning of July Dolmetsch had settled down perfectly in his new surroundings, and in a letter to his pupil Jean Sinclair he has once again, chameleon-like, assumed the colour of his habitat:

> 4, Tanza Road,
> Hampstead, N.W.
>
> London is better than Paris for me; most of my engagements were here, and my instruments mostly went to English people. Having lived in London 25 years before going to America, I am well known here and have many good friends. Then my wife is English, and her family, which is large, and well disposed towards our children helps to make life easy and pleasant. We have a very nice home, pleasantly situated close to a magnificent park,[7] and we feel much more comfortable than in France.... I am a musician as well as a mechanic—neither one severally could have done what I have—Now, I have a workshop here and am making the instruments on my own account.[8]

Ten days later, Dolmetsch sends out his printed notices on expensive paper, as always, extolling the virtues of the virginals and spinets as opposed to the piano: he claims that they are decorative, small enough to fit into any room, and that their lightness allows them to be carried about with ease. 'The crispness of their touch and facility renders them ideal for students; it develops their sensitiveness and nimbleness of fingers which is the despair of piano players, and it replaces the dreary hours usually spent in pursuit of technique by the performance of enjoyable and mind-improving music.' He announces that he has organised an efficient workshop and now proposes 'to make a virginal of a simple form, without costly decoration, yet pleasing to the eye, with a compass of five octaves (sufficient for all the music up to Beethoven, and a good deal besides) at a cost not exceeding 25 guineas, if not less than twelve orders are given.' He adds that the price will, naturally, depend upon the number of orders he receives. The payment should be made in three instalments: '8 guineas with the order; 8 guineas as soon as the instrument is strung, and the balance on delivery.' And finally, 'They will be ready by July 1915 so that the owners will be able to take them away with them on their holidays.'

Roger Fry was one of the first to place an order for a set of virginals and asks if his can be made in such a way that he can decorate it at the Omega Workshop.[9] He further suggests that perhaps they could come to an agreement whereby he could order several (at a special rate) and have them decorated. It is not known if this suggestion was ever taken up: it is highly unlikely since Dolmetsch had an aversion to anyone outside taking part in the production of his instruments. Herbert Horne and Selwyn Image (see p. 101) were rare exceptions, whilst the Burne-Jones experiment had proved a disaster (see p. 122). Charlotte Shaw did not keep Dolmetsch waiting very long: she felt she must have a set of virginals but since war had just been declared (11 August) she is concerned as to whether it will make any difference to the price; if so, she will have to give up the idea.

With the outbreak of war, the price of a set of virginals became of secondary importance. The separation from his family in France caused Dolmetsch much anxiety. His aged mother was still in Le Mans and his favourite brother, Albert, was making pianos in Colombe. He writes to say that he has enlisted in the local army (a similar organisation to that of the English Home Guard in the Second World War); they are armed with pistols and patrol constantly; the company on watch the previous evening had taken two German prisoners. He also sends news that the house of Erard closed down the previous day. On 30 August, Albert writes saying that this may be his last letter as things are very serious: the 'bandits' are coming to Paris by the north and are already in the Somme, Aisnes and Champagne with a battle line stretching for 400 kilometres.

In another letter, dated 9 September, Albert tells of the terrible difficulty in making enough money to live. Erard has reopened for two days a week and he is one of the lucky ones who are employed for four days a month, for which they receive 20 francs. This and two or three tunings from private customers is all that he can manage to find in the way of employment. But Albert also seems to have struck a good bargain with the local grocer, with whom he is in debt for one hundred francs: he teaches piano to the grocer's three children, working off the debt at the rate of 25 francs monthly. 'I pay the father with tunes ... this is a great work as I consider these pupils as future artists ... I don't know what *kind* of artists!' (Trans.) On New Year's Eve, Dolmetsch's mother writes to wish him good luck with his book and hopes it will bring the advantages he desires, but that as it is written in English even if he sends her a copy she will not be able to read it.

Dolmetsch always had a very French concern for his family's welfare and was worried that he might never see his mother again unless the war ended soon: and there seemed little likelihood of that. In Hampstead he was settled and happy but by no means prosperous. The workshop kept him occupied and the children also: both girls remember having to plane and finish the various parts of instruments; they made and assembled jacks and tongues using both circular and band-saws.

It was Rudolph's job to grind tuning-pins on a revolving grind-stone and he was in the habit of dropping the mis-shapen ones down a mousehole rather than incur his father's wrath. Rudolph was the least interested in the workshop activities. As he was recognised as being the most talented, he was often released from these duties so that he could practise. Even the baby, Carl, was beginning to play a little on the recorder and the viol, although he was never allowed in the workshop.

The Bohemian atmosphere of Hampstead village suited the family down to the ground and once more Dolmetsch looked forward to settling in one place. It was not to be. The battlefields of Flanders were a long way from Hampstead Heath but London had not yet been visited by those silver monsters that would bring the real meaning of war to London and its people—the Zeppelins.

NOTES

1. Neville Lytton, artist, morris-dancer and writer, was said to be the only person to play the 18th-century flute at this time.
2. Dolmetsch, Arnold, *The Interpretation of the Music of the XVII and XVIII Centuries*, Novello 1915, p. 292, Dandrieu.
3. Unfortunately we do not know the nature of these 'queries' as no other correspondence is extant; but we observe Dolmetsch's rare submission to another's opinion without argument.
4. Dolmetsch gave a series of three concerts at the New Hall of The Artworkers' Guild in Queen Square and he also supplied music for The Shakespeare League concert on 24 April.
5. Dolmetsch is reputed to have left Gaveau in great haste—almost overnight without announcing his departure; but there is no trace of events at this time since Gaveau's archives were destroyed by fire in the war of 1914-18.
6. Italian clavichord (unidentified).
7. Hampstead Heath.
8. 5 July 1914.

9. Omega Workshops were founded by Roger Fry in 1913 for the purpose of regularly employing artists on a part-time basis (30s. a week for three half-days) so that they would not starve. It was organised to decorate every kind of furnishing, mostly designed by Omega and made elsewhere; the artists then decorated. It was handicapped by the war of 1914–18 and finally distintegrated in 1919–20 but had considerable influence in its time.

CHAPTER XVII

Lost At Waterloo

DOLMETSCH'S manuscript was finished by the end of the year and in the spring of 1915 he writes to Ernest Newman (15 April) that he has sent a set of proofs to Henri Verbrugghen, the Belgian conductor, who as a result was 'immediately convinced and converted!'[1] However, the main purpose of the letter was to let Newman know that many of the interpretative points from his book would be introduced at the first two concerts of the Bach-Beethoven-Brahms Festival at Queen's Hall the following week, in which he was to take part; the London Symphony Orchestra was to be conducted by Henri Verbrugghen. Dolmetsch, together with his pupil Mrs. Violet Gordon Woodhouse, would be playing the Bach concerto for two harpsichords; but it was in the concerto for two violins that they were to introduce 'new readings that will *startle* the critics who have ears (?)'. Dolmetsch continues:

> Then I play the solo part of the Concerto in F, on a real *Violino Piccolo* ... as we give no warning of our intentions, there might be, there *ought* to be, discussions if the critics have ears!

Newman replies that he will be at the concert and promises to listen with the greatest interest to phrasing, etc. Although he is glad to hear that Dolmetsch's principles will be put into practice, he does not think that they need anticipate much discussion: 'The majority of the people—more's the pity!—won't know that there is anything new in the matter at all.'

In this forecast, Newman was underestimating the interest shown by the critics. As for their 'ears', they were certainly not charmed by the conductor's attempts at authenticity. The *Daily Telegraph* makes a quip about the contrast between serious musicians who have been crusading on behalf of British composers whilst a Belgian conductor is holding a festival of German music at the Queen's Hall. 'The surprises were that the whole of Bach's orchestral suites in C and D were given, instead of merely the overtures as originally announced.' Verbrugghen is criticised for his slavish attempts to produce original balance by engaging nine oboes instead of the normal two: 'The result may have been truthful to the original, but truth is not always pleasing, and the prominence of the oboe tone became somewhat trying to sensitive ears.'

The writer was no happier about the solo part in the Brandenburg Concerto on the violino piccolo: 'In the slow movement the thin tone of this small-sized violin may have suggested to some minds the antiquity of the music, but in the final allegro all the efforts of the soloist, Mr. Arnold Dolmetsch, could not prevent the entrance of comic element consequent on the rich tones of the London Symphony Orchestra's strings with those of the baby violin.' The same critic was more generous towards the concerto for two harpsichords, in which 'a beautiful balance of tone was secured'.

Dolmetsch's book, *The Interpretation of the Music of the XVII and XVIII Centuries*, was finally published in December 1915. The reviewers were kindly disposed towards it and considered it a well documented, scholarly work. Dolmetsch is praised for the order he has produced out of the chaos of ornamentation: 'In no other textbook has the great subject of ornamentation in the old music been more thoroughly and convincingly discussed than it is here.' Ernest Newman[2] puts the case for Dolmetsch: he longs for some millionaire to publish, in a cheap form, the best of the out-of-the-way music of the 17th and 18th centuries and declares that 'the greatest service Mr. Dolmetsch's book will do will be to demonstrate the necessity not merely of publishing these almost forgotten texts, but of applying to the editing of them the full fruits of modern research into the period that gave them birth'. Newman doubts whether there exists in England at the present time five people competent to undertake such a task.

The important point drawn by Newman is that Dolmetsch has spent a lifetime in the study of ancient music but not 'in the spirit of mere antiquarianism but of unquenchable love for the old music as a living thing. . . . It is this sense of moving about among presences not dead, but living, that is conveyed by Mr. Dolmetsch's book, that differentiates it from the late Edward Dannreuther's two large volumes on *Musical Ornamentation*.'[3] He admits Dannreuther's work to be of value, but considers that it unconsciously gives the impression of treating the subject as a dead one, 'while from Mr. Dolmetsch's eager pages one gets the idea that for him it is not only alive, but almost the only subject that *is* alive. For he has so steeped himself all his life in this old music that he sees and hears it, so far as any man of the present day can, as a product contemporary with himself.' The article runs to two and a half columns of solid advocacy.

Despite the excellent reception of Dolmetsch's book on both sides of the Atlantic, its appearance in the sixteenth month of war, when the chances of victory still seemed remote, inevitably reduced its impact. Furthermore, the manpower shortage meant that it was virtually impossible for Dolmetsch to find an assistant to help him in the workshop: most skilled men who had not enlisted were making munitions. Orders for clavichords and virginals still came in and Dolmetsch seldom had more than a few hours' sleep in his effort to get the work done. Then there were general shortages of tools and raw materials. Although the demand for concerts and lectures had diminished, there was still sufficient to 'spoil his work at the bench', as he put it in a letter to Newman (17 March 1916).

The Dolmetsch children were as yet untouched by these difficulties: they enjoyed living so near the heath and walked over it each day to attend a small private school run by Miss Isobel Fry, of the well-known Quaker family. Their classmates were mostly children of the poets, writers and artists living in the neighbourhood and it was here that they first met the Sturge Moores and Judith Masefield and formed life-long friendships with them. Whilst the children were at school, Mabel helped her husband in the workshop and gave dancing lessons. Her research into the old dances was considerable and she had by now learned sufficient to instruct others: besides which, the money was very useful.

One of her pupils at Tanza Road was a young woman destined to become 'one of the principal architects of English ballet',[4] the Polish-born Miriam (now Dame Marie) Rambert. A friend had written a ballet for her in two parts, one depicting a Fra Angelico Chapel and the other a Renaissance scene with Botticelli naked nymphs. She wanted to do the Chapel scene to music by Corelli but couldn't find the right style. Someone suggested to her that she should consult Mrs. Dolmetsch. When she was 80, Dame Marie recalled how much she had learned from Mabel: 'Her work on the dances was a tremendous contribution . . . nobody had written these steps down . . . in modern times. Mrs. Dolmetsch seemed rather old to me then . . . she must have been over forty but she danced *beautifully* . . . she reminded me of a mediaeval picture.' It seems that whenever she arrived for her lesson the family were in the kitchen baking: 'Then we all trooped into the dining room and had tea with freshly baked bread and cakes.'

Dolmetsch's diaries, which begin in 1917,[5] although written in telegraphic-style French, give us a vivid picture of his and the family's activities at the time. He records concerts, lessons, appointments and auction sales: he appears to have attended several of these and made a number of purchases, most likely to sell again for profit. Every piece is entered, and in comparison with today's prices he seems to have struck an extraordinary number of bargains. For instance, on 20 May Beatrice Horne (presumably on his behalf), 'acheté la vielle à la vente Cummings [d. 1915] pour £3 prix très bas'. This scoring off his old enemy must have given Dolmetsch considerable pleasure.

The most consistently recorded events are the two main preoccupations of Dolmetsch's life: his garden and the weather. Every sowing, flowering, picking, is known to us, as is the appearance of the sun, mist or storm. 'Jardin, Cécile sème Beet, radish' . . . 'le 1er semé qui donne peu' . . .' 'mangé grand plat d'haricots beurre' and then 'Mauvais temps' . . . or, 'Belle journée d'été—Repas au jardin'. Family illnesses, with the changing temperatures of the patients such as in an epidemic of influenza, are all there, together with a daily bulletin of their progress.

Unfortunately this idyllic picture was soon disrupted by the first air-raids. On 7 July, we read: 'Air Raid—Cécile et Mabel en danger'. Although the horticultural activities continue as before, there are increasing fears as the raids persist. On 4 September, '2 raids pendant la nuit à 11.50 et à 12.30. Torpedoes [bombs?] bomber près d'ici notre canon tire plusieurs fois on entend les aéroplanes au dessus de notre maison on ne voit rien.'

By disturbing nights already shortened by the demands of the workshop, the raids had a deleterious effect on Dolmetsch's health. He found he could no longer concentrate properly and was in constant fear for his family's safety. Beatrice Horne came to the rescue. Normally she lived in town but she also owned a small cottage at Thursley in Surrey and Mabel occasionally took the three younger children to stay. When Dolmetsch reached the stage of being unable to work in Hampstead, Beatrice Horne offered them her cottage in return for a modest rent. They arrived there in the middle of September and the few weeks of tranquillity did much to restore both Dolmetsch's health and his temper: the children in turn regained the vitality they had lost through constantly disturbed nights. But true to the pattern of living to which they had grown accustomed, no sooner had they settled down than the owner became unable to bear the air-raids herself and asked for the return of her cottage. So most of the autumn of 1917 was spent looking at properties in neighbouring villages.

House-hunting may have kept them busy but it did not prevent Dolmetsch and his wife undertaking a concert tour of Ireland, for which they received a fee of 35 guineas. It is interesting to note that apart from the fees the only entry for this tour was that on 1 November, when Dolmetsch purchased a leg of smoked bacon from a celebrated pork butcher in Cork for £3 4s. 6d. Ten days later Dolmetsch bemoans: 'Perdu le lard d'Irlande!'

It seems that it was difficult to find a house large enough for their needs and to suit their pocket. Dolmetsch was now almost 60 and he wanted this move to be the last. On 22 November we read in his diary: 'Mabel et Cécile vont à Witley et Haslemere voir des maisons. Trouvent "Jesses", qu'elles pensent convenable.' The next day: 'Visité "Jesses" Approuvé. Offert à l'agent de la prendre 9 mois à partir de Noel à £50 par an. avec option achat pour £1,050. Appris qu'il y a hypothèque pour £930.'

Mabel had first seen their new home in the snow, the surrounding trees sparkling white in the winter sunshine. It was of dark red brick, built about 1844 on high ground in the style of an old Sussex farmhouse: its long front garden stretched to meet the road below, which joined the villages of Grayswood and Haslemere. Mabel Dolmetsch has often been accredited with having second sight. When she first set foot in the porch of the new house, she is reputed to have said that if they moved there they would never have cause to leave it. Considering the ubiquitousness of their existence to date it was certainly a rash statement, but she proved to be right for both she and her husband died at 'Jesses' and two generations of the present family are still there today.

It was when they were living at Thursley that Dolmetsch and his wife had become acquainted with French-Canadian troops stationed at Witley Camp: the soldiers had overheard the couple speaking their native language and had introduced themselves. Subsequently the Dolmetsches had entertained them on numerous occasions and in addition gave concerts to the troops at the camp, with the result that when the family made the move to Haslemere on 20 December the unit produced horse-drawn waggons and men, who made short work of transferring all the Dolmetsches' possessions to the new house: indeed a fortuitous association, for no form of haulage was readily available to private persons at this time.

The winter of 1917 was a hard one, and snow lay deep on the ground as they unpacked, shivering in the unheated house. But within a few hours the indefatigable Mabel had found some oil stoves and produced a meal of sorts. On Christmas Day she served the traditional dinner with plum pudding and all the festive accompaniments, cooked on an old kitchen range that she had met for the first time only five days before.

The family settled down well at 'Jesses' and Dolmetsch chose for his workshop the room on the ground floor that today houses the Library. He continued to make and restore instruments, and gave concerts in neighbouring villages and in the local St. Christopher's and later Haslemere Halls. The children attended St. George's Wood, a girls' school just across the road from their own house. The rules were waived in order to allow the two boys to attend, but Rudolph's good looks were alleged to have impaired several schoolgirls' concentration when he was in sight.

It was at St. George's Wood that Dolmetsch once again took up music class-teaching and raised the standards considerably during this time: he again adopted the individual methods that he had used at Dulwich and within a short time had two school orchestras (in which the headmistress, Miss Kemp, took part), operating with considerable success. Dolmetsch writes to Ernest Newman (15 July 1918) about a performance of *The Tempest* in which his pupils, 'the little band of musicians I started *this term* and none of which had ever touched a string instrument before, are performing all the necessary music and dance tunes, Elizabethan of course. This is a fact of such interest, showing the possibility of a general revival of true home music that I think it would be well worth while for you to come all the way from Birmingham here, to report upon it.'

Dolmetsch stresses the fact that these players had not been specially selected but that they are just average schoolgirls. He is confident that the same result can be obtained with adults, even if they are old. It is unlikely that Newman would have travelled all the way from Birmingham to attend a school concert, but Dolmetsch's enthusiasm would not have been any the less had Newman lived in the Hebrides.

A sad note enters a later letter (21 October): 'Hélène Dolmetsch, who is coming to play the viola da gamba in Birmingham next December, is a daughter of mine from a former marriage, not a happy one like the present! We have been estranged for 15 years. She acted badly towards me and would not forget it. I would . . . However, she is gifted, musically. I thought you had better know this, as you will go to her concert.'

By this time the Dolmetsch children were full members of the family consort: Rudolph, in particular, was fulfilling his early promise. At the age of nine he could read from a figured bass without difficulty and by his tenth birthday was giving remarkable interpretations of Bach and Couperin on the keyboard instruments. Dolmetsch proudly described his continuo playing to a friend as being 'the best . . . I ever had'. And this happy situation continued in spite of the wartime difficulties which beset their concert-giving. But on 11 November Dolmetsch, always balancing so delightfully between the serious and the ridiculous, entered in his diary:

Fin de la Guerre, nouvelle vient à 11 heures. 2 vaches passent dans le jardin et mangent 13 choux.[6]

Six months later, Dolmetsch makes another entry:

May 26 1919

À Bedales arrangé avec Mrs. Fish que j'irais 2 fois par semaine pour 2 hr ½ a 10/6 l'heure.[7]

A week later he started giving lessons to the pupils at Dunhurst, the preparatory department of Bedales School: thereby began an association which was to last until the war of 1939. At first Dolmetsch taught in the classes himself but later he was assisted by Rudolph and other members of his family. Eventually his children and their families took over completely. Miles Tomalin, Dolmetsch's pupil, also took a very active part in teaching at Dunhurst and applied his considerable gifts of writing and composing to great effect.

Dolmetsch very soon improved the existing musical standards and saw to it that the children were given reasonably good instruments to play. He would go to auctions in London and buy suitable instruments and carry out all the restoration and repair himself. At Dunhurst he again introduced his specialised methods of teaching based on Playford (see p. 17) and although he came in for a certain amount of criticism, the results proved beyond doubt that his system worked for the majority of his pupils. He could inspire the most indifferent child with a desire to make music. A charming pen-picture by one of his pupils during this period, Inès Walter (now Lady Burrows), gives us some idea of how he was regarded by the young under his care:

> When I think of AD my mind is instantly full of pictures: his carved ivory, intensely mobile face, small hunched figure in its baggy black trousers, black skull cap, strong, thick waving white hair tucked behind his ears. A fine, extremely arresting head, alive, restless black eyes darting, piercing, brilliant. His smile, which was a little alarming because you were not at once quite sure that it was not a snarl (perhaps over a remembered wrong note in a phrase during orchestra practice before lunch?); but once established that it *was* a smile, then full of charm and impish humour . . . His way of covering his ears with both arms (while holding a fiddle in one hand and a bow in the other) in mock—but not altogether mock— agony over a wrong note; and his crushingly derisive imitation (in front of the assembled orchestra of 6–12 year olds) of a young performer whose performance displeased him, scraping the strings of his own violin with his bow until the delinquent's spine bristled with shame, and the others, not this time selected for derision, thanked God for their escape.

Lady Burrows is quite convinced that, without exception, he was held in absolute respect by all the children. In this context an extremely strong impression remained with her that his own children were as much in awe of him as were his pupils: a consoling thought for these youngsters, who were unaccustomed to be treated in anything but the most courteous manner.

Another remembered picture is that of the orchestra assembled under the old beech tree on the lawn on a hot summer afternoon ready for a rehearsal:

> Dolmetsch would arrive with Rudolph, probably arguing over a point of technique—which Dolmetsch would win—and then Rudolph would be brusquely ordered to go to a certain place—he [Rudolph] goes without protest. The children are transfixed and watch him [Arnold] gravely, holding their breaths. When he is

ready there is absolute silence and after telling them how they should play, a nod indicates that the first notes may be sounded. If there is a slip, he raps his bow on the chair, exclaiming loudly, making a terrible grimace of pure anger. It is completely effective. There is no mistake the second time. The anger passes as if it had never been, he is in a world of music: it matters not that the music is played most imperfectly by under-teenage children. For a moment of time everyone is united in the pure enjoyment of creating music. This is all that matters. . . . He himself plays with the first violins and conducts at the same time . . . There is no sheet music to read, it has all been learnt by heart. Looking back and wondering what was strange and unique about it all, I think this is described by the *seriousness* of the attitudes involved, and the immense trouble AD took over the progress of his pupils. All the children in the orchestra were treated as adult musicians, and as such with complete seriousness. . . . He demanded their complete concentration, their comprehension and above all simple good taste.

Once when talking of these children at Dunhurst, Dolmetsch said: 'Music is for their delight and it deserves that they should bring to it all their devotion—or leave it alone! It is meant to be enjoyed; this can be done most easily by children who have more capacity for natural innocent uninhibited enjoyment than anyone else. By starting young and imbibing the kind of music I give them, their ear will be imperceptibly trained and they will forever after be unlikely to fall into the usual errors of taste—musically. A high standard of appreciation acquired at the age of seven or even earlier can never altogether leave you, however much you superimpose upon it—however much you add to and widen your knowledge. And this has nothing to do with being a professional musician.'

Dolmetsch did not believe in professionalism as we know it today: he believed in music for and by the family. It was the Elizabethan idea. By the same token we do not today wear ruffles, but we still enjoy the work of artists who have captured the period for us in their paintings.

*   *   *

The freedom and pace of rural life had always suited the Dolmetsches and in Haslemere they were able to enjoy the village atmosphere that went so naturally with their own old-world activities. Gradually they became acquainted with a few artistically inclined neighbours who were also wealthy, but in a letter to his pupil Jean Sinclair Buchanan, Dolmetsch shows a marked interest in the lesser orders:

Jesses
March 2nd 1919   Haslemere,
Surrey

All the cheap seats at a concert were filled by the shop-keepers and small local people. I am delighted and proud to see how keenly they delight in our music and how intelligently they appreciate it. For 200 years it has been witheld from them.

They never were in sympathy with the foreign, mostly German, music that was pressed upon them. Consequently it was said they were not musical. But I know this was not true.

And in an earlier letter to Mrs. Buchanan we have a positive glimpse of his integrity. Apparently he had received an order with payment from an American musician, Lotte van Buren. He was constantly short of money at this time, but despite this he writes:

Jesses,
Haslemere,
Surrey.

January 26th 1919

I have become seriously doubtful as to whether these virginals will stand the climate of America. I have not been able, on account of war conditions, to make them as I intended. It seems to me it would be better all round that I should dispose of it here, and return her the money she has paid on account. I could get her a reliable instrument later on.

From this correspondence we also learn that Dolmetsch was trying to organise a more effective workshop: he is awaiting the demobilisation of one or two skilled craftsmen who have promised to work for him, so that soon he may finish more clavichords and virginals.

But on 30 April of that year an incident occurred that would result in Dolmetsch becoming known the world over, although at the time he was in despair.

The family had been performing at a concert at the Artworkers' Guild in London and were assembled on Waterloo Station awaiting the train for Haslemere. However weary they might have been, the children were delegated to carry some part of their equipment. It was the seven-year-old Carl's job to carry the bag of tools in which were also kept the two recorders. When it arrived they boarded the train and settled down for the journey: little Carl was asleep before the train had moved from the platform. During the run, Dolmetsch needed something from the bag and to his horror he saw it was not on the rack. It was characteristic of him that the greater the disaster, the calmer he became. He would be violent and noisy over trifles, but this occasion was a grave tragedy, shared by all the family: Carl Dolmetsch recalls it as being decidedly 'non-violent'. But the entry in Dolmetsch's diary that night is perhaps the greatest insight into this extraordinary man's thinking:

Concert Londres AWG. Grd Succès—Baba abandonne mon sac à main contenant le recorder et mes outils etc., à Waterloo en face de la plateforme No 5 Désespoir! Belle journée.[8]

Every effort was made to retrieve the lost bag but without success. Assiduous tours of second-hand shops and promises of rewards brought

La Société des Instruments Anciens, 1897

Music room in Dolmetsch's house in Cambridge, Mass.,

Suzanne Bloch,
1934

Dolmetsch family, 1925
Back row (l. to r.) : Rudolph, Arnold
Front row : Cécile, Nathalie, Carl and Mabel

Arnold Dolmetsch
with Robert Donington,
1935

Rudolph Dolmetsch
recording for Columbia
Studios, 1929

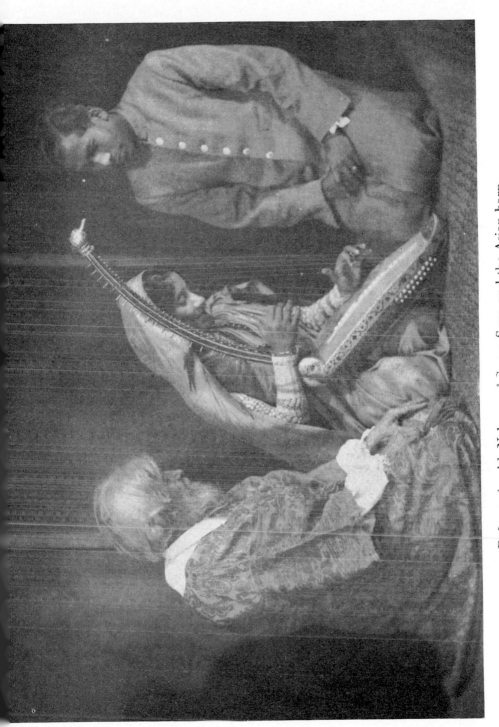

Dolmetsch with Nelun and Surya Sena and the Asian harp
which he made for them in 1935

Aged 75, in the garden at Haslemere

With Mabel at his
80th Birthday Concert at
the Art Workers' Guild

Teaching at Dunhurst Junior School, Bedales, *c.* 1921

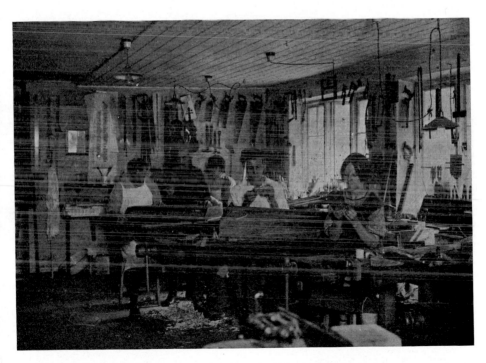

The Dolmetsch family workshop, Haslemere

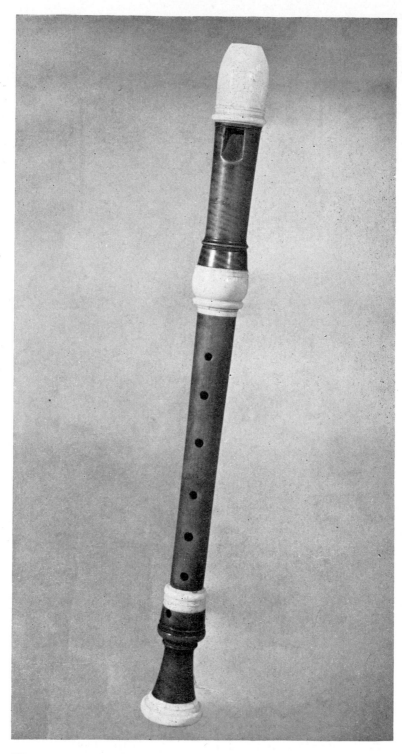

The recorder by Pui Bressan, the loss of which in 1918 caused
Dolmetsch to make the first modern recorder

nothing.[9] The bag in itself was an inconvenient loss, for many of the tools had been made by Dolmetsch: but the recorders were impossible to replace. There were virtually no others to be had in playing condition. Canon Galpin had one or two which he and his family used for their private musical evenings and there was the 'Chester' set in the museum belonging to that town. Since he had now successfully introduced a fair amount of recorder music into his programmes, Dolmetsch was loath to abandon this repertoire.

At first he thought it would only be necessary to do so until replacements could be acquired, but he was wrong. Fortunately he had taken down all the measurements of the lost instruments; his favourite was the one he had bought in the Taphouse sale in 1905,[10] so he set to work on making a copy. He then spent the following year experimenting, rejecting model after model because the right intonation constantly eluded him. He would produce a beautiful looking instrument, every turn accurate to a fraction of an inch and a mouthpiece that exactly matched that of the missing instrument, but no amount of drilling or filling would produce the intonation he desired. On August Bank Holiday, when he finally solved the problem, he rushed into the kitchen shouting 'Eureka! Eureka! I've got it!' and danced round the room repeating his newly-found note like a two-year-old with a birthday whistle. Dolmetsch, at 60, had perpetuated the legend by achieving yet another seeming impossibility: one that would result in his prototype being reproduced in millions before the century had reached half its span.

*　　*　　*

The 'gramophone' had become a household word by the early twenties, its success mainly due to the recordings made by the world-famous tenor Caruso. After the human voice came the military bands, the instrumentalists and the pianists: it was therefore not surprising that The Graphophone Company (later Columbia) should approach Dolmetsch to make some recordings of early music. Percy Scholes[11] was concerned in this particular series and a letter to him from Mabel Dolmetsch on 5 January 1921 discusses making an appointment for them to meet. No more information is available until 31 December of the same year, when Dolmetsch writes to Scholes:

> Jesses
> Haslemere,
> Surrey.
>
> The Gramophone [sic] Co. have taken some records of our instruments, separately and in various combinations. Ten or so. They seem to me very good. The timbre

of the instruments is reproduced very faithfully. They don't sound as loud as Caruso's but they are, I think, quite loud enough.

They might interest only a small section of the public, but from the educational point of view, they are worth having.

Now, the Committee of the Gram. Co., think they are not powerful enough to publish. I differ from them. I am probably wrong. Anyway, I should like to have an independent and impartial opinion on the point. Would you like to hear them? Anyway, they *are* interesting.

The archives are silent as to the progress of these recordings, but it would seem that Dolmetsch was the first person to make recordings of music played on the harpsichord, viols and recorder, even if these early attempts were never issued to the public. The first person to record harpsichord-playing was his pupil Mrs. Violet Gordon Woodhouse in July 1920.

During the time that Dolmetsch was negotiating to make the gramophone records, he was also making inquiries as to the cost of building a workshop adjacent to the house: one of his young pupils, Marco Pallis,[12] had offered to finance this undertaking. At an estimate of £632 the work was put in hand in February 1921: the extra space would enable Dolmetsch to increase his intake of apprentices and pupils, and there would be additional room to accommodate a few permanent craftsmen whom he had trained himself. It was an amusing twist of fate that at the same time as Dolmetsch put his signature to the estimate for his own workshop to be built, he received a letter from Gaveau in Paris. They were now reorganising the firm after having suffered considerable damage during the war, and were most anxious to know if Dolmetsch would be interested in returning to work for them. Dolmetsch's diary eschews an entry but his reaction is not difficult to imagine.

The workshop was completed by the autumn of 1921 at a figure considerably higher than the original estimate. The extra space and plant helped in increasing production, but there was still the question of how to pay the wages. Dolmetsch, at this time, had two excellent craftsmen in his employ—Bernard Unwin, a member of the publishing family and Oskar Dawson—but they never knew if they would be paid at the end of the week. The workshop and the household were run together on a rob-Peter-to-pay-Paul system and it was no more unusual for a workman to ask Mrs. Dolmetsch for half a crown to post a package than for her to resort to the petty cash for a few shillings to pay the domestic help.

Somehow she always managed enough food for the family and could accommodate an unexpected guest without much ado: the children never lacked warm clothing and Dolmetsch certainly was not denied his bottle of wine, although its source was Mabel's own secret. She had a genius for making ends meet, even if they seemed a hundred miles apart. Despite her own comfortable upbringing, she was as adept at getting the most out of every penny as if she had been born in the slums: and she could accept, with almost royal grace, gifts that were offered by their more discerning admirers.

Dolmetsch's individual attitude to money never changed: for himself he needed little: he always wore the same clothes—a William Morris suit, knee breeches, thick woollen stockings and an orange silk tie. Apart from his favourite strong-smelling Brazilian tobacco, he never spent a penny on himself. Money for the workshop was quite another matter: he seemed to have little regard as to where the resources came from as long as his work could survive. This approach did not stem wholly from a lack of concern for others: the scientific and logical bent in his nature visualised the end product rather than the means, and therefore did not regard the gifts as personal but rather more as a contribution to music as a whole. In the light of the advances made in early music today, it is doubtful whether anyone could claim that at the time his opinions were unjustified.

Apart from a long working day[13] and a brain that never stopped thinking, Dolmetsch regularly attended sales at Puttick and Simpson and made a number of purchases, all of which are recorded in his diaries: he seldom profited much on re-selling the instruments, for prices were not high at this time.

Another entry of a more private nature, in his diary, reports: 'Arrivée d'Hélène' on 17 January. The reconciliation was brought about by Mabel, who had sought her out at her London home. When his daughter returned to London, Dolmetsch notes: 'Hélène nous quitte- guérie apparament.' She paid a second visit to Haslemere in April and all their differences were discussed and resolved completely. It remained an occasion that Dolmetsch could never recall without emotion. Then on 7 July he writes in his diary: 'Hélène morte à 7 h du matin.' On the following Wednesday he and Mabel attended her funeral in Dulwich. All the associations must have made it a very sad time for Dolmetsch. A heart condition had weakened Hélène's already frail constitution and death was caused by a stroke, which brought on total paralysis; but she lived only a few days in this terrible state. She was forty-six when she died, but had become very embittered over the years. When Mabel went to collect her belongings she discovered a complete trousseau neatly folded in tissue paper: when she became engaged, or to whom she hoped to be married, has remained a mystery to the present time.

Even death in the family could not keep Dolmetsch down for long. Throughout the spring and early summer he had been giving concerts at the Haslemere Hall, The Artworkers' Guild and the Grotrian Hall: in

March he travelled up to Liverpool to give a series of concerts in the Rushworth and Dreaper Hall which had been arranged simultaneously with an exhibition of early musical instruments organised by Marco Pallis and Cyril Goldie, an art teacher and 'cellist who had become an enthusiast and skilled performer on the viola da gamba.

That last Liverpool tour of 1924 set Arnold Dolmetsch thinking of yet another new plan. He had spent his life taking his music to the people of the British Isles and beyond. Why should they not now come to him? On the train journey back from the north he began working out a scheme: he would start a festival in Haslemere. By the time he had reached home, his eternal optimism had overtaken him and had envisaged an event that would bring music lovers from all over the world. He may have been a little premature, but this time he was right.

NOTES

1. An interesting letter from Verbrugghen, 18 February 1934 (Jesses) tells how he has been assisted by Dolmetsch's work. He writes that Dolmetsch has started him on a path which he has followed ever since, preaching Dolmetsch's gospel in the Antipodes and America. He comments that he found it odd that so many musicians, indisputable proof notwithstanding, still ignored the methods of the 'olden days'.

2. Newman, Ernest, *The New Witness*, 13 January 1916, pp. 318–20.

3. Dannreuther, Edward, *Musical Ornamentation*, Novello, Ewer & Co., 1893, Volumes I and II.

4. *Everyman's Enclycopaedia*, J. M. Dent, London, 1958, p. 423.
   In the 1920s Marie Rambert took the celebrated dancer, Leonide Massine, to Haslemere. He was greatly impressed with Arnold Dolmetsch's work and confirmed this admiration in a letter to the writer in 1968.

5. Several earlier diaries, written mostly in English, from 1902–16 are extant. Then a larger set (French) 1917–39.

6. End of the war: news came in at 11 o'clock. Two cows come through the garden and eat thirteen cabbages.

7. At Bedales—I arranged with Mrs. Fish that I would go twice a week for $2\frac{1}{2}$ weeks at 10s. 6d. an hour.

8. Concert at AWG (Artworkers' Guild Hall), London—great success. 'Baba' [Carl Dolmetsch] left my bag with the recorder and my tools etc., in it on Waterloo Station in front of platform No 5. Despair! Beautiful day!

9. Eventually the recorder was purchased by the clarinettist Geoffrey Rendell in a second-hand shop in the Waterloo Road for 5s. He visited Dolmetsch to show him his 'bargain' but as soon as Rendell pulled out the mouthpiece, Dolmetsch recog-

nised it as his lost instrument. Rendell straightaway gave it to Dolmetsch and was later presented with one of the first Dolmetsch recorders.

10. Recorder in F by Pui Bressan *c.* 1720–24 described in the Sotheby catalogue in the Taphouse sale as: 'Recorder or Flute à Bec, English, ivory, about 1730.'

11. Percy Scholes, 1877–1958, English musical author and lexicographer.

12. Marco Pallis was one of Dolmetsch's pupils at Haslemere in the early '20s. He later worked enthusiastically for the Dolmetsch Foundation and wrote articles for *The Consort*. He became a good performer on the viols and later formed The English Consort of Viols: he is now Professor of Viols at the Royal College of Music.

13. A fine instrument made at this time (1924) was a clavichord for presentation to Robert Bridges, Poet Laureate, on the occasion of his 80th birthday. It was beautifully decorated with paintings by Mabel and inscriptions in gilded lettering by Cécile. There is a picture of this instrument in *Early Musical Instruments* by Philip James, Davies London (1930), plate no. XVIII.

CHAPTER XVIII

The Voice of the Nightingale

WHEN Arnold Dolmetsch had an idea his enthusiasm could not be contained. Long before arrangements for the forthcoming festival of chamber music had been completed, it was being widely discussed among critics and musicians. Whether they scoffed or speculated, curiosity made brothers of them all. The Dolmetsches were regularly criticised for being under-rehearsed and for appearing on the platform in quaint costumes that had never seen an iron. Now the patriarch of early music was in charge and there would be no restraining hand. Certainly it was a prospect to liven the accustomed quiet of the summer season.

Although Dolmetsch welcomed controversy, he was shrewd enough to know that a festival would attract more attention if he could persuade a celebrity to open the proceedings with a few friendly words. It was to Shaw, who had helped him so much in the past, that he wrote, but the request was rejected with characteristic wit and good advice. Shaw told Dolmetsch that nothing would induce him to 'dose' this audience with 'chin-music'. He praised Dolmetsch's special gift for entertaining audiences by commentaries and considered that any 'distant nervous utterance' from either critic or historian would ruin the festival. Dolmetsch's 'personality . . . rare power of speaking . . . with complete and instantaneous intimacy (not possessed by one per cent of our best public speakers) . . . delightful foreign accent which never checks the rush of . . . English words' were all of such value that to give the speeches to an outsider would be like abandoning the lute and substituting 'an ophicleide played by a Teddy bear!' He advised Dolmetsch to keep the whole affair in his own hands and to behave exactly as he did in Queen Square with the Art-workers' Guild concerts. Shaw knew that he himself would not draw a musical crowd and reminded Dolmetsch that his business was to fill the seats with people who will want to come again for the love of the music, not with 'idiots' who come to gape and never return.

No concert was ever safe from comment by Dolmetsch, so that there was no fear of deprivation on this score. Nonetheless, he insisted upon a speaker and at the first concert (25 August 1925) Joseph King, a business man and ex-MP with a love for music, made the introductory speech.

The evening was warm and the little Haslemere Hall was packed. There were musicians, men of letters, politicians, publishers; there was a professor from the Berlin Conservatory, travelling at his government's expense, and a woman writer from the *New York Times*. There were 12 concerts in all, every evening except Sunday for two weeks; four were devoted to Bach,[1] two each to English music and concerted music for viols, and one each to the music of French and Italian composers. The remaining concerts were given to Haydn and Mozart and 'Composers of Various Nationalities'. Though Dolmetsch was then nearing 70, only a handful of his patrons realised that his work had been before them for some 35 years before the first festival opened its doors. Almost every item in the programme had been heard previously, many at his own concerts in the 1890s.

If the private patrons were not fully aware of what the festival meant, the critics knew that something extraordinary had happened in the musical world, and the wide and mainly enthusiastic coverage reflected their interest. Of course there were still those who pleaded for the 'cello instead of the gamba and complaints that the clavichord could not be heard. But whichever side they were on they couldn't stay away.

The *Daily Telegraph* critic orginally intended to cover the first two concerts but was so captivated that he persuaded his editor to allow him to stay for the entire two weeks, sending daily reports—something unheard of in 1925. He points out that many people will have met for the first time the tenor violin, the lyra-viol, double-bass viol (violone) and the viola d'amore. The tenor violin was being heard for the first time since it went out of use, and people could judge for themselves whether or not its voice should be heard in the string quartet or indeed in the orchestra. On the use of the 'older violin'[2] for an unaccompanied prelude and fugue, he writes: 'To hear Bach's music played "in native worth" is to realise how very much a man of his own time he was; with contemporary forms of expression he was always in touch and through this touch, the forms throbbed with a life and energy that have not yet been exhausted.' *The Times* critic tells us that Mr. Dolmetsch has given us 'Home music' (instead of a concert) in that 'he talked as well as played to us—and claimed with every justification that the concerto in D minor for harpsichord and strings to be played there and then by his family, would reproduce the conditions existing in Bach's own family'.

It seems that Dolmetsch was in genial mood but he 'could not altogether forbear from chastising the faithful in the manner of popular preachers for the blindness and shortcomings of the unregenerate'. The writer says that, as always at Mr. Dolmetsch's concerts, one feels some guilt at having been present at all and rather wondered how he had been persuaded to broadcast some of the concerts of this festival.[3] Having indulged in his innocent fun at Dolmetsch's expense, he writes:

> It was a valuable experience to hear his music as Bach himself heard it. The scale of the concerto accompanied by one instrument to a part (violins, gamba and the sweet-toned violone) is smaller . . . the concert grand pianoforte, and passages where there is a toccata-like figure for two manuals (in the first movement for instance, just before the final reinstatement over a pedal bass) or where there are little cascades of sound (as at the very end of the concerto) had a peculiar beauty in this, their historically correct rendering. We cannot give up our big orchestral performances but these chamber representations are the more valuable as necessary correctives and as reminders that Bach has an elusive charm besides his more austere and his more vigorous qualities. *Plus fait douceur que violence* is the apt motto on the lid of Mr. Dolmetsch's new clavichord, the beauties of which were unfolded in performances of 2 preludes and fugues and the chromatic fantasia.

Every account draws attention to the exceedingly gifted Rudolph, then not yet 19. *The Times* critic is in no doubt:

> The harpsichord playing of the evening showed not only a technical mastery that made one happy, but a musical instinct for the subtleties of phrasing that marked him as an artist who, though very young, may no longer be called, promising: as a harpsichordist, he has arrived.

In addition to the evening concerts an exhibition of their instruments, together with books and manuscripts, was held every morning in the Haslemere Hall, with pupils and younger members of the family in attendance to answer questions and give demonstrations. Parties of visitors holding concert-tickets were also taken over the 'Jesses Workshop'; the *Daily Telegraph* (27 August) representative had been one of these, and was impressed that Dolmetsch had 'trained his followers to be both artists and artisans. . . . There was a curiously mediaeval atmosphere in the workshop—mediaeval save for a few examples of modern machinery. These, I was made most carefully to understand, were only used when an instrument was required urgently, or when one small section was holding up the rest of the construction. Otherwise the work is most jealously preserved for the encouragement of handcrafts and such machinery as there is has been adapted and adjusted for the making of the old instruments, since it is obviously impossible to obtain a ready-made device from a modern market.' He adds that 'William Morris would have delighted in this close alliance of the arts and crafts'.

Basil Maine, who wrote those first notices in the *Daily Telegraph*, became a regular annual visitor to Haslemere. In a book which came out some five years afterwards,[4] he suggests that Dolmetsch was perhaps the only musician at this time who was truly 'self-dependant and self-sufficient'. The yearly festivals proved his courage and conviction and there are signs that 'the vigour of his faith is compelling more and more people to revise their preconceptions as to the true nature of music'.

After the close of that first summer festival, orders for instruments came in from many places abroad and offers of engagements poured in from all over the British Isles. Concerts involving long train journeys never did much more than cover expenses but they did promote interest, and that was enough for Dolmetsch. However, he was now forced to be more selective in accepting engagements too far afield, but London appearances could never be resisted. Three December concerts in a series at the Chenil Galleries in Chelsea were particularly successful. At the first of these he received an enthusiastic response from the press for his playing on the clavichord of the Bach Prelude and Fugue in B flat major (Book 1) and the Chromatic Fantasia.

＊　＊　＊

Dolmetsch's knowledge of the Bachs and their music had gained him the respect of F. T. Arnold, whose book[5] has remained an authority on accompaniment from a figured bass. Subsequently, the two men became close friends but met infrequently. Arnold would pay an occasional visit to Haslemere when there was something important that could only be settled by private discussion, but their main intercourse was through the written word. Arnold was a voracious correspondent and the letters to Dolmetsch which have survived throughout the period from 1924 to 1938 are packed with information and discussion, each musical example drawn in faultless manuscript. The letters are also very amusing. A gourmet and a renowned connoisseur of wine, Arnold possessed a well-stocked cellar of Edwardian proportions. Dolmetsch was the frequent recipient of cases of wine, liqueurs, plover's eggs, mussels, oysters and truffles from the Pyrenees. Arnold would also invite Dolmetsch to drink to Bach's 246th birthday, or Corelli's 282nd. If such an anniversary occurred on the date on which he was writing, he would head the letter with the composer's name: i.e. 'Handel's 249th birthday'.

Although a recognised expert on the art of thorough bass, Arnold's letters reveal that time and time again there arose a point where his own knowledge would not provide the answer and he would turn to Dolmetsch for advice. Dolmetsch generally supplied an explanation to the most obscure problem and it was for this that Arnold showed his gratitude with gifts of wine and rare foods. Unfortunately not one letter from Dolmetsch to Arnold has survived but the Arnold writings are so detailed that they indicate the content of Dolmetsch's letters.

Dolmetsch greatly respected Arnold; in a letter of 21 October 1925 he notes no fewer than 22 errors in Dolmetsch's own book and kindly suggests that in some future edition these should, for the sake of accuracy, be rectified. Although Arnold's advice was taken only in part, it does not appear to have had a disruptive effect upon their friendship. In a letter dated 21 December 1925, Arnold informs Dolmetsch that he is sending him a bottle of 1904 cognac to greet him on his return from Ventnor, where he has been resting. He also tells him that he has now finished his article for the new Grove's *Dictionary* on thorough bass which will replace the present one by Rockstro:

> 9, Pulteney Street,
> Bath
>
> I remember now that I wanted to mention it, but felt ashamed to do so, as I felt that it was you and not I who ought to have been asked. When I get the proofs I should be very grateful if you would let me send them to you as I should greatly value your opinion, even though it would not be possible now to make any very extensive alterations.

Arnold writes that 'he had a good slap at Vaughan Williams (of course without mentioning his name) and all the "Musicians" who perform Bach without the figured bass accompaniment and excuse the omission by saying that the harmony is supplied by the instrumental or vocal parts'.

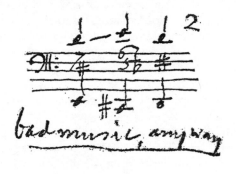

Park View House,
Brock Street,
Bath.

22nd April 1926

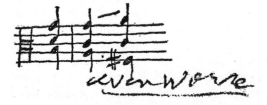

In the following spring Arnold writes a long letter filled with questions which Dolmetsch had evidently answered satisfactorily. And although the actual reply has not survived, Dolmetsch made a few pencilled notes beside the musical examples in Arnold's letter. Of a 'transferred resolution' by Ph. E. Bach from *Versuch Ch. I s 67*, Dolmetsch writes 'bad music anyway' and of a further example he writes 'even worse'. For examples see opposite page.

Then, in typical F.T.A. fashion, he adds:

> One more question: Do you like cream? Because I can get very good Devonshire cream here *without preservative* and should like to send you some plover's eggs, but they seem to have come prematurely to an end.

With much apology and considerable pleading, Arnold writes again to Dolmetsch on 29 May 1926 asking him for a favour:

> Park View House,
> Brock Street,
> Bath
>
> I go on Tuesday next (1 June) to Cambridge . . . to deliver the MS of my book[6] at the University Press, for approval . . . I don't think any of the people to whom the book will be submitted have any idea of the importance of the subject or sufficient knowledge of it to make them competant critics—They will only realise that it is very *long*— If you, who are so universally acknowledged as an authority, wd. write a few lines concerning the *need* for some such work and adding anything that you cd, conscientiously say about my qualifications for the task (you know that I have, at all events, a genuine interest in the music of the period) you wd. be doing me a great service, and it might just turn the scale between acceptance and rejection.

By October, Arnold is full of more questions on a passage from Agazzari, translated by Praetorius. But after two pages he returns to an epicurean inquiry as to whether Dolmetsch has the wherewithal to open oysters. Arnold is sending some 'delicious' ones from the Army and Navy Stores, 'small, but very plump'. These will be accompanied by some fine Dutch mussels. The letter closes with precise instructions as to how to open oysters with an ordinary knife, should Dolmetsch have no other means available.

Opening oysters was not Dolmetsch's main concern that summer. His plans for the second Haslemere Festival were going ahead. He had reconstructed the complete family of viols and violins (including the tenor), but he wanted to achieve a recorder consort.[7] He realised that ambition on 25 August, the second night of the 1926 festival with a Purcell Chaconne in three parts from *Dioclesian* and Couperin's *Les Fauvettes Plaintives*, also in three parts. The first five part consorts for descant, two trebles, tenor and bass were performed on 30 August at the same Festival. However, it was at an all-Bach programme on the opening night that Dolmetsch brought about another 'first' performance, once again taking a practical step to recreate a sound which had not been experienced by any British audience since Bach's own family music-making: it was the Brandenburg Concerto No. 4 in G major with Dolmetsch on the solo violin and his son, Rudolph, and Miles Tomalin playing the 2 'Flauti d'Echo' recorders in G. He had finished these two instruments in time for the festival and Dolmetsch himself explained: 'It is possible to play very softly upon them without lowering the pitch, and so produce the lovely "echo" effects demanded in the Andante of that Concerto. I had previously made Recorders in F only, but having now succeeded with the smaller ones in G, I tried a larger one, a Tenor in C, which was wanted for Consorts. It also succeeded. Then came a booming Bass in F and a small Descant in C, with a voice like a nightingale. We then had a whole family, one Descant, two Trebles, Tenor and Bass.' The critics were well-pleased with the second Haslemere Festival and devoted much space in praise of Dolmetsch's newest instruments.

Arnold Dolmetsch had always dreamed of founding a centre where his work could flourish and develop; from their very inception, the first two festivals achieved this without anyone being aware of it. The Haslemere 'centre' had attracted the attention of a number of younger people anxious to break away from the established musical scene. Marco Pallis was already working hard for the cause and he brought several of his young friends from Liverpool. Then there was Gerald Hayes[8], a musicologist who first came for advice and stayed to write, under Dolmetsch's guidance, several books on early music and its instruments. Miles Tomalin,[9] a brilliant young Cambridge graduate, who was said to be (apart from Carl Dolmetsch) one of the finest recorder players ever heard at Haslemere.

Perhaps the most significant figure at that period was the young Robert Donington. Already living at Haslemere with his family, he met the Dolmetsches when he was still a schoolboy, before he became interested in early music. When first he attended their concerts he was still far more concerned with Wagner and Beethoven. During the third Festival in 1927, he went every night to the concerts and was captivated by the sheer beauty of the English consort music. One evening, after a programme consisting wholly of viol consorts in five and six parts, he was so moved that he broke away from his parents and accosted Dolmetsch backstage, telling him that he wanted to become his pupil. The old man was astonished at the confrontation but 'absolutely charming' and handed him over to Mabel, who knew how to deal with such incidents. This was the beginning of an association that was to last many years: today, Robert Donington[10] is still the most important historical link between Dolmetsch's genius and the academic world. His first lessons with Mabel were highly successful: an excellent teacher, sensitive and extremely tolerant, she always gave her pupils every encouragement. She usually taught in the kitchen 'with one eye on the soup', but neither pupil nor brew appears to have suffered.

As Donington progressed he had lessons with Rudolph and later with Dolmetsch himself: these he found very rewarding. He was able to study at close quarters the many facets of Dolmetsch's extraordinary character. On the one hand, helping in overcoming a pupil's nervousness and sympathetic to small faults: on the other, when in a different mood, he could be utterly contemptuous of the slightest misinterpretation of his teaching, and nothing would go right.

Donington has a theory that there are parallels between Dolmetsch and Mabel and Richard and Cosima Wagner:[11] they were both marriages of fiery genius and docile peacemaker. If one wanted to approach Dolmetsch, one had to go through Mabel, in a similar way as with Cosima and Wagner. Donington is convinced that this obsessiveness is inseparable from greatness: a part of the picture, and it is necessary to know both sides. He acknowledges that many people knew 'A.D.' well, loved him sincerely and benefited from his teaching, but at some time or other they all felt the sharpness of his tongue.

One of the few people who can remember Dolmetsch's violin playing in the early twenties, Donington confirms that it was 'wonderful', although later, lack of practice, illness and approaching age, physically prevented his maintaining his old technical mastery. But he could 'get *inside* a piece of baroque music in the way that nobody else could . . . he had just the right tone-colourings and articulation . . . the two things impeccably right'. Donington is sure that if one were gifted enough one knew it was right: he has never claimed to be more than a good chamber musician able to understand through his ear and to express himself through his writing. He has since written extensively on interpretation of the music of the period, but he has the greatest respect for Dolmetsch's book: 'There has never been such a solid important piece of work . . . I simply found out things that Dolmetsch would have discovered himself if he had lived longer. I never had to undo the things done by Dolmetsch.' He compared Dolmetsch's work with that of his contemporary, Dannreuther: 'indeed a valuable pioneer but his work was never as sound as Dolmetsch, chiefly because his judgement wasn't too good. His work has been done over and over again, whereas Dolmetsch's work has not been done "better", but "more".'

* * *

It was shortly after the 1927 festival that a band of Dolmetsch's pupils and supporters began working upon what was later to become The Dolmetsch Foundation. There was a growing concern for the fact that the family were living from hand to mouth to keep workshops, concerts and festivals going. If Dolmetsch died, his work could easily pass into obscurity. By December of that year, the foundation had been registered with Marco Pallis, Gerald Hayes and W. E. Muir as hon. secretaries and an imposing list of names on the council: F. T. Arnold (musicologist), Dr. Robert Bridges (Poet Laureate), Dr. Percy Buck (musical scholar and organist), Sir Walford Davies (composer), Sir Henry Hadow (scholar, educationist and musician), Selwyn Image (Slade Professor of Fine Art, Oxford), Rt. Hon. D. Lloyd George, MP, Sir Richard Terry (organist and musical scholar), Dr. W. G. Whittaker (Bach scholar, composer and conductor), and H. E Wortham (music critic).

Having thus obtained such eminent approval, Gerald Hayes wrote to leading musicians and men of letters asking for their 'moral support' before opening an appeal to the general public. The entire cost of registration and corporation and other expenses had been defrayed privately so that money contributed by the public in the first year would go directly to fulfilling its objectives. Presided over by their treasurer, Mr. W. H. J. Whittall, the governors of The Dolmetsch Foundation held their first meeting on 14 June 1928 at the London School of Economics. Their main objectives were quite clear. Of the greatest importance was that the renaissance of early musical instruments and its music should be encouraged: then that the results of Arnold Dolmetsch's researches in that field should be preserved and extended so as to be available to future generations. They also realised at the outset that it would be necessary to enlarge the Dolmetsch workshop. The circular letter had embraced all these aims and had received an encouraging response—with the notable exception of George Bernard Shaw, who wrote:

> Ayot St. Lawrence,
> Welwyn
> Herts
> 2nd Nov. 1927

Dear Mr. Whittall,
    The prospectus is utter nonsense. I am of course quite friendly; but I can't sign a statement that I approve of a proposal which I think absurd.
    If a society were formed (or rather a subscription list) of the Friends of the Haslemere Festival, like the Friends of the Fitzwilliam Museum, etc., etc., or even bluntly, the Friends of Dolmetsch, the matter would be simple enough. There would be no capital, no liabilities, no impossible Councils, nothing but a clear understanding that the money would be handed over unconditionally to A.D. to help him work himself to death . . .

Amid laughter, Mr. Whittall said that he regarded the last sentence as an epigram, not an epitaph for Dolmetsch. Shaw's letter closed with the final suggestion that much expense could be saved by opening a Friends' Fund as they would have no dealings with registration fees and company law and such like; furthermore, 'there would be no pretence of controlling A.D., who is quite uncontrollable—fortunately.'

Whittall agreed that Dolmetsch was an uncontrollable person; he also considered that he could be subjected to control in spite of himself. He felt that Mr. Dolmetsch was in fact being controlled already by circumstances over which he had no 'control'—money, or lack of it. The meeting closed with the declaration that 70 famous people had given support to the idea, 42 people had subscribed sums of money, and their funds had now reached the £200 mark. The foundation was now a reality.

By the spring of 1928 a capital sum of £2,500 had been raised: this provided a small income for Dolmetsch and his family, support for the workshop and the annual festival: in addition, two scholarships had been awarded. The first was to John Challis[12] from Yipsilanti, Michigan, a pupil of Madge Quigley who had herself studied with Dolmetsch. The second was to Elizabeth (Betty) Brown from Liverpool. Hers was a musical scholarship: a keyboard player and singer, she studied both harpsichord and viol-playing during her four years at Haslemere. She was no newcomer, for she had already spent a number of vacations at Jesses performing in the early festivals. It was here that she met her future husband, Robert Goble, then an assistant in the workshops. After their marriage they lived in Haslemere until 1937, when they moved to Oxford to start up on their own account. Today they are known everywhere for their fine instruments but both acknowledge the debt they owe to Dolmetsch, whose techniques are still faithfully practised in their own workshops.

Betty Goble admits that from the time she was first taught by Dolmetsch, she never looked at a piece of music in the same way again. 'He definitely showed one the meaning of the music . . . if you couldn't see the proper sequence of a phrase, he would get very cross and say, "Nonsense! *This is speech!* You must not just follow your eye but use your ear and brain. This will tell you *musically* what to do with a piece much more than your eye!" Dolmetsch would then expostulate on the inaccuracies of some of the old editions and stressed the importance of doing "what you felt to be right". Since the Bach Gesellschaft editions had no phrase-marks at all, it is easy to see how Dolmetsch's advice could be misunderstood and subsequently criticised.'

Robert Goble saw Dolmetsch in a different light: 'There wasn't anyone who didn't have an occasional brush with him, but if there was any trouble,

one could go to him and he would be very reasonable and understanding.'
Convinced in retrospect of the greatness of the man, Goble wishes that he
had taken more notice of all he said and played. On one occasion Goble
brought an old hurdy-gurdy to Dolmetsch, who decided to use it in one
of the dance shows at the festival. He took one look at it, re-strung it and
started to play: after a couple of days' practice he played it at the festival
as though he had been familiar with it for years.

Meanwhile the Dolmetsch Foundation was steadily gaining a foothold
and further lists of celebrities were added frequently to their list of
supporters. This growing interest, together with the unaccustomed
luxury of financial backing, inspired Dolmetsch to branch out into making
new models of instruments. He may have been 70 but his inventive
powers seemed to have diminished very little.

Early in April of that year Dolmetsch completed the first treble viol
made at Haslemere—apart from the varnishing.[13] For many years he had
sought to perfect a certain kind of varnish and said at the time to a pupil:
'I wanted to capture the light and reflect it under the varnish. This
indescribable effect, which the old masters knew how to obtain, has little
to do with the varnish itself; it depends upon the finishing and preparation
of the wood before varnishing. My amazing luck brought me the discovery
just in time.' By the end of the month his viol was varnished and so pleased
was Dolmetsch that he went on to make his first violin from the wood that
had been carried twice across the Atlantic and several times over the
English Channel before the family had settled in their Surrey home.

Until this violin of his own make had been constructed, Dolmetsch
always preferred instruments made by the old masters from Cremona or
their contemporaries when playing the early music. He deplored the way
in which modern makers and repairers were changing instruments to
meet the demands of the larger concert hall. So when making his own
instrument he sought to maintain the principles of the old masters, such
as the flatter bridge and shorter neck and fingerboard. But he added one
touch of his own: the bass-bar made in one with the table. He also
designed a bow which could best be described as a compromise between
the old and the modern: although still fluted and out-curved, it was a little
longer than the early bow but not as long as the modern one.

In the autumn of 1928 both violin and bow were exhibited at the Arts
and Crafts Society at Burlington House, together with other instruments
of Dolmetsch's own make. It was following this exhibition that he was
made an honorary member of the Society, on which he commented: 'This
honour has been conferred only once before and it profoundly touched
my heart.'

However, for the most remarkable achievement of that year we must return to the spring, when he had completed his first 'improved' or 'New Action' harpsichord.[14] For some years Dolmetsch had been trying to avoid the minute 'click' of the 'fall-back' of the jack on the harpsichord; he wanted a completely pure sound in which the mechanism would not be heard. The constant criticism being levelled at the harpsichord comparing it unfavourably with the modern piano, and its capabilities may have prompted him to begin his experiments. Eventually, he worked out a device that allowed the jack to fall back clear of the string. He then went even further and invented a sustaining pedal so that it could be used in the same way as a piano pedal, he also achieved a vibrato effect similar to that obtained on the clavichord. His scientific turn of mind caused Dolmetsch to make several small models in great detail and at times he almost despaired of achieving any results at all. However, once set on his course, there was no turning back and he spent a great deal of time and foundation money trying to perfect it.

When it was finished, Rudolph played the new instrument at a concert at the Rudolf Steiner Hall on 29 May 1928 and the critics received it well. *The Times* of 11 May jests that if Mr Dolmetsch continues his researches long enough he will discover the piano. Their critic is of the opinion that his latest instrument 'is still more harpsichord than piano, but it does embody among its numerous "effects", two piano-like features. It contains a damper pedal which does something towards sustaining the tone by sympathetic vibration, as on the piano, and one of its "stops" gives almost the impact of a hammer in one of the old sweet-toned square pianos. But it is essentially a plucking instrument and with its couplers, which add 16-foot and four-foot tone, it now has enough power to be adequate to provide the continuo part in the large works of Bach and Handel. For solo purposes a stop has been invented which gives an effect similar to that of the direct pressure of the finger on the string of the clavichord. An improvement throughout the machine is an increased sensitiveness to touch. . . . The only criticism that can be levelled against such a demonstration is moral, not aesthetic: it rouses the sinful feeling of covetousness in the breasts of the auditors.'

Unfortunately, the new action harpsichord never truly fulfilled Dolmetsch's expectations. When it worked it was as beautiful a tone as the critics described; but the mechanism was extremely complicated and frequently went wrong. Dolmetsch here showed the intractable side of his nature: having once committed himself to the new model, he would not abandon it and refused to acknowledge it as having been ill-advised or imperfect in any way. His supporters found it difficult to obtain money for this instrument to be made and the so-called 'improvement' nearly ruined the family, who were already not very rich. Mabel, as always, stepped into the breach, and it was she who was forced to sell some of their most lovely instruments. The ebony and ivory Harton lute, made in 1598 that Dolmetsch had unwittingly purchased at an auction in 1890; a Richard Meares viola da gamba of 1615 and an English treble viol by John Strong, *c.* 1590, all went to the USA in the Folger Collection.[15]

Lack of money was not the only problem Mabel Dolmetsch had to face that year. The strain of overwork, no doubt increased by anxiety over the new-action harpsichord, had been undermining Dolmetsch's normally robust constitution for some time. He was as obstinate about his health as he was about most things; on the one hand he complained almost daily of his aches and pains, whether real or imaginary, and on the other, refused to rest or slow down his pace. Eventually the matter was taken out of his hands. In the summer of 1928, after the festival, he suffered his first bout of real illness: a slight heart attack followed by respiratory trouble and a disturbance of the liver, the culminating effects of a condition that had built up over the years. Dolmetsch's age was against him and his resistance was low, but he was still an infuriating and demanding patient. After several weeks in bed he agreed to a period of convalescence at Hyères in the South of France, accompanied by his son, Carl; this trip was naturally at the invitation of an admirer, Miss Lucy Ellis, a cousin of Lord Howard de Walden.

The first sizeable place east of Toulon, the old town of Hyères remains unspoiled today. A few miles inland, surrounded by hills and spreading pine forests, the sheltered town enjoys the best of all worlds: palms and cacti in abundance and begonias and mimosa blooming cheerfully through the late autumn.

Dolmetsch's letters were at first in praise of the locality and the fine situation of the Ellis's villa overlooking the distant sea. Every page contained detailed description of his health, almost hour by hour: how he had slept and his personal reaction to the prevailing weather. After a week in which he no longer appeared to be suffering, he reports a visit with his hosts to Aix-en-Provence. The old zeal returning, he writes of going directly to the library, where he had found a very interesting book on the lute containing a hundred French songs and some Italian ones written by a 16th-century Provençal composer. He tells Mabel he has copied a dozen of these and in addition has made photographs of six pages showing ornaments, inscriptions and proverbs which will be very useful to her for her decoration of instruments. They will go on to Marseilles and spend the day looking for wood. On 30 October, Dolmetsch writes that he had taken Carl with him to the wood market and given him a lesson in the art of choosing the best pieces: he reports that he has found three bars of old grenadillo, 'un beau bois, *excellent* pour fair des recorders'. But together with ebony purchased at Hyères, this is all that he has obtained: the market has neither sycamore nor boxwood, so he is unable to find the wood they need for violin-making.

The following account of a Children's[16] Concert given by Robert (now Sir Robert) Mayer at the old Central Hall, Westminster, in December 1928, is proof that Dolmetsch's health had been restored. Mayer had been unsuccessfully trying for some time to persuade Dolmetsch to appear at one of his concerts. His programmes, especially arranged to suit the level of the young audience's understanding and cultivate their musical taste, were of necessity composed of 'movements' rather than entire works. Soloists seldom were given more than a few minutes to themselves; this, coupled with his refusal to appear on a platform with artists outside his own *coterie*, were Dolmetsch's reasons for resisting Mayer's repeated offers. However, Mayer, also a small man, equally determined and, like Dolmetsch, a pioneer of European origin, was not easily overcome. Finally, on the condition that he and Rudolph would be given the maximum 15 minutes' solo playing time, Dolmetsch agreed to appear.

For the rest of the programme Dr. (later Sir) Malcolm Sargent was conducting some Berlioz, two of Arnold Bax's four orchestral pieces and the *scherzo* and *finale* from Beethoven's Fifth Symphony. 'Amid the wealth of orchestral luxury'[17] Dolmetsch pleaded for the 'soft complaining flute',[18] which he told his young audience had so gained in popularity that 400 people now played his instrument. He reminded them that in days gone by, people all over Europe came to this country to study music: he predicted that history would repeat itself as this increasing interest in his work on early music signified. Then he told them that they must not applaud. But 4,000 children, captivated at first by Dolmetsch's charm and then by the clear soft tone of the recorders in duet, forgot the warning. The applause was deafening. Dolmetsch, gesticulating wildly first with arms in the air and then hands capping his ears, shouted, 'Stop! Stop!' until the noise subsided. But the children were equally delighted with Simpson 'divisions' on a bass viol and a Purcell 'ground' on the harpsichord and again ignored his request. By the end of the 15 minutes Dolmetsch had become attached to his audience and had no intention of letting them go. Sargent and Mrs. Mayer were both waiting in the wings, one to make his entrance, the other to thank the retiring artist. Dolmetsch was adamant. Muttering half to himself and half to the audience that he was obliged to go against his will, he waited until the last moment before stamping off. While this little comedy was in progress, the orchestra had quietly slipped into their places and the conductor had mounted the rostrum. As the first few bars of the *scherzo* could be heard, Dolmetsch swept past his hostess and pointing an accusing finger at the orchestra, shouted: 'And you expect me to leave ze platform for zat circus! Bah!'

Sir Robert, recalling the incident some 40 years later, said: 'It was really his opinion of Beethoven compared with the rarified music he played himself . . . and who knows, he might have been right if the performance of Beethoven is bad. But what he did was so impeccable in regard to the purity of the music. We both admired the integrity of the man to stick to his convictions. It marks the man as a musician of great character and neither my wife nor I shall ever forget him.'

*   *   *

15.12.1928   Jesses,
                                                                       Haslemere,
                                                                         Surrey

At twelve o'clock I arrived at Haslemere: suddenly I saw it all with my own eyes . . . the reality of what I had seen only in pictures before. On my way to 'Jesses' I noticed a small woman going in the same direction and I recognised her from pictures as being Mrs. Dolmetsch. As soon as she saw my violin case, she asked if I were Mr. Hellwig. A burst of eloquence in English and French fell upon my ears. When we entered the house the old man appeared: a grown-up dwarf with piercing eyes and a robustness and activity phenomenal for a man of seventy years. He ordered his eldest son, Rudolph, to the harpsichord and the younger son, Carl, to play the recorder. I must confess I was astonished at their performance. I never expected this . . . his daughters also work in the workshops—one lacquers and the other carves heads, and so on. Mother Dolmetsch also works in the firm . . . she paints harpsichords, ottavinas, does the accounts and deals with the correspondence.

This extract from a letter written to his mother by the young German, Günther Hellwig,[19] gives a graphic picture of his first impressions of the Haslemere atmosphere. Hellwig had already completed his training at the famous Violin School at Mittenwald and had come for a further course of study with Dolmetsch. Today he is Germany's most famous maker of viols and is celebrated for his valuable researches on the instruments of Joachim Tielke.[20] In those early days he enjoyed working with the Dolmetsches; he delighted in being able to look out from his window over his bench to see green trees and fields: 'there is nourishment here for the soul as well as the mind.'[21] He applauds Dolmetsch's perfect understanding of the necessity to cease working from time to time and reflect a little upon inner things. On the principles of the workshop, he writes: 'Take as much time as is necessary for the work to be done in the best possible way.'[22]

For Hellwig, born in Berlin and accustomed to the correctness of German behaviour, it must have been a paradise. He writes a great deal about the 'spirit' that rules the musicians, and about the 'love' that Mrs. Dolmetsch puts into playing the gamba. 'She has an unbelievable knowledge about old instruments too . . . it is not only Dolmetsch himself who knows.'[23] Hellwig also joined in the dancing: 'It was mainly the boys from the workshop and young girls from the village who danced. Mrs. Dolmetsch was the leader and when she danced she looked more like a girl of sixteen than a grey-haired woman. The old man, sitting quietly in the corner, beat a small drum smiling contentedly.'[24]

Tranquillity is a word seldom used in any aspect of Dolmetsch's volatile character, but as he grew older the fiery outbursts were less frequent. They were replaced by an increasing bitterness as the recognition he had hoped for constantly eluded him. Ironically, it was the time when musicians and scholars were beginning to see the true value of his work, and had he been a little more approachable he might have won their confidence.

One thing that was infallible in restoring his good temper was a new project: all the old eagerness would return. In December the Columbia Graphophone Company approached Dolmetsch with a view to making several commercial recordings. An entry in his diary tells us that he has accepted their offer to complete the work in several sessions, extending over a period of two weeks, at £20 per session and a further 10 per cent on wholesale price sales. Dolmetsch was again at his peak: before the first programme had been sketched in, he had mentally provided the world with gramophones; he imagined handles that would wind endlessly so that the sound of the viol, the lute and the harpsichord would reach a public that had never heard of either Haslemere or Dolmetsch. The old man was *en forme*, with a vengeance.

NOTES

1. Of the works by J. S. Bach performed at the first Haslemere Festival, the following had been played at Dolmetsch's own concerts on the original instruments.
Sonata for Harpsichord and Viola da Gamba,

No 1 in G major	19 March 1892
Chromatic Fantasia for Clavichord	4 July 1893
Concerto in D minor for Harpsichord and Strings	6 December 1894
Prelude and Fugue in C major (Book I, No. 1.)	7 July 1896
Prelude and Fugue in F minor (Book II, No. 12)	18 May 1898
Partita No. I in B flat for Harpsichord	29 May 1900

2. The 'older' or 'Baroque' violin is an instrument which has been allowed to remain

in its original state: pre late 18th century. From this date onwards the desire for greater power and raised pitch caused drastic alterations to be made to some of the finest instruments of the time: *viz*, the raising and arching of the bridge, which in turn caused the end of the fingerboard to tilt, thus forcing the neck back to an angle. The tension of the strings was increased and the neck lengthened by half an inch; the greater tension on the belly necessitated a stronger bass-bar. Today, there is a welcome return to playing the earlier instrument. Eduard Melkus, the celebrated Austrian violinist, has a Matthias Klotz in original state. N.B. It is important that these violins should also be played with the 'early' or 'outcurved' (Corelli) bow.

3. From *The Times*, 28 August 1925: 'Portions of the Haslemere Festival of Chamber Music under the direction of Mr. Arnold Dolmetsch will be broadcast from both 2 LO and 5 XX tonight. At 8 o'clock from Daventry four pieces relayed from Haslemere Hall will be transmitted, consisting of early English Consorts for viols. The concert will continue for an hour, and at 9 p.m. another hour of music from the same festival will be relayed to London and broadcast from 2 LO.'

4. Maine, Basil, *Reflected Music*, Methuen, 1930, pp. 69–80.

5. Arnold, F. T., *The Art of Accompaniment from a Thorough-Bass as practised in the 17th and 18th centuries*, Oxford, 1931.

6. ibid.

7. descant (c″), 2 trebles (f′), tenor (c′) and bass (f). (In the USA the descant and treble recorders are known as 'soprano' and 'alto' respectively.) The smallest member of this family is the sopranino (f″), mainly a solo instrument.

8. Hayes, Gerald R., *The Treatment of Instrumental Music*, Vol. I in a series, *Musical Instruments and their Music, 1500–1750*, Oxford, April 1928.
On the whole well reviewed but *The Times*, 25 April 1928, calls it a 'propagandist pamphlet rather than treatise . . . militates against its own success by the touch of fanaticism with which it argues an interesting but questionable case'. G. H. acknowledges the help he has received from Dolmetsch and it it doubtless from this influence that the disciple has become more fanatic than the master. The second book in the series, *The Viols and other bowed instruments*, appeared in October 1930.

9. Miles Tomalin, writer, musician, son of H. F. Tomalin, founder of Jaeger, the well-known wool retailers. He was a campaigner in the Spanish Civil War of 1936–39, and took his Dolmetsch descant recorder with him: the name of every campaign and place of instruction is carved on it. There is a charming account of Miles Tomalin's association with Dolmetsch in *The Recorder and Music Magazine* 'Early Days', December 1973, pp. 271–4. Carl Dolmetsch completes the picture in 'In at the Start', ibid., March 1974, p. 325. His father was one of the first supporters of the Dolmetsch Foundation and provided much financial assistance.

10. Robert Donington, English Musical scholar, author and editor: Professor of Early Music studies at Iowa School of Music, University of Iowa, USA.

11. Donington, Robert, *Wagner's 'Ring' and its Symbols*, St. Martin's Press, New York, 1963, 1969, pp. 44, 200, 201.

12. John Challis is today one of the most important builders of harpsichords in the USA (New York City). He also handed on many of Dolmetsch's skills and principles to his pupils, now prominent harpsichord-builders in the USA.

13. Dolmetsch had already produced lutes, treble and other viols at Chickering's in Boston, 1904–11.

14. Extract from Dolmetsch's application for a patent for his 'new action' harpsichord: 'In the old harpsichords, the plectrum, actuated by a jack, on its return after plucking, glides upon the string whilst it is still vibrating. This causes a rattling, which impairs the clearness and beauty of the tone. To overcome this the present invention provides for a return of the parts to initial position, after plucking, without contact being again made with the string.
   'A vibrato is produced by means responsible to vertical rocking of the key and adapted to alter the pitch of the string just as does the rocking of a violinist's finger upon the strings of his instrument.
   'Pedal operated means may be provided to vary the volume of tone, and dampers may be fitted adapted to be operated by pedal as well as by the keys.
   'In the carrying out of the invention, a tongue is employed below its associated string, and under this tongue is arranged a jack resting upon the key. In action, this jack raises the tongue and with it the string. When the string has acquired the proper degree of tension, the jack, under the control of an escapement, suddenly quits the tongue and the string is left to vibrate freely, for the tongue, by reason of inherent springiness of the material of which it is constituted, or its construction, recedes from the strings.
   'On its return, the jack glides on the side of the tongue without touching the string, spring means serving to urge the jack back to its original position under the tongue.' There are several pages of technicalities, together with a diagram, in the Dolmetsch Library at Jesses, Haslemere.

15. Later these instruments were deposited in the Folger Shakespeare Library, Washington, DC, where they have been preserved in perfect condition: (see pp. 32–3, 226

16. Sir Robert and Lady Mayer introduced orchestral Children's Concerts into England in 1922. They were originally held at the Central Hall, Westminster, but by 1938, 27 centres had been formed throughout the British Isles.

17. *Times Educational Supplement*, 3 December, 1928.

18. ibid.

19. Günther Hellwig, extracts from letters to his mother, 15 December 1928.

20. Hellwig, b. 1903, Charlottenburg, Berlin, is preparing a book to be published shortly on the instruments of Joachim Tielke.

21. Letter to his mother (Hellwig), 20 December 1928.

22. Letter to his mother (Hellwig), 15 December 1928.

23. ibid.

24. Letter to his mother (Hellwig), 15 December 1928.

CHAPTER XIX

The Dolmetsch Foundation

A severe attack of bronchitis kept Dolmetsch to his bed during the last week of December 1928 so that the recording sessions with Columbia had to be postponed until February. But by the end of January he was in Dublin with his family playing to delighted audiences. His warmth of personality appealed particularly to the Irish. A critic in *The Irish Statesman* (2 Feburary 1929) writes that 'Mr. Dolmetsch's infectious enthusiasm conveyed by spoken words as well as by music . . . moved his audiences deeply'.

In June and July Dolmetsch appeared at the Grotrian Hall, London, in a series of five concerts.[1] The *Musical Times* notes that 'One of the most interesting features was a "Brandenburg" Concerto, where the timbres of the individual instruments, including harpsichord, viole de [sic] gamba, and violone, and their general balance, reproduced the composer's intentions, which are treated with scant regard in so many of our concert-halls.' He also praises a prelude for lute in one of the Bach programmes: Dolmetsch, who had been 'gallantly wrestling with its difficulties for some years, has now attained sufficient mastery to convince one that in sheer loveliness of tone it is unsurpassable'. He also commends Rudolph's 'masterly performance' of the *Goldberg Variations*, on the harpsichord, and goes on to say that 'During the course of these concerts this young musician performed on half-a-dozen different instruments, and seemed equally at home on all of them'.

The informal atmosphere of this particular concert has been well captured in a letter[2] by a member of the audience:

> During the first quartette [sic] Mr. Dolmetsch stopped the players, explaining that he was not satisfied with his son's entry on the recorder. 'Not incisive enough, you understand' he told us. And when the passage was repeated we were asked if we had noticed the improvement? We agreed, and the recital continued.
>
> Then Mr. Dolmetsch told us he proposed playing, on the lute, an ancient piece of music which was particularly difficult and he was not at all sure he could manage

it! Having played it through once he was not satisfied, and asked our permission to play it a second time. It was most necessary, he told us, that we should hear a correct rendering of such a lovely and historic piece of music. And still, after all these years, I picture that dignified, devoted figure and the enchantment of his playing on that ancient instrument. . . .

That Dolmetsch recital was a unique musical experience. From being an aloof audience waiting to be entertained, we found ourselves to be part of the family circle as if we were old friends. We were talked to and consulted till we felt equally responsible with the performers for the success of each item. And the personality of Arnold Dolmetsch made it all seem perfectly natural.

Dolmetsch was often criticised for these false starts and repeats. In this sense he was proudly amateur in the true meaning, not the present-day corruption of the word. There was also much of the showman in his performances: he could not have otherwise exercised such enchantment. Fundamentally, his motives were genuine, and when one reads that his personality 'made it all seem perfectly natural', it does not seem to matter how much was artifice and how much was not. The important point was that people listened to him in a way they would not have listened to a musicologist lacking his charm of delivery. We have many parallels today through culture promoted by radio and television, with the consequence that more people find they are developing a taste for subjects that were formerly the prerogative of the experts. On the television screen, Dolmetsch would have been an instant success.

The following August the festival again drew a large following and over 30 performers took part: Leon Goossens, playing the oboe d'amore in Bach's Cantata 152, was the first of many celebrated soloists who were attracted to Haslemere for its unique performing opportunities. Dolmetsch, delving into his vast store of music, once more provided an interesting variety of programmes from the music of the English composers of the Stuart period and their Italian, French and Spanish contemporaries to Bach and Handel. The two songs he had unearthed in the library at Aix-en-Provence[3] the previous autumn were heard on the all-French programme. The dancing, which had been introduced at the third festival, now took up two evenings, the last being in the form of a masque, a tradition that was to continue for another ten years. Mabel Dolmetsch, choreographer, producer, dancer, cook and musician, also designed and made many of the costumes, and much of the scenery: most remarkable of all was the unruffled calm she sustained throughout.

It was at this festival that Dolmetsch played the hurdy-gurdy brought to him by Robert Goble (see p. 224); *The Times* correspondent, caught in the spell, writes: 'Mr Dolmetsch, in becoming costume, suddenly appeared carrying a hurdy-gurdy; everyone was delighted, and still more so at its quaint, bagpipe-like sounds, when it helped to accompany Miss Cécile Dolmetsch and Mr. Miles Tomalin, also in costume, in their dancing of a 17th-century French bourée and minuet. These dances have all been carefully deciphered by Mrs. Dolmetsch from contemporary records, and they certainly have very attractive figures and steps. She herself with castanets showed us the gracefulness of a Spanish sarabande and a French one, in *slower* tempo, set to an English tune by William Young.'

'In the world of chamber music . . . the Columbia Company[4] has achieved something of a "scoop" by the issue of the first record made by the world-famous Dolmetsch family—two Fantasies by the Elizabethan Morley and a Fantasie for six viols by Richard Dering, musician to Charles I. The pieces are beautifully played and almost faultlessly recorded,' writes a special correspondent of the *Morning Post* (5 September 1929). The *Sunday Graphic* (8 September) places it on their list of 'Pick of the Records' and an extract from *The Gramophone* gives some indication of the growth of intelligent criticism that was now replacing the downright rejection of Dolmetsch's performances in some of the earlier reviews. After acknowledging the fame of the Dolmetsches both at home and abroad, the writer thinks it rather surprising that we have not had records of their playing until now: 'That the performances are not always perfect is well known. Their value lies at times more in spirit than in truth; but the influence of the craftsmanship and art that the family has carried on for the last fifteen years at Haslemere has been deep and profitable for music. . . . Some people will miss the vibrato in this viol-playing. I am rather glad to have the clear tone of the strings, for once, without the vibrato, of which in general players give us too much.'

When Dolmetsch was living in Paris before the First World War, he had made the acquaintance of a young Frenchwoman, Marie Thérèse de Lens. An accomplished musician, she had played regularly in Dolmetsch's concerts both in Paris and London and the families had kept in touch over the years. Shortly after the war, Mlle de Lens had left France and taken up residence in the Arab quarter of Meknes in Morocco, where she spent the rest of her life studying the native music. Knowing that her researches would interest Dolmetsch she invited him to spend a holiday there with his wife and younger son, Carl. Since all expenses were to be paid by his hostess, Dolmetsch accepted with alacrity, left Haslemere in late September and stayed away for a month.

Later, writing of his own musical discoveries in North Africa,[5] Dolmetsch admits that he found there a solution to one of his many problems. For many years he had been puzzled as to the suitability of accompanying songs of the mediaeval and Renaissance periods. He knew that they were

sung to the viol, lute, harp and other instruments and that the original
MSS contain sometimes, though rarely, indication of instrumental parts,
but which are insufficient to build upon. 'I wrote accompaniments to
some of these songs; yet in spite of my repeated efforts, the result was
never satisfactory and I came to the conclusion that these melodies were
incompatible with the tonal and harmonic systems of later periods.' He
then refers to his discoveries of Spanish songs in which 'The lute part is a
free Fantasy consisting of embroideries, divisions and imitations forming
an independent framework to the melody. It can be compared to the gold
background on which medieval figures are painted. Here and there a
final chord shows a tendency towards harmony, but the melody is never
dogged by chords.' Dolmetsch then explains that at Meknes he heard a
quantity of Arab music, some of it dating back at least 800 years, as yet
unspoiled by European influences. He likens the songs to those of our
own troubadours. It seems that one Arab lutenist recognised some of our
melodies but said to Dolmetsch that he should not be playing them
'plain'—that he should 'embroider' them. He then discovered to his
delight that the Arabs do indeed embroider in 'the freest, most daring and
effective way', and that this tradition has remained unbroken. Dolmetsch
then admits that when he applied this new style to his own accompaniment
he was surprised how well the songs came to life again. One of these, the
15th-century song *L'Amour de Moy*, was reproduced with the article,
written in lute tablature with a transcription suitable for virginals or other
keyboard instruments. The words are in French with a translation into
English by Dolmetsch's old friend Arthur Symons.

Meanwhile the Dolmetsch Foundation, now steadily gaining membership from musicians as well as the general public, launched its first
magazine, *The Consort*, in October 1929. Edited by Gerald Hayes and
limited to 500 copies, it was the first publication of its kind in this country.
It contained a concise bibliography of early treatises on music with brief
comment on each work. Lionel Glover gave a progress report on the
foundation and Arnold Dolmetsch contributed an article on 'Home
Music'. W. G. Whittaker wrote on Bach's ornamentation and Ll. Wyn
Griffith on 'John Jenkins', illustrating his piece by a supplement of his
own manuscript copy of the Jenkins' *Fantasy for five viols*. A poem, 'Rose'
by Walter de la Mare, seemed strangely out of place and the inclusion of
'Death of the Old Governess', a fragment from an unpublished novel by
Storm Jameson, had nothing to do with music of any period. Dolmetsch
was furious. In his diary of 14 November he writes: 'Journée detestable—
Reçu le "D.F." *Magazine, Horreur*!!' The second issue of the *Consort* did
not appear until 1931.

If the future of the foundation's literary ventures were doubtful, the writing talents of their 72-year-old *paterfamilias* were still in demand. Some six months earlier, Dolmetsch had received a letter from Nils Ericsson, who had served him so loyally in Boston and in Paris. Ericsson was now the curator of the Belle Skinner Collection of old musical instruments in Holyoke, Massachussets. A wealthy spinster, philanthropist and amateur musician, Belle Skinner, had acquired a Ruckers two-manual harpsichord in her youth: from thenceforth she had become an ardent collector, and at the time of her death had amassed close on a hundred instruments. She had begun to list the items herself but the work was never finished. As a memorial to his sister, William Skinner decided to have a handsome illustrated catalogue printed and sought the curator's advice. Ericsson then wrote asking Dolmetsch to contribute an introduction. Naturally, the old man was delighted. On 27 January 1930, Otto Kinkeldy, chief of the Music Division, the New York Public Library, wrote to Dolmetsch on William Skinner's behalf, telling him how the project stood at that time: 'Perhaps', he writes, 'this knowledge will give you some ideas for your introduction, although, of course, you are to remain absolutely free to write . . . [it] on perfectly general grounds, if you so choose.' Then follows a paragraph that must have set Dolmetsch's teeth on edge:

> Before the task of working out the purely musical and mechanical details was handed over to me, Mr. Skinner had had a tentative description made by . . . (Mr. Carl Freund), a furniture collector, antiquarian and art dealer of New York. Mr. Freund confined himself mostly to a detailed description of the exterior of the instruments, but Mr. Skinner had a few copies of his inventory struck off in print to be used as a working basis for future elaboration. I do not believe all of Mr. Freund's historical judgements will stand close scrutiny, nor do I think it safe to accept certain of his ascriptions of the decorative features to famous artists. Still, his descriptions will suffice to identify the various items of the collection and you could base your judgement of its general character upon this list.

and later:

> If you are inclined to go ahead with a general introduction on the basis of what you know of the collection, Mr. Skinner says he will be delighted to have whatever you choose to send him at any time, the sooner the better.

In order to appreciate the full significance of the request, we must return to the year 1908, when Dolmetsch was in Boston, working at Chickering's, and first made Miss Skinner's acquaintance. On 12 April 1908, Dolmetsch wrote to her regarding a Hoffmann clavichord[6] she wished to purchase from him. We observe the care he bestowed upon his instruments during their transportation and the affection he retained for them long after they had passed from his hands:

Chickering & Sons,
Pianoforte Makers,
Boston

Dear Miss Skinner,

The clavichord is packed, ready to go. I forgot to tell you that the oak case was originally beeswaxed. I have had it waxed afresh, as the wood was rather hungry in places. This should be done in 3 or 4 years, and the instrument well rubbed with a dry, soft, woollen rag, as often as necessary. It gives it a soft, dull polish very agreeable to the eye, and which imparts the delightful feeling of a well cared for thing.

Very sincerely yours
Arnold Dolmetsch

Belle Skinner also purchased a harpsichord of Dolmetsch's own make which was to be sent by express on 5 May, but he is more concerned with the little clavichord he is forced to sell:

11, Elmwood Avenue,
Cambridge,
Mass.

May 11 1908

Indeed, I do not like to sell my clavichord. But I want money *now*, and this would help me out of a difficulty. So if you will give me $1,000 for it, you may have it. It is in perfect condition and stands in tune marvellously!

My regret at parting with it would be softened by the feeling that it could not be in better hands than yours, and that I shall be likely to see it again. I suppose you would have no objection to my examining it, in case of need, for my new clavichords are made practically on its model, and I might want to refer to it later.

A postscript tells of the instrument's origin:

This clavichord was in the collection of Mr. Taphouse of Oxford. I exchanged it for a priceless little book which he coveted. I restored the instrument myself, in England, and used it for years for my concerts.

The American climate affected it somewhat, I strengthened the bottom and the back, and did some small repairs to it in Chicago in the summer of 1905, and it has proved perfectly reliable since.

The fact that it took him four months to reply to William Skinner is clear proof of Dolmetsch's integrity. The Skinners were extremely wealthy and would have spared no expense on a fitting memorial to their sister. Her collection was worth a fortune and the catalogue that finally emerged runs into some 200 pages, copiously illustrated and sold for $10.00 in 1969. It would have been easy for Dolmetsch to have submitted a pleasing account saying all the 'right' things; moreover, in 1930 he needed the money. Instead, he wrote the following:

May 14th 1930   Jesses,
                                                                  Haslemere,
                                                                  Surrey

Dear Mr. Skinner,

I must explain the reason of my delay with the catalogue.

The proofs you sent me showed such amazing ignorance, carelessness and bad style (in 3 languages!) that I was frightened at the idea of correcting such a mass of nonsense and blunders.

My first idea was to send the lot back and have nothing to do with it.

Yet, it could not be published as it is; it would have been less than worthless from the point of view of education and an insult to the memory of Miss Skinner.

I decided to tackle the problem; but it was shelved for the present! One of my difficulties is that I have never seen many of the instruments. Photographs and colourprints can help, a little, but in many cases I have not even photographs; only these confused and, often, ridiculous descriptions through which I must try to discover enough truth to make reasonable statements.

The authenticity of some of the early instruments is very doubtful. That of the Clavicytherium of Pope Gregory XIII is more than doubtful. It is an obvious fake. The painter of these two angels on the doors is probably alive and thriving.

There are plenty such fakes in most collections; many in the Metropolita n Museum of New York! I make a war on them for they do a great deal of harm.

I strongly advise you to get the opinion of an *expert*, a real one, *on the paintings*; this will bring light on many points.

I do not like to see the names of great painters taken in vain! For example, the lovely Ruckers Harpsichord I restored for Miss Skinner is decorated with charming paintings; but I would not attribute them to François Boucher without good reasons.

The fact is that an *expert* opinion on the paintings would facilitate my work of description.

I am sending herewith an Introduction to the catalogue which you will probably like. This, I am responsible for. My name should be appended to it.

But, although I shall correct or rewrite the body of the catalogue, I *would not sign* it, as I must not be associated with doubtful specimens, unless it be to expose them!

The Introduction deals with some instruments in particular, i.e. the double keyboard harpsichord by Johannes Rückers, No. 63 in the catalogue:

She entrusted it to my hands for restoration. With care and love, I brought it back to its pristine condition and it proved to be an exquisite instrument, unquestionably one of the finest of that style and period in existence.

It shoud be noted here that when the famous Blanchet of Paris took it in hand in 1750, he did not merely *repair* it, but he *remade* it, which means that using the perfect shape, tone producing material and string proportions of Johannes Ruckers, he turned it into an instrument capable of rendering the masterpieces of Couperin, Scarlatti and J. S. Bach, which made demands upon the harpsichord undreamed of in the previous century.

Dolmetsch goes on to describe the history of the harpsichord, how it was never given a chance to achieve perfection owing to it being ousted by the piano. He continues:

> The most precious and rarest of Miss Skinner's instruments is that little gem of a piano made in 1611. . . .
> The piano has revolutionized history by proving that a century before the invention of the instrument, according to the 'Authorities', the instrument existed—The genuineness of its hammer action has been doubted by 'experts' who pretended that it was originally a clavichord. Challenged by me to show how this could have been done, they did not reply. I am convinced that it is genuine. I examined it most carefully before it came into the possession of Miss Skinner and I can do no better than reproduce the description I gave of it in my book:[7] . . . I wish I could speak of the many valuable instruments added to Miss Skinner's collection since I left America; but to my regret, I have not seen them and my statements would consequently lack authenticity.

There was no further correspondence and Dolmetsch's introduction never appeared. There is none in the 1933 publication, still in use today, and even in the foreword, consisting mainly of acknowledgements, the word order of the paragraph in which Dolmetsch's name is mentioned speaks for itself:

> These notes have been compiled by Fanny Reed Hammond and by the curator, Nils J. Ericsson, an expert maker of violins, at one time associated with Arnold Dolmetsch of England in the restoring of old musical instruments, and with Etienne Gaveau, in Paris, and Chickering and Sons in Boston, in the making of clavichords and harpsichords.

*   *   *

Although Dolmetsch himself seemed more adept at refusing money for his work than accepting it, he was a genius at attracting wealthy patrons. H. F. Tomalin, owner and director of Jaeger, was one to whom he was particularly indebted. Tomalin was rare among business men: he believed that music could be developed in the same way as design and decorations had been used to benefit business itself, rather on the lines of the Liberty slogan of 'Beauty draws more than oxen'.[8] So he thought of the novel idea of giving a luncheon in Dolmetsch's honour at the Jaeger store then in Oxford Street, followed by a week of invitation concerts to be held there each evening. It was an instant success. Viols, recorders and keyboard instruments were displayed in the windows and members of the Dolmetsch family were available all day for advice. During the first week over 1,000 people applied for tickets, so the project was extended for a further seven days.

At the 1930 festival Dolmetsch introduced the Concerto in C major for 3 harpsichords and strings by J. S. Bach. The *Daily News* critic (2 September 1930) writes:

> Tonight this clever family played a Bach Concerto for 3 harpsichords and strings. Probably this unique work has never been played in England before: certainly not in the memory of living men.
>
> The 3 harpsichords have all been made by Mr. Dolmetsch and his sons and daughters at Jesses . . . apart from their beautiful musical tone, they are works of art from a decorative point of view. . . . One could visualise the grand old man of Leipzig and his friends in his house playing this work just as the quaint old man of Haslemere and his little coterie played it to night, each for his own satisfaction.

The idea that the work had never been played 'in the memory of living men' was typical of the limited span in which Dolmetsch's work was regarded in 1930. A man would have only to be in his early fifties to have heard Dolmetsch's first performance of it at his house 'Dowland' in Dulwich in 1894.

From the reviews of the 1930 festival we observe a general improvement of standards. One critic describes the Dolmetsch family as having 'grown up in every sense'. Whilst there were still 'little breakdowns . . . the improvement both in the individual playing and the ensemble work is very marked', and 'the greater certainty of the performances has been gained moreover without sacrificing the domestic intimacy which has always been a pleasing feature of the Dolmetsch performances'. He goes on to claim that 'No chamber concerts anywhere else in the world offer the same extraordinary variety of instruments, and for that reason if for no other Mr. Dolmetsch's concerts have never been dull.'

The critic had questioned Dolmetsch on his opinion of the International Festival currently being held at Liège in Belgium. Dolmetsch had no doubts about some of the contemporary music being performed there: he thought these 'eccentric' works attracted more notice than they deserved. 'You people [the critics], visiting on me the sins of the whole critical fraternity, rush after those novelties as if they were something that really mattered, while neglecting the things that positively do matter, such as the Haslemere Festival, because it happens to be here at home and under your very noses.' Dolmetsch's growing chip on his ever-bending shoulder prevented him from acknowledging that anyone else could achieve something worth while—if it infringed the least fraction upon his own activities. This was never to be improved despite encouraging comment such as that of the closing paragraph in the same article from the *Liverpool Post* (6 September 1930). After a flattering description of the instruments they were producing and praise for the virtuosity of both Rudolph and Carl on their respective instruments, with an extra compliment to the latter for his craftsmanship, we read:

> Thus everything seems to conspire at the moment towards the perfecting of a life-time of labour, carried out with a unique persistence, and in face of the apathy which the English reserve for original genius.

There was in the same month (13 September 1930) an excellent article in *Week End Review* by Dyneley Hussey, entitled 'A Great Craftsman'. His closing paragraph is significant:

> The most vital part of Mr. Dolmetsch's work is . . . not that which is done in public, but his teaching, whereby he passes on to others the technique which he has revived, and his craftsmanship which has put into our hands once more the most beautiful domestic instruments of the past.

Dolmetsch was suddenly reminded of that past—the early days of his first instrument-making—for he received a letter from his old friend, William Rothenstein:

13, Airlie Gardens,
W.8.

15.10.30

My dear Dolmetsch—in some reminiscences I am writing,[9] I mention a visit Horne, Frank Harris and I paid you, when Harris wanted to buy the clavichord (was it a clavichord?) painted by Helen Coombe. Am I right in thinking that F. H. ordered another similar instrument for himself? that the price was then only £20? and that when the lovely thing was done, Harris rather wanted, at first, to get out of his bargain? Not that I would mention the last matter—but that is what remains in my mind. I shall be glad if you will correct me, if I am wrong. I always remember the days at Bayley Street with particular pleasure. I hope these days bring you more practical sympathy, and that y[ou]r workshop is as active, or more active, than when I was last at Haslemere. My warmest greetings from house to house. Always most sincerely y[ou]rs.

William Rothenstein

Dolmetsch answers promptly:

Oct 22 1930

Jesses,
Haslemere,
Surrey

Concerning the Harris Clavichord, your story is not quite correct. I never made a clavichord for £20. This one was a specially fine one and the price was, I think, £70. Harris had known me through the piano I made for Cecil Rhodes.

One evening, Runciman brought him to me; they were both rather drunk. H. got very enthusiastic about the clavichord, and he gave me an order for one. But when it was finished, he had lost interest in it. After some trouble, however, Runciman got him to pay.

He gave the clavichord to Runciman[10] who was very pleased to have it. . . .

Do you remember an evening in Bailey [sic] St., I think, when you, Image, Horne and others of that set were there and George Moore came, in his most characteristic mood; whilst he was talking, you made a caricature of him, with a blue pencil and sealing wax?

I have it still a *delightful thing*!

*   *   *

The second of Gerald Hayes' books was published in October and received favourable comment from the press. *The Listener* called it:

An unassailably documented book, the result of immense research in the original sources . . . Much of it will probably come as a surprise even to musicians with a fairly extensive knowledge of the early music . . . The work is an accurate encyclopaedia of very wide interest, its proper reward will be a revival of the viol consort.

*   *   *

Dolmetsch instruments could now be heard in many places, but the most important order the workshops had yet received was that of a large two-manual harpsichord for the BBC.[11] How this came about is best described in Dolmetsch's own words on a postcard to Dorothy Swainson, then living in Paris:

30 April 1931   Haslemere
                                                                 Surrey

The B.B.C. (wireless) have had an open fight between a Pleyel Harps. and mine. Judges, Adrian Boult with half a dozen Directors etc. It ended in laughter. The Pleyel was 'hors de combat' at the first Chord . . . They have ordered one of mine.

Yours ever,
Arnold Dolmetsch

*   *   *

Although the following account is today interesting merely from the academic point of view, it is an example of how authorities consulted Dolmetsch when a controversy arose. He was seldom lost for an answer. The correspondence began with a letter from Gerald Hayes (16 April 1931) in which he tells Dolmetsch that he has had an exchange of letters with Dr. Sanford Terry and has been able to give him the information he wanted, all except on one point:

37, Clanricarde Gardens,
W.2.

He [Dr. Terry] was speaking of the high treble clef used for violin music by the French in the 17th century with G on the lowest line. He then says: 'Bach used it

for the Flauto as distinct from the Traversière. Here is a fact for which there must be some practical reason, which as yet eludes me. Normally the Flauto was not a transposing instrument. But in his Cantata 18 Bach undoubtedly uses an instrument in B flat apparently transposing down a ninth!

This Cantata is, I suppose, the one on the words, 'Gleich wie der Regen und Schnee von Himmel fällt' with violas, cello, violone and 2 Flauti. I have not got a score but doubtless Terry has his facts correct. A Recorder in B flat is, I suppose, a tenor (the Treble is usually in F isn't it?) and why the music for this should be written in the treble clef with G in the lowest line I am unable to say. I assume he's correct in saying that it sounds a ninth lower than written, but you can perhaps correct this?

However, Terry had already written to Dolmetsch asking the question himself since their 'common friend, F. T. Arnold'[12] encouraged him to believe that he may venture to tax his unique knowledge. He asks: 'There is no other instance in Bach's scores in which he prescribes a transposing Flauto, and the score in question is an early Weimar one. If you can enlighten my ignorance on this point I shall be most grateful . . Charles Sanford Terry.'

On 17 April, Terry writes to say that the recorder is, after all, a transposing instrument in B in Cantata 106. Terry has written to Johannes Wolf in Berlin to get 'an indication of the Recorder score as it reads *in the original,* and not as adapted by Rust for the BG. Edition. Till one is quite certain as to Bach's actual autograph one may miss something essential. So that I am afraid I have given you an imperfect statement.' Terry closes by saying that his immediate hope is to learn why the French violin clef was used for the Blockflöte and not the Traversière. 'And, secondly, any guidance you can give me as to the Recorders in general. I hope I am not unduly trespassing on your time and good nature.'

Terry writes again (undated), presumably the same day, telling Dolmetsch he is afraid his last letter posed a question that must have appeared ill-informed. He has now received from Berlin 'a clear statement as to the actual notation of the Blockflöte parts in the autographs there'. He had conjectured from Cantata 18 that Bach treated the instrument as transposing. Terry had worked out a compass table and claimed that it 'plainly shows that he never used the Bass, Tenor or Basset flute à bec, and quite rarely the Alto. He never takes the instruments below

His German flutes are almost invariably d'.

The following day, Terry writes again that he had posted a letter to Dolmetsch before receiving his 'very kind reply' to his enquiry:

> I felt quite sure that Monty Hauptmann's supposition that the Recorder in Cantata 18 transposed down a ninth is absurd!

Terry says he will not burden Dolmetsch with a transcript of the score, but he foresees occasions ahead when he may have cause to 'trespass' upon his 'unique knowledge' again, and that Dolmetsch's kind letter encourages him to do so. In Terry's last letter he confers an exalted form of address upon his mentor:

Westerton of Pitfodels
by Aberdeen

26 April [1931]

Dear Dr. Dolmetsch,

I am presuming on your kind willingness to instruct me.

I have made out and enclose a complete table of Bach's Recorder scores, stating not only the compass of the several instruments in each score, but also (in case the detail is relative to the key of the instruments) the key or keys it serves. Owing to the modernizing of the parts by the editors it is rarely possible to determine the pitch of the Flute used by Bach—I can do so in Cantatas 18, 103, 106, 152, 161. But those stated as 'C' are purely speculative, and others I do not attempt. Can you give me the lacking information?

As to the instrument itself—taking the compass as given, by Praetorius and L'Encyclopedie—it looks as though Bach generally used only the discant (c" – c" ') excepting the 2 piccolo scores. I don't know the compass of your quartet, or of the Bärenreiter set. But I suppose the following will be approximately correct?

Discant	c" – c" "
Alto	f' – f'''
Tenor	c' – d" '
Bass	f – d"

Riemann's article says of 'die grossen Flötenarten in B bei Bach Kantate 18' that they 'veraltet sind'. Also, he adds, are the Fl. piccolos in Kantate 103. So far I can not understand why this is so.

Please do not let me take up your valuable time too greatly—But if you could pencil some guiding notes on the enclosed paper I am sure I should see daylight where darkness at present broods.

The correspondence ends here. The original handwritten table is extant[14] at Jesses but the space for remarks remains blank. Whether Dolmetsch replied without returning the sheet is a question as yet unanswered. It is unlikely that he ignored the request since he probably knew more about Bach's use of the recorder than anyone else at the time: furthermore, it was not in his nature to leave things unresolved. However, this apart, it is interesting that the whole question has remained problematical up to the present time and it is doubtful if a definitive answer can be found. All contemporary performances use the treble in F and Alan Davis[15] says, 'Whatever the reason for Bach's ingenious notation the point is of little practical importance as the parts can be played with no difficulty on treble recorder in F.'

From a letter written by Dolmetsch to the young Edgar Hunt (then a flautist), we see that Dolmetsch's interest in giving performances on the early wind instruments was increasing, but his method of instruction remained as dictatorial as ever:

13th June 1931

Jesses,
Haslemere,
Surrey.

Dear Mr Hunt,

I am sending you by registered post the old flute I promised. I send you herewith a copy of the best methode for the old flute. 1709—it is in old french which you may find difficult to understand. Anyway, the 'Tablature' at the end gives all the fingerings; also the shakes—and, in the book, the interpretation of the ornaments.

The G clef on the 1st line is used right through, as usual at the time in France—

I am not sending the part, I prefer you should have the first impression of it *from me*. This will save trouble.

You will see that the performance is on 22nd July *afternoon*. There will be a final rehearsal that morning. Please let me know when you can come here for a couple of hours to learn the part. Almost anytime, any day, Sundays included, would suit me at a pinch, but, give me some choice, if possible, and please *come as soon as possible*; I am naturally anxious about that!

sincerely yours,
Arnold Dolmetsch.

During the summer of that same year Dolmetsch made the acquaintance of another musician, one whose admiration for him and his work was total and uninhibited. On 12 July 1931, Dolmetsch received the first letter from a man who would become a life-long friend and indefatigable supporter of his cause: Percy Grainger.

Lilla Vrån,
Pevensey Bay,
Sussex.

Dear Sir,

For years I have felt admiration and thankfulness for the unique and priceless work you are doing for the cause of musical culture. Just lately I have heard with delight of your Haslemere Festivals. . . .

Yours, in admiration,
Percy Grainger.

Grainger tells Dolmetsch that he and his wife are in England and hope to attend four of the festival concerts, but he has written specifically to express his thanks and 'pay homage to all you have done and are doing for music'. Dolmetsch was overjoyed. He knew that Grainger was a 'free soul', in many ways rather like himself and he respected the work that Grainger was doing with the revival of folk-song and 'natural' music.

On 30 July Dolmetsch received another letter thanking him for playing a Lawes fantasy especially for Grainger on the previous evening. He writes:

Lilla Vrån
Pevensey Bay,
Sussex

I enjoyed it even more than the week before. It certainly is one of the most glorious and subtle compositions of any school or period and is just the kind of work I, personally, enjoy and admire above all others.

The concerts Grainger attended were 'a great education . . . as well as a keen artistic delight'. He suggests that if there was such a thing as a Nobel Prize for music 'to be given to the man doing most good to the cause of music itself and all it stands for', it should certainly be given to Dolmetsch: he confesses that he can think of no one living who is 'doing so much for *so many sides* of music' as he is. Grainger then lists all the aspects in which he considers Dolmetsch pre-eminent:

Your whole activities are the result of a complete understanding of the true and normal relation of art to life; the result of an inspired vision of *what is most needed* in modern (or any) life. As a result of this unique insight your whole endeavo[u]rs are informed with *perfect cultural virtue*—a virtue that enables you to do things that most men (even most exceptional ones) would deem impossible.

Grainger is a self-confessed modernist in music in that his inner ear is listening continually to the music of the future. But he also realises that true art has no 'oldness or newness'; that all periods of human life produce great art, and that all artistic culture depends upon knowledge of the past, an understanding and love of the past. He also appears to be aware of the great difficulties in obtaining access to this knowledge of the past and acknowledges that the musical world should be grateful to Dolmetsch for 'putting this knowledge so easily, so fully and so charmingly within our reach'. Dolmetsch's concerts are 'the most liberal education' he has ever witnessed and the most enjoyable he has ever heard. He enjoyed the early instruments altogether, but best of all he liked the viols, 'for they give a loveliness of instrumental tonecolo[u]r and a perfect *balance of sound* such as one finds in a good *a cappella* choir—but which one never finds in a string quartet or a symphony orchestra or military band'.

In Dolmetsch's reply he suggests ways of using Grainger's appreciative remarks for publicity purposes. Unfortunately, these letters from Dolmetsch have not come to light[16] but Grainger is such a meticulous correspondent that we have a good general idea of the contents. Grainger is full of ideas for promoting interest in the Haslemere Festival and once again draws up a list of ways in which he can achieve this plan. He will mention the festival to interviewers on his return to America in September as 'the most interesting and instructive experience' of his European trip, 'pointing out the vast *educational* scope' of Dolmetsch's work. Grainger has soon to write an article for Schirmer's *Musical Quarterly* on the subject of 'Tonal Variety and Tonal Balance in Orchestration', and he intends to mention in this the 'perfect tonal balance' that Dolmetsch achieves with the viols etc. Grainger also offers to write to the famous Mrs. Coolidge[17] and urge her to engage him and his family to play at one of her chamber music festivals in Washington, DC:

> She tries very hard to present the best in chamber music for purely aesthetic reasons and I would like to point out to her that such tonal variety and tonal balance as yours is never heard in modern chamber music, and that the Fantasies for Viols, as you do them, are a far more subtle and exalted form of string 'music' than any of the usual 'quartets' that are everlastingly heard.

Grainger asks Dolmetsch if he would like to write an article for the *Musical Quarterly*: if so, Grainger will approach Carl Engel, their president. He has ideas also for publishing some of Dolmetsch's manuscripts, such as the fantasies for viols and also some of the recorder music, which he thinks would be equally suitable for wind ensembles, whilst the string pieces can be published with alternative markings for modern strings. And in case Dolmetsch should react unfavourably to this suggestion, Grainger points out that he knows that the lovely old music can only be done justice to by the authentic instruments and that performance on modern instruments would be 'a sort of travesty'. On the other hand he suggests that a collection of examples of the old music (in each case stating the authentic orchestration and that these instruments may be obtained from Dolmetsch and studied with him) might lead many an enthusiastic young music-lover to a knowledge of the old music and a wish to study it with Dolmetsch. He then makes a declaration that must have warmed Dolmetsch's heart:

> It seems to me that some means (such as publication) should be taken to make a *world public* realize that the old music and the old instruments (made available and practical by you) is a *necessary part of musical study* (alongside the study of Beethoven, Bach, Wagner, etc.) and that it can be studied, as *living music*, from you!

A later letter poses (21 August 1931) a question about Bach's Brandenburg Concerto No. 3 in G major for ten strings and cembalo. He asks:

> What would have happened in Bach's time, in the 2 Adagio chords that lead from the first to the last movement?
> Would the cembalist have played arpeggios, or other figuration along Chromatic Fantasia lines, over these, or what? I would be very thankful to learn this detail from your wisdom and experience when we meet!

Since the reply was verbal we have no idea of Dolmetsch's ruling, but it was certainly not a difficult question for him to answer. It is included here simply as yet another instance of the lack of knowledge that existed at the time concerning the playing of early music, and in particular that of Bach.

After his return to the USA, Grainger writes from White Plains on 12 October thanking Dolmetsch for his wonderful hospitality and the artistic delights that Dolmetsch and his family showered upon them when he visited them just before sailing. Grainger has already spoken to Carl

Engel of Schirmers and there are plans for publishing some of Dolmetsch's music. The *Musical Courier* has commissioned Grainger to write some articles and the second one is to be about Dolmetsch and the 'wondrous "revival" work' he is producing. He has also kept his word and spoken to Mrs. Coolidge and to Engel about the possibility of some chamber-music concerts. No doubt it would have materialised if times had been normal, but it was the time of the depression in the USA and eventually the idea had to be abandoned.

Meanwhile, on Dolmetsch's own side of the Atlantic there were discussions as to the formation of a '48 Society'. Their intention was to record all the preludes and fugues of J. S. Bach on the clavichord, the instrument for which they were written. And who better to play them than Arnold Dolmetsch?

NOTES

1. Dolmetsch played the violin in the Sonata in E minor for violin and harpsichord (Rudolph Dolmetsch). He used an instrument, now in the Dolmetsch Collection, designed and made by himself.
2. Extract from letter from Mrs. Marjorie Claisen, 28 September 1967.
3. Two songs with lute accompaniment:
   i. *La belo Mourentino*, 16th century, Provençal.
   ii. *C'est a ce jolly Moys de May*, 15th century, French.
4. *Columbia History of Music Through Ear and Eye*, edited Percy Scholes, Oxford University Press,
   Album I, Period I, London (1930);
   Album II, Period II, London (1931).
5. The *Consort*, Haslemere, 1931, pp. 4–5. There is in the same issue a more detailed account of the trip by Mabel Dolmetsch, pp. 12–17 (illustrated).
6. Belle Skinner Collection of Old Musical Instruments. Now part of the Yale Collection of Musical Instruments, New Haven, Conn.
7. Dolmetsch, Arnold, *The Interpretation of the Music of the* XVII and XVIII centuries, Novello, London, 1915, p. 431, rep. etc.
8. Liberty and Co. were founded in 1875 in Regent Street by Sir Arthur Lazenby Liberty as importers of Eastern silks in an attempt to improve the design and colour of British mass-produced textiles. They subsequently printed their own designs which were influenced by the muted eastern designs and colours. Later they branched out into jewellery, silverware and furniture. Today they still retain the highest standards of printing and design and their textiles are world-famous.
9. Rothenstein, William, *Men and Memories*, Vol. I (1872–1900), Faber & Faber, London, 1931.
10. See p. 112 FN 6.
11. Unfortunately the instrument ordered by the BBC was destroyed by the bombing

of St. George's Hall in 1940. Subsequently, after the death of Rudolph Dolmetsch in 1942, the BBC bought the instrument which had belonged to him.

12. F. T. Arnold (1861–1940), English musical scholar, *The Art of Accompaniment from a Thorough-Bass as practised in the 17th and 18th centuries* (Oxford, 1931), recognised as the standard authority.

13. This is the fundamental note (c) of a tenor recorder.

14. Jesses.

15. Davis, Alan, *Recorder and Music Magazine*, 'Bach's Recorder Parts', June 1972, pp. 49–50.

16. Repeated attempts to obtain copies of letters from Arnold Dolmetsch to Grainger believed to be in the Grainger Museum in Melbourne have been unsuccessful. A catalogue is in process of being made and it is hoped that these letters will emerge eventually. Other correspondence has been made available by the courtesy of the Library of Congress, Washington, DC.

17. Mrs. Elizabeth Sprague Coolidge (1864–1953), pianist, composer and patron of music. Founder of Coolidge Foundation at Library of Congress, Washington, DC (with auditorium presented by her) for concerts, festivals and awards of prizes and medals to contemporary composers of all nationalities.

CHAPTER XX

The 'Forty-Eight'

IF Arnold Dolmetsch was the *enfant terrible* of the early music revival, Landowska represented a formidable rival to the female title in the same field and equal to him both in zeal and temperament. Originally a pianist, Wanda Landowska was born in Poland but came to Paris early in her career. Although she arrived at the harpsichord much later than Dolmetsch she devoted all her energies to the playing of this instrument and had by 1932 achieved a reputation of some importance. She became a brilliant but controversial exponent and attracted a number of talented keyboard players to study with her at the École de Musique Ancienne, which she founded and directed at Saint-Leu-la-Fôret near Paris. One of her students was the young American, Ralph Kirkpatrick.[1] After a visit to Boulogne-sur-Seine to hear Dorothy Swainson play the clavichord that Dolmetsch had made for her, he writes to his family:

21 rue Jacobi
Paris VI

Feb 29 '32

It was a beautiful instrument, better than the one in Cambridge. [Harvard University, Mass.] She played beautifully, producing an amazing variety of effects, many of which I had not discovered. She is a pupil of Dolmetsch and renews my conviction that there is a great deal to be gotten from him.

Two months later, in another letter, Kirkpatrick describes his meeting with Dolmetsch:

April 18th 1932

I found a hump-shouldered little old man with long straggly white hair and a thin gray beard and wizened face with sharp brilliant brown eyes . . . he does know a great deal and admits it to be only a small fraction of potential knowledge, although he is conceited to the utmost and will tolerate no disagreement. But his egoism and 'shouting down the world' differ from that of Landowska in that they are directed more at a cause than at personal glory, and they seem to be perfectly honest.

Ralph Kirkpatrick complains that most of the afternoon was spent in musical gossip and histories of his more famous quarrels but that he also 'played the clavichord with an extraordinary variety and beauty of tone colour'. And so the summer of that year found Kirkpatrick at Haslemere, attending the festival and having lessons with Dolmetsch on the clavichord.

It did not take the young man long to find, as did all the others, that life with Dolmetsch was not easy. In later letters he tells his family that he begins to wonder who is the more difficult, Landowska or Dolmetsch, and issues a warning: 'If I ever get like that, I implore you either to beat it out of me or to seclude me at the bottom of a pond in the company of a millstone!' However, he goes on to admit that it is more Dolmetsch's strongly-ingrained ideas, combined with degenerating health, rather than his personal character that makes him difficult. What Kirkpatrick really wants is 'conversation with him purified (the impossible) of all irrelevant digressions'. He finds Mrs. Dolmetsch 'very kind, and apparently the most accessible . . .' and hopes to find out about the old dances from her as she has spent much time reviving them. His last letter, dated 24 October 1932, is when he collects the instrument he had ordered from Dolmetsch:

> I am much pleased with the clavichord. Tonally it is even better than I expected, with a fine resonance, perfect evenness, and the utmost sensitiveness. The entire instrument seems to vibrate for each note. As the wood ages and becomes still more resonant, it ought to become perfectly marvellous.[2]

Ralph Kirkpatrick has since become one of the world's leading harpsichordists and musical scholars. His views on Dolmetsch's instruments have not changed: 'I think the Chickering harpsichords were most remarkable for their time because for the next 30 or 40 years they were the only instruments that had much relation to 18th-century harpsichords . . . Pupils of mine now come and play this instrument[3] and are astonished at the degree of congruence with current fashions in the return to 18th-century reconstruction. It certainly presented me with an ideal of sound that was otherwise not available in the average French or German instrument of the time. It was really only an achievement that has been caught up within the last 15 years by the Boston School of harpsichord makers. And to a certain extent now spreading elsewhere. It was an extraordinary piece of pioneering; and also with what was obviously a great deal of intelligence being applied to technical problems in the Chickering Factory. A very high standard of workmanship was maintained throughout.'

It seems that most of the instruments Dolmetsch made at this time were practically forgotten some 20 years after they were made and were gradually brought out of obscurity, so that in a way they could be said to have been

40 or 50 years too early. Kirkpatrick's first instrument was originally made for Busoni (see pp. 175–6) and remained in his apartment in the Victoria Luise Platz in Berlin until he died. The instrument was then returned to the Chickering factory, purchased by Lotte van Buren, the American harpsichordist, and subsequently acquired by Kirkpatrick, who used it in his earliest recordings.

The Boston or New England school of harpsichord makers are without doubt the logical continuation of the principles set down by Dolmetsch at Chickering's, although there was a decided break for some 20 years and an American had to cross the Atlantic to pick up the chain once more: it was John Challis, the first Dolmetsch Foundation scholar-craftsman, who, in terms of inventiveness and materials, took up where Dolmetsch left off. Although Challis, whose metal-framed instruments with special action are today the subject of much controversy, many of his attitudes or 'Dolmetschisms' are preserved in him intact. Ironically it is also through Challis and the New England school that Dolmetsch[4] has such a great influence in the USA today. The two leading members of the school have direct links with Dolmetsch: Frank Hubbard studied at Haslemere and William Dowd was a pupil of Challis; the young William Post Ross (who has a workshop in the original Chickering factory) was in turn a pupil of Dowd.

One thing that Kirkpatrick has retained from his association with Dolmetsch is his way of tuning: 'I first began to tune when I got that clavichord. He [Dolmetsch] used the "c" fork and fundamentally from my way of thinking it is always from "c". I still use an "a" fork sometimes, but the basic thinking is "c", in 5ths round the circle of the sharp side as far as c sharp, then round the circle on the flat side to d flat, testing along all the way . . . It was from him that first I got the trick of tuning the unison strings ever so slightly apart and which Challis still does and most other clavichord makers don't.'

* * *

It was in that summer of 1932 that 'The 48 Society' first approached Dolmetsch asking if he would undertake to play all the Bach preludes and fugues for a set of seven 12″ 78 rpm recordings. In a letter to Mabel on 19 July the Columbia Graphophone Company show considerable interest in the project but add a proviso that 500 subscribers must be found to make the deal financially viable. The foundation members lost no time: by 19 October The 48 Society had achieved a president in Sir Henry Hadow and proudly declared itself on printed notepaper. The secretary writes to

Mrs. Dolmetsch to tell her that they now have a total number of sub-scribers sufficient to justify them going on with the scheme. In a letter to Dorothy Swainson in Paris, Dolmetsch writes saying that he never personally believed in the project but now that it has become a reality he is delighted. He tells her that subscriptions have been coming from all over the world from places as far afield as Japan, the Sandwich Islands, France and Germany: in the British Isles, George Bernard Shaw was the first to send his cheque for two guineas.

Recording was due to start in November but Dolmetsch became ill and the sessions were postponed for a month. The first recordings were successful enough but Dolmetsch disliked doing things to order—especially where machines were concerned: he was almost 75 and too old to withstand the unavoidable hustle and bustle of a studio. On the way to the Columbia Studios, his taxi swerved to avoid a cyclist and Dolmetsch was thrown across the interior; he was considerably shaken, although apparently uninjured. However, a pain in his chest some days later warned him that something was wrong: it was then discovered that he had cracked two ribs, so the second session also had to be postponed.

When he had recovered sufficiently to face the microphone, but not the travelling, there followed a procedure that must have been unique for the time. For about ten days or so, Jesses became a temporary recording studio, with technicians appearing out of nowhere and the household apparently going on much the same. Dolmetsch's temper was somewhat more testy but Mabel took the upheaval with all her usual calm, consoling herself that her beloved Arnold would not have to travel to London after all. Dolmetsch was allowed to play as and when he felt inclined. His health was now failing considerably and he found the effort too much at times. So he would rehearse, agree to play and everything would be set up: then he would suddenly decide that he didn't feel like it after all and would shuffle away and fortify himself with a drink, whereupon he would return to his clavichord again and make another attempt. Perhaps it would go well. Sometimes it did with all the old magic; at others it was difficult and he would make mistakes to the extent that he would suddenly throw up his hands in the air and exclaim 'It is impossible!' (with the accent French-style on the last syllable). 'I cannot play today! We will try again tomorrow.'

Despite this unorthodox method of working the results were extra-ordinary. Unfortunately the series was never finished but the records which were actually issued, the preludes and fugues numbers 5, 6, 10, 22, 25, 31, 36 and 39 and the *Chromatic Fantasia* in d minor, are remarkable examples of his great gifts and insight. Although many who knew him in his earlier days knew that he was not at his best at the time, in general these recordings survive as proof of his mastery of the true technique of the clavichord, and he brings out the intricacies of ornaments and rhythm in the style which he knew instinctively was the correct contemporary interpretation. This instinct, previously recorded in his book and confirmed in later writings by others, is indisputable—even today, when authenticity has become almost more important than the music itself. The *Sunday Times* considered that 'these are notable records. The tone and character of the clavichord are admirably reproduced, and there is no doubt that we are listening to these works as they were first conceived in Bach's mind. Mr. Dolmetsch gives to each part its fullest expression, so that every phase of this delicate contrapuntal music sings with its own meaning. Those who are not whole-hearted Bach lovers may find here too great a severity; to others they will be the final interpretation of some of the world's masterpieces.' A writer in the *Gramophone* (April 1933) was impressed: 'His [Dolmetsch's] high skill in the management of the clavichord will probably win for it adherents, though it is perhaps not everybody's love.' He went on to say that Dolmetsch makes these instruments and that it might not be a bad thing if 'we all had to do that before we got any music!' He recommended the clavichord as 'a sweet creature to have in our modern thin-walled houses, and noisy life', but warned that we need to attune our minds to its tiny tone and forget the iron-clad-nine-foot grand—advice Dolmetsch would have endorsed most willingly. The writer also praised Dolmetsch's notes for the player, one being that rules for fugue-making would not have troubled Bach, for 'he wrote music containing fugues, not fugues constricting music'.

Reviewers everywhere were equally enthusiastic and stressed that the records were important for many more reasons than that they were the first recordings of the clavichord ever put on the market. They all were enchanted by the actual playing, which says a great deal for the fact that Dolmetsch was so old and tired when he made them. The *Daily Telegraph* (25 March 1933) wrote: 'The runs throughout are brought out with exquisite clearness, and the recitative passages have a thrilling quality owing to the vibrato which the piano is of course unable to produce.' *London Town* (1 April 1933) claimed that 'Mr. Arnold Dolmetsch feels also the lyrical side of Bach's genius. By research into the style and tradition of performance in Bach's time, and by a lifetime's study of the earlier music, Dolmetsch has recaptured the spirit of the composer in all its poignancy and emotional appeal. His performances on the clavichord have been a revelation to music-lovers who had previously been unable to enjoy Bach's music and scarcely less to those who had appreciated only his austerer moods.'

Finally, Ernest Newman writing a year later, in the *Sunday Times* (11 March 1934), contributed an interesting comparative study in an article entitled 'The Two Bachs'. It appears that the Bach Society had also brought out the first records of the '48' played by Edwin Fischer on the piano. Newman makes it plain that he does not intend to discuss either set from the point of view of technical performance, but solely from that of interpretation: 'For in the two albums we have two quite different Bach's; and if one of them is the right Bach the other must necessarily be the wrong one—or, to put it in less sweeping terms, in proportion as the one set of records is right on this little point or that, the other must be wrong. Detailed comparison of the two sets is not possible, because while Mr. Fischer intends to work his way steadily through the series from No. 1 to No. 48, Mr. Dolmetsch gives us, in his first album, selections from both parts, with the *Chromatic Fantasia* thrown in.' Newman warns that those of his readers who are unfamilar with the tones of the little clavichord will be a little puzzled by the sound of it, whilst they will be even more puzzled by what Dolmetsch does with the works. He speculates upon the effect it would have upon Bach himself if he should be able to revisit this earth, and thinks that Bach would be more puzzled still if he heard the piano being used for his music. He does not rule out that Bach might be delighted with the new instrument and the possibilities it might open out for him, but he is 'tolerably certain he would say that at a hundred points Mr. Fischer and the rest of us moderns look at his preludes from a wrong point of view. He might not agree with everything that Mr. Dolmetsch does, but on the whole he would say, I think, that it was thus, and not in Mr. Fischer's way, that he himself and his contemporaries played the pieces.'

Newman comes down on Dolmetsch's side as being 'a profound student of the ancient music', and that he has shown conclusively in his book[5] that notes invariably 'do not mean what they say' and from a mass of evidence on the subject quotes Couperin[6]—'We write differently from what we play'. He maintains that Dolmetsch's careful examination of all the ancient theoretical treatises has led him to 'certain conclusions the general truth of which cannot be disputed; and on these conclusions he boldly acts in his playing of Bach'. Newman takes as one example (the B flat minor prelude from Book 1) the modern practice to play all the groups of semiquavers just as they are written, with the two small dots in each group being of equal value. 'Mr. Dolmetsch plays them throughout as a dotted semiquaver followed by a demi-semi-quaver. Frequently he converts a dot into a double dot, as Handel's contemporaries, there can hardly be any doubt, did with the dots in the first movement of the overture to *The Messiah*. When the rest of us arrive at one of those chords of the diminished seventh which Bach loves to plank down just before his final cadence, we play it as a simple chord and pass on to the next note.

Mr. Dolmetsch will sometimes turn the chord into an expansive arpeggio flourish (see, for instance, the end of the D major Prelude of Book 1). He generally treats the closing rhetorical chords in a still more rhetorical fashion than the notes themselves suggest.'

Newman goes thoroughly into Dolmetsch's treatment of long notes that stretch over a bar or more in slow time. For the slow trills or series of insistent demi-semiquaver tappings of the too-retiring note, he says Dolmetsch would gladly supply chapter and verse to any challenge. 'All kinds of technical points spring to notice in Mr. Dolmetsch's readings that are not perceptible in a performance on the piano; the polyphony is often clearer, ostinato notes or figures stand out more boldly, and, in general, the polyphony is clearer, because, in the absence of the wash of that tone that the piano leaves behind it in rapid passages, the bare bones of the part-writing show up better.'

Dolmetsch was greatly pleased by this wonderful response from the critics, especially as another set of the Columbia recordings, in which the whole family were playing viols, virginals and recorders, was equally well received: Rudolph, in particular, was praised for his Domenico Scarlatti sonata in D major on the harpsichord. But some of the best publicity he had ever received came in the form of the promised article from Percy Grainger, published in the *Musical Quarterly* in April 1933.[7] Under the apt title of 'Arnold Dolmetsch Musical Confucius' he blazoned the trail for any aspiring student of the early music in an irresistible account of Dolmetsch's work following an assessment of the present state of musical interest. His broad and comprehensive knowledge of the music of other cultures enabled him to see more clearly the importance of Dolmetsch's researches and he suggests that, in order to offset the 'long-standing musical impoverishment' of the present time, the first 'cure' is provided, ready-made by the genius and activities of Arnold Dolmetsch, who:

for more than forty years has played the role of a musical Confucius, holding up to our ears the perfections of a great variety of ancient European music and preaching its value with persistence, yet without exaggeration or undue partisanship. If by the term 'a genius' we mean one who has not allowed his great natural gifts to become narrowed and withered by specialization, but instead has kept a manly, full-blooded, all-round approach to art and life, then we must acclaim Arnold Dolmetsch as a genius indeed. From the very start of his artistic life he has shown a breadth and universality of vision, a combination of theoretical deduction with practical handicraft, a blend of aesthetic intuition with scientific fact-hunger and unbending truthfulness that is truly breath-taking to review.

Prior to the article appearing, Grainger had written sending a copy to Dolmetsch asking him to alter or suppress anything he thought unsuitable.

It is doubtful if he changed anything, for such glowing praise did not come his way so often.

1933 started well for Dolmetsch. The recording sessions had tired him but as soon as the responsibility was over he regained his usual vigour and shortly after celebrating his 75th birthday in February he had given a series of three concerts at The Artworkers' Guild Hall. Once again he managed to produce something new for his audiences. He had long been inspired by the pictures of Fra Angelico and the combination of instruments he depicted, such as lute, harp, rebec, recorder and viol. He had imagined the 'heavenly sounds' suggested by such a choir but their realisation had now become possible through the successful construction of a little mediaeval harp with strings of brass that had been completed during the previous year in his own workshop.[8] After the concert one critic wrote 'that the effect was strange but pleasant, the entry of the recorder in the first piece like a ray of light in a dusky room'. (*The Observer* 26 March 1933.) At the second concert Dolmetsch gave his audience 'An Evening of the Music of J. S. Bach on the clavichord'. The *Daily Telegraph* suggests that there had probably never been a clavichord concert in London: nor anywhere else, the writer might have added, and certainly no one but Dolmetsch had ever played the instrument in public. Dolmetsch's instructions to the audience as to how they should behave was seldom allowed to pass without comment. This critic gives a tongue-in-cheek account of how the audience may not clap nor shuffle their feet: ' "Quiet", Dolmetsch had said, "was the medicine the modern world wanted". So with one or two broadsides at contemporary musicians and contemporary critics he bent over his clavichord in a dim religious light and played preludes and fugues from the 48.' Applause being forbidden, it seems that Dolmetsch managed to deduce from 'sighs and exclamations' that the audience wished to hear certain pieces again and he proceeded to repeat some of the more familiar ones. However, Dolmetsch confessed that, although the clavichord was beautiful, it was also a ruthless instrument and 'if a devil got on his shoulder, what could he do?' Nothing, says the critic, 'except be honest, admit he has made mistakes and start again. It was worth while. For the interest of hearing these supreme little classics on the instrument for which they were written far outweighed such little contretemps as were caused by emissaries of the Evil One.'

A new set of recordings and the making of two new instruments would have seemed enough for a septuagenarian to sit back and take a bow, but Dolmetsch was never a man to rest on his laurels: a remarkable state of affairs when it is realised how very few accolades actually came his way. His letters convey that he is always pressed for time: his excuses are not complaints but simply that the day is not long enough to do all the jobs at hand. As soon as the spring concerts were over he had to attend to the coming festival, the ninth. His advance notices made certain that his patrons were left in no doubt as to their past achievements. Since 1925, some 1,200 pieces had been performed and, after deducting repetitions, there were about 1,000 new works. Dolmetsch points out that a certain number of these were already known to concert-goers in an adapted or altered form but would be presented at Haslemere on the instruments for which they were composed. At this festival he would present a little mediaeval harp that had been introduced at the Artworkers' Guild concerts in the spring. In a programme consisting entirely of French music from Saint Louis to Louis XV there was a *Basse Danse* for a consort of recorders, rebec, lute, harp and viols (published by Pierre Attaignant in 1529) and a 13th-century troubadour song to the harp, *Bele Doette as Fenestre se siet*. The instrument was to be used again for 'French and English Dances and Courtly Masquing Airs' and a programme of 'English Intimate Music'. But the star item in that festival was to be the Bach concerto for four harpsichords and strings, adapted by Bach from a concerto by Vivaldi for four violins. It was to receive its first performance on the opening night, Monday 17 July. On 31 March, Dolmetsch writes to Dorothy Swainson in Paris asking her if she will take part in this work. He already has Rudolph, 'le virtuose in excelsis, Betty (née Brown) qui joue bien . . . A.D. votre serviteur . . . et . . . *Dorothy Swainson* la dernière *sur cette liste* mais pas dans mon estime . . . C'est -à-dire, si ladite D.S.' Dolmetsch has evidently heard from Landowska, who, it seems, is also a possibility. 'Il y a bien W. Landowska, qui m'a écrit qu'elle viendrait avec un groupe d'élèves . . . En tous cas, même si elle vient, elle n'aura pas à refuser de jouer dans le Concerto!' Unfortunately neither Dorothy Swainson nor Landowska played on that occasion and it seems doubtful whether the latter ever attended herself, with or without her group of pupils. It would be interesting to find out if Landowska ever knew that she was on Dolmetsch's 'reserve list'. The fact would not have pleased her. The concerto was finally played with Douglas Brown as the fourth harpsichordist.

The festival now attracted wide press coverage and a greatly increased attendance from followers throughout the world. Although the critics still considered the standards of performance less than perfect, they generally acknowledged that Dolmetsch's work was now to be reckoned with as a serious contribution to the musical life of the country. *The Times* of 22 July 1933, after a generally appreciative and occasionally critical assessment, sums up that

> The pleasant thing about these concerts, apart from Mr. Dolmetsch's own rare combination of deep scholarship and high enthusiasm, is the sense that for all the participants a festival is merely an intensification of their music of everyday.

Several writers remark upon the growing interest shown abroad. In countries like Germany and Switzerland early-music societies had already been founded, mostly taking their lead from Haslemere: the Germans had rediscovered Schütz, whom they now recognise as the greatest composer of the Thirty Years War period, whilst Italy had recently published two volumes of the works of the two Gabrielis of Venice. And although the concerto by Bach for four harpsichords was well-received at Haslemere and acknowledged as being the first performance in this country, E. Van der Straeten, that eminent critic and firm supporter of Dolmetsch, points out that the work had been heard in Germany the previous year in a performance by the Chamber Music Society of Hagen-Kabel (Westphalia) under its director, Herr H. E. Hoesch. However, the two Bach chorales played on four recorders seem to have been enjoyed by everyone and the *Observer* (23 July 1933) advises its readers to make the journey to Haslemere for the next three concerts as the recorders are to be heard again and should not be missed. The playing of the young Carl Dolmetsch on this instrument was now being noticed, as was Rudolph's on the harpsichord. Mabel Dolmetsch, too, was complimented upon her dance programmes and is especially praised for her diligent researches into the old dances and their relationship to the rhythms and tempi of contemporary music: music that would have served originally as an accompaniment but which had subsequently become detached and, inevitably, corrupt.

Although authenticity and rarity were words used to describe Dolmetsch and his activities, occasionally—and providentially—he succumbed to the very human desire to fill his impoverished pockets by more modern means. Such occasions were when he and his entire family played the music for the films, *The Lady of the Lake*, and later, *Colonel Blood*.

If Dolmetsch's purse was strengthened by a little popular entertaining, his brain had been vibrating on a very much higher plane. All through that year he had been working on two of his greatest discoveries, both of which he wrote about in the *Consort*[9] of June 1934. They were the deciphering of the Welsh Bardic MS and his scoring of Pérotin le grand's four-part *organa* from the 13th-century school of Notre Dame in Paris. Many opinions have been voiced since these discoveries were published and the rights or wrongs of Dolmetsch's interpretations will no doubt be argued for many years to come. For the potential researcher who can approach the subject without prejudice, there is much literature available; but if the material is viewed from a purely academic standpoint he will have little success. Dolmetsch's instinct and insight were often of more use to him than academic underpinnings and yet he was sought after by the academics when they needed his help. One instance of this was when Dom Anselm Hughes[10] had approached him asking if he would supply two players 'on such instruments as your expert judgement would suggest'[11] as the Columbia Graphophone Company were shortly making two records of some vocal music from the Old Hall MS *c*.1450. The introduction had been brought about through their mutual friend Percy Grainger. In writing to Grainger on 28 February 1934, Dom Anselm tells him that he and Dolmetsch are laying their heads together about the whole question of instrumental accompaniment for early mediaeval music:

Nashdom Abbey,
Burnham,
Bucks

It is a queer partnership, for the old man appears to despise all musicology, and to rely upon his artistic instinct and experiences alone. Yet I somehow feel it is very good for the antiquarian to be forced into collaboration with a musician of that type. I have met people, especially at the International Congress, who do not seem to care about the music itself, and if their work goes no further than that I do not see the use of it. I am very grateful to you for having given me the first idea in this direction, as it may lead to great things.

Today, Dom Anselm remembers that meeting well and with some affection. He recalled Dolmetsch as 'an extremely picturesque figure . . . very friendly indeed . . . I was asked to take a meal with him in his kitchen which he told me was a great honour and very few people were allowed the intimacy of his kitchen where they all ate together.' Later, Dom Anselm quite rightly realised that this signal honour was paid to a great many others. 'Whether it was a little piece of shop window or not, I don't know. . . . There was a good deal of shop window about the old man.'

Nevertheless, Dom Anselm has no doubts as to his greatness and the importance of his work: like many others who had dealings with him, he regrets that the old man had such a chip on his shoulder when 'wherever I went, I found people appreciated him and his work and thought very highly of him'. He confirmed that Dolmetsch's instinct was a rare gift that was quite unique. He gave as an example the occasion when he took a piece from the Worcester MSS[12] to Dolmetsch to try out in different ways to see how they sounded. 'We tried out a certain number in a new way with 3 viols and a voice part supplied by me. . . . It was a new interpretation of the music and I am quite sure it was the true, the right interpretation that no academic minds would ever have stumbled across, but Dolmetsch, with his extraordinary flair, had found the true interpretation and when it was over he said . . . "This has been the greatest day in my musical life!" '

It was an article by Professor Jacques Handschin in the *Musical Times* of August 1933 that first called Dolmetsch's attention to Pérotin's *organa*: the professor called the MSS what Dolmetsch described as 'the fearsome and inaccurate name of *Choralbearbeitungen*'. In his article Dolmetsch goes into careful detail and states, most convincingly, his reasons for disputing the professor's theories: it would seem that once more he has presented the case for having the music performed before arguing its merits from a purely musicological viewpoint. The discussion is fully covered in the *Consort* and Dolmetsch's scoring for four rebecs instead of voices was performed at the Tenth Haslemere Festival. In the same article we have Dolmetsch's version of the deciphering of the Bardic Penllyn MS.[13] The opinions expressed as to the pros and cons of his arguments could easily fill a large book, but the fact remains that Dolmetsch left no original source unmolested: however controversial, his findings are the work of a brilliant and independent mind. The pieces were also performed that summer at the festival, played by Mabel on the little Celtic harp and on the crwth[14] by Dolmetsch, yet another instrument recently constructed in the workshops and making its first appearance.

The Bardic MS transcript caused a great deal of comment from the press and much correspondence, especially from Wales; Dolmetsch was later invited to lecture at the museum in Cardiff. Eventually his supporters founded *The Early Welsh Music Society* (Cymdeithas Cerddoriaeth Gynnar Gymreig).[15] They were very active for some time and sponsored gramophone recordings of harp and crwth pieces played by the Dolmetsches and issued in 1937.[16]

With so many novelties on their programmes, the 1934 Haslemere Festival provided a field-day for the press and they turned up in their numbers: the more serious papers devoted columns to the concerts, whilst the popular press published photographs of Dolmetsch playing the crwth. A clear account by Gerald Hayes in the *Monthly Musical Record* (September 1934 p. 158) gives a fair summing up of the important points:

> There is very strong evidence of supposing it [the Bardic] MS to represent a corpus of Bardic Music established at a famous eleventh century congress. It need hardly be said that such music would for centuries before and after be handed on solely by oral tradition. Mr. Dolmetsch has said that he thinks it cannot be later than the eighth-century and, though he rarely gives a speculative opinion, when he does, his views have a special value.
>
> It is too early to see the full implications of this reversal of all accepted ideas of development, but it may suggest that our ordinary scale of today is really very ancient and that the modal system, which left its impress on European musical idiom until the eighteenth century, was a 'modernist' innovation, introduced by the Church and propagated by all her immense powers of ubiquity, in opposition to the secular music of pagan origin.

Although the musical establishment regarded Dolmetsch and his pursuits with certain reservations, they were unstinting in praise of his book, which had now been in print for 20 years. It is a curious fact that no one had sought to make a translation. Eventually it was his pupil, Dorothy Swainson, then living and working in Paris, who decided to make a start in the French language. At Dolmetsch's recommendation she was being assisted by Bernard Steele, a close friend of Dolmetsch's who was a French scholar and a man of considerable influence in publishing in that country at the time. For the past year there had been exchanges between master and pupil with suggestions and counter-suggestions, but by the beginning of 1935 the work was assuming some shape. In a letter of 2 January, Dolmetsch tells Dorothy Swainson that her work is admirable and that she has never misunderstood a text, whether it be his or a translation. And then:

> Jesses,
> Haslemere,
> Surrey

L'Edition des Couperin de Brahms et Chrysander est *mauvaise*! Vous allez sauter, mais, attendez—Je la croyais bonne—Les notes sont correctes et les signes d'ornements aussi, bien que corrompus dans la forme. Récemment, j'ai dû renseigner des Pièces de Couperin à une élève qui jouait sur cette édition. Nous sommes arrivés à des difficultés! Ces idiots d'éditeurs ont confondu ⌐⌐ avec ⌒ aboli le premier et tout réduit au second—C'est fondamental dans bien des cas! Comme j'ai l'édition originale je ne m'étais pas servi de l'autre et n'avais pas remarqué la faute.[17]

According to another letter of 11 January, Dorothy Swainson had asked Dolmetsch why a certain pupil of hers found difficulties when trying to interpret the composer's intentions in the 6th and 7th preludes by Couperin in his *L'Art de toucher de clavecin*. Unfortunately Dorothy Swainson's letter has not as yet been traced but Dolmetsch's reply is revealing:

> Jesses,
> Haslemere,
> Surrey

11 Janvier 1935

Ma chère Dorothea,

Votre bien légitime curiosité sera satisfaite—J'ai même l'idée que vous auriez pu la satisfaire vous même, car vous ne manquez ni de logique ni de perspicacité.

Il faut cependant que je vous reproche sérieusement d'avoir supposé que Couperin, si méthodique, si soigneux, si précis, si Français enfin ait pu employer côte à côte deux signes *complètement différents* pour produire un seul effet! Pour bien saisir le principe il faut voir *l'Edition originale*. Vous y verrez que l'arc ⌒ indique toujours la prolongation *d'une même note*. En dessous ou en dessus de l'arc, il peut y avoir des notes détachées.

Le signe du phrasé, qui correspond le plus souvent avec la liaison est la ligne droite, ou presque droite ⌐⌐ ⌐ ⌐――― . Cette même ligne droite est plus ou moins privée de(s) crochets quand ils sont inutiles: c'est à dire quand les notes sont disposées de telle façon qu'on puisse les relier *directement* par la ligne droite. Même alors on voit souvent une trace de crochet à l'extremité de ces lignes.

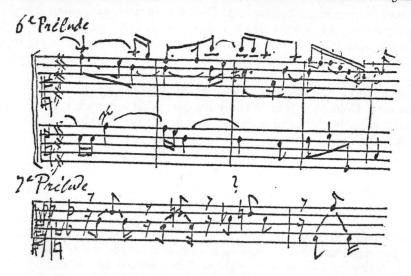

Il est évident qu' à la 4e mesure de la ligne en haut, on ne pourrait pas mettre les traits entre les notes—mais, à la 3e ligne, on le peut et on le fait! Et voilà la raison pour laquelle votre fille est muette.[18]

* * *

Throughout the years Dolmetsch had continued his practice of sending out informative advance notices of the forthcoming festival programme: in 1935 he excelled himself by producing a 'Preliminary Discourse' running to nine pages of close print. His introductory chapter concerns the oratorios and cantatas of the 18th century, principally in the works of J. S. Bach where 'one finds occasional pieces using special instruments more or less uncommon and quite different from the Strings, Oboes, Flutes, for which the bulk of the Music is scored'. His claim being, rightly that they 'enhance the effect . . . often [being] one of the most beautiful pieces in the work'. He attacks the organisers and conductors who, despite his 50 years' crusade and example, 'continue to suppress these pieces, or worse still, they use some common instrument as a substitute, however incapable it may be of reproducing the intended quality of tone. Today, it would be unthinkable to employ any but the correct instruments in a fully professional performance of, say, the *St. John Passion*, the bass Arioso 'Betrachte, meine Seele', which is accompanied by two Viole d'Amore and Lute. It is therefore significant that when writing of this piece Dolmetsch needed to explain: 'As some of the lower notes do not exist on our instruments, we use a second lute specially tuned to fill the gaps. The Continuo will be played on my Schnetzler Organ alone. It has been recognised that the harpsichord and the Lute do not blend well together. In the Tenor Aria, of which the above is an elaborate introduction, two Viole d'Amore have important parts, but no mention is made of the Lute; and yet, obviously, the lute must have continued to play the accompaniment of this song, although no obligato part is written for it.' And: 'The Lute has made great progress lately. Not long ago, one Lute was all that we had. Now we are having some pieces performed as they were intended, by a Consort of 4 Lutes.[19] As each Lute can, and does play in full harmony, the harmonic richness of the ensemble may well be imagined. It is strange that such beautiful instruments, which nothing else can replace, should have disappeared; but the Art of Music, even more than the other arts, seems to suffer from a desire for novelty at any cost.'

After some discourse on neglected composers like Christopher Tye, about whom Dolmetsch appears to know a great deal, and some detailed description of what his little Schnetzler organ can achieve when properly coaxed, he goes on to an important discovery in the study of 15th-century dancing. Dolmetsch has seen a facsimile edition of a MS in the Bibliotheca Magliabecchiana in Florence. The manuscript is 72 pages long and contains, among other interesting matter, the complete description of the steps of a 'Bassa Danza' called *Venus* and composed by Lorenzo di Piero di Cosimo de Medici, known as Lorenzo il Magnifico, lover and protector of the arts. Dolmetsch claims that he can identify it with the 3-part song *Venus tu m'a pris* which is in the *Odhecaton* published in Venice in 1501, and the first music book ever printed. The dance, he promised, would be performed at the first dance evening, 27 July.

In a further paragraph on another manuscript from which Dolmetsch had made a copy, this time, 'Le Manuscript des Basses Danses de la cour de Bourgogne'[20] from the Bibliothèque Royale de Bruxelles, he proves the advantage of the practical approach. He tells us that many musicologists from Dr. Burney to Ernest Closson of Brussels (who, in 1912 published an extensive monograph on this book) had tried to understand it and failed. Such a problem, claims Dolmetsch, could be solved only by the combined efforts of a dancer who understands the steps and a musician for whom the music of that period has no secrets. He writes:

Under the notes of Music, the 'Tablature' of the Dance records the various steps in a system of notation which resembles closely that of Thoinot Arbeau in l'Orchésographie, 150 years later.

The symbols of the steps are apparently distributed so precisely under the notes of music, that at first sight one would think that they correspond. Moreover, the text says that each step occupies '*une note de Basse Danse*'. Yet these apparently positive premises lead to an absurd conclusion. Marguerite d'Autriche [to whom it belonged in 1523] would have been intensely surprised if you had told her that the airs as noted would have to suffice for a whole Dance; for, in order to accomplish this, each note of the air would have to be stretched *four times* longer than common sense and the ear dictates. No tune could be recognisable, or even exist under such conditions.

Dolmetsch solved this problem by the most obvious means: he played the music on the harpsichord and Mabel danced the steps. Admittedly, Dolmetsch was already so well acquainted with the music of the period that the music itself presented no difficulties. Finding that the steps corresponded to the tablature of those in the *Orchesographie*, Mabel in turn was able to realise the dance directly from the open book. When Dolmetsch played the melody as he was 'used to treat music of that period', his tune fitted her steps. But he found that he had to play the tune four times through to fit the dance. As he explains:

And this follows exactly the original directions, which we find in the treatise on dancing by Arena (c.1525). He, Thoinot Arbeau and others explain that 'une note de Basse Danse' or 'quarternion' takes four beats, i.e. one bar of modern common time.

Dolmetsch does not neglect to acknowledge that, but for Ernest Closson's facsimile reproduction of the book, his work would have been impossible. Contrary to the statements made by later students that Dolmetsch made little of other people's discoveries or assistance, the author has found this to be unfounded. He had many dark sides to his nature and he could be very unfair: but he never lacked gratitude.

The 11th Festival was highly successful and achieved a greater number of visitors than ever before, especially from abroad. Most of the reviewers had by now become accustomed to the unpredictability of the concerts and almost welcomed the spirit of adventure that was part of the game. One writer described it as being 'like a journey through Aladdin's cave',[21] which, he goes on to say, is what all music ought to be, 'but is usually too terribly efficient to succeed in being'. He tells us that this music was by no means efficient: 'Mrs. Dolmetsch broke a string of her harp, and when she essayed the six-stringed viol somebody gave her husband the wrong music, and he still got a good many notes right. Never mind! We had it again, right. One laughs but one would not have it otherwise!'

Behind this façade, which everyone enjoyed, including Dolmetsch, there was a lifetime of research: the planning of the programmes could not have been undertaken by anyone else at this time. He knew this perfectly well and cannot be blamed for sometimes playing up to it. At this festival Dolmetsch gave them the dances he had mentioned in his Preliminary Discourse[22] and the music ranged from the 8th-century Bardic MS to Beethoven, the latter played on a piano built in 1799. However, both the Welsh MS and a Beethoven sonata for violin and piano had been heard the previous year. Dolmetsch was expected to produce something entirely new and he had no intention of disappointing his audiences. This year it was music for lute: lute solos, lute for the accompaniment of songs and music for two and four lutes. Diana Poulton and Suzanne Bloch, 'two pupils of whom he [Dolmetsch] may be justly proud[23] . . . The many bravura passages in the works for two lutes[24] gave these two a chance to display real virtuosity, the more attractive for its obvious good companionship. The pieces for 4 lutes had almost certainly never been played in public since the days of the "Golden Age".' It caused the same critic to write:

> The depth and feeling of this music made one regret the feeble romantic associations that a dead school of poetry has foisted on the word 'lute'. It is earnestly to be hoped that Mr. Dolmetsch will find others to train on the right road—which is emphatically not the guitar road.[25]

Suzanne Bloch, the young pupil previously mentioned, was the daughter of the composer Ernest Bloch, and already a trained musician. She had been struggling to learn the lute for some time and during the summer of the previous year had come to Haslemere to take some lessons from Dolmetsch, whom, she had been told, was the only person who knew anything about the instrument. She wrote to him on 25 May 1934 from her home in New York; the letter is a typical example of how Dolmetsch could inspire the young and often the old:

> Dear master,
>   . . . Of course I shall play in your concerts. I shall do everything, dance, sing, play the harp, the lute! And I shall smile . . .
>   The world is in chaos: uncivilized at the present time. People need music and instruments like yours which bring peace and courtesy . . .
>   I will come to you as a humble disciple to work hard and try to become a real lute player, not a drawing-room amateur. . . . Your example is a very great inspiration to me and I hope to become worthy of you.
>   Your devoted,
>   Suzanne

She recalled their meeting with amusement. When she arrived she was greeted by Carl and then Mabel: finally Dolmetsch was brought in but refused to talk to her. Mrs. Dolmetsch then tactfully explained that this was because his English was not good, but it was more likely to have been because she was in the first instance Ernest Bloch's daughter and in the second a professional musician. Suzanne seized her opportunity and burst into French: the temptation was too much for Dolmetsch and he beamed. 'That was it', said Miss Bloch 'We got along splendidly after that. . . .' When I showed him my lute, he said, 'You've got a cigar-box there!' She then understood why she had met with such difficulty and straightaway ordered a lute for the following year, when she would be able to afford it. Then she broached the subject of her previous training but he was not interested. 'Trained musician!' he would say, 'C'est un crétin!' The greatest excitement was being taken into his workshop. Everything was there to hand, tools, old rags, pieces of sharkskin, manuscripts, pieces of bread on the window for the birds and a sofa when he felt in need of a rest. It was on that first day that Suzanne Bloch was instructed into the way of handling precious documents: 'I wanted to look at a book of manuscript lute tablature and he said, "Let me see your hands . . . and no *ink* . . . only pencil!" Then he made me wash my hands before he would allow me to touch it. It is something I have never forgotten.'

Nonetheless the lessons proceeded well and Suzanne Bloch was invited to play at the festival the following year. Her arrival that next summer was quite different. 'He invited me to lunch and very proudly showed me his garden with all the herbs growing . . . I always think of AD when I go into my own garden in Vermont, where I also grow herbs.' Of Dolmetsch's playing she says: 'Sometimes there were wrong notes, but when there was that moment of truth the beauty of his playing was in excess of anything I have ever known . . . I have known many people much later who had all the perfection of technique but they never achieved that sound. . . . And it was just the same with the clavichord.'

Miss Bloch tells a delightful story of how they overcame some of the difficulties of stringing the lutes when rehearsing for the Vallet four-lute pieces. It seems that they used gut strings purchased from a well-known dealer but these kept on breaking; every time this happens it is four-times for each unison set, which makes four times nineteen for the whole lute. In the end they used surgical gut, which was marginally better, but the problem was by no means solved. Then Suzanne Bloch purchased some silk strings from a violin dealer and used them without mentioning a word to Dolmetsch. He was against silk strings. One day he noticed that everyone else's strings were breaking except hers. Then she told him she was a 'free soul' and had decided to have silk strings. Dolmetsch made no comment but sat up the whole night inventing a machine to make his own silk strings. 'You see he wasn't going to be beaten. That was what was so marvellous about the man.'

Suzanne Bloch also admits that she soon changed her ideas about becoming a disciple as expressed in her first letter. She found that she achieved much better results when she stood up to him and argued. 'He was wise enough and *French* enough to know that I was on his side and in a way he enjoyed the badinage. . . . I think my attitude was preferable to those who worshipped him so much they almost grovelled at his feet.'

A final story that tells a great deal about the way in which the Dolmetsches showed their gratitude for services rendered. For many years Suzanne Bloch became a kind of unofficial shipper of recorders when the instrument was becoming better known: Carl Dolmetsch would send them to her home in Greenwich Village and she would despatch them to the individual addresses. The cheques would go direct to Haslemere and they would refund the postage. When she next visited England she ordered a set of virginals from Dolmetsch which she knew would cost about $250. She asked Mrs. Dolmetsch how much she owed, expecting that they would give her some small deduction for the work she had put in on the recorder mailing. Firstly Mabel Dolmetsch said she would like to make her a present of the costume she had worn in the masque at the festival; then she said that Suzanne owed them 75 dollars for the virginals and she would not take a penny more. The Dolmetsches have sometimes been criticised for being difficult over money, but this was certainly proof against it and, as Miss Bloch says, 'They needed that money! They *always* needed the money!'

The little set of virginals is still in excellent shape today. 'I wouldn't part with that instrument for anything! It has gone everywhere with me . . . on planes and trains, and it has the best sound of any instrument I have ever played.' Suzanne Bloch sums up the essence of Dolmetsch with telling accuracy: 'You never knew what would happen at concerts. I can remember moments that were so beautiful that I could never forget them. The musicologists only remember the bad ones!'

Musicological opinion had never made much impression on Dolmetsch: he was in every sense a practical man. He always preferred to be getting on with doing something rather than spend precious time on argument or speculation. In this he was not necessarily right and had to pay for his mistakes. But, nevertheless, his advice was now being sought in the most promising quarters.

The issue of the gramophone recordings, 'The Columbia History of Music Through Eye and Ear', had certainly opened the door for Dolmetsch at Oxford University Press, who had published the textbooks accompanying the series. In the spring of 1935, Hubert Foss, then musical editor of OUP, approached Dolmetsch for his opinion of a scheme to publish English instrumental music before 1700. In a long letter he presents his plans for a 'properly organised and authoritative edition' of the texts of this music. He admits that, until now, scholars have paid too much attention to the sacred and secular *vocal* music of the period, thus accounting for the existing gap in the instrumental music. He acknowledges that there is evidence of isolated and varied activities being carried out but he envisages a major edition on well-considered lines, properly co-ordinated lest editions of doubtful origin begin to appear sporadically and so prejudice both the music itself and the prospects of an authentic edition.

He suggests that a series of volumes be printed under central direction, representing a corpus of all that is of permanent value in English music between 1500 and 1700. He mentions the uncompleted Purcell Society editions, and a new edition of the Fitzwilliam Virginal Book, both of which could be included. Violin music, too, by Purcell and earlier composers, Gibbs, Locke, Simpson and Jenkins, etc., could be issued in a cheap form to make it accessible for students. He suggests that the viol music could be issued in score, since there are not enough viol parties to justify a playing edition.

Foss asks for Dolmetsch's general views on the project and if he would allow him to use his name as a supporter of the scheme. He suggests the formation of a preliminary committee to consider the practical points of the problems in detail. He welcomes Dolmetsch's 'frank comments'.

Dolmetsch's reply on 6 April is indeed frank:

> Jesses
> Haslemere,
> Surrey
>
> Your letter of the 5th is interesting. It is gratifying to see that my discovering of the English Instrumental music 1500–1700, and 50 years of hard work on my part have not been entirely wasted. My ideas are at last being not only recognized but even worked upon by a number of musicians more or less capable of doing so. But the immensity of your scheme is simply *appalling*. The works of Bach, Handel, etc., are nothing in comparison. Mayer (?) gives a list of ab. 1000 Fantazies to which I could add many more—but this does not include the Pavans, Galliards, Suites, pieces with Lute, recorder, virginals, Organ, nor the violin music—it would fill *hundreds of volumes*—Moreover, it cannot be classified properly—Some of the music urgently wanted now might be coming in 50 years. I suggested to you a few years ago that you should begin the publication of the Repertory of the Haslemere Festival. This was practical, bringing out pieces that *are in demand*. It could have led to anything. You declined! Now an American publisher offers me the very same thing. The sales in America are ten times larger than here. Yet for sentimental reasons I would prefer to see this English Music issued here than abroad—As to the use of *my name* as a *supporter* of the scheme you know very well that I could not be a *figurehead* in such a scheme. I must be *responsible* for all that is done or keep out of it.

I have an invaluable assistant in my son Rudolph, who has a life long experience of this music and is an incomparable musician.

None of the 'others' would be any good to me.[26] If my letter does not discourage you right off, we ought to discuss the matter personally.

The outcome of this correspondence is unknown. There is no existing evidence that an American publisher had approached Dolmetsch, although it must have been true. He was not afraid of speaking his mind and would never have made the statement simply to impress. It is more than likely to have been through Percy Grainger with his own publishers in New York. There is no further exchange of letters between Foss and Dolmetsch so that the scheme was obviously never taken into consideration. But it is an interesting example of how far ahead of his time Dolmetsch was in comparison to his contemporaries, and furthermore how he was regarded by the music publishers.

NOTES

1. Kirkpatrick, Ralph (b. Leominster, Mass. USA, 1911). Celebrated harpsichordist, clavichordist, lecturer and author. Published edition of Bach's 'Goldberg' variations and biography of Domenico Scarlatti: 60 Sonatas, Domenico Scarlatti, 2 vols: edited Ralph Kirkpatrick; G. Schirmer inc. New York, 1963.

2. Ralph Kirkpatrick has made several recordings on this instrument: they include the two- and three-part Inventions, the Little Preludes, two suites, and Book 1 of the *Wohltemperierte Klavier*.

3. No 60 dated 1909 (with 16ft) Dolmetsch took this instrument with him to Europe: it was acquired by Ralph Kirkpatrick in 1948 and used in his 1952 recordings of the harpsichord portions of Bach's Clavier Übung.

4. This applies to Dolmetsch keyboard instruments. The influence of lecturing and performing has been perpetuated by Carl Dolmetsch through his annual tours of the USA.

5. Dolmetsch, Arnold, *The Interpretation of the Music of the XVII and XVIII Centuries*, Novello, London, 1915.

6. ibid., p. 20.

7. Grainger, Percy, 'Musical Confucius', *Musical Quarterly* (USA), April 1933, Vol. 19 XIX 2, pp. 187–98.

8. Celtic harp or clarsach with 27 brass strings. The modern instrument is metal-strung.

9. *The Consort* (Haslemere), June 1934, pp. 1–20.

10. Hughes, (Dom) Anselm, (b. 1889) English musicologist, musical editor, author and composer. Hon. secretary and treasurer of *The Plainsong & Mediaeval Music Society*, 1926–35.

11. Letter from Dom Anselm Hughes to Dolmetsch, 27 January 1934.

12. *The Consort* (Haslemere), June 1934, pp. 1–5.

13. The *Penllyn* or 'Welsh' MS, British Museum (Add. MS. 14905).

14. The crwth is a bowed lyre from the 13th century which survived in Wales in the 19th century. It has four bowed strings and two plucked drone strings tuned in octave pairs GG, CC, DD. A unique feature of the crwth is its bridge, which has one short foot resting on the soundboard and a longer one passing through one of the soundholes which rests on the back of the instrument to act as a soundpost. When the crwth was first heard at the Haslemere Festival in 1934, Lord Ponsonby of Shulbrede (1871–1946) was said to have remarked: 'The crwth is stranger than fiction!'

15. Founded June 1936 (London) and Hafan, Ruthin, Wales.

16. These recordings are at Jesses, Haslemere.

17. The Brahms and Chrysander edition of Couperin is *bad*! You will start with surprise but wait, I also thought it was a good one—the notes are correct and the signs for ornaments, too, even though they are corrupt in form. Recently, I had to teach some pieces by Couperin to a pupil who played from that edition. We encountered difficulties! Those idiots of editors have confused ⌐⎯⎤ with ⌒ abolishing the former and reducing all to the latter. It makes a fundamental difference in many cases! As I have the original edition, I did not use the other and had not noticed the fault.

18. Your quite legitimate curiosity will be satisfied. I even have an idea that you could have satisfied it yourself for you lack neither logic nor perspicacity. I must, however, reproach you severely for having supposed that Couperin, so methodical, so careful, so precise, in short, so French, could have used 2 *completely different* signs side by side to produce only one effect. In order to grasp the principle, one must refer to the *Original Edition*. You will see that the arc ⌒ always indicates the lengthening of the *same note*. Beneath or above the arc, there can be detached notes.

   The phrase mark, which corresponds most often with the slur is the straight line, or almost straight ⌐⎯⎤ ⌐⎯⎤ ⌐⎯⎯⎯⎤ . This same straight line more or less does away with hooks when they have no use! That is to say when the notes are disposed in such a way that one can link them *directly* by a straight line. Even then one often sees a trace of hook at the extremity of these lines. It is clear that at bar 4 of the top line, one could not put straight lines (dashes) between the notes but at the 3rd line, one can and one does! And there is the reason for your girl being silent [dumb].

19. Two pieces for four lutes by Nicholas Vallet 1619:
    i. 'Gaillarde'   ii. 'Un jour de la semaine'
    Treble   Arnold Dolmetsch
    Alto   Suzanne Bloch
    Tenor   Diana Poulton
    Bass   Tom Poulton
    Friday, 2 August 1935

20. 'Bassa Danza in Tre', *Venus*. The dance composed by Lorenzo de Medici *c*. 1470, music by De Orto. Performed at the sixth concert, Saturday 27 July 1935.

21. *Hindhead and Haslemere Herald*, 3 August 1935.

22. Dolmetsch, Arnold, *Preliminary Discourse*, 1 June 1935, Jesses.
23. *The Monthly Musical Record*, September 1935, p. 158.
24. Two pieces for two lutes, Jane Pickering's Lute Book
    i. The Quadrant Pavan
    ii. The Quadrant Galliard
    Performed at the 10th concert, Thursday 1 August 1935.
25. *The Monthly Musical Record*, September 1935, p. 158.
26. This could mean the co-operation of the gramophone companies, or the 'isolated and varied activities' of the 'others'. It is not quite clear.

CHAPTER XXI

The Final Recognition

IT was Marco Pallis who brought the Sinhalese musicians Nelun and Surya Sena[1] to Haslemere. He had attended one of their London concerts where they presented programmes of Asian folk song and dance, playing their native instruments, all of which were originally intended for intimate music in the drawing room. When asked to perform in large halls they experienced some difficulty in being heard: what they needed were instruments which were oriental in timbre but with greater carrying power. Their first encounter is described by Devar Sena as 'a happy meeting of pristine music of East and West' and 'seldom have we had such instant rapport with any family . . . from the moment we set foot in Jesses'.

To celebrate the occasion, Marco Pallis presented Sena with a tenor rebec made by Dolmetsch. Delighted though he was to receive it, he admitted that it solved only half their problem. For some time he had been carrying with him a postcard reproduction of a Mughal painting depicting the hunter, Amir Khusra, on horseback aiming at deer with his bow and arrow. His consort, seated beside him, was playing a triangular-shaped harp which rested on her lap. Sena showed the picture to Dolmetsch, asking him if he could make one like it for his wife. After looking at it intently for a moment, Dolmetsch exploded: 'Mais voyez vous, c'est très difficile à construire une harpe comme ça!' But he pocketed the card with a grunt. He would think it over. A month later, Sena received a note, 'J'ai commencé à construire l'harpe'.

This is a typical example of the way Dolmetsch went about his work. He had spent weeks looking up pictures of Burmese and Persian harps and made a number of tests to find out which kind of wood could stand the extra strain imposed upon the instrument by the absence of a front pillar. Also, to preserve the oriental timbre, it would have to be strung with wire instead of gut. When it was finished the Senas were delighted. Indeed, it was a beautiful instrument,[2] with a graceful curving neck attached to a boat-shaped hollow resonating body. Dolmetsch had used pine for the deck, sycamore for the body and ash for the neck. Mabel Dolmetsch had carried out the decoration in white and gold paint, bordered by a leaf design in the peacock colours of green and blue. It had 19 strings with a range of over two octaves, the lower ones being like the lower strings of a guitar wrapped in copper wire whilst the higher ones were made of plain steel. Inside the body, Dolmetsch had inscribed 'L'orient inspire l'occident! Cette harpe à été faite pour Nelun Devi par Arnold Dolmetsch'.

In the late autumn of 1935 Dolmetsch's health began to decline steadily His liver had always bothered him and this condition was not helped by the considerable amount of wine he was in the habit of taking. He also had bouts of chest trouble, indigestion and sundry other irritations which were aggravated by his stubborn insistence upon working to the utmost every day. Fortunately when things became too much for him there was usually a friend willing to pay for some form of recuperation, so in December Dolmetsch found himself once more in Hyères, where he stayed again with Lucy Ellis and her family. Perhaps he became too demanding even for his admirers, for after a few days he moved to an hotel but was still visited daily by the faithful Lucy. His letters to Mabel, who had stayed to look after things at home, are quite up to his usual standard, with daily bulletins of his health, the weather and the delectable food he appeared to be enjoying. But perhaps the most remarkable aspect of all is that, despite the hypochondria, it is impossible to realise that the letters are written by a man approaching his 79th year. They are forward-looking, almost restless to be getting on with something. His descriptions of the forest, the beauties of the countryside and the changing moods of the sea are all most evocative, and clearly those of a man whose enthusiasm and optimism will survive as long as he has breath. As soon as he feels rested sufficiently to work, we find him repairing Lucy's spinet and then, after a visit to the museum where he has checked on a manuscript, he writes: 'Je mets au clair des pièces de Luth de Nic[olas] Val[e]et—Merveilleuses!'[3]

Dolmetsch returned to England in January considerably refreshed, but by the end of March he was again taking a compulsory change of air— this time nearer home at Niton, on the Isle of Wight, where he was staying at a small inexpensive hotel. He writes to Mabel that the food is 'British' and will therefore please her. But for himself:

> J'ai souffert ces derniers jours de soupes et ragoûts *brun foncé* et de 'greens' couleur aniline. Aujourd 'hui, j'ai réclamé—une soupe légère, une petite côtelette d'agneau et des choux nature![4]

Throughout the weeks that followed his return, Dolmetsch's diaries show him to be as active as ever. He is very excited about a new Handel cantata he has discovered, *Tra le Fiamme*, for soprano, 2 recorders, viola da gamba, obbligato strings and harpsichord. There is no indication as to where he found the manuscript, but it received its first performance at the festival that summer.[5]

Meanwhile, unbeknown to Dolmetsch, Robert Donington (then secretary to the Foundation) had written to a number of well-known public figures asking them to support an application for a Civil List pension for their *paterfamilias*. His letter outlines the appalling state of affairs that had persisted, despite the partial recognition Dolmetsch had achieved at this time:

> Pittance Farm,
> Smithwood Common
> Cranleigh,
> Surrey.
> July 1936
>
> I am sorry to say that Mr. Arnold Dolmetsch is in great need of help. His health has become very precarious of late and it is imperative that he should be relieved now of the need to support himself by strenuous concert-giving. His life has been a very disinterested one, and his financial position has recently been terribly difficult and obscure.

Shaw had drafted the letter of support to be sent to the Prime Minister, and Donington carefully points this out to the potential signatories.

Separate letters were sent to the Prime Minister, Stanley Baldwin, from Ramsay MacDonald, Donald Tovey and R. C. Trevelyan; the list of supporters contained 31 names, amongst whom were G. Bernard Shaw, John Masefield, W. B. Yeats, T. S. Eliot, Laurence Housman, Walter de la Mare, Siegfried Sassoon, Bertrand Russell, The Earl of Lytton, Lord Berners, David Lloyd George, Sybil Thorndike, Walford Davies, Vaughan Williams, Henry J. Wood, Thomas Beecham, Adrian Boult, Henry Hadow, Arthur Somervell, Percy Scholes, Granville Barker and Granville Bantock. But if the musical world in general remained unconvinced of Dolmetsch's unique contribution to the researches of his time, the artistic following in particular responded to Donington's request with extraordinary enthusiasm. The appeal was successful and in March 1937, Dolmetsch was awarded a pension of £110 per annum.

Impoverished he might have been, but in a letter marked 'Important', written on 20 January 1937 to his pupil Jean Buchanan[6] in New York, we have one of those charming insights into his personal sense of values:

> My *crop of sweet corn* failed last year—My gardener had got crazy—He froze the young plants and burned them later! So, I have no seeds of my own breed. I cannot get the right kind here; but I think you might get a good seedsman in New York to send me half a pint, or a pint of 'Early Golden Bantam', which is a good kind, or something similar—only the early kinds have a chance of ripening here.

He then goes into much detail as to the state of his health but his closing lines show that the old spirit is still very much alive: 'However, I can work, which is life to me.'

Jean Buchanan writes soon to say that she has sent him a pound package of the seeds as a gift as she cannot imagine the Dolmetsch garden without sweet corn. On 10 March Dolmetsch acknowledges receipt of the seeds and is pleased that they are just the kind he wanted. But he cannot sow them yet as the weather has been particularly bad, with blizzards and violent storms. There was also another reason:

> My health has been very bad. For days could not do any work. Keep in bed, which I hate—I have felt very much depressed, being incapable of getting over my sufferings. I was very weak. Yet a few days ago, I felt better! Now I am almost well . . . I have been able to work. I have finished the transcription of the *Bardic Music* a most difficult work, but of immense value.

He tells her that the records of the Bardic music will be issued shortly and concludes the letter with descriptions of the wedding of his son Carl to Mary Ferguson. Now all four of his children are married.

Festival plans went forward as usual but they relied less on Dolmetsch himself and more on Mabel and the younger members of the family. Every one of Mabel's letters to her friends betrays her growing anxiety about Dolmetsch's health, but if he rallies well enough to play at a concert she clings to the hope that the improvement will continue. What Mabel never told her friends was that he was a very difficult patient. Even at the best of times he was obstinate and demanding but as he grew older, and weakened by illness, these tendencies increased. One of his pupils once wrote: 'There was no room for divided opinion in his proximity.'[7] Certainly his great gifts needed much room for expansion and it was Mabel Dolmetsch who made this possible. Calm, uncritical and tolerant in the extreme, Mabel sought to smooth the way for her 'genius'. The Cosima-Wagner relationship, as suggested by Robert Donington (see p. 221), is a very fair analogy. In the days before he became ill she saw that Arnold had his daily glass of wine: not much, but always choice. She procured his favourite foods, even when the purse was empty and the cupboards bare, and stood resolutely between her husband and his critics, whether they were personages of import or pupils with trivial problems: not in grim defiance but with tacit obdurance and an exterior show of calm and sweetness that none could resist. If Dolmetsch thought something was right, it was right. If he held the reverse opinion, the matter was dismissed without question. She bowed to his superior knowledge in all but the dancing and here she had proved herself an undisputed authority. Arnold always gave her full credit for her scholarship in this subject. But even the dancing was originally undertaken in order to help him in his work. He had transcribed the music of many dances but knew nothing about choreography. Mabel, working slowly and assiduously in addition to her household duties and bringing up a family, had mastered the choreographic tablature by which the French dancing masters of the Renaissance and the Baroque periods recorded their steps and figures, and similarly with the more elusive Italian School. She learnt the steps, she taught her own children and later, when dancing was introduced into the festival, the informal family lessons had led to a regular class. 'Her teaching was by direct method: she showed the class by action and example with just enough verbal instruction to minimise confusion . . . She was herself so excellent a dancer that to imitate her came naturally enough. Like her husband, she had the unmistakable quality of style.'[8]

The festival took place in July with dancing and all the regular items, but Dolmetsch's appearances were strictly limited according to the state of his health. The opening night was evidently a good one in this respect. J. A. Westrup, from the *Daily Telegraph*, wrote:

> July 20 1937
>
> Arnold Dolmetsch, bearing his advanced years with a zealot's unconcern, opened his festival of old chamber music this evening with a characteristic speech, in which he praised the glories of the past and his own undisputed services in revealing them and gaily accused previous explorers of criminal stupidity and ignorance.

Of a fantasy and two almains for six viols and harpsichord by Martin Pierson, Westrup commented:

> Music so tranquil and clear-flowing is a refreshment in a noise-ridden world, and certainly more than an historical document. The players kept step and tune with true family accord and careful musicianship, and all was done without fuss or showmanship.
>
> Even more delightful was a brace of pieces for three recorders, led by Carl Dolmetsch, who excels on this instrument, as his brother does on the harpsichord. Here, smooth and crystalline, was the faithful echo of domestic music-making of three centuries and more ago.

At the second concert, Dolmetsch produced his newest reconstruction, a vihuela. On the printed programme we read that he will also play it; however, according to *The Times* of 24 July 1937, he produced an instrument 'which was as pleasing to the eye as it was enchanting to the ear. He confessed that he had not learned to play it adequately and handed it to a competent pupil [Diana Poulton]. But, if, as we understood, this instrument was the product of his own workshop, his hand has lost none of its cunning, nor its intuitive skill in fashioning acoustically fine musical instruments.'

Today, it is difficult to appreciate the necessity for J. A. Westrup to make the following comment in the *Daily Telegraph* on the Purcell and Bach concert:

26 July 1937

Haslemere performs a double service. It gives us unfamilar music and also offers familiar music in an unfamiliar, that is to say, authentic form. It was a valuable experience to hear the celebrated contralto air from the St. Matthew Passion, 'Erbarme Dich, mein Gott', with the background of a double continuo—organ and harpsichord—and the bright pizzicato of the fretted violone, a sound unknown in the modern orchestra.

The performance, though unpretentious, was sincere and truthful. Elizabeth Goble sang with taste and musicianship, and Arnold Dolmetsch's playing of the violin obbligato (with the old type of bow) was remarkable for a man in his 80th year. Another aria, from the same work 'Komm süsses Kreuz' contained an elaborate obbligato for viola da gamba, skilfully handled by Mrs. Dolmetsch.

Finally, the *Musical Times* of 1 August offered advice on the festival and its future:

Everyone who has to produce music of the Bach Handel period should at least be familiar with the violone, which gives an entirely different character to the instrumental bass. This instrument also has the advantage of being easier to play than the double-bass, by reason of its frets; and its clear bright tone is a most welcome change from the tubby sound of its modern supplanter.

It is well to be frank about the performances at Haslemere, since they have proved a stumbling block to many. There are certain obvious and essential virtues. The instruments are always in tune, and the performers keep time. What one misses is the energy and intensity that turn a casual reading into a living recreation. We know that the Dolmetsch family believe in what they play; but too often their playing seems to give the lie to their enthusiasm. A richer tone is wanted, a better attack, a more springing rhythm, and—in a word—the practical evidence of conviction.

The writer went on to chastise them further for their uncertainty over repeats, false starts and disagreement about the length of a pause, but his advice was meant to be constructive and was almost certainly justified. He maintained that, despite all this, Haslemere 'remains a unique review of old music performed on the instruments for which it was designed . . .' and he concludes:

Mr. Dolmetsch's insistence on the importance of the continuo in all music of the 17th and early 18th centuries is not the least of his services. The ignorant disregard of this principle shown by many modern conductors is distressing . . . The affirmation of principles of this kind, organ, harpsichord, viola da gamba and violin in the St. Matthew Passion gives Haslemere a peculiar and instructive value and justifies its continuance.

Dolmetsch had long been the subject of countless newspaper articles and the more sensational press invariably illustrated their piece depicting him as a 'character' sitting on his doorstep playing one of his instruments, woollen socks and knee-breeches well in evidence. But until now no one had attempted a serious biography: the nearest approach to this had been Robert Donington's *Works and Ideas of Arnold Dolmetsch*, published at Haslemere in 1932. So Jean Buchanan, his American pupil, herself a writer and university lecturer, decided to undertake the task herself.[9] Her first step was to confirm the need for such a work with some of the famous people with whom Dolmetsch had been associated during his lifetime. Her replies were encouraging. Sir Henry J. Wood thought the idea 'an admirable one':[10] Professor H. F. Davies of the University College of North Wales, wrote:[11]

> It is of the greatest importance that a reliable and detailed record of Mr. Dolmetsch's activities during his long and fruitful life, should be placed on record ... Many European countries are indebted to Mr. Dolmetsch for his researches, while we in Wales owe him a debt which we can never repay for his genius and untiring labours in solving the problem of the manuscript of ancient bardic music.

Sir Donald Tovey, then Dean of the Faculty of Music at Edinburgh University, thought that 'such a book is already needed while that unique craftsman is still alive as the doyen of luthiers, and it will become more and more necessary as time passes'.[12] Ernest Newman put the matter succinctly: 'I cordially support your plan for a book on Mr. Dolmetsch. He has done a great work for music, which is still insufficiently recognised. And the work doesn't end in itself, as a purely personal matter: it concerns the correction of many of the accepted notions about the older music.'[13] Not surprisingly the most evocative letter came from George Bernard Shaw:

28th August 1937

4, Whitehall Court,
London, S.W.1.

Dear Mrs. Buchanan,

Arnold Dolmetsch's work has been of the greatest importance both historical and practical in English music. I have been *au courant* with it from the beginning, when I was a professional critic of music; and you will find his name recurring in my reprinted criticisms pretty frequently. It was by the rarest of chances that the skill of a master craftsman in musical instrument making was combined with a fanatical devotion to XVI-XVII century music. How astonishingly Dolmetsch brought it to life after centuries of neglect and oblivion can be appreciated only by those who remember, as I do, how absurdly it was handled before—when it was handled at all.

No musical subject could be more worthy of endowment.

Faithfully,
G. Bernard Shaw

There is a P.S. in Shaw's handwriting:

'Today's papers announce that he has been given the Legion of Honour by the French Government for his services to music.[14]

Dolmetsch had indeed been nominated and accepted for the award of la Croix de Chevalier de la Légion d'Honneur by the country of his birth. The idea had come originally from his young friend and pupil Marie Thérèse de Lens, now living in Morocco. She had prevailed upon other friends and supporters to approach the government through various cultural societies in France and had finally met with success. Dolmetsch could not let the award be achieved without a jibe; to Dorothy Swainson he wrote:

Jesses,
Haslemere,
Surrey

30 Aôut 1937

J'ai reçu une très charmante lettre de l'Ambassadeur de France à Londres m'annonçant que le Président de la République m'avait décerné la Croix de Chevalier de la Légion d'Honneur en reconnaissance des services que j'ai rendus à la musique, en géneral, et l'Art Français en particulier. Il semble que cette dignité est fort appréciée en Angleterre. Il est vrai qu'elle est très rarement donnée à un étranger[15] à moins qu'il n'ait inventé quelque nouvelle machine pour mieux détruire les gens.[16]

*   *   *

Dolmetsch had now been making recorders for 18 years,[17] during which time the sale of this instrument had increased greatly. It was becoming popular in schools and several musicians were beginning to take it more seriously. Edgar Hunt (see p. 245) had been inspired in his twenties by Dolmetsch and his work and in 1932, had spent a holiday at Haslemere studying the recorder. He eventually specialised in playing and teaching on this instrument and had also written a textbook on it for students. In October 1937 the Society of Recorder Players was formed and Dolmetsch agreed to become its president, with Edgar Hunt and Carl Dolmetsch as joint hon. musical directors. The aims of the society were to form a centre where all who were interested in the recorder could meet periodically to exchange ideas and it was also hoped that information could be collected and redistributed to its members. Above all, the society was most keen to raise the general standards of playing; to bring this about they would encourage and assist the formation of groups of players in different districts. Today the Society of Recorder Players has over 1,000 members and Edgar Hunt is now head of the Department of Early Music at Trinity College,

London, where the recorder can be taken as a first study and is therefore eligible for a diploma—a far cry from the description of the recorder in a London newspaper announcing the foundation of the Society as, 'this old flageolet kind of instrument'.[18]

Now that the recorder was achieving a more secure position and the harpsichord that Dolmetsch had sold to the BBC was in regular use, it would seem that his work was at last being recognised. It is true that he was being regularly consulted by the experts, as his correspondence with Canon Galpin, Ansermet, a number of teachers and university lecturers proves, but to so many who should have known better he was still the inspired enthusiast who lacked the academic qualifications to substantiate his theories. He may not have had a university degree but he was a thoroughly trained musician and craftsman. There are also two sides to the previous assumption. For the most part, Dolmetsch's phenomenal intuitive powers served him well: sometimes they did just the reverse. It was then that Dolmetsch could not lower his guard and admit that he had made a mistake and it was these mistakes that his so-called 'enemies' would seize upon to attack him. In doing this they forget that his work had prevailed from a time when early music was in almost total neglect. Dolmetsch had battled so long with 'authorities' and he was now a sick man fighting to complete his work before his powers were decimated. When his 80th birthday celebrations took place in February 1938, he gathered all those friends from the past around him and in his speech there were small notes of bitterness which indicated that he could never quite forgive the injustices that had been done to him in the past.

The celebration took the form of a musical party held at the Hall of the Artworkers' Guild in Queen Square, Bloomsbury, on Saturday afternoon, 26 February, two days after Dolmetsch's actual birthday. The programme consisted of music composed or arranged by Dolmetsch over the period 1888–1936 and played by his family and friends. The earliest examples were two pieces for strings and harpsichord and the most recent, the song, *Hark, Hark, the Lark*, from *Cymbeline*, rediscovered and set with an accompaniment for recorder, viols and harpsichord in 1936. In between there was a fantasy for 3 recorders (1932) and a *Woodland Chorus* from *Sakuntalá*, the Hindu classic, first performed on 3 July 1899. There was a song for soprano accompanied by lute and viol and another for contralto and a fantasy for 5 viols on the theme of E.A.D.G. (Eugène Arnold Dolmetsch Guillouard, 1932). The final item was Dolmetsch's Easter hymn *Il est Ressuscité*, for tenor, piano, organ and violin obbligato (1890).

In the interval Dolmetsch had the chance to meet again the few surviving friends of his Bloomsbury days, besides many of his admirers who had known him only through the Haslemere festivals. Mrs. Mackail,

Burne-Jones' daughter, Robert Steele, Madame Marchesi, Violet Gordon Woodhouse and W. A. (Will) Boxall, his one-time 'black sheep' from Dulwich College in the 1880s, were all there to wish him well. There was much excitement when Dolmetsch cut his birthday cake with 80 candles burning brightly upon it; then suddenly a second cake arrived from Paris, sent especially by Dorothy Swainson, his faithful pupil who was too ill to leave France. Dolmetsch was touched to tears. Then came the presentation itself and the French Ambassador, M. Roger Cambon, made a most appreciative speech in recognition of Dolmetsch's services to the artistic life of France. As the minister bent to take the Croix de la Légion d'Honneur from its case, Dolmetsch was observed to be giving one of his characteristic shrugs accompanied by a grunt—interpreted by those who knew him well as being the equivalent of 'About time too!'

None the less, the old man was very proud when he had the cross pinned on his jacket and after the illuminated address had been presented to him, together with a purse collected by the Central School of Arts and Crafts and the Dolmetsch Foundation combined, Dolmetsch made a speech in reply. He professed himself as being at his wits' end to know what he could do to show his gratitude; therefore he had decided that he could not do better than go on with his work. Two accounts of the occasion, one by A. H. Fox-Strangways in the *Observer* (27 February 1938) and another by Ernest Newman's deputy in the *Sunday Times* of the same date, give some idea of his obvious gifts coupled with a totally unexpected and uncharacteristic modesty. The first, on his compositions:

> I have known him [Dolmetsch] for over fifty years, but his modesty is such that I had never heard of them. They are all straightforwardly musical, tuneful, and expert.

the second, on the same accomplishment:

> The music showed him possessed with the simple direct eloquence of the period in which he is steeped, and in entire sympathy with the constructional devices of those days.

The congratulatory letters and telegrams poured in from all over the world, and perhaps for the first time in his life the old man began to feel that his work was beginning to be understood. A particularly touching letter came from Günther Hellwig, now back in Germany working on his own account as Geigenbaumeister in Lübeck:

Burgtorhaus
Lübeck

25th Feb 1938

> ... Without you I would never have become the man I am now. If you could come to Lübeck and see my workshop and my instruments and the way I do my work,

I hope you would perceive that a good deal of your spirit is alive here—and I hope you would be pleased and not repent having taught me and had me as your pupil over in England for almost four years. . . . I wish that you will have a good many years to live yet, in good health, spiritual and physical strength and good mood. Many people may still learn from you and carry out your ideas and work in their lives . . . your thankful pupil,

Günther.

Although Dolmetsch knew that his 80th birthday and its accompanying award would attract certain attention from the press, it is unlikely that he expected such extensive coverage as it received. The national daily and weekly papers and most of the leading provincial publications gave long and appreciative accounts of the man and his work. His picturesque personality was a gift to the journalists and they made full use of it. The *Observer* thought that he looked 'like something out of the Old Testament, painted by Rembrandt. The dark eyes are capable of flashing patriarchial fire.' The same writer noticed that, despite his keen ear and having been resident in England for 60 years, Dolmetsch still spoke with a strong French accent. They knew also how to arouse his anger by the mere mention of the modern piano:

'The modern piano,' says the Sage, 'is the impurest, the beastliest, instrument the world has ever seen! There are some nice ones—my own Broadwood, fifty-seven years old, has a beautiful tone.'

After agreeing that no one had rendered such a service to English music as he had, Dolmetsch answered a question on official recognition:

Lately—yes! But when you English do a good thing you make a secret of it. Last year the King (to whom I had the honour of playing when he was still Duke of York) granted me a Civil Pension in recognition of my services to English music. This aroused only mild comment in the English Press. But when it became known last summer that the French Government had made me 'Chevalier de la Légion d'Honneur' for my services to French music, the English papers made a great song of it and trumpeted it in all directions.

In other parts of Europe there were calls of a very different kind. Austria had been annexed by Germany earlier in the same year; in the autumn the fateful agreement of Munich would leave only twelve months before Europe was plunged into war. Dolmetsch could know nothing of this except the general feeling of unrest, but having reached 80 years, and in poor health for most of the time, he became reconciled to having to delegate more and more responsibility to the younger members of his family.

At the 14th festival, which opened on 18 July, he made very few appearances on the concert platform. He accompanied one of his daughters in a

French song but for the most part merely came on to introduce this or that talented pupil. The festival that year gave much prominence to the English school of the 16th and 17th centuries, thus making a survey of Dolmetsch's life work in the reconstruction of instruments and the resuscitation of the music of the period. One of the more unusual works presented at the ninth concert on 27 July, was J. S. Bach's *Peasant Cantata* (*Mer hahn en neue Oberkeet*).[19] Few people at that concert would have heard the work performed before the Haslemere era, although Dolmetsch had presented it several times at his early concerts in Bloomsbury some 50 years earlier.

However, this rustic revelry was short-lived. Soon after the festival Dolmetsch was taken ill again. Within a few days he and his wife set off for Le Mans in France, where Dolmetsch was installed at a clinic where the doctor's methods were scientific and based on diet. He diagnosed Dolmetsch's condition as being a rare form of dropsy and prescribed an entirely salt-free diet. The regime was very drastic for a man of his years but both Mabel and the doctor were confident that it would help. By the beginning of September he had progressed sufficiently to be brought back to England but the return journey was a nightmare. The ambulance broke down on the way to Dieppe and when after hours of waiting at the road-side, they obtained another, it rushed them at great speed to the port, hooting and ringing like a fire-engine, catching their boat within minutes of its sailing. But Dolmetsch's resilience was such that within a week he was walking around the garden inspecting his plants and even spent short spells at the clavichord. By 12 September, Mabel writes to Dorothy Swainson that 'he is beginning to think of resuming his musical activities and explorations'. In the same letter she explains that Dolmetsch has to restrict himself to an almost vegetarian diet, and drinking only light wine, diluted, tea and Vittel water. She adds, optimistically, that she is confident he is resigned to this prospect.

As Dolmetsch progressed, the light wine became less and less diluted and the Vittel water was taken under protest. It is doubtful if he ever took the tea at all. Certainly the 'cure' had given him a temporary respite, for quite soon he was able to despatch to Schirmer of New York the first draft copy of his viol fantasies edited by himself. Dolmetsch was to receive $1,000 for this work, probably more money than he had seen for many a day. But there were difficulties—a fact that emerged very early in the new year, a year that would bring war to Europe and a halt to all Dolmetsch's practical musical activities.

NOTES

1. Devar Surya Sena (b. 1899–), baritone singer and barrister, educated in England: practised at Colombo Bar before making singing his profession. With his wife, Nelun Devi, he made a study of Asian folk song and dance and together they travelled extensively throughout Europe, India and Ceylon (see Grove's *Dictionary of Music* 5, pp. 696–7).

2. *The Consort*, June 1937 (illustration).

    The harp was not only beautiful but kept pitch and could be heard at the back of the largest hall. Today, 40 years after it was made, it is still unique. Despite being in constant use throughout the years it has not deteriorated and, remarkably, keeps in tune.

3. Letter to Mabel from Dolmetsch, 22 December 1935.

4. Letter to Mabel from Dolmetsch, 17 March 1936.

    I have suffered the last days with dark brown soups and stews and 'greens' the colour of 'aniline' [indigo]. Today I demanded—a light soup, a small cutlet of lamb and boiled cabbage!

5. Performed 27 July 1936. Original edition in Dolmetsch Library.

6. Jean Sinclair Buchanan, pianist, studied with Hans Seifert, E. A. MacDowell, Tobias Matthay, Leschestizky and others. Teacher of harmony, ear-training and history of music, Vassar College, New York, for five years. Later studied clavichord with Dolmetsch and gave lecture recitals on early music.

7. Marco Pallis in an article on Mabel Dolmetsch (1874–1963) in *The Consort*, Summer 1964, pp. 253–8.

8. Donington, Robert, 'The two roles of Mabel Dolmetsch', ibid., p. 262.

9. Her biography was never published.

10. 29 June 1937, Free Library of Philadelphia.

11. 30 June 1937, ibid.

12. 30 June 1937, ibid.

13. 6 July 1937, ibid.

14. 28 August 1937, ibid.

15. Dolmetsch had become a naturalised British subject on 17 September 1930.

16. I have received a very charming letter from the French Ambassador in London announcing that the President of the Republic of France has conferred on me the Cross of the Chevalier of Honour in recognition of services rendered to music in general and French Art in particular. It seems that this honour is greatly appreciated in England. It is true that it is rarely given to a foreigner, unless he has invented some new machine for better destruction of the people!

17. In 1926 Dolmetsch handed over the entire responsibility of research and production to his son, Carl.

18. *The Star*, 14 December 1937.

19. Performed at the Haslemere Festival, 1931.

CHAPTER XXII

The Last Battle

SCHIRMER'S entered into negotiations with Dolmetsch to publish the viol fantasies on Percy Grainger's recommendation, but a letter from Carl Engel, the president, expresses disappointment upon examining the submitted manuscript copies:

G. Schirmer Inc.,
3 East 43rd Street
New York

Jan 20th 1939

> For our practical purposes there remains a great deal to be done to these pieces before we can issue them. As you know, one of our aims, in issuing these pieces, is to supply material suitable for our schools. Not many school teachers of music are endowed with the knowledge and discrimination that would be required to present this old music without your edition containing a great deal more than is to be found now in your copies.

He then refers to a fantasy by John Jenkins and one by William Lawes, both manuscripts having been arranged from Dolmetsch's transcriptions by Percy Grainger. These copies have been 'carefully edited, with all the indications necessary to instruct the performers. Your copies lack tempo indications, lack bowings, lack phrasings; they should furthermore contain, as do Grainger's copies, markings to show which instrument should stand out in the ensemble at certain points of the piece.' He goes on to suggest that it would be more practical if it could be indicated which of the modern string family of instruments could be substituted if necessary. He continues:

> In some cases the writing of the piece in alla breve eight-quarter time adds to the difficulty of the reading, especially for younger and untrained players. Whether to halve the time values or halve the measures [bars] with a dotted bar line will have to depend on the tempo of the piece. But your copies contain not the faintest trace of tempo indications, they do not show whether the piece is a fast or slow one, nor whether there are to be any retards. In other words, what we have are the notes and not much more. We propose to have a competant musician, such as Mr. Adolfo Betti, prepare these copies for publication. But in order to avoid any

conflict with your views, I should be grateful to you if you would let me know, at least roughly, what is the speed at which you play the different pieces you have sent us.

Dolmetsch's reactions were always unpredictable. One might have anticipated a stormy outburst with insults piled upon the heads of Betti and Engel. On the contrary, Dolmetsch responded very diplomatically whilst still driving home his own criticism of the editor's intentions. In the beginning of his letter Carl Engel had excused himself for not writing sooner on account of his ill-health. Dolmetsch, replying on 12 February, thanks him for his 'interesting' letter and hopes that he is now fully recovered. Then, fox-like, he proceeds:

> With regard to the marking of the Fantasies, believing you to be in a hurry to receive the scores, I posted them as promptly as possible with the intention of marking on the rough proofs, which I expected to receive within a few weeks, those indications of tempi, bowing and phrasing which would enable others to render the works in a fashion similar to that heard at my concerts and festival. I had also intended to write, and to send to you with the corrected proofs, an explanatory preface on the interpretation and phrasing of viol music.

He then points out that if Engel arranges his viol scores for violins before he has sent Dolmetsch the rough proofs 'to correct and mark in the way both of us intend', he will not only destroy the music by incorrect interpretation but he will lose the entire value and individuality of the publication. He also stresses that with a score fully marked with expression marks, phrasing, etc . . . 'any intelligent musician should be able to give a good rendering'. It is important to remember that V or the forward bow of the viol is the accented stroke, and in order to adapt this authentic edition for the use of ordinary string players, it is a simple matter of stating at the top of each fantasy, 'read V as the accented stroke'. Dolmetsch then suggests that if, after all this has been done, that another arrangement for schoolchildren is indispensable there is no reason why they should not produce one, provided that his discovery and scoring of the works is acknowledged. 'My dear friend Grainger or Betti could do this perfectly well: such things have already been done for years.' He adds that he is quite in agreement with the idea of placing dotted bar-lines if it is any help, but he points out that in the original MSS there were no bar-lines at all; the 'music flowed unhampered'. And finally:

> It may interest you to know that in England, and even more so on the Continent, there is a growing public of viol players, and these are eagerly awaiting an edition of authenticity upon which they can rely.

Carl Engel was far from happy with Dolmetsch's reply and he sends a copy of it, together with his own original letter, to Grainger with the following comment:

> Dolmetsch's reply is in so far disappointing as he has failed to let me know anything about the speed at which he takes the various pieces. It is not practical to engrave the music and then have the tempo, expression marks, etc., added to the final proof. This should all be done in the MSS before it goes to the engraver.
>
> You will easily realize in what an embarrassing and rather hopeless position we are at present. I wish that I could discuss this whole situation with you . . . I don't see that much can be expected from Dolmetsch, and therefore we will have to put our heads together and try our best. I am greatly relying on your valued advice.

From later correspondence from both Grainger and Mabel Dolmetsch, we gather that they also considered photographing the original MSS but the idea was abandoned because most of these, having been copied down some 40 years earlier by Dolmetsch, were in too shabby a condition to be reproduced in this way. Mabel also pointed out that the MSS parts are not all in Dolmetsch's own hand: several other members of the family had copied them at various times. Grainger writes from Norway on 8 June 1939:

> Norway
>
> I have been thinking about the matter of Schirmer's reproducing the Dolmetsch MSS of the Fantasies in facsimile—by means of photography. I do not see that it makes any difference whether all the MSS are in Mr. Dolmetsch's hand or not. As far as I saw, all are written *with exquisite beauty and clarity*, thus reviving in the music-writing field that same old-time beauty of craftsmanship that Mr. Dolmetsch has injected into all his work. Is it not a wonderful proof of the practical vitality of the Dolmetsch tradition that several members of the same family can all produce these clear and exquisitely beautiful manuscripts?

Grainger hastens to point out that the affair is entirely between Schirmers and Dolmetsch and he has no wish to suggest anything that is unsympathetic to either party. He does, however, make several suggestions how this could be carried out and has written a letter to Schirmers giving them his views. The final outcome was that the pieces were returned to Dolmetsch, who made the necessary additions and the music was engraved and printed in one operation. The extra edition for adaptation to modern instruments was edited by Percy Grainger.

In March of that year, Dolmetsch received an honour that was long overdue. Durham University offered him an honorary degree of Doctor of Music, and he was delighted with the prospect of travelling to Newcastle in the summer to have it conferred upon him.[1] In Mabel's letters to her friends she is looking forward very much to the occasion, but she is also concerned about the state of her husband's health. In one letter he seems to be deteriorating and on a strict diet, whilst in another, only a few days later, he 'is beginning to agitate about musical matters, and resume the clavichord lessons of a pupil he likes very much.'[2] In a letter to Artemy Raevsky[3] she writes, 'A.D. continues to get stronger and to refuse to admit it'. And, truth to tell, although now very thin and frail, Dolmetsch survived extremely well. When the 15th festival came around, he managed to play the clavichord on the opening night and also made a brief appearance in the masque that Mabel had devised from *Le Roman de la Rose* for the last night. It attracted a large audience and an appreciative but objective account appeared in the *Observer*, 23 July 1939, written by A. H. Fox-Strangways.

He and Dolmetsch had first met at Dulwich College when they were both teaching there. Fox-Strangways had not always been kind in his reviews of the festival and there was a period when the two were distinctly hostile. Nonetheless, he knew perfectly well that Dolmetsch's contribution to the world of music was unique. In a private letter on 20 July he writes:

> 13, Prince's Gardens,
> West Acton, W.3.
>
> Well, you've done a stout piece of work in your time, and cheered up a lot of people and given them something to think about, who might otherwise have led hum-drum lives. And you've always put 'music first', and there are not too many public performers who have done that—and yet it's the only thing worth doing.
> Bless you,
> Yours very sincerely,
> A. H. Fox-Strangways

A hot-house plant could not have been given more care and attention than Dolmetsch throughout the last months of that year. Now on a strict diet of milk foods, fruit and vegetable soups, he was in bed most of the time, or sitting in his chair. He could not even walk around the room without assistance. The doctor in Le Mans had given him six months at the most and he had survived well over a year. Mabel's letters to friends at Christmas are full of optimism.

During the latter half of January and the first part of February, Dolmetsch went through a wonderful period of renewed vitality. He was even able to resume working on some manuscripts with Mabel, who acted as his night nurse for most of this time. She described how she would make little meals for him and take tea herself in the 'Sarey Gamp' fashion, whilst they talked of their life together and of their achievements. He managed to play the clavichord and walk without help and he even played the violin again. One day he surprised Mabel by talking about the next journey they would make to France.

It is certain that during this time he had illicit access to the wine bottle and in addition had defied all orders for rest; he even resumed some trapeze exercises[4] that he had been doing for some time until his recent illness. The exercises were too much for a sick man and as a result he burst a blood vessel internally and was ordered ten days' rest. On his 82nd birthday he seemed to have improved sufficiently to get up for a little but he then caught influenza and was back in bed the next morning. It was the last order that he obeyed. He rallied a little on the Tuesday but on the Wednesday evening 28 February the crisis developed and within an hour it was all over: 'The Grand Old Man of Music', as one newspaper heading described him, was dead. It was announced the next day from the BBC on the 6 o'clock news, then a signal honour paid to the few.

Following a lifetime of agnosticism, Arnold Dolmetsch had re-entered the Catholic faith, into which he had been born, only a few weeks before his death, and was buried in the cemetery at Shottermill, Haslemere, on Saturday 1 March (1940). This was a family affair with a few close friends, but on 17 March a memorial service was held at Portsmouth Catholic Cathedral and over a thousand people attended. Dolmetsch's own composition, *Il est Ressuscité*, an Easter hymn, was an appropriate choice for one of the musical items. The entire family took part to form the small orchestra, poignantly significant of the determination they shared that his work should not be neglected.

Many accounts appeared in the press, but they were stories rather than obituaries, the writers being reluctant to miss the opportunity to write about the passing of such a legendary figure. This fact had not escaped Ernest Newman. In the *Sunday Times*[5] he declared that he had seen only one obituary notice and the terms of that one seemed to indicate that, as far as the larger public of this country is concerned, Dolmetsch had lived in vain:

> If the obituary notice to which I am referring[6] is typical of others, the current British notion of him is that of an amiable old gentleman who made, and encouraged other people to make, queer sounds on queer instruments, and showed a regrettable preference for the music of the past over that of the present. Relatively few people, seemingly, are aware that Arnold Dolmetsch was a scholar of a rare type, who added considerably to our knowledge and understanding of the older music.

Ernest Newman's piece goes on to an objective and unemotional assessment of Dolmetsch's work. Today, many of Dolmetsch's principles have become commonplace, but it is extremely doubtful if the majority of early-music enthusiasts have the remotest idea of how much they owe to that 'amiable old gentleman who made, and encouraged other people to make, queer sounds on queer instruments'.

NOTES

1. The honour was awarded but never received personally by Dolmetsch as he never recovered sufficiently in health to make the journey.
2. Ruth Mott, now Lady (Neville) Mott.
3. Artemy Raevsky, a White Russian refugee with a fine deep bass voice. A pupil of Blanche Marchesi he took part in the festivals and sang solo on many occasions, especially in the music of Bach in the Passions.
4. Dolmetsch used a 'Dr. Roberto self-exerciser' which consisted of parallel bars suspended from the ceiling. They are still at Jesses in the room where he worked and slept.
5. *The Sunday Times*, 17 March 1940.
6. It is not clear as to which notice Newman refers: there were, in fact, obituaries in both *The Times* and the *Daily Telegraph* and a number of provincial papers. There were also several on the lines that Newman suggests in the pictorial dailies, with lurid headlines.

CHAPTER XXIII

Dolmetsch, The Scholar

THERE are countless letters from well-known musicians in Dolmetsch's files asking his advice upon tempi or interpretation of the early music. A detailed quotation from a letter from Ernest Ansermet[1] shows Dolmetsch's careful method of replying: it concerns the correct application and execution of double-dotting and *notes inégales* with particular reference to Bach's Suite no. 4 in D major for orchestra and the fugue from the 5th Prelude and Fugue in D major, from Book I of the '48'.[2]

The correspondence makes it clear that Dolmetsch advocates flexibility, and that one's own judgement should be used, in the application of double-dotting, *notes inégales* and the length of the appoggiaturas. The interesting point is that, despite the fact that so much work has been done by scholars on the subject, the arguments still persist today. In 1929 research on early music was extremely limited. Dolmetsch was practically the only person available for questions and similarly the only one who could attempt the answers with any confidence.

We must be grateful that Dolmetsch lived to record at least some of the Bach preludes and fugues, although it is regrettable that the opportunity came too late for him to complete the two books of the '48'. Had he been approached even ten years earlier by a recording company, he would probably have included the *Goldberg Variations* and The Italian Concerto. However, the recordings that he did manage to complete aroused considerable interest in the USA. In the *Musical Record*, July 1933, Ernest Brennecke Jr., wrote:

> After two or three hearings we are converted to Dolmetsch ... [he] adds ornaments, he flourishes arpeggios where Bach indicated none, and he even changes note-values, willfully (as it seems) changing eighths to sixteenths to thirty seconds.[3] His reading of the appoggiaturas is revolutionary ... and what seems at first in the highest degree capricious and irreverent turns out to be, on close acquaintance, quite in keeping with the spirit of the work. Again and again it brings into a moribund passage an astonishing flow of vigour and sap. The curious and sceptical may find abundant justification for it in Dolmetsch's book.

An interesting appendage to this is Ernest Newman's story of how, when he had written an article on Dolmetsch's recording of the Bach works (see pp. 253–7) and that this would serve to show us how a clavichordist of Bach's time would have played, he received an indignant letter from a pianist who protested against the 'liberties' Dolmetsch had taken with the music. Newman commented: 'The poor man was evidently unaware that Dolmetsch had chapter and verse for every departure from modern routine in these performances of his, and that it is the present-day method of playing the old music precisely as it is written that is to a great extent wrong.'[4]

Then there were the letters from F. T. Arnold; despite these being concerned with truffles fresh from the Pyrenees and how Dolmetsch could avoid 'Madeira stink' by decanting the wine and leaving the stopper out all night, the main part of the correspondence deals with questions for which Arnold required an answer, each query accompanied by an immaculate little piece of manuscript. No doubt Dolmetsch answered satisfactorily, for although Arnold was known to be a benevolent man, it seems unlikely that he would have kept Dolmetsch so well supplied with such a regular delivery of choice wines if his knowledge had been found wanting.

Percy Scholes was another who plied Dolmetsch with queries at every step of his Columbia[5] recordings. Dolmetsch's exacting replies were not always popular with Scholes. Percy Grainger, one of his most regular correspondents, put Dolmetsch's elusive qualities into a nutshell: 'You seem to me to have more artistic commonsense than any musician I have ever met.'[6] Grainger attended the festivals whenever he was in England, often bringing other musicians: Cyril Scott and Roger Quilter both came with Grainger. When Dolmetsch died, Grainger financed the publication of the *Four-Note Pavin*[7] as a memorial tribute: Dolmetsch had edited the piece and become closely identified with it over the years.

There were many other poets, writers, artists and musicians who recognised Dolmetsch's outstanding gifts, but there were also as many who criticised him or dismissed him as a crank. Why? His childhood and youth have been discussed in the early chapters of this book. We know that his irascible nature angered people but this alone would not have discouraged them had they respected his work. There are countless difficult men of genius in the musical world who would never have gained a hearing if a sweet temper was a prerequisite of musical respect. The main reason for Dolmetsch's lack of recognition was his inability to channel any one of his many talents into a main stream at the expense of all the others. Commercially, the former practice is generally more successsful, but it was not Dolmetsch's way: and it was this very trait that made him unique.

He was trained as a craftsman and as a musician, with a good working knowledge of science and mathematics. In the days of his youth he was an excellent violinist, and his craftsmanship was impeccable. It was perfectly natural that when he discovered a whole period of music that had been neglected for hundreds of years, he could not resist the temptation to try it out and make it work. This is the point in Dolmetsch's life when he was faced with the vital choice: should he become a full-time violinist or must he pursue the unknown and change the face of musical history? Once, when he was old and frail, he went for a walk in the country with a young pupil; they came to a choice of ways, the one flat and easy, the other steep and challenging. Dolmetsch chose the latter and nearly missed his footing several times. When he had conquered the climb he said: 'I have always chosen the most difficult path, but in the end it is the only one that matters.'

Sir George Grove had confirmed in Dolmetsch's youth that researches on early music would not be easy but that he would be rendering a great service to music. The rest of the story has been told in the pages of this book, and perhaps we can now appreciate that when he set out he had nothing but his books and his intuition upon which to base his interpretations. There were no 'experts' to consult who had themselves studied the performing styles of early music. The only books were those written contemporary with the music concerned. There were naturally plenty of musical historians who knew the facts, but of practical performance they had no idea at all.

The Victorian mania for collecting had fostered some of the finest musical instrument collections of all time: Cummings, Taphouse, Galpin, Dr. Watson and Donaldson in Great Britain, and De Witt, Fétis and Mahillon on the Continent. But apart from Galpin and the last two named these were 'museum-minded' men who gave lectures and sponsored exhibitions: if the instruments did not work when they took them out of the glass cases, they put them back and murmured 'How nice' or 'How quaint'. They continued to advise on them, left them mute, and continued to play Purcell on Steinway grand pianos.

What did Dolmetsch do? He decided that the only way to fulfil the requirements of the early music was to restore the instruments to playing order—an art in which he had been trained. When he wanted more than a handful of people to play he knew he must make modern reproductions. It was a logical decision made by a logical man. So far, so good. It is quite possible that any good instrumentalist with training at the bench could have copied out the music and then restored or reconstructed the instruments for which it was written. But Dolmetsch went further, and this was when he found himself being eyed with suspicion. It is one thing to be a crank putting on drawing-room soirées for the denizens of Bloomsbury or the nobility of Knightsbridge: but it is quite another if one gives concerts to the general public to which critics are invited, some of whom actually defend the cause of this archaic music.[8] Furthermore, when the concert-giver starts lecturing the professors on the performing styles of this music, and in no uncertain terms tells them that they have been doing it all wrong, if indeed they have done it at all, then we have heresy of the first order on our hands. And the musical Establishment treated Dolmetsch in the way that all heretics have been treated through the ages: they may not have burnt him at the stake but they made it as hot for him as they dared.

Having chosen his course, Dolmetsch studied every facet of presenting early music, from the collecting of manuscripts to the restoring and making of instruments. He consulted every available manual on performing styles and there is no doubt that he contributed more in this respect to our musical heritage than any other man in this century or the last. This vast undertaking meant that he was always overworked, therefore his performances were often under-rehearsed, especially those of the early festivals. The pundits sneered at the lack of professionalism but where else (at that time) could they have ten to fourteen concerts of early music played on the original instruments in authentic style? How much did this matter? All that mattered to Dolmetsch was that the musical value was of the highest order, so if there were false starts, then better to hear the piece again and trust it would be an improvement. There would certainly not be another opportunity to hear the work again unless Dolmetsch presented it.

Today we have early music virtuosi on every hand, but in their efforts to play every note correctly and in strict tempo, have they perhaps lost the spirit of the music? It is a debatable point. Dolmetsch sometimes played very *badly*, especially when he was old and his ageing fingers would not obey the still agile mind; but even then he could always capture this spirit. His uncanny intuition led him to an interpretation which appeared much nearer the composer's intentions and this feeling invariably reached his audience. Few who heard him would dispute this assertion.

Dolmetsch was one of the first music researchers to realise that an old score is not what it seems. He pioneered a branch of musicology that has now come into its own. In more modern times the late Thurston Dart, Robert Donington and many others have pursued the musicological aspect of early music and, aided by their indisputable scholarship, have edited and written extensively on the subject. But Robert Donington's comment (see p. 221) that he and others have not so much improved on Dolmetsch's basic work as extended it in a way that Dolmetsch would have done, had he lived, is still valid.

The modern way of committing musical ideas to paper by way of staff notation has long been proved an unsatisfactory one because none of the conventional symbols for duration, dynamics or tempi can convey anything but an approximate idea of what the composer had in his mind when he wrote the music. As Ernest Newman once said: 'If they [the written notes or "symbols"] do not say all they mean, at least they mean what they say'. And certainly the modern composer does not write one set of note-values expecting the performer to play something quite different. But we tend to forget that this happy state is a fairly recent development. As Couperin put it: 'We write our music differently from the way we play it.' And so there arises from this all the argument about dots and double-dots as quoted in the opening paragraphs of this chapter: they are still rife today as we hear in the varying interpretations of the first part of the overture to Handel's *Messiah* according to the whim of the conductor.

It was Dolmetsch's artistic ardour, combined with the self-discipline of the true scholar, that caused him to research so thoroughly into the musical literature of the 17th and 18th centuries until he had satisfied himself that he had found the nearest and clearest instructions for performance based on this contemporary evidence. He then wrote his book[9] and for the rest of his life put his principles into practice.

Newman, who felt very strongly on the subject, once wrote that 'scholars do not, as a rule, perform; while not one performer in a thousand has any pretensions to scholarship'.[10] Today this is no longer true: the percentage on each side has increased and we produce both scholarly performers and performing scholars. But how many of them have had to begin their studies of the early music with nothing but a formal musical training and flair?

NOTES

1. Ansermet, Ernest (1883–1969), Swiss conductor: founded the Orchestre de la Suisse Romande.
2. *The Consort*, July 1975.
3. American notation.
4. Newman, Ernest, *The Sunday Times*, 17 March 1940.
5. Scholes, Percy, *History of Music Through Eye and Ear*, London (see p. 249).
6. Letter from Percy Grainger to Dolmetsch, 3 September 1935.
7. *The Dolmetsch Collection of English Consorts*, edited Grainger, G. Schirmer inc., New York, 1944.
8. George Bernard Shaw.
9. Dolmetsch, Arnold, *The Interpretation of the Music of the XVII and XVIII Centuries*, Novello, London, 1915.
10. Newman, Ernest, *The Sunday Times*, 17 March 1940.

Postscript

MABEL DOLMETSCH survived her husband by 23 years and in that time maintained the traditions set down by him. She continued to play the gamba, violone and celtic harp in concerts and at the Haslemere Festival until 1961. She also presented her programmes of early dances each year until 1963, the year of her death. She wrote two books on dances[1] and one of her personal recollections of her husband.[2]

CECILE DOLMETSCH (b. 1904, Dorking, England) Dolmetsch's eldest daughter, continued to take part in the festivals at Haslemere, singing, dancing and playing several of the instruments introduced by her father. She has made a speciality of playing the much neglected pardessus de viole.[3] She married Leslie A. Ward, a fine craftsman who had received his early training under Arnold Dolmetsch. They were both for many years directors of the Arnold Dolmetsch Workshops: known since 1938 as Arnold Dolmetsch Ltd.

NATHALIE DOLMETSCH (b. 1905, Chicago, USA) Dolmetsch's younger daughter has perpetuated her mother's tradition of the early dancing and has specialised in playing the viola da gamba: she has also published a book on the viola da gamba and many valuable editions of literature for the viols. She founded the Viola da Gamba Society in 1948. Nathalie married George Carley, also a skilled craftsman, who later became a director of Arnold Dolmetsch Ltd.

RUDOLPH DOLMETSCH (b. 1906, Cambridge, Mass., USA, d. December 1942) Dolmetsch's eldest son had a brilliant career as virtuoso harpsichordist and viola da gamba player, and was for many years his father's closest assistant. His wife Millicent is also a musician.

Rudolph was the first Dolmetsch to take an interest in modern music and achieved considerable success as a conductor. (Attended the Royal College of Music and studied conducting with Sir Adrian Boult.) Although he eventually broke away from the Haslemere traditions, he continued to play in the annual festivals until 1939.

A number of his compositions survive, and his *Two Movements to be played following the Borodin Unfinished Symphony No. 3 in A minor*, has received two performances in Moscow under Rozhdestvensky and has also been broadcast from London, Moscow and Warsaw. During the 1939–1945 war he served in the Royal Artillery and was lost at sea in 1942.

CARL DOLMETSCH (b. 1911, Fontenay-sous-Bois, France) Dolmetsch's younger son began on the viol at the age of four but later planned to become a violinist and studied with Carl Flesch and Antonio Brosa. At the age of 14 he was ordered by his father to learn the recorder as there was no one else available at the time: he succeeded admirably on this instrument and in so doing, became the first recorder virtuoso of the 20th century whilst still a very young man. He was also required to play the lute, rebec, viola d'amore, viola, pipe and tabor when necessary. Although he also plays all the viols and keyboard instruments, he has specialised in the recorder and treble viol. After his father's death he inherited the responsibility of the *Arnold Dolmetsch Workshops* (Arnold Dolmetsch Ltd.) of which he is now Chairman and Managing Director. He has been Musical Director of the Haslemere Festival since 1940 which celebrated its Golden Jubilee in 1974. The workshops still make instruments according to the principles set down by Arnold Dolmetsch and there are waiting lists for almost every instrument in their catalogue. Their hand-made wooden recorders are in great demand the world over and production of these instruments together with mass-produced school recorders now exceeds 5,000 per week.

Carl Dolmetsch has written articles for various journals both on the musical and technical side of instrument-making as well as tutors on recorder playing at all levels. He has edited and published much solo and ensemble music chiefly for Universal Edition and Schotts of London. He regularly gives concerts and lecture-recitals all over Great Britain and tours abroad including Europe, USA, South America, Canada, New Zealand, Australia and Japan. From 1929–74 he has recorded extensively for Columbia, Decca, EMI, Angel and Orion (USA). He was co-founder of the first recorder summer school at Roehampton in 1948. For the past two years under his direction the Dolmetsches have run their own Summer School, which now takes place at the University of Surrey. Carl Dolmetsch married Mary Ferguson in 1937; she is also a Director of Arnold Dolmetsch Ltd.

FRANÇOIS DOLMETSCH (b. 1940, Haslemere) Carl Dolmetsch's eldest son, studied music as a child and took part in concerts and recordings with his father, brother and sisters, but did not follow the family to pursue it as a career. He became a professional photographer and as such achieved considerable success. He is married and lives in Colombia, South America, and frequently visits this country at which time he joins the rest of the family at the Festival playing the bass and treble recorders.

JEANNE and MARGUERITE DOLMETSCH (b. 1942, Haslemere) Carl Dolmetsch's twin daughters were taught by their father and later received a formal musical education at the Royal Academy of Music: they play viols, recorders and violin in the *Dolmetsch Ensemble* with their father. They also play with the *Dolmetsch Concertante*, a group of outstanding young soloists (directed by Jeanne Dolmetsch) who perform early music on the instruments for which it was written, and contemporary works written for the same instruments. Jeanne Dolmetsch, a brilliant performer, specialises on the recorder and treble viol, and Marguerite Dolmetsch on the recorder, tenor and bass viols.

RICHARD DOLMETSCH (b. 1945, Haslemere) Carl Dolmetsch's younger son, was undoubtedly the most gifted of the younger generation. He died tragically at the age of 21 after a long nervous illness. He, like his father's half-sister Hélène, and his uncle Rudolph, showed highly developed musical talent from early childhood. He first played in public at the age of six and began composing about the same time. A virtuoso recorder player, a brilliant violinist and keyboard player, he frequently appeared as a soloist on all these instruments. Throughout his short life he distinguished himself whenever music was present. At Charterhouse, his house 'Lockites' won the Inter-house Music Competition year after year under his leadership and he won the coveted Gold Medal of 'Le Royaume de Musique' in Paris in 1961.

NOTES

1. Dolmetsch, Mabel *Dances of England and France* (London 1949)
   Dances of Spain and Italy   (London 1954)
2. Dolmetsch, Mabel *Personal Recollections of Arnold Dolmetsch*
   (London 1958).
3. *Pardessus de viole* is the Descant member of the viol family and tuned a fourth higher than the treble viol. It usually had five strings, tuned C, E, A, D and G, but they were also made with six or even seven strings.

Select Bibliography

ABRAHAM, GERALD   *A Hundred Years of Music*, Duckworth (London, 1964).

ALBARDA, JAN   *Wood, Wire and Quill*, The Coach House Press (Toronto, 1968).

ALDRICH, RICHARD   *Concert Life in New York 1902-4*, Putnam (New York, 1941).

Bedales School   *Bedales School and its Founder, John Haden Badley, 1865-1967*, ed. Gyles Brandreth and Sally Henry (Petersfield, 1967).

BISPHAM, DAVID   *A Quaker Singer's Recollections*, Macmillan (London, 1920).

BLOCH, SUZANNE   'Saga of a Twentieth-Century Lute Pioneer', *Journal of the Lute Society of America* ii (1969), 37.

BONAVIA, F.   'Dolmetsch's Haslemere Festival', *N.Y. Times* (25 August, 1951).

BRENNECKE, Jr. ERNEST   'Bach in the Nude', *Musical Record*, USA, Vol. I, No. 2 (July 1933).

BUCKLEY, JEROME HAMILTON   *The Victorian Temper*, Frank Cass (London, 1966).

BURDETT, OSBERT   *The Beardsley Period*, Bodley Head (London, 1925).

BUSONI, FERRUCCIO   *Briefe an seine Frau*, edited by Friedrich Schnapp (Zurich & Leipzig, 1935).
Letters to his Wife, translated by Rosamond Ley, Arnold (London, 1938).

COLLAER, PAUL   '*Les IXm Festival de Musique Ancienne*', p. 218. *La Revue Musicale* (Paris, Sept.–Oct. 1933).

DANNREUTHER, EDWARD   *Musical Ornamentation*, I, Vol. I, Novello, Ewer & Co., 1893.

DART, THURSTON   *The Interpretation of Music*, Hutchinson's University Library (London, 1954).

DAVIES, J. H.   *Musicalia* (Sources of information in music) second edition, Pergamon Press (London, 1969).

DOLMETSCH, ARNOLD

(a) WRITINGS

'The Consort Viols; the Viola d'Amore, the Lyra Viol; and the Viola da gamba', *The Hobby Horse* (London, 1893), No. 2.

A Lecture at the Society of Fine Arts, *The Journal of the Society* (18 Dec. 1896).

'The Lute: I'. *The Connoisseur*, viii (1904), Apr., p. 213.

'The Lute: II', ibid., ix (1904), May, p. 23.

'The Viols', ibid., x (1904), Nov., p. 134.

'Un cas d'ornementation chez Bach', *Journal of the Société Internationale de Musique* (Paris, Feb. 1912).

The Interpretation of the Music of the XVII and XVIII Centuries, Novello (London, 1915), 2/1946, rep. Washington (1969) with new preface by R. A. Harman.

'Home Music', *The Consort*, No. 1, p. 12, Oct. 1929.

'Instrumental Accompaniments of Early Songs', ibid., p. 4, Dec. 1931.

'Ancient Welsh Music'. Address given at Seaford House, London, Jan. 1935. Pub. *Transactions of the Cymmrotraian Society* (London, 1933–1935).

'The Truth About the Piano', *The Listener* (London, 27 Dec. 1934). Also *Glasgow Herald* (Glasgow, 9 Feb. 1931).

'Concerning My Recent Discoveries', *The Consort*, No. 3 p. 1 (June 1934).

'*An Analysis of the Harmonies and Forms of the Bardic Music*, ibid., No. 3, p. 12.

'Eastern Light on Music', ibid., No. 4, p. 14, June 1937.

'*Alterations of Rhythm*', ibid., No. 8, p. 18, June 1951.

(b) EDITIONS

Corelli: Sonatas arranged for Violin and Piano, Novello, Ewer & Co. (London, 1888).

Corelli: Six Trio Sonatas arranged for Violin, Cello and Piano, Novello, Ewer & Co. (London, 1888).

Handel: Six Sonatas arranged for Violin and Piano, Novello, Ewer & Co. (London, 1890).

Four Venetian Dances of the 16th and 17th Centuries transcribed for pianoforte, Cocks (London, 1895).

Select English Songs and Dialogues of the 16th and 17th centuries, Boosey & Co. (London, 1898, 1912).

Divertissement in B flat by J. Haydn, for oboe, violin, viola da gamba and bass, with a part for harpsichord, with introduction, notes and table of ornaments, Oxford (London, 1927).

English Tunes of the 16th and 17th centuries for Treble Recorder in F and Pieces for 2, 3 and 4 Recorders (Haslemere, 1930).

'L'amour de Moy', 16th and 17th century airs for Recorders in 3 and 4 parts, *The Consort*, Dec. 1931.

'A Traditional Welsh Song to a Harp Piece', ibid., 1934, Loose-leaf.

Music for Virginals by English composers of the XVI century Album of 11 short pieces (Haslemere, 1935).

Translations from the Penylln Manuscript of Ancient Harp Music. Transcriptions from Add. MS 14905 British Museum. Pub. by *The Early Welsh Music Society* (Llangefni, 1937).

Select French Songs from the 12th to the 18th century, Boosey & Co. Ltd. (London, 1938).

The Dolmetsch Collection of English Consorts, ed. Grainger, G. Schirmer inc. (New York, 1944).

DOLMETSCH, CARL F.   'Interpretation', *The Consort*, No. 5, April 1948, p. 7.

'On Playing the Recorder', ibid., No. 7, July 1950, p. 18.

'Some Peculiarities of Musical Instruments', ibid., No. 9, June 1952, p. 9.

'Charles Avison on Some Early Composers', ibid., No. 11, July 1954, p. 34.

'A Practical Approach to Bach's Violin Sonatas', ibid., No. 12, 1955, p. 15.

'A Prospectus by Thomas Stanesby, Junior, Recorder Maker (1692–1754)', ibid., No. 13, July 1956, p. 14.

'The Recorder and the Flute', ibid., No. 14, July 1957, p. 18.

'Specialising in Versatility', ibid., No. 15, July 1958, p. 26.

'An Introduction to the Recorder in Modern British Music', ibid., No. 17, July 1960, p. 47.

DOLMETSCH, CÉCILE   'The Crwth', *The Consort*, No. 13, July 1956, p. 23.

'Personal Recollections', ibid., No. 15, July 1958, p. 18.

DOLMETSCH, MABEL   'The History of the Viol', *The Consort*, No. 6, October 1949, pp. 7–12.

Dances of England and France, Routledge & Kegan Paul (London, 1949).

Dances of Spain and Italy, Routledge & Kegan Paul (London, 1954).

Personal Recollections of Arnold Dolmetsch, Routledge & Kegan Paul (London, 1958).

DOLMETSCH, NATHALIE   'The Chest of Viols', *The Consort*, No. 7, July 1950, p. 18.

'John Taverner', ibid., No. 13, July 1956, p. 18.

'John Jenkins', ibid., No. 14, July 1957, p. 18.

'Le Mans', ibid., No. 15, July 1958, p. 23.

DONINGTON, ROBERT   *The Work and Ideas of Arnold Dolmetsch* (Haslemere, 1932).

The Instruments of Music, Methuen (London, 1949).

The Interpretation of Early Music, Faber & Faber (London, 1963), Third ed., Spring 1974.

'The Two Roles of Mabel Dolmetsch: An Appreciation', *The Consort*, No. 21, Summer 1964.

Wagner's Ring and its Symbols, St. Martin's Press (New York, 1969).

The Performer's Guide to Baroque Music, Faber and Faber (London, 1974).

DOWNES, OLIN   'Dolmetsch's Revival of Old Scores', *New York Times*, 20 Sept. 1934.

'Dolmetsch Reveals New Old Music', ibid., 19 Aug. 1934.

ELLMAN, RICHARD   *James Joyce*, Oxford, 1959.

FERGUSON, N. D.   'The Development of the Dolmetsch Movement', *Hinrichsen's Musical Year Book*, p. 419 (London, 1947).

FIELD, MICHAEL   *Works and Days*, ed. Sturge Moore, John Murray (London, 1933).

FRY, ROGER   *Letters of Roger Fry*, ed. Denys Sutton, 2 vols., Chatto & Windus (London, 1972).

GROVE   *Dictionary of Music and Musicians*, Fifth Edition, Eric Blom Macmillan (London, 1954).

GOLDIE, CYRIL   'Arnold Dolmetsch', *The Recorder News*, London (1939–40) pub. SRP.

GRAINGER, PERCY   'Arnold Dolmetsch, Musical Confucius', *Musical Quarterly*, New York, April 1933, p. 187.

GRIFFITHS, LL WYN   'Early Welsh Music', *The Listener*, London (8 Aug. 1934).

HINRICHSEN   *Music Libraries & Instruments* (1961).

HAYES, GERALD R.   'Old Ways for New in Violin Training', *Musical Times*, London, March 1926.

The Treatment of Instrumental Music, Vol. I, Oxford (London, 1928).

The Viols, and other bowed instruments, Vol. II, Oxford (London, 1928).

'An Estimation of Arnold Dolmetsch's Life Work written Thirty Years ago', *The Consort*, No. 15, July 1958, p. 31.

HERRIN, EDWIN   'Arnold Dolmetsch', *Weekly Review*, 21 March (London, 1940).

'Arnold Dolmetsch', *The Consort*, No. 15, July 1958, p. 33.

HIPKINS, A. J. and GIBB, W.   *Musical Instruments, Historic, Rare and Unique*, A & C Black Ltd. (Edinburgh, 1888).

Historical Concerts Edinburgh Music Class Rooms: Programmes and Notes.

HONE, JOSEPH   *The Life of George Moore*, V. Gollancz (London, 1936).

HOUGH, GRAHAM   *The Last Romantics*, Duckworth (London, 1949).

JAMES, PHILIP   *Early Keyboard Instruments*, Davies (London, 1928).

JACKSON, HOLBROOK   *The Eighteen Nineties*, Jonathan Cape (London, 1913) rep 1934 ed. Karl Beckson, Capricorn Books (USA, 1966).

JOYCE, JAMES   *Ulysses*, Shakespeare & Co. (Paris, 1924).
Dubliners, Guild Books, 1914, Jonathan Cape, 1947.

MAINE, BASIL   *Reflected Music*, Methuen (London, 1930).

MACE, THOMAS   *Musick's Monument*, 1676.

McNAUGHT, W.   'Arnold Dolmetsch and his Work', *Musical Times*, p. 153 (London, April 1940).

MOORE, GEORGE   *Evelyn Innes*, T. Fisher Unwin (London, 1898).

Musical America   'Arnold Dolmetsch's Search for the Music of Past Generations' (24 Aug. 1907).

Musicians, Worshipful Company of, *English Music*, The Walter Scott Publishing Co. Ltd. (London, 1906).

NEWMAN, ERNEST   'Interpretation of Old Music', *Musical Times* (London, Dec. 1915).
'New Light on Old Music', *New Witness* (London, 13 Jan. 1916), p. 318.
'Arnold Dolmetsch', *Sunday Times* (London, 17 March 1940).

New Oxford History of Music, The·   'The Age of Humanism 1540–1630', Vol. IV, Oxford (London, 1968).

PALLIS, MARCO   'Mabel Dolmetsch (1874–1963) A pen-portrait from Memory', *The Consort*, No. 21, Summer 1964.

PLAYFORD   *A Brief Introduction to the Skill of Musick*, 1664.

POULTON, DIANA   *John Dowland*, Faber & Faber, London, 1972.

ROTHENSTEIN, WILLIAM   *Men and Memories* (1872–1900), Faber & Faber (London, 1931).

SCHOLES, PERCY A.   *Columbia History of Music Through Ear and Eye*, Periods I and II, Oxford (London, 1930).
The Oxford Companion to Music, London 7th ed. Oxford (London, 1947).
The Concise Dictionary of Music, Oxford, 1912.

SHAW, GEORGE BERNARD   *Music in London*, Vols. II and III (1890–94), Constable, 1932.
Collected Letters, ed. Dan Laurence, Reinhardt (London, 1965).

SPEAIGHT, ROBERT   *William Poel and The Elizabethan Revival*, Heinemann (London, 1954).

SKINNER, WILLIAM   *Belle Skinner Collection of Instruments. A Descriptive Catalogue*, Holyoke, Mass., USA, 1933.

STEELE, ROBERT   'Let the Viols Speak', *The Gamut* (London, June 1928).

STRAETEN, E, VAN DER   'Arnold Dolmetsch', *The Strad* (London, June 1931).

STRANGWAYS, A. H. FOX-   'Dolmetsch Festival: The True Spirit', *The Observer* (London, 6 March 1936).

SUPPER, UTA   *A Catalogue of the Dolmetsch Library*, Haslemere, 1967. 'Treasures of the Dolmetsch Library Unveiled', *The Consort*, No. 26, 1970, pp. 433–44.

SWAINSON, DOROTHY   'Un Grand Musicien Français, Arnold Dolmetsch est Mort à Londres', *La Sarthe* (France, 11 March 1940).

SYMONS, ARTHUR   *Poems, of*, Vol. II, Heinemann (London, 1912). *Plays, Acting and Music*, Jonathan Cape (London, 1928).

TERRY, CHARLES SANFORD   *Bach's Orchestra*, Oxford (London, 1932).

TOLBECQUE, AUGUSTE   *L'Art du Luthier*, Niort, 1903.

YEATS, W. B.   *Autobiographies*, Macmillan (London, 1926). *Letters*, edited Wade, Rupert Hart-Davis (London, 1954).

VALLANCE, AYMER   'Decorative Art of Sir Edward Burne-Jones', *The Easter Annual Advertiser* (London, 1900).

Viola da Gamba Society Bulletin

WELCH, CHRISTOPHER   *Lectures on the Recorder*, Oxford (London, 1961).

WORTHAM, H. E.   *A Musical Odyssey*, Methuen (London, 1934).

General Index

An Index of Musical Instruments follows on page 316

Index of Musical Instruments